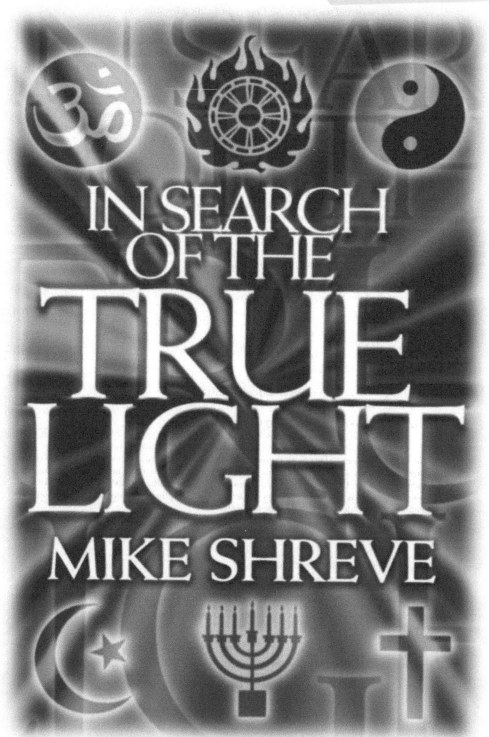

IN SEARCH OF THE TRUE LIGHT

MIKE SHREVE

Original Edition: First Printing 2003, Second Printing 2004
(under Pivotal Publications, an Imprint of Deeper Revelation Books)

Updated Editions 2019, 2023: Missing citations were inserted and the presentation of the material was polished and perfected, especially Part Four. Updated information was added in both new editions. Significant changes were made, but not enough to label this edition a revision.

ISBN: 0-942507-73-8 (10-digit)
ISBN: 978-0-942507-73-7 (13-digit)
In Search of the True Light is also available as an e-book.
Comparative Religion Website: www.thetruelight.net
The Catholic Project Website: www.toCatholicswithlove.org
Primary Ministry Website: www.shreveministries.org

Publisher's Cataloging-in-Publication
(Provided by Quality Books, Inc.)

Shreve, Mike.
    In search of the true light / Mike Shreve. — Rev.
version.
    p. cm.
    Includes bibliographical references.
    LCCN: 2006927468
    ISBN-13: 978-0-942507-73-7
    ISBN-10: 0-942507-73-8

    1. Religions. 2. Shreve, Mike. 3. Jesus Christ.
4. Yoga. 5. Mysticism.   I. Title.

BL80.3S55 2009   200
                QBI08-700244

The True Light Project—This is an outreach especially geared toward those who are seeking truth through Buddhism, Hinduism, Sikhism, Taoism, New Age Spirituality and the study of Yoga, to introduce them to the One who declared, "I am the way, the truth, and the life" (John 14:6). The hub of the project is this book with its associated website, that contains articles, personal transformation stories, interviews, and video podcasts.

Author Contact Info: P.O. Box 4260, Cleveland, TN 37320 / mikeshreve@thetruelight.net

Cover design by Jeff Johnson—www.j2arts.com

Illustration on page 8 donated by: Mia Lane Studios—www.mialaneart.com

Back Cover Explanation—The picture in the background of the back cover is an ink-sketch portrait of Mike Shreve when he was a teacher of Kundalini Yoga, drawn by one of his yoga students in 1970.

Published by Deeper Revelation Books
Revealing "the deep things of God" (1 Cor. 2:10)
P. O. Box 4260 * Cleveland, TN, USA 37320-4260
Phone: 423-478-2843, Fax: 423-479-2980
www.deeperrevelationbooks.org

SYMBOLS OF WORLD RELIGIONS

On the front cover of this book are symbols commonly associated with six of the eleven main living religions presently active in this world. The remaining five symbols are included with them in this explanation section. Each symbol conveys a foundational belief emphasized in the worldview it represents. We should learn the meaning of these symbols that we might better understand the belief systems they typify. A brief history of each religious group or teacher mentioned in this book can also be found near the end of this book and on the website.

BUDDHISM (THE WHEEL OF DHARMA) — The Sanskrit word *dharma* means, "that which is established." It refers to both truth and duty: the way of life a person embraces in order to achieve enlightenment. Buddhists are taught to take refuge in "the *dharma*": the teachings of Buddha. Adherents of this religion believe that Buddha's instructions to his disciples "set the wheel of *dharma* in motion." The eight spokes represent "The Eightfold Path."

CHRISTIANITY (THE CROSS) — The cross is the primary symbol of Christianity. This belief system revolves around the truth that Jesus Christ, the Son of God, died on the cross to provide forgiveness for sins and the availability of reconciliation with God for those who believe. Christians are also called to share the cross by dying to self and living sacrificial lives focused on meeting the needs of others.

CONFUCIANISM (THE WATER SYMBOL) — Though this worldview is recognized as one of the eleven main living religions, it has no standard symbol or icon representing its belief system. Quite often, this Chinese ideogram for water is utilized. It represents the "source of life" in Chinese philosophy.

HINDUISM (THE SACRED SYLLABLE) — This is the Sanskrit symbol for the word "OM." Adherents claim that this was the primal sound-vibration uttered by God in the beginning of creation. By repetitiously chanting this single-word mantra during long periods of meditation, yoga advocates believe they can access oneness with the Absolute, the Source of all things.

ISLAM (THE CRESCENT MOON) — The lunar calendar determines the Islamic year with its system of religious devotions. The Qur'an explains that Allah created the stars to guide people to their destinations. According to Muslims, these are the reasons the crescent moon *(hilal)* and the star *(najm)* have become the traditional dual symbol of Islam.

JAINISM (THE RAISED PALM) — The open palm is a sign of peace, adopted by Jains in 1975, the 2,500th anniversary of the proposed enlightenment of the founder, Mahavira. The palm has the word *Ahimsa* written on it, meaning non-violence. The wheel represents the *dharmachakra*, meaning the resolve to stop *samsara* (the cycle of death and rebirth) by practicing *Ahimsa*.

JUDAISM (THE MENORAH) — The seven-stemmed menorah was a primary article of furniture in both the Tabernacle and the Temple. It first represents God's light shining in Israel; second, it speaks of Israel's calling to shine God's light in this world. The menorah is associated in Scripture with Zechariah 4:6 (a seven word prophecy in Hebrew), "Not by might, nor by power, but by my Spirit."

SHINTO (THE TORII) — Shinto shrines are believed to be the dwelling place of *kami* (various gods, spirits or sacred powers that are worshipped). A *torii* is erected at the entrance of the shrine. It consists of two columns crowned by two beams. This signifies the shrine is a sacred area set apart from the profane, outside world.

SIKHISM (THE KHANDA) — The Khanda symbol consists of three swords. The two outer swords symbolize spiritual and temporal power. The inner, two-edged sword represents the Sikh's responsibility to balance these two types of power. The inner sword and the circle also symbolize the One Eternal God.

TAOISM (THE YIN-YANG SYMBOL) — In this worldview, the opposite forces underlying all things are termed *yin* and *yang*. Taoists believe that these complement each other. *Yin* is associated with darkness, negative, passivity, earth, winter and the female. *Yang* is representative of light, positive, activity, heaven, summer and the male. Each force contains the seed of its opposite.

ZOROASTRIANISM (THE GUARDIAN SPIRIT) — This icon is a *fravashi*, a "guardian spirit." The *fravashi* is different than the soul that incarnates in human flesh. It is the preexistent 'higher Self,' the eternal essence that is said to be one with Ahura Mazda (the righteous God of Zoroastrianism). Adherents believe this is the very nature of God within a person, and that the *fravashi* subtly guides the individual soul on its journey through this world.

Doctrinal views from a number of other religious groups and teachers have also been included, such as: Astrology, Bahá'í, Benjamin Creme (Share International), Brahma Kumaris World Spiritual Organization (Raja Yoga), ECKANKAR (Paul Twitchell, Sri Harold Klemp), Egyptian mythology, Gnosticism, Greek mythology, Guru Maharaj Ji (Divine Light Mission), Helen Schucman (*A Course in Miracles*), ISKCON (International Society for Krishna Consciousness, founder A.C. Bhaktivedanta Swami Prabhupada), Kabbala (Mystical Judaism), Kriya Yoga (Swami Sri Yukteswar and his chief disciple, Paramahansa Yogananda, who later founded Self-Realization Fellowship), Kundalini Yoga (Yogi Bhajan), Meher Baba, Sai Baba, Theosophy (Helena P. Blavatsky, Henry Steel Olcott and Annie Besant), Transcendental Meditation (Maharishi Mahesh Yogi) and United Church of Religious Science (Ernest Holmes).

ACKNOWLEDGMENTS

I appreciate the following persons, many of whom gave freely of their time, discussing and confirming the doctrinal position of their particular worldviews: Dr. Yigal Levin, professor with the Department of Philosophy and Religion at University of Tennessee at Chattanooga (Judaism), John Algeo, international vice-president of the Theosophical Society, Myrna Belgrave, Nandi and Surya of Raja Yoga (BKWSU), Preet Mohan and Yuktanand Singh of Sikhism, Bansi Pandit, author of *The Hindu Mind*, Swami Varadananda of the Vedanta Society, Tom Egenes, professor of Sanskrit at Maharishi University (TM), Brahmachari Lynn of Kriya Yoga (Self-Realization Fellowship), Laurent Weichberger, Daniel J. Sanders and Markar, devotees of Meher Baba, Livia Kohn Ph.D., Professor of Religion at Boston University and recognized authority on Taoism and Chinese religion, Lynn Robert Farny, Public Relations Department, Church of Scientology International, James C. Stephens, founder and president of Sonrise Center for Buddhist Studies, Dr. Richard Jones, Assistant Professor of Anthropology of Lee University, Dr. Ed Moodley, Assistant Professor of Intercultural Studies of Lee University, Kabir Helminski, co-founder of the Threshold Society and representative of the Mevlevi tradition of Sufism (founded by Jalaluddin Rumi), Professor Shaul Magid of the Jewish Theological Seminary and many others. *Sincere thanks to all of you!* Though most of us hold differing views concerning the nature of truth (in areas of major importance), we agreed on one essential point—a willingness to interact with kindness and gentleness, as we discussed the differences and commonalities of our belief systems.

Many thanks are also to be expressed to my faithful proofreaders, Winnie Shreve (my precious mother who has since passed on to her heavenly reward) and Jeannie Obee, and to my diligent and committed typesetter, Bunny Bateman. Her selfless commitment to this project is beyond description. What an amazing friend she has been! Mia Lane, an excellent artist and dear friend, supplied the illustration on the dedication page. Many thanks to her.

I also would like to express my deepest, heartfelt gratitude to those who have supplied the financial backing for this project (the book, the website and the outreaches). Respecting their privacy, I have not mentioned their names, but I am quick to say that their help has been essential for the success of this venture. Certainly, the very truth they have supported will undergird them on their journey through this world into the next.

CONTENTS

DEDICATION

I dedicate this book to every sincere seeker of truth, regardless of culture or religion—every wandering sadhu, every Hindu chanting a mantra, every Buddhist seeking nirvana, every Sikh in a meditation pose, every Jainist practicing non-violence, every Jew rocking his body as he prays, every prostrate Muslim facing Mecca, every whirling Sufi, every college student studying Zen, every housewife doing yoga and every corporate executive practicing TM.

I especially dedicate this book to every knee that bends and every head that bows before the glorious Creator of heaven and earth. May the breath of life that flows through these pages bring inspiration to all those who dare to look beyond the transitory things of life in order to find that truth which endures forever. May the living God manifest himself to you in great love and great power!

There is a common thirst in the hearts of all who seek the truth.
Only one revelation can quench that thirst.

INTRODUCTION

My main purpose for writing *"In Search of the True Light"* is fourfold: first, to reveal the areas of unity and similarity that exist in the various religions of this world; second, to honestly assess the differences; third, to share the details of my own personal, spiritual journey; and fourth, to reveal the *"True Light"* that alone imparts completion, spiritual rebirth and life-transformation.

I was a teacher of yoga and meditation at four universities. Every day was consumed with an intense and detailed system of yogic disciplines. As I increasingly devoted myself, it seemed the night of spiritual uncertainty was giving way to the dawn of spiritual illumination.

Hundreds of yoga students were looking to me for guidance. Then, for my own sake and theirs, I began to reevaluate some of the concepts that initially I had accepted as unquestionable truth—and I began to reassess my own personal motivations. Had I based my beliefs on irrefutable evidence? Or because of a deep longing to transcend the natural realm and experience the supernatural, had I allowed myself to become impressionable and at times, even gullible? The fine line of my doctrinal stance became more and more blurred as these and other pertinent questions occupied my thinking.

In this book I share the inward struggle I experienced in searching for the *"True Light."* I also share some very insightful, powerful and convincing conclusions—the result of nearly fifty years of reflecting on eternal mysteries.

I do not thoroughly examine the history or the tenets of each religion, sect or religious leader mentioned. Such a complete study was never my objective. There are other books that accomplish that goal quite well. Instead, I pinpoint certain basic issues that are essentially important in any religious system of thought. Then I objectively contrast the views that various religions and sect leaders offer with regard to these pertinent issues. These perspectives sometimes complement and, at other times, contradict each other. Dealing with these comparisons presents us all with the challenge of distinguishing between what is true and what is false, what should be included, or what should be excluded from our philosophy of life.

For those who are thirsty, this book will be a stream of living water— flowing, not from the sharp tongue of an opinionated orator, but from the soft heart of a fellow pilgrim. We are all traveling this road together. We are part of the same human family. And if there's anything I believe—I believe those who find *"True Light"* are constrained, both by duty and by love, to share it with those who are yet groping through the darkness. Yes, we are our 'brother's keeper,' both naturally and spiritually.

Regardless of their religious persuasion, I feel a deep, soul-to-soul connection with all who are seeking Ultimate Reality, those who are not satisfied with a mere sensual or temporal existence, those whose hearts cry out for more than doctrines, creeds, traditions, ceremonies and the extraneous trappings of religion.

For this reason, I often quote persons whose worldviews are quite different than mine. Why have I risked such a choice? For several reasons: first, to show the areas of commonality that exist between various cultures, religions and people groups; second, to recognize truth wherever it is found; and third, to find common ground so a bridge of communication can be successfully built.

I have spent many hours, days, weeks and months laboring over this manuscript. At times, I havev even wept over the words—knowing they would fall like seed into the hearts of those who long for the fruit of divine wisdom to grow in their lives. The fact that you have picked up this book to examine its contents persuades me you are a person of such spiritual caliber.

So quite possibly, our hearts beat with a similar pulsation, a shared love for that which has infinite value, a longing to experience transcendent reality, a mutual desire to have our entire being illuminated with the *"True Light."*

My heartfelt prayer is that, in a spiritual sense, this book will be bread on your table, oil in your lamp and a steppingstone—lifting you from this present world into the glory of what is yet to come.

Mike Shreve

PART 1

THE QUEST OF EVERY HEART

"Just as the ocean woos every spring, every river, every frothing waterfall into itself—so the ocean of God's infinite love draws the hearts of men."

Mike Shreve

"The soul is a never ending sigh after God."

Theodor Christlieb[1]

"He who has no vision of eternity has no hold on time."

Thomas Carlyle[2]

Most human beings are searching. Searching for purpose. Searching for fulfillment. Searching for identity. "Who am I?" is a question that echoes deep in the heart of collective humanity. "Why am I here?" is the question that follows close behind. Then inevitably, "Where am I going? What's my destiny in this world and what's going to happen to me after death?"

Darkness is a good description of the condition of our minds before discovering the truth. We are born in darkness—the darkness of sense-consciousness. Initially, we are able to define life only by the input that comes to us through the five sensory gates. Many years are spent, from infancy through adulthood, in the development and maturing of these senses. In the process, human beings tend to relate to themselves only within these experiential boundaries. What a mistake it is to stop at these gates, for if our motivation is only toward the gratification of bodily cravings, how empty is that most important and most enduring part!

Life in this world teaches us that daylight always follows the darkness of night. In like manner, no person confronted with the spiritual darkness that drapes humanity should despair, thinking that light-producing answers are not available. In a spiritual sense, light also follows darkness, especially for those who hear the truth and have an opportunity to embrace it.

How insightful it is that all living things—the child in the womb, the embryo in the egg, and the tiny sprout in a germinating seed—enter this world in a bowed position! Maybe, just maybe, this is a subtle hint from the Creator that we have all been created for one main purpose: to "bow" before him adoringly all the days of our earthly sojourn.

Though some have dared to question his existence, nature herself imprints on the minds of men the idea of God. It is impossible to meditate on the intricate beauty of a flower, the complexities of the human body, or the vastness of the universe without being filled with awe toward the magnificent One who fashioned it all. From microcosm to macrocosm, creation sings an inspiring song—a song that all human beings can hear regardless of their chosen belief system. The psalmist David said it beautifully:

⌣• "The heavens declare the glory of God; and the earth shows His handiwork...There is no speech nor language where their voice is not heard." *(Psalms 19:1, 3, Judaism/Christianity)*

Writings from other worldviews express a similar observation:

⌣• "Whatever is in the heaven and on earth doth declare the praises and glory of Allah." *(Qur'an 64:1, Islam)*

⌣• "Your Name is affirmed by the mantle of the forest; your infinity proclaimed by every blade of grass." *(Jaap Sahib 1, Sikhism)*

⌣• "The light of the sun, the sparkling dawn of the days, all this is for your praise, O Wise Lord..." *(Avesta, Yasna 50.10, Zoroastrianism)*

Being filled with wonder when viewing the grandeur and beauty of the creation should come as natural as breathing to any human being. The next gasp of inspiration, however, should be an even greater sense of wonder concerning the Creator himself. When this happens, a holy metamorphosis takes place—mind-ruled seekers of truth suddenly become heart-led adorers of the Author of truth. At this stage of the journey, language is left behind. Earth-born words on the lips of finite men simply cannot express the full glory of the heavenly, infinite One. I believe Guru Nanak, founder of Sikhism, was overcome with this kind of spiritual elixir—this love that defies language—when he authored the following verse:

"Were I to live for millions of years,
And drink the air for my nourishment,
I should still not be able to express Thy worth.
How great shall I call Thy name!"
(Siri Rag 2.1, 3)

Though I no longer embrace Sikhism, I agree with the passion for God expressed in this quote. Yes, God's greatness is inexpressible. Even so, our daily duty—rather, our moment-by-moment privilege—is to find creative, ever-increasing ways of declaring his eternal majesty, beauty and value. Though in this life, we may never reach the top of the ladder that stretches from earth to heaven—we must each "awake from sleep" (as Jacob, the grandson of Abraham did) and declare, "Surely, the Lord is in this place and I knew it not!" *(Genesis 28:16)* What a grand discovery— God can be found, he can be known, he can be experienced—in this wearisome and sometimes heartbreaking world!

The Most High God always has been, and always will be, our "natural habitat." How can a fish survive once removed from the water? How can an eagle be content in a cage, once accustomed to the windy heights? And how can human beings, created to enjoy communion with the Source of all things, ever be truly alive or content without the realization of this supreme privilege?

RELIGION—THE HUMAN PHENOMENON

The concept of religion is a dominant theme within the human race. Though the following individuals often embrace conflicting viewpoints on vitally important doctrinal issues, still, their definitions of this essential facet of the human experience often strike a harmonious chord:

Mahatma Ghandi made the profound comment:

> *"Religion is...more an integral part of one's self than one's body. Religion is the tie that binds one to one's Creator and while the body perishes, as it has to, religion persists even after death."*[3]

Henry Pitt Van Dusen's definition pries the door open further:

> *"Religion is the reaching out of one's whole being—mind, body, spirit, emotions, intuitions, will—for completion, for inner unity, for true relation with those about us, for right relation to the universe in which we live."*[4]

A.W. Tozer, a popular Christian writer, proposed:

> *"True religion confronts earth with heaven and brings eternity to bear on time."*[5]

Meher Baba emphasized:

> *"The real meaning of religion is to know God,*
> *to see God and to be one with God. Everything else*
> *about religion is an exercise in rites and rituals."*[6]

The motto of the Theosophical Society (taken from the *Mahabharata*) reduces all of these definitions to their simplest essence—*"There is no religion higher than truth."*[7]

Most worldviews concur, if we are really "religious," it should strongly impact our character and our day-to-day existence. Consider the following quotes:

↵· Edmond Burke—*"Religion is essentially the art and the theory of the remaking of man. Man is not a finished creation."*[8]

↵· Kahlil Gibran—*"Your daily life is your temple and your religion."*[9]

↵· Albert Einstein—*"True religion is real living; living with all one's soul, with all one's goodness and righteousness."*[10]

↵· Ralph Waldo Emerson—*"Religion is to do right. It is to love, it is to serve, it is to think, it is to be humble."*[11]

↵· Ramakrishna—*"Common men talk bagfuls of religion but act not a grain of it, while the wise man speaks little, but his whole life is a religion acted out."*[12]

↵· Maharishi Mahesh Yogi—*"Religion should forward a way of life...[that] every thought, word, and action of the individual may be guided by a higher purpose."*[13]

After reading these similar sounding quotes, some readers might feel a compulsion to immediately dive into the deep waters of full religious syncretism. However, before you jump off the cliff, you need to closely inspect the nuances, the subtle shades of meaning, conveyed by each of these statements. Often, you will find them to be at opposite ends of the theological spectrum. For instance, the Theosophical quote above is powerful and correct, yet a Theosophist's interpretation of "truth" is quite different than A.W. Tozer's (or mine). And the idea of "knowing" God has a unique slant when coming from Meher Baba, for he professed to be an incarnation of God, a claim adherents of many other religions would quickly challenge and refute (including myself). Then why should I even offer all these quotes on religion, since there are irreconcilable differences between the religions or types of spirituality represented? Simply to show that there is a common cry in the heart of humanity.

A dark and negative view flowed from the atheistic pen of Karl Marx. This architect of communism dubbed religion "the opium of the people."[14] He was apparently suggesting that religion distorts the senses, granting a false sense of euphoria that prevents religious persons from dealing with reality. Actually, the opposite is true. Materialism and sensualism are the real culprits, the 'opiate-like' influences that distort reality. These have a drug-like, even addictive influence on human beings causing them to be consumed with temporal things. Those who seek fulfillment in the pleasures of this life often seem lulled into a false sense of security, the deception that these things will somehow go on forever. Those who are wise recognize the transient state of this world and seek those things that have eternal value.

The world is teeming with countless expressions of religious devotion. These are primarily the product of man's longing to embrace, not the transient, but the transcendent. Almost every culture and people-group possesses a distinctive worldview and path that promises to lead thirsty seekers to the cool waters of spirituality. This includes doctrines, ceremonies and traditions designed with the hope of entering and maintaining a right relationship with some kind of Deity. Being able to even conceptualize such a possibility is one thing that sets man apart in his uniqueness.

William Howells, the American novelist, observed that man is a "creature who comprehends things he cannot see and believes in things he cannot comprehend."[15] Though at the beginning of life's journey God is incomprehensible to all of us, those who are lovers of light dare to believe they can overcome this time-locked, earth-bound, carnal-clad condition of existence. Eagerly, they seek to comprehend—but lacking confidence in their own ability to discern the truth, they usually gravitate toward those who appear very confident. Thus, religions are brought to birth in this world: the unsure placing their trust in those who claim to be very sure, with regard to understanding the mysteries of life.

This term "religion" has an interesting origin. Quite possibly, it stems from the Latin word *religio* which can mean *something done with meticulous care*. Then again, it may be derived from the verb *religare*, which can mean *to bind back or to bind together*. Cicero believed it came from two words—*re legere*—which mean *to read again or reflect upon*, certainly a reference to the practice of meditating on the Scripture to ascertain its meaning. He also felt it came from the root word *leg* meaning *to take up, gather, count or observe*.

All of these interpretations have value, because as seekers of truth *meticulously and carefully observe* the patterns of life and as they *study* those communications believed to be divinely inspired, they *gather* a harvest of beliefs—about the earth, the cosmos, our relationships with other human beings, and the "Power" that brought all things into being. This ordinarily results in a sense of holy obligation, the seeker *binding himself* to those concepts in the hope of possessing greater meaning, purpose and destiny in life. Moreover, those of common beliefs tend to *bind* themselves to each other—forming a community that often transcends geographical, political, social, racial and cultural boundaries.

There are, at least, four different types of religion.

(1) **Natural religion** occurs because of four fundamental influences that affect almost all people: first, the innate, God-given desire that many human beings feel to know and serve their Creator; second, our ability, at times, to rationalize the existence and basic attributes of the Eternal One; third, the subtle, subliminal influence of the Holy Spirit who woos the human race by convicting the consciences of all men; and fourth, the automatic, resulting sense of responsibility and accountability that such affected persons often feel toward this grand Designer who designed their existence. Quite often, seeing the amazing beauty and complexity of the universe awakens "natural religion" in the souls of the children of this world. This excites a response of worship, though the full identity of the worshipped One is uncertain.

(2) **Invented religion** usually has its roots in "natural religion," but religious architects go beyond their initial, inspired insights to interpolate all kinds of self-created doctrines, concepts and traditions. This results in the development of a belief system that is primarily the product of human imagination and often bears little or no resemblance to the natural religion that spawned it.

(3) **Revealed religion** is pure truth, disclosed by the Source of truth himself. Recipients of revealed religion do not always seek such intuitive insights; these flashes of truth come at the will of the Almighty. Being divinely authored, they are infallible and irrefutable. (Of course, the adherents of many "invented religions" erroneously claim their worldviews fall under the heading of "revealed religions.")

(4) **Augmented religion** takes place when recipients of "revealed religion" add humanly devised concepts and traditions to what God has revealed. The result? Either the dilution or the pollution of the truth.

Only one of these four types of religion has the power to actually bring fulfillment and completion to its adherents. However all of them *seem* to impart certain benefits—whether real or imagined—to those who follow the rules, participate in the rituals, and embrace the doctrines.

In his book titled *The World's Living Religions*, Robert E. Hume summarized these proposed benefits. The following list is drawn primarily from his observations, but condensed into a more readable format:

> *"Religion gives to a person what he can obtain from no other source"*—

- Confidence in the outcome of life's struggles.

- An added sense of power and satisfaction.

- Help to bear the troubles of life uncomplainingly.

- A solution for the problem of evil.

- Improves the quality of this present life.

- Offers the hope of a better life in the future.

- Outlines an ideal society and influences others to achieve that goal.

- Sets forth a working plan of salvation.

- Strengthens human relationships by granting a fulfilling sense of community.

> *"The distinguishing function of religion, in contrast with that of philosophy or ethics, or any of the idealizing or cultural activities, is to give to a human being the supreme satisfaction of his life through a vital relationship with what he recognizes as the superhuman Power, or powers, in the world."*[16]

Admittedly, there are many conflicting ideas offered in world religions concerning the nature and identity of this "superhuman Power," as well as the correct "solution for the problem of evil" and "working plan of salvation." Yet in all the contradictions, there are some common elements. These commonalities are not discovered in the upper levels of theological teaching, but at the base. They usually concern foundational issues like guidelines for moral and ethical behavior, the need for character development or a simple longing to believe in God, to know God and to serve God. At times, certain basic ideas are not only similar; they are universally acceptable.

On the next seven pages you will find quotes, drawn from books considered sacred in various religions, on seven fundamental subjects. Please be assured I am not validating or endorsing the belief systems that are included in these lists of quotes; rather, by highlighting these similar sounding admonitions, I am laying the groundwork for some very important conclusions later in this book.

THE
GOLDEN
RULE

The social, relational concept termed "The Golden Rule" is found in the teachings of almost all religions, as well as popular philosophical sources. Sometimes, it is worded in the positive *("Do unto others…")*; at other times, it appears in the negative *("Do not do to others…")*.

FOUND
IN ALL
RELIGIONS

Bahá'í: "Choose…for thy neighbor that which thou choosest for thyself." *(Bahá'u'lláh)*[17]

Buddhism: "Hurt not others in ways that you yourself would find hurtful." *(Udana-Varga 5, 18)* "Consider others as yourself." *(Dhammapada 10.1)*

Christianity: "Therefore, whatever you want men to do to you, do also to them, for this is the Law and the Prophets." *(Matthew 7:12)*

Confucianism: "Is there one maxim that ought to be acted upon throughout one's whole life? Surely it is the maxim of loving kindness: Do not unto others what you would not have them do unto you." *(Analects 15, 23)*

Greek Philosophy: "Treat your friends as you would want them to treat you." *(Aristotle, Lives and Opinions of Eminent Philosophers, 5:21; Bohn Library translation, 188)* "Do not do to others what you would not wish to suffer yourself." *(Isocrates, Isocrates Cyprian Orations, 149)*

Hinduism: "Men gifted with intelligence and purified souls should always treat others as they themselves wish to be treated." *(Mahabharata 13.115.22)*

Islam: "Not one of you is a believer until he loves for his brother what he loves for himself." *(Forty Hadith of an-Nawawi 13)*

Jainism: "A man should treat all creatures in the world as he himself would like to be treated." *(Sutra-keit-anga)*

Judaism: "Don't take vengeance on or bear a grudge against any of your people; rather, love your neighbor as yourself: I am the Lord." *(Leviticus 19:18)* "What is hateful to you, do not to your fellowman. That is the entire Law; all the rest is commentary." *(Babylonian Talmud, Sabbath 31a)*

Sikhism: "As thou deemest thyself, so deem others. Then shalt thou become a partner in heaven." *(Kabir's Hymns, Asa 17)*

Taoism: "Regard your neighbor's gain as your own gain, and your neighbor's loss as your own loss." *(T'ai Shang Kan Ying P'ien)*

Zoroastrianism: "That nature alone is good which refrains from doing unto another whatsoever is not good for itself." *(Dadistan-i-dinik 94, 5)*

SEPARATION FROM THE WORLD

"Separation from the World" is another common theme found in almost all religions. Most worldviews agree that to experience their perception of Ultimate Reality, there must be some kind of renunciation of that which is transitory. To experience that which is pure, there must be a renunciation of that which is evil.

Bahá'í: "O my brother! A pure heart is as a mirror; cleanse it with the burnish of love and severance from all save God, that the true sun may shine within it and the eternal morning dawn." *(The Seven Valleys and the Four Valleys, 21)*

Buddhism: "Come behold this world, which is like unto an ornamented royal chariot, wherein fools flounder, but for the wise there is no attachment." *(Dhammapada 171)*

Christianity: Jesus said of his disciples, "They are not of the world even as I am not of the world." *(John 17:16)*

Confucianism: "To conserve his stock of virtue, the superior man withdraws into himself and thus escapes from the evil influences around him." *(I Ching 12: Stagnation)*

Hinduism: "He becomes immortal who seeks the general good of man, who does not grieve and who can renounce the world." *(Mahabharata 5.46.20)*

Islam: "Renounce the world and Allah will love you." *(Forty Hadith of an-Nawawi 40, 31)*

Jainism: "He who is rich in control renounces everything, and meditates on the reflections of life…Like a ship reaching the shore, he gets beyond misery." *(Sutra-Kritanga Sutra 1.15.4, 5)*

Judaism: "You are to be holy, for I am holy." *(Leviticus 11:45)* "Learn not the way of the heathen." *(Jeremiah 10:2)*

Shinto: "Leave the things of this world, and come to Me daily and monthly with pure bodies and pure hearts." *(Oracle of the Deity Atago)*

Sikhism: "Yoga consists not in frequenting tombs and cremation grounds, nor in falling into trances; nor lies it in wandering about the world, nor in ritual bathing. To live immaculate amidst the impurities of the world—this is true yoga practice." *(Adi Granth, Suhi, M.1, p. 730)*

Taoism: "If one have done deeds of wickedness, but afterwards alters his way, and repents, resolved not to do anything wicked, but to practice reverently all that is good, he is sure in the long run to obtain good fortune." *(Tai-Shang Kan-Ying Pien, characters 1200–1230)*

PRAYER

"Prayer" is another vital subject. Most religions affirm that in order to commune with the Creator or penetrate Ultimate Reality, its adherents must use methods of prayer and/or meditation deemed to be effective in that worldview. F. B. Meyer commented, "The great tragedy of life is not unanswered prayer, but unoffered prayer."[18]

Christianity: Jesus taught, "Whatever things you ask when you pray, believe that you receive them, and you will have them." *(Mark 11:24)*

Hinduism: The instruction of Deity is: "Worship me through meditation in the sanctuary of the heart." *(Srimad Bhagavatam 11.5)*

Islam: "Prayer restrains one from shameful and unjust deeds; and remembrance of God is the greatest thing in life, without doubt." *(Qur'an 29.45)*

Judaism: "Prayer should not be recited as if a man were reading a document." *(Jerusalem Talmud, Berakhot 4.3)*

Meher Baba: "The ideal prayer to the Lord is nothing more than spontaneous praise of his being."[19]

Roman Philosophy: "Live among men as if God beheld you; speak with God as if men were listening." *(Seneca: Epistolue ad Lucilium)*

Shinto: "Pray in all righteousness and the Deity will be pleased to listen to your supplication. Foolish is he who, in impatient eagerness and without following the path of righteousness, hopes to obtain divine protection." *(Shinto-Uden-Futsujosho)*

Sikhism: "Of all the prayers of the heart, the best prayer is the prayer to the Master to be given the grace of properly praising the Lord." *(Adi Granth, Maru Ashtpadi, M.5, p. 1018)*

Theosophy (Bhagavan Dass): "It is not enough to pray, however sincerely, that God's Will be done on earth; it is necessary also to know what that Will is; if we are to…act in obedience to it."[20]

United Church of Religious Science (Dr. Ernest Holmes): "Some prayers are more effective than others. Some only help us to endure, while others transcend condition."[21]

Zoroastrianism: "The pure whom you have found worthy for their righteousness and their good mind, fulfill their desire, O Wise Lord, let them attain it! I know that words of prayer which serve a good end are successful before you." *(Avesta, Yasna 28.10)*

CHARACTER
DEVELOPMENT

"Character Development" is something that is normally emphasized in all religions. Moral and ethical guidelines fill the doctrinal base of most writings considered sacred. All tend to agree that human beings cannot achieve their highest potential until they rise above the sense-driven aspect of their lower nature.

Buddhism: "By degrees, little by little, from time to time, a wise person should remove his own impurities as a smith removes the dross from silver." *(Dhammapada 239)*

Christianity: "We also glory in tribulations, knowing that tribulation produces perseverance; and perseverance, character; and character, hope." *(Romans 5:3–4)*

Confucianism: "The moral man's life is an exemplification of the universal order...the vulgar person's life is a contradiction of the universal order." *(Doctrine of the Mean 2)*

Greek Philosophy: "The end of life is to be like God, and the soul following God will be like him." *(Socrates)*[22]

Hinduism: According as one acts, so does he become. The doer of good becomes good; the doer of evil becomes evil. One becomes virtuous by virtuous actions; bad, by bad actions." *(Brihad-Aranyaka Upanishad 4.4.5)*

Islam: Abu Huraira reported God's Messenger as saying, "The believers whose faith is most perfect are those who have the best character." *(Hadith of Abu Dawud and Darimi)*

Jainism: "Right belief, right knowledge, right conduct, these together constitute the path to liberation." *(Tattvarthasutra 1.1)*

Judaism: "Study of Torah leads to precision, precision to zeal, zeal to cleanliness, cleanliness to restraint, restraint to purity, purity to holiness, holiness to meekness, meekness to fear of sin, fear of sin to saintliness, saintliness to the Holy Spirit, and the Holy Spirit to life eternal." *(Babylonian Talmud, Avoda Zara 20b)*

Sikhism: "Liberation comes from living the holy Word." *(Adi Granth, Sri Raga, Ashtpati, M.1, p. 62)*

Taoism: "Do not swerve from the path of virtue...lest you cast away that which links you to God." *(Kwang Tze 29.2)*

Zoroastrianism: "Next to life, purity is for man the greatest good. That purity is in the religion of the Wise One for him who cleanses his own self with good thoughts, words and deeds." *(Vendidad 5.21)*

FAITH

"Faith" is the heart-pulsation of any worldview, pumping the 'blood' of spiritual vitality through the veins of its adherents. Those who are 'full-of-faith' tend to become 'faithful'—loyal to their chosen belief system, whether it is true or untrue.

Bahá'í: The "essence" of faith is "fewness of words and abundance of deeds." *(Tablets of Bahá'u'lláh Revealed after the Kitab-i-Aqdas, 156)*

Buddhism: "Faith is the best wealth to man here." *(Sutta Nipata 181: Coomara Samy, Sutta Nipata 48, Alavaka Sutta 2)* "By faith you shall be free and go beyond the world of death." *(Sutta Nipata 1146)*

Christianity: "Now faith is the substance of things hoped for, the evidence of things not seen." *(Hebrews 11:1)*

Confucianism: "Heaven makes hard demands on faith." *(Shi King 3.1.2.1.3)* "A people without faith cannot stand." *(Analects 12.7.3)*

Hinduism: "Without faith, whatever offering or gift is made or work done or penance performed, it is reckoned "not-being" both now and hereafter." *(Bhagavad-Gita 17.28)*

Islam: "The true believers are those whose hearts are filled with awe at the mention of God, and whose faith grows stronger as they listen to His revelations." *(Qur'an 8.2)*

Jainism: "Without faith there is no knowledge, without knowledge there is no virtuous conduct, without virtues there is no deliverance, and without deliverance there is no perfection [Nirvana]." *(Uttaradhyayana Sutra 28.30)*

Judaism: "The just shall live by his faith." *(Habakkuk 2:4)*

Sikhism: "Inexpressible is the state of faith; whoever attempts to describe it shall in the end regret his rashness. This state pen and paper cannot record, nor cogitation penetrate its secret. The great, immaculate Name of God may only be realized by one whose mind is firmly fixed in faith." *(Adi Granth, Japji 12–15, M.1, p.3)*

Taoism: "Faith, if insufficient, is apt to become no faith at all." *(Tao-Te Ching 17.1; also 23.3)*

Transcendentalism: "All that I have seen teaches me to trust the Creator for all I have not seen." *(Ralph Waldo Emerson)*[23]

United Church of Religious Science (Dr. Ernest Holmes): "In order to keep faith, we must allow nothing to enter our thought which will weaken this conviction."[24]

LOVE
AND
COMPASSION

"Love" and **"Compassion,"**similar to the **"Golden Rule,"** are also unifying components in all the positive religious approaches in this world. In a world sick with senseless hate and selfish lust, the revelation of love provides a healing balm. This quality injects meaning and purpose into that which can appear, at times, to be meaningless and purposeless.

The **humanist** poet, Petrarch, suggested:

> *"Love is the crowning grace of humanity, the holiest right of the soul, the golden link which binds us to duty and truth, the redeeming principle that chiefly reconciles the heart of life, and is prophetic of eternal good."*[25]

These two choice, related character traits are celebrated, proclaimed and evidenced in many of the religious communities that make up the global family:

Bahá'í: "Love is the light that guideth in darkness, the living link that uniteth God with man, that assureth the progress of every illumined soul...Love is the most great law that ruleth this mighty and heavenly cycle...Love revealeth with unfailing and limitless power the mysteries latent in the universe." *(From the writings of Abdu'l-Baha, p. 27)*[26]

Buddhism (Tibetan): The Dalai Lama, the most visible religious leader of Tibetan Buddhism, warns: "Love, compassion and tolerance are necessities, not luxuries. Without them, humanity cannot survive."[27]

Christianity: Jesus, the embodiment of divine love, urged his followers, "Love your enemies, do good, and lend, hoping for nothing in return; and your reward will be great, and you will be sons of the Most High. For He is kind to the unthankful and evil." *(Luke 6:35)* "By this will all men know that you are my disciples, if you have love for one another." *(John 13:35)* John, the beloved disciple, added, "God is love, and he who abides in love abides in God, and God in him." *(1 John 4:16)*

Jainism: "Charity—to be moved at the sight of the thirsty, the hungry, and the miserable, and to offer relief to them out of pity—is the spring of virtue." *(Kundakunda Pancastikaya 137)*

Judaism: "Administer true justice. Let everyone show mercy and compassion to his brother." *(Zechariah 7:9)*

Sikhism: "Those immersed in the love of God feel love for all things." *(Adi Granth, Wadhans, M.1, p. 557)* "Hear ye, for I speak the Truth, only those who Love will experience the Almighty!" *(Tav Prasad Savvayaa, Guru Gobind Singh)*

Sufism (Mystical Islam): "The essence of God is love and the Sufi path is a path of love...Love is to see what is good and beautiful in everything... The aim of the Sufi is to be accepted as a lover by the Beloved, that is, by God."[28] "Love means that the attributes of the lover are changed into those of the Beloved. Now he lives in accordance with the saying of God: 'When I love him, I will be his eye by which he sees and his hearing by which he hears and his hand by which he reaches out.'"[29]

Universalist Lebanese poet, Kahlil Gibran, writes, "When you love you should not say, 'God is in my heart,' but rather, 'I am in the heart of God.' And think not that you can direct the course of love, for love, if it finds you worthy, directs your course."[30]

And there is no more inspiring definition of compassion than one shared by the **Buddhist** teacher, Sharon Salzberg:

"Compassion makes the narrow heart as wide as the world."[31]

If we are truly prayerful, inspired, sensitive persons—certainly this will be the case. Our hearts will widen to embrace this world with its amazing diversity, to deeply love those who may be quite different from us, culturally and religiously. When this happens to us, we may well stumble on a profound realization—that in all of these quotes on various subjects there can be heard an echo of the heart-cry that connects us all.

Passion for God Should be Respected

Being a follower of Jesus, I believe in the exclusivity of Christ. However, I also appreciate passion for God whenever and wherever it is found. One of the most evident examples of such spiritual fervor is discovered in Sufism, the mystical branch of Islam. Traditional Muslims emphasize the idea of the transcendence of God—that God is far too lofty and holy, and man, far too degraded and sinful, for any kind of personal indwelling and relationship to take place.

On the other hand, Sufis accentuate Mohammed's teaching that God is "nearer than your jugular vein." *(Qur'an 50:16)* They contend that deep, personal communion with God is possible, and ecstatic, spiritual experiences with him, obtainable. The Sufis are world renowned for their "love-poetry"—religious ardor captured in verse toward the desirable

Eternal One, the Beloved. None is more inspiring than the following excerpt from a Persian devotional poem by 'Abdallah al-Ansari:

> *Thou, Whose breath is sweetest perfume*
> *to the spent and anguished heart,*
> *Thy remembrance to Thy lovers bringeth*
> *ease for every smart.*
> *Multitudes like Moses, reeling,*
> *cry to earth's remotest place.*
> *"Give me sight, O Lord," they clamor,*
> *seeking to behold Thy face.*
> *Multitudes no man hath numbered,*
> *lovers, and afflicted all,*
> *Stumbling on the way of anguish,*
> *"Allah, Allah" loudly call.*
> *And the fire of separation*
> *sears the heart and burns the breast,*
> *and their eyes are wet with weeping*
> *for a love that gives not rest.*
> *...Oh God, all other men are drunk with wine:*
> *the wine-bearer is my fever.*
> *Their drunkenness lasts but a night,*
> *while mine abides forever.*[32]

Such poetry gets to the heart of what true religion should be—longing for God, for a real experience of God, not just intellectual concepts about God. All who are parched spiritually, all who feel this "unquenchable thirst," can relate to such poetic language even if they do not believe in the concept of God as presented in Islam. Where the Islamic name for God appears ("Allah"), I can insert the name of the Lord of glory ("Jesus") and quote the rest of the poem sincerely, with watering eyes.

Though the *externals* of religion often leave participants dry and unfulfilled, this longing for an *internal* experience of Ultimate Reality is what binds true seekers together on our pilgrimage, our quest for understanding. It is this emphasis on the importance of the *"internal state"* as compared to the *"external"* that gave birth to the Sufi maxim:

"Love the pitcher less, and the water more."[33]

This is a valuable truth that needs to resound in our minds again and again. We need to love the "pitcher" less—the form, the rules, the rituals, the dogma. And we need to love the "water" more—the deep flow of divine influence that alone can quench our thirst. You see, "religion" is the pitcher; "relationship" is the water—the living water—that alone can overflow the heart and fill the life. Many religions have conceptualized the means of possessing this spiritual panacea. The Sufis and others have fervently sought it. Only a select people have actually found it. Is it shrouded in esoteric mysteries understood only by a few initiates? No, not really. Actually, the way is so plain, it is often overlooked. Jesus said, "If anyone thirsts, let him come to Me and drink" *(John 7:37)*.

INTERPRETING THE NAMES OF VARIOUS RELIGIOUS GROUPS

In searching for common elements in various religions, it is helpful to inspect the interpreted meanings of the names of these groups. Together, they strike quite a harmonious chord.

A Buddhist is one who seeks "enlightenment."

A Christian is one who seeks "Christ-likeness."

An ECKANKAR devotee is one who seeks to be "a co-worker with God."

A Jainist is one who seeks to "conquer" attachment to this world.

A Jew is one who seeks to be a source of "praise to God."

A Kabbalist is one who seeks to "receive" an experience of the Divine (through the practice and contemplation of the Torah).

A Muslim is one who seeks "submission" to God and to the truth.

A Sikh is one who seeks to be a "disciple," a "follower" of God.

A Sufi is one who seeks "purity" and "mystical insight."

A Taoist is one who seeks to live in "the Way."

A Theosophist is one who seeks "divine wisdom."

A Yoga devotee is one who seeks to be "yoked with God."

Without controversy, the interpreted meanings of the names of these religious groups are descriptive of characteristics that should be the goal of any sincere seeker of truth.

Many who see these evident similarities immediately assume that all of these belief systems must, therefore, spring from the same source, that "True Light" radiates from every one of them. At one time, this would have been my conclusion as well. However, as a believer in Jesus Christ, I abide securely within well-defined doctrinal walls, yet I am very willing to admit that commonalities like these exist outside those walls. But how did they get there? This is an all-important issue that will be resolved powerfully in Part 5 of this book.

THE COMMON PULSE OF SPIRITUALITY

True spirituality involves being receptive and responsive to supernatural realities. When sensitivity in this area lights on a society in a positive way, it normally pollinates that people-group with a desire to aim for higher ideals. Those so influenced tend to blossom with righteous character and bear the fruit of compassionate works. This is of great benefit—whenever, wherever and however it happens. We live in a world that is far too often bent on pleasure-seeking and self-gratification. How refreshing it is to find people in every culture who want to lift their world to a better place! How reassuring it is to know there are still those who reach for virtue, kindness and goodness!

Just as every individual cell in the human body pulsates with the pulsation of the heart, so all positive religions appear to have a common pulsation. This has caused many to conclude, as Theosophist Annie Besant:

> *"Each religion has its own mission in the world,*
> *is suited to the nations to whom it is given and to*
> *the type of civilization it is to permeate."*[34]

Or dramatist George Bernard Shaw, who proposed:

> *"There is only one religion, though there are a*
> *hundred versions of it."*[35]

Pause for a moment. Think deeply. Dwell on the full ramifications of such an idea. For many thoughtful and compassionate persons, reaching such a conclusion erects a pleasing portal, especially those whose hearts groan for unity among men. However, those who entertain this proposition must be prepared to answer another important and related question:

> *Just because certain basic beliefs appear to have*
> *equal value and validity, do we leap to the conclusion*
> *that ALL of the doctrines of these various religious*
> *groups are valuable and valid?*

Asking such a question does not show lack of love or narrow-mindedness. It merely reveals a longing for genuineness. I believe Buddha was a passionate seeker for "True Light." At one point, he also must have dwelt on this pivotal issue.

Upon reviewing the conventional belief system ingrained in his particular culture, region and era, Buddha dared to go against the grain. Not only did he reject many traditional beliefs as invalid, he urged his hearers, if they encountered questionable doctrine, to do likewise. His admonition is still relevant today:

> *"Believe nothing...merely because you have been told it...or because it is traditional, or because you yourselves have imagined it. Do not believe what your teacher tells you merely out of respect for the teacher. But whatsoever, after due examination and analysis, you find to be conducive to the good, the benefit, the welfare of all beings—that doctrine believe and...take it as your guide."*
> (Kalama Sutta, Anguttara Nikaya III.65)[36]

Though I differ with Buddha on many major issues, I can shout an "Amen" to this statement. Seeking hearts must be neither gullible nor skeptical. But allow me to take it one notch higher. Genuine seekers cannot discover truth by their intellect alone. They must have the help of the Holy Spirit to discern what is of the "True Light"—and there are certain criteria that must be met for this to take place.

The rationalist philosopher Voltaire proposed:

> *"If God didn't exist, it would be necessary to invent him."*[37]

Though I disagree with any insinuation that God could be a mere invenntion of the imagination, I must admit this statement nudges my heart toward another important consideration.

Many human beings crave ultimate answers for the mysteries of life. So could it be, that in many cases, lacking true revelation (from the Holy Spirit), they have actually invented various concepts about God and his universe? Or being unsure of themselves and easily influenced, have they merely accepted someone else's invented worldview? Participants in either one of these scenarios may be quite sincere in striving for answers and quite sincere in arriving at conclusions—but sincerity is not always an indication of veracity.

Part of finding the "True Light" involves discerning correct doctrine from that which is the product of man's propensity for inventiveness in spiritual matters, his impressionable nature and his passion for religious tradition.

PART 2

WORLDVIEWS CONTRASTED

- ⌣· *The Three Essential Themes*
- ⌣· *The Seven Pillars of Wisdom*

> *"The chief end of life is the desire to enquire into truth."*
> (Bhagavata Purana 1.2.10)
> (* See special note: p. 329)

> *"God is a Spirit, and they that worship him must worship him in spirit and in truth."*
> (John 4:24 KJV)

> *"Wisdom has built her house, she has hewn out her seven pillars."*
> (Proverbs 9:1)[1]

Through the centuries, fervent voices have been heard in every kind of cultural setting promoting diverse notions about God's nature, man's condition and what the future holds for all of us. From thatched roofs to towering skyscrapers, from mountaintop stone altars to temples overlaid with gold, from isolated caves to high-spired cathedrals—the expression of religious opinions is as endless as the shifting images of a kaleidoscope. As a yoga teacher, I explained that these differences, though often appearing contradictory, are actually complementary and compatible. An ancient Hindu parable illustrates this stance quite well:

A king gathered a number of men who were born blind. He positioned them around an elephant, then asked each one to de-

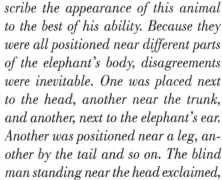

scribe the appearance of this animal to the best of his ability. Because they were all positioned near different parts of the elephant's body, disagreements were inevitable. One was placed next to the head, another near the trunk, and another, next to the elephant's ear. Another was positioned near a leg, another by the tail and so on. The blind man standing near the head exclaimed, "The elephant is like a pot!" *The blind man who was near the trunk argued,* "The elephant is like a hose!" *The one who handled the ear insisted,* "No, the elephant is like a fan!" *The one who touched the tail countered,* "The elephant is like a rope!" *In like manner, the rest submitted their differing observations: the elephant was like a pillar, a wall, a brush, a branch and so forth.*

The evident "moral of the story" is a unifying statement, an attempt to blend together the whole assortment of spiritual hues and shades that color this planet. At one time, I would have wholeheartedly embraced this analogy. Without hesitation, I would have instructed my yoga students that just like the elephant, religious groups whose doctrines seem radically opposed actually unite to make one homogeneous whole. Then, after an encounter with Ultimate Reality, I learned to my own amazement that the elephant trunk hanging next to me actually belonged to a different animal altogether—and the elephant tail being gripped by another truth-seeker was really a man-made rope.

Constrained by deep love for God, for truth and for all men, I embarked on what has since become nearly a fifty year pilgrimage— exploring the tenets of the eleven main living religions and numerous smaller religious sects and groups. As I crossed cultural boundaries and journeyed into various worldviews, I discovered many notable similarities, but I also encountered stark contrasts, remarkable differences of opinion on key issues.

The following seven categories emerged, in my thinking, as the most important subject areas. These deal with the revelation of God, the nature of the universe and the understanding of man's condition: past, present, and future.

These seven categories are the primary supporting pillars that uphold the doctrinal ceiling of most religious expressions encountered in this world.

> ***The Origin and Nature of the Universe***
> ***The Nature of God***
> ***The Origin and Nature of Man***
> ***The Nature of Salvation, Liberation, or Enlightenment***
> ***Dimensions or Planes of Existence***
> ***The Spiritual Journey and Ultimate Destiny of Man***
> ***Cycles, Ages, and the Ultimate State of the Universe***

Notice that three of these categories deal primarily with the universe *(The Origin and Nature of the Universe, Dimensions or Planes of Existence,* and *Cycles, Ages, and the Ultimate State of the Universe)*; three deal primarily with man's situation *(The Origin and Nature of Man, The Nature of Salvation, Liberation, or Enlightenment,* and *The Spiritual Journey and Ultimate Destiny of Man)*; and one category deals with the central and supreme subject: *(The Nature of God)*. So there are three main areas of revelation, three essential themes, on which we will be focusing our attention—(God, Man, and the Universe)—but under these headings there are seven divisions of important and insightful information.

You will quickly detect, as you continue reading, that in this section I make no effort to prove or disprove any doctrinal stance. My objective is to offer an unbiased examination of each religion's position concerning these "seven pillars of wisdom." Showcasing the beliefs of the eleven main religions is the major emphasis in this section and usually, in each category, viewpoints from all of these primary religious groups are included.

At times, the beliefs of certain smaller or more modern sects, individual teachers, and even some extinct religions are also inserted, if the additional information is unique and warrants inclusion. Some of those included are: Astrology, Bahá'í, ECKANKAR, Egyptian mythology, Gnosticism, Greek mythology, ISKCON, Kabbala, Kriya Yoga, Kundalini Yoga, Raja Yoga, Scientology, Theosophy, and the United Church of Religious Science. Sometimes different opinions can be found on a given subject within separate sects of the same religious group. Sometimes I include all these opinions; at other times, I emphasize the viewpoint that seems to be the most predominant.

An eighth category of essential wisdom that could have been included in this section is "The Origin of Evil." However, since this is a negative subject, I decided to deal with it later in the book. The seven subjects included here are all primarily positive.

As you gaze into this kaleidoscope of concepts, I believe you will marvel at the unique patterns that emerge. I think you will also be challenged to answer a crucially important question. Is it really true…is it even remotely possible…that all of these religious groups and doctrinal views actually make up…*one elephant?*

THE SACRED JOURNEY

You are now standing at the threshold. You are poised, ready to go forward in this journey of all journeys. The wisdom concepts you are about to explore deal with those areas of revelation most essential for any seeker of "True Light." Two paths will lead you through this spiritual terrain: the long path and the short path. You will learn far more on the long path, but the short path may be more appealing. You decide.

The long path—This involves reading all the detailed information contained in this section (Part 2). By the time you finish, you will possess an overview of the doctrinal stance of the eleven main living religions, and many smaller religious groups and individual teachers, with regard to "the seven pillars of wisdom." This is by far the most informative path to take.

The short path—If you feel it would be too laborious to read through the large amount of information presented in this section, you could simply scan it, and pick out those categories that most interest you. Then you could flip forward to the more concise, summarized contrasts offered on page 153 (the section subtitled, *Acknowledging the Contradictions)* then continue on through the rest of the book. You will miss a lot on this shorter path, but it leads to the same garden-like destination—where mind-probing questions take root, receive nourishment, and blossom into long-branched conclusions hanging heavy with everlasting fruit.

Whichever approach you choose, as you progress into this section, I urge you to read with a sense of great anticipation. For the final outcome of this overview will be the grand discovery of Ultimate Truth. After passing through the wilderness of humanly manufactured ideas about religion and spirituality, those who persist on this spiritual trek will surely encounter "Holy Ground" and a "Burning Bush" out of which God speaks.

THE THREE ESSENTIAL THEMES

THE SEVEN PILLARS OF WISDOM

"WISDOM HAS BUILT HER HOUSE,
SHE HAS HEWN OUT HER SEVEN PILLARS."

(Proverbs 9:1)

GOD

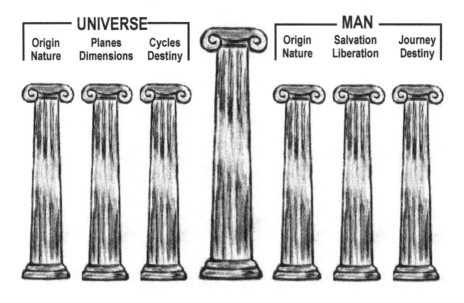

"GOD IS A SPIRIT, AND THEY
THAT WORSHIP HIM MUST WORSHIP
HIM IN SPIRIT AND IN TRUTH."

(John 4:24 KJV)

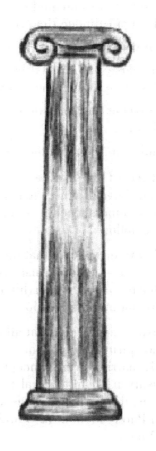

1

THE ORIGIN AND NATURE OF THE UNIVERSE

✳ **The Origin of the Universe**—There are seven main ways the existence of the universe is explained in various religions of the world:

(1) The universe is eternal and uncreated.

(2) The universe was created by God out of nothing *(ex nihilo)*.

(3) The universe was created by God (or various gods) or emanated out of Ultimate Reality using a preexisting substance.

(4) The universe was created by God, yet is separate from him.

(5) The universe was created by God. Though it is not God in manifestation, God is the essence of life within it.

(6) The universe was emanated out of God *(ex Deo)*. Therefore, it is divine in essence.

(7) The universe is simply the result of causal actions.

✳ **The Nature of the Universe**—Some religions teach the material universe is an illusion; others teach it is real. Some teach that it has a divine essence; others teach it is separate from God. The various views are defined as follows:

⌣· **Dualism:** the concept that the universe is composed of two distinct parts—mind and matter, or "being" and "non-being"—and that there is a distinct difference and separation between the Creator and his creation.

⌣· **Monism:** the concept that all things in the universe, natural and spiritual, are of one essential substance. Monism is usually married to the concept of pantheism. If "All is One" (monism), it is only logical that "All is God" (pantheism). There are three types of monism—the belief that the universe is: (1) Purely Mental; (2) Purely Physical; (3) A Mixture of Both Views.

⌣· **Monistic Theism:** a blend between monism and dualism. According to this view, during the soul's evolution, God temporarily "appears" to be transcendent, separate from the universe and from us. Ultimately, all things will blend together in undifferentiated, monistic oneness. In monistic theism God is both transcendent and immanent. This allows for a personal relationship with God on the way to an undifferentiated union with an impersonal God.

⌣· **Pantheism:** the idea that creation with its substances, laws and forces, is an emanation of God. In the most extreme form of pantheism, God does not exist apart from these—"All is God, and God is All."

- ⤸ᐧ **Panentheism**: the teaching that even though he transcends creation, yet God is the essence of life within it—"All is in God, and God is in All."

- ⤸ᐧ **Pluralism**: the idea that reality is comprised of a number of parts. No single belief system can sufficiently explain the nature of the universe and of God.

- ⤸ᐧ **Theism**: the view that creation is separate from God, that he is transcendent, existing apart from the material universe. The "life" of animate things is distinct from God. It is a gift *from* God, but it is not an emanation *of* God.

Some religions are very precise in their cosmogony; others are vague. A few even discourage speculation in these areas. Regardless of which view is held, most of us can agree with Sir Thomas Brown that:

"The created world is just a small parenthesis in eternity."[1]

THE ELEVEN MAIN LIVING RELIGIONS

Buddhism: This worldview presents a non-theistic approach to existence of the universe (also described as "atheistic monism.") "The world exists because of causal actions, all things are produced by causal actions and all beings are governed and bound by causal actions. They are fixed like the rolling wheel of a cart, fixed by the pin of its axle shaft." *(Sutta-Nipata 654)* The universe was not "created'; neither is it permanent.

Three things identify the true nature of this world: impermanence *(anitya,* also spelled *anicca)*; suffering *(dukkha)*; and insubstantiality or not-self *(anatman or anatta—no enduring essence in anything).* Buddhist scholar, Nyanaponika Thera, warns, "Ignoring or distorting the three basic facts ultimately leads only to frustration, disappointment and despair...the clear comprehension of impermanence, suffering and not-self will bring us a saner outlook on life. It will free us from unrealistic expectations, bestow a courageous acceptance...against the lure of deluded assumptions and beliefs...By seeing thus, detachment will grow, bringing greater freedom from egoistic clinging..."[2]

A fourth doctrine that further identifies the nature of things is *sunyata,* a word meaning "emptiness." This term communicates that all things are "empty" of lasting value or that they are "empty" of anything substantive. All things are mere "appearances," temporary illusions, possessing no lasting reality or substance. So in essence, they are "empty."

Realizing this as the basic character of the material world imparts an attitude of detachment that ultimately serves to free a person from suffering. In conclusion, therefore, even though interpretations of these terms may differ slightly from one Buddhist school to another, the following line of logic is generally accepted—All things are empty *(sunyata)*, impermanent *(anicca)*, devoid of essence *(anatman)* and marked by suffering *(dukkha)*. Buddhists contend that such a view is neither optimistic nor pessimistic, simply realistic.

Christianity: God created all things out of nothing *(ex nihilo)*. He did this by a series of verbal commands (e.g., "Let there be light," "Let there be a firmament in the midst of the waters," "Let the dry land appear," etc. Genesis 1:3; 9). All things in creation continue to be upheld by "the word of His power." *(Hebrews 1:3)*

Enhancing the Genesis account of creation, later Scripture explains, "By the word of the Lord the heavens were made, and all the host of them by the breath of His mouth." *(Psalms 33:6)* Just as words manifest out of our mouths accompanied by breath, so in the creation, the spoken commands of God manifested out of him, accompanied by divine "breath." The Hebrew word *ruach* is translated both "breath" and "spirit," so this is most likely a reference to the Spirit of God, sent forth during the act of creation to execute his word. The word "host" is probably referring to the multitude of heavenly bodies (stars, planets, asteroids, etc.), but could also be a reference to the angelic "host" of heaven.

The natural creation is separate from God, not an emanation of his own being. The material world is not an illusion; it is real, a gift from God.

Confucianism: Confucius did not offer any speculations concerning the origin of the universe. He was more concerned with the practicality of perfecting human character and relationships. However, some simple inferences are made, such as: "All things originate from Heaven." *(Li Ki 9.2.8)* Prior to the start of all things, there was nothing.

Hinduism: Different creation stories and Creator personalities exist side-by-side in Hinduism. The word "OM" (pronounced AUM) is described as the primal sound out of which the universe came forth. The creator-god is usually identified as Brahma, the first god in the Hindu triad. He is brought to birth in a lotus that emerges from the navel of Vishnu, the second god at the head of the Hindu pantheon. Brahma created the universe simply by opening his eyes. When he closes his eyes at the end of each eon, creation ceases to exist. Another cycle then ensues. In the *Visnu Purana*, Brahma is described bringing forth demons out of his thigh. He then abandons his first body, and it becomes the night. After creating the gods out of his mouth, he abandons his second body and it becomes the day.

In the Laws of Manu 1:5–14, a different creation story is told. The eternal "Divine Self-existent...desiring to produce beings of many kinds from his own body, first with a thought created the waters, and placed his seed in them. That seed became a golden egg, in brilliancy equal to the sun; in that egg he himself was born as Brahma, the progenitor of the whole world...The Divine One resided in that egg during a whole year, then he himself by his thought divided it into two halves; and out of those two halves he formed heaven and earth." *(See also Shatapatha Br. 11,1,6, Rig Veda 10,90.v)*

The Hindu Trimurti (the three highest gods) consists of Brahma, Vishnu and Shiva. Hindus ordinarily refer to Brahma as the "Creator," Vishnu as the "Preserver," and Shiva as the "Destroyer." However, Saivites (followers of Shiva) insist that Shiva is the primal person and source of the universe. Vaisnavites (worshippers of Vishnu) believe that he is the creator-god and relate him to the omnipresent, primeval waters believed to exist before the creation of the world.

Basic to Hinduism is the belief that the creation came from a primordial substance referred to as *prakriti*. Many teachers in Hinduism propose a pantheistic, monistic view of creation—that the universe, with its substance, laws and phenomena, is actually an emanation of God and that all things in the universe are of one essential substance. This monistic view is termed *Advaita*—a concept that also insists the natural creation is not real. It is an illusion, perpetrated by God—a condition called *maya*.

In absolute pantheism, God does not exist apart from the physical universe. In traditional Hinduism, however, there is both a manifested and an unmanifested aspect to Brahman: simultaneously, 'It' is both immanent (as the underlying life of creation) and transcendent (apart from creation). God being manifested as the universe, both physical and spiritual, was a result of the inner divine constraint, "Let me become many, let me be born." *(Taittriya Upanishad 2,6,1)*

There are other Hindus who believe in a dualistic approach concerning the Creator and creation called *Dvaita*. Madhva, one of its main proponents, felt "it is blasphemous to accept that a perfect God changes himself into an imperfect world."[3] He also taught that God and the soul are eternally distinct and separate from one another, and that the world is a reality, not an illusion perpetrated by Brahman. According to this worldview, the universe was not created; on the contrary, three things have existed eternally: God, souls, and the universe. There is also an interpretation that arrives midway between these two extremes called *Vishishtadvaita*, which is a qualified non-dualistic approach.

In Hindu cosmogony, there is no absolute beginning point assigned to the creation of the universe. Instead, there are an infinite number of cycles of creation and dissolution. The creation stories are understood to mean the periodic emanations of God into the form of the material universe. Furthermore, the word for creation in Sanskrit is *srishti*. It does not imply creating something out of nothing; it rather means the transformation of a subtle or spiritual substance into a physical or material one. So the more proper description might be that the universe is the "projection of the Supreme Being," not an act of creation.[4] It should also be mentioned that the earth is acknowledged as a deity in Hinduism and is referred to as a goddess with names such as *Bhumi* or *Prithvi*.

Islam: Muslims believe that God brought creation into being by the power of a spoken command, "Be" *(Kun)*. The material world is separate from God.

Jainism: Considers the world eternal and uncreated. Their Scripture states, "Those who on arguments of their own maintain that the world has been created do not know the truth."[5] The universe is made up of six basic elements or components that are infinitely indestructible. However, these are in a constant state of flux. These fundamental elements *(dravyas)* are: "soul, matter, time, space, the principles of motion, and the arrest of motion."[6] Only living matter contains a *jiva* or soul (consciousness). Non-living matter is *ajiva*. To a Jainist, matter is reality, not an illusion perpetrated by an emanating Force that temporarily takes upon "Itself" the "appearance" of matter.

Judaism: Creation beliefs are basically identical to the Genesis account offered under "Christianity," being the first book of the Old Testament. Other Jewish sources offer additional interpretations and legends. For instance, a tradition exists that in the Temple there was *Even Shetiyyah* (the foundation stone), "which was so named because upon it the world was founded, and from this as a center the earth was created." *(Babylonian Talmud, Yoma 54b)*[7] "Since the Holy Land was God's chosen country it must have been first in creation; and because the site of the Temple was the most sacred of all places, the process of creation must have begun there. The legendary stone also points to another widespread belief in ancient times which is explicitly mentioned in Rabbinic literature, viz.: "The Holy One, blessed be He, cast a stone into the primeval sea from which the world was formed."[8]

Shinto: In the Kojiki, the creation myth depicts a cosmic egg splitting to form heaven and earth. Revealing a "yin-yang" kind of cosmogony, the better, positive portion of the egg-shaped substance rises to form the sky; while the inferior, negative portion descends to produce the earth and sea.

Unique to Shinto tradition is the belief that the Japanese islands were one of the first acts of creation. After the initial creation of the heaven and earth, the god Izanagi and the goddess Izanami (the last of seven generations of gods) were standing on a floating bridge in the heaven. Izanagi was stirring the ocean water with his jeweled, celestial spear. Once raised, the droplets of salt water fell from the spearhead forming the Japanese island of Ono-goro-jima. To this island the divine couple descended, where they married and gave birth to other deities, the other Japanese islands and the Japanese people.

Sikhism: Maintains that this world was created by a divine decree *(hukam)*. "With a single command creation was unfurled..."*(Japji 16)* The whole creation and individual destinies are maintained and preserved by the complementary principles of justice *(nian)* and grace *(nadar)*.

Sikh doctrine is strongly against the pantheistic notion that all substances, forces and laws in this universe are essentially God in manifestation. However they do embrace what has been termed "panentheism": the idea that God, though transcendent, is the essence of life within creation. The universe is not God, but his container. "The world is God's own form." *(Adi Granth 922:6)* So most Sikhs would conclude, "This creation is divine since God is present in the creation in His Immanent form."[9]

Contrary to the Hindu belief that the world is an illusion *(maya)* and the Buddhist doctrine that all phenomena in this world are ultimately empty *(shunyata)* and unreal, Sikhism is world affirming. Guru Nanak taught, "Real are Thy realms and real Thy Universe. Real are Thy worlds and real Thy created forms." *(Adi Granth p. 463)*

Taoism: Taoism is pantheistic in its view of the material world. The origin of the universe is explained: "[Tao] is its own source, its own root. Before heaven and earth existed it was there, firm from ancient times. It gave spirituality to the spirits and gods; it gave birth to heaven and to earth." *(Chuang-Tzu 6)* "It is Nameless...the origin of Heaven and earth." Yet it is "Namable...the mother of all things." *(Tao-te Ching 1)* The primal 'Life Force' that initiated all things and continues to permeate the universe is referred to as *ch'i* (pronounced both "chee" and "key"). The pre-creation state is called *Wu Chi*: ultimate nothingness.

THE ORIGIN AND NATURE OF THE UNIVERSE

A reliable source of orthodox beliefs speaks of a "Primordial Breath" that split into two parts: the light yang breath brought forth heaven; the heavier yin breath formed earth.[10] It also explains how "pure energy rose up [out of the primordial chaos] and became heaven, turbid energy sank down and became earth, and the conjoined energies in the middle became yin and yang" [which brought forth humanity]. *(Huai-nan-tzu 3)*

In certain sacred texts Lao-Tzu, the founder of Taoism, is deified as the original personification of the Tao, who brought forth creation and abides with all men. Sacred literature also speaks of "three basic energies of creation—mysterious, beginning, and primordial" that combined to make a "heavenly sound" (similar to the Hindu concept of the word "OM"). Also, from the three basic energies, over vast periods of time, were brought forth the Three Treasure Lords (also called "the Three Pure Ones" and "the Celestial Lords of the Three Pure Realms"). They are—the Lord of Heavenly Treasure, the Lord of Numinous Treasure, and the Lord of Spirit Treasure. These three Original Deities were emanated from Lao-chün (the deified aspect of the founder, Lao-tzu). Together these deities brought forth the nine energies out of which came all of creation.[11]

Coincidental with the formation of earth was the creation of the first man, named Pangu. When this progenitor of the human race died, his body was transformed into various parts of the material world: "His breath became the wind and clouds; His voice became the thunder. His left eye was the sun; His right eye was the moon. His four limbs became the four compass points...His blood and body liquid turned into streams and rivers. His muscles and sinews became solid earth...His hair turned into stars. His body hair turned into grass and trees. His teeth and bones were transformed into gold and minerals...His sweat was the rain and moisture of the land. The germs in his body were carried off by the wind; they became the mass of the people." *(from the Yuanqi Lun)*[12]

Zoroastrianism: According to this worldview, there are two eternally existent gods: Ahura Mazda, the "Wise Lord" and god of light, who created both the spiritual and material worlds (during the second 3,000 year period of history) and Angra Mainyu, god of evil and darkness, who later created six demons and a rival material world: including undesirable creatures such as serpents and flies.

OTHER RELIGIONS, SECTS OR TEACHERS

Bahá'í: "The material universe has always existed, albeit in different form, but its generating impulse was the Word of God."[13] It is made up of individual parts of creation (such as stars, planets, trees, animals, people, etc.) that do originate in time. However, though the individual parts may be subject to change, decay or cessation of existence, "creation as a whole has neither beginning nor end."[14] The biblical creation account is to be taken figuratively, not literally.

Benjamin Creme (Share International Foundation): "Esoteric science postulates seven streams of energy, or rays, whose interaction, at every conceivable frequency, creates everything in Cosmos...three primary rays, or rays of aspect, and four secondary rays of attribute." The "Rays of Aspect" are: (1) Power, Will or Purpose; (2) Love-Wisdom; (3) Active, Creative Intelligence. The "Rays of Attribute" are: (4) Harmony through Conflict, Beauty or Art; (5) Concrete Science or Knowledge; (6) Abstract Idealism or Devotion; (7) Ceremonial Order or Magic or Ritual or Organization.[15]

Brahma Kumaris World Spiritual Organization (Raja Yoga): The earth was never created. It has always existed. Time, space and matter are all infinite, though constantly in a state of change. The Supreme Soul and all individual souls are also eternal. There are five basic elements in the universe: earth, water, fire, ether and air.

Egyptian Mythology: Originally only the ocean existed. Then Ra, the sun, emerged from an egg that appeared on the surface of the ocean. Ra produced four offspring, two gods Shu and Geb, and two goddesses Tefnut and Nut. Shu and Tefnut were transformed into the atmosphere. They stood on top of Geb, who became the earth. Then they elevated Nut, whose metamorphosis produced the sky.

Gnosticism: The original lofty and unknowable Creator generated a number of lesser deities by emanation. "The last of these, Sophia ("wisdom") conceived a desire to know the unknowable Supreme Being. Out of this illegitimate desire was produced a deformed, evil god, or demiurge, who created the universe" (the material world).[16] This demiurge is usually identified as Yahweh or Jehovah, the God of the Jews. Because of its negative origin, matter is considered corrupt and evil.

Greek Mythology: "Chaos generated the solid mass of Earth, from which arose the starry, cloud-filled Heaven. Mother Earth and Father Heaven, personified respectively as Gaea and her offspring Uranus, were the parents of the Titans."[17] One of the Titans, Prometheus, created men, then went up to heaven and secured a torch lit with the fire of the sun. Bearing this gift of fire back to earth, he earned the wrath of Zeus who reacted by chaining Prometheus to a rock. Zeus is considered the father of all gods and mortals, yet he did not create either of these. He fills a fatherly role only in the sense of being the head of the Olympian family, the ruler of the world and protector of all.

THE ORIGIN AND NATURE OF THE UNIVERSE

ISKCON (International Society for Krishna Consciousness): According to ancient, standard, Vedic teachings, Krishna is described as the Creator of all things. "In the beginning of the creation...there was no Brahma, no Siva, no fire, no moon, no stars in the sky, no sun. There was only Krishna, who creates all and enjoys all."[18] "Krsna [preferred spelling of Krishna] who is known as Govinda, is the Supreme Godhead. He has an eternal, blissful, spiritual body. He is the origin of all. He has no other origin, and He is the prime cause of all causes."[19]

Kabbala (Mystical Judaism): God created the universe by manifesting a series of ten rays or intelligences, which descended from him. These ten emanations are called *Sefirot*. These are considered personifications of various attributes of God. (See "Kabbala" under *The Nature of God* for a detailed description of these emanations.)

Creation is comprised of four major realms of consciousness, called worlds or universes, plus a fifth that could be called the realm of origination. These "are not separate universes, but are concentric, one within the other. *Assiyah* is the world of physicality; *Yetzirah*, the world of emotions; *Beriyah*, the world of the intellect; *Atzilut*, the world of the spirit; and *Adam Kadmon*, the primordial source."[20]

There are two other unique concepts that need to be emphasized:

(1) **The Mystical Power of the Hebrew Alphabet**—In the Sefer Yetzirah (the Book of Formation), believed to have been written by Abraham about 4,000 years ago, an in-depth explanation is offered describing how the Creator used numerous combinations of letters in the Hebrew alphabet to bring forth the physical universe. "Each letter has a specific energy, and each reveals a particular aspect of the Creator."[21]

(2) **The Shattering of the Vessel**—This idea begins with the premise that a dominant characteristic in the Creator ("the Light") was and is an infinite and boundless desire to share of "Itself." This necessitated the creation of a "receiving entity." Thus, "the Vessel" came into being, formed from the Light. At a certain point, the Vessel wanted to become more like the Creator, but was unable to do so, as long as it could only receive and not give. So to achieve its goal, the Vessel resisted the Light and the Light pulled back. Overwhelmed with desire to be restored and refilled, the Vessel drew on the Light, which then rushed into the Vessel with even greater force. "The result was the defining moment of all kabbalistic teaching. At that instant, the Vessel shattered. It exploded into an infinite number of fragments, which became our universe" (both matter and energy). This concept is promoted as being in harmony with the "Big Bang Theory."[22]

Kriya Yoga (Swami Sri Yukteswar): Creation sprang into being from four *manus* (primal thoughts): the Word, Time, Space and the Atom. The utterance of "Aum" (synonymous with Amen) brought all things into being. The universe is the body of God and is comprised of the same five elements as men's bodies (earth, water, fire, air and ether). **(Paramahansa Yogananda)** Corresponding to a belief that Ultimate Reality is an impersonal being (a being that does not feel or experience emotion), he taught, "creation came into being by a desireless desire of spirit."[23]

Meher Baba: Taught that God did not actually, consciously create the universe. "It started automatically. First there was God and nothing else. In God was everything: experience, power, knowledge and existence. But he had no consciousness that he was God. All this bother and headache you see around you is to gain that consciousness."[24] Prior to the act of creation, God was in a state of "infinite unconsciousness."[25] God himself passes through three levels or states of consciousness: (1) His Original State (unconsciousness); (2) Helplessness (by expressing himself in the form of helpless humans); (3) All-powerfulness (by unveiling his divinity in enlightened beings).[26]

Meher Baba also proposed that matter does not exist because "there is nothing but God...the existence of matter is due to the existence of the mind. When the mind disappears, matter also vanishes."[27] "The whole world is created and carried on by the force of the imagination."[28] Actually, it is only God who appears as the universe. "The manifold evolving universe arises from the mixing of the one Reality and Nothing...It is an outcome of Nothing and is nothing. It only seems to have existence."[29] Meher Baba proposed that there are other universes. Within this universe, "there are 18,000 worlds in creation which are inhabited...but the value of our Earth...is inestimable. For it is here and here alone...that God-realization can be attained."[30]

Scientology: Foundationally, the cosmogony of Scientology is similar to Buddhism—"Before the beginning was a Cause and the entire purpose of the Cause was the creation of effect."[31] However, the full explanation of this "cause" goes beyond the boundaries of the Buddhist worldview.

Human beings are comprised of three parts: mind, body and *thetan* (pronounced thay´-ten). The *thetan* is the real person, "the continuing and persisting identity which transcends the body which it inhabits. It is said to be immaterial and immortal, or at least to have the capacity to be immortal, and to have an infinite creative potential."[32] *Thetans* originally existed in a pre-creation, spiritual state with unhindered, divine, godlike abilities and attributes. For their own pleasure, they brought the material world into existence. However, in the distant past, once creating MEST

(Material-Energy-Space-Time), *thetans* became entrapped by it, and lost the awareness of their initial, transcendent state.

Sufism (Mystical Islam): The "universes" (and there are many) are an expression of God's Infinite Compassion and came into existence through the utterance of the Divine command, "*Kun* (Be)!" One of the early Sufi mystics, Suhrawardi (1153-1191 C.E.), explained that the "Light of God" brings all things into existence and sustains them. He also offered the unique teaching that Gabriel is the guardian angel of the human race and that all things were created by the sound of his wings.

Most adherents of this worldview insist that no true Sufi would ever claim a pantheistic view of the universe (though non-Sufi theologians who evaluate the doctrines of this religion, at times, conclude otherwise). However, they do embrace the idea of the Unity of All Being, the relationship of all planes of existence as an expression of the Divine Reality. The term "panentheism" may come closer to fitting inside the Sufi mold: the idea that the universe is not God in manifestation, but he is the life at the core of all things. Speaking of the Divine Spirit, one more modernistic Sufi explained, "every atom of this universe, mental or material, is an outcome of that source and cannot exist without having a part of that heavenly radiance within it."[33]

Theosophy (H.P. Blavatsky): "We believe in no *creation*, but in the periodical and consecutive appearances of the universe from the subjective onto the objective plane of being, at regular intervals of time, covering periods of immense duration." "No one creates it...We, Occultists and Theosophists, see in it the only universal and eternal *reality* casting a periodical reflection of *itself* on the infinite Spatial depths. This reflection, which you regard as the objective *material* universe, we consider as a temporary *illusion* and nothing else. That alone which is eternal is *real*."[34]

United Church of Religious Science (Dr. Ernest Holmes): "Creation is God making something out of Himself, or Itself, by becoming the thing He creates...We must understand that *Creation* does not mean making something out of nothing, but means the passing of Substance into form."[35] "Creation is the passing of Being into be-coming: the flowing of the Invisible into the visible."[36] Just as God and man have a "trinity," so the universe has a "trinity" aspect: (1) The Physical World; (2) The Mental World; (3) The Conscious World. Human beings are one with all three.

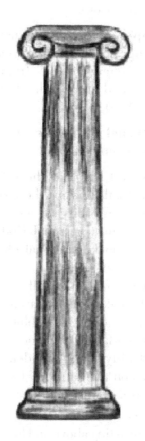

2

THE NATURE OF GOD

✳ **The Nature of God**—There are three main ways "Ultimate Reality" is defined in the religions of this world:

(1) **A Personal Being** (one who thinks, remembers, hears, speaks, plans, responds, expresses emotion, demonstrates character, exercises will and makes choices and judgments based on reason).

(2) **An Impersonal Being** (a non-thinking, non-hearing, non-speaking, non-emotional, non-volitional, non-responsive "cosmic energy force" from which all personal beings originate and into which all personal beings will ultimately be absorbed).[1]

(3) **An Eternal Principle** (a system of rules and laws that govern the universe).

Many would say that these three interpretations of "Ultimate Reality" are actually one and the same. Though appearing to be uniquely different, they can easily be merged in syncretistic harmony. But is that possible? Can a personal God who constantly expresses himself emotionally and makes rational choices be the same as a "Universal Principle" that exists apart from emotion and is governed by nothing more than a system of cosmic laws? If all world religions spring from the same eternal Fountainhead—as separate, yet related "divine streams," they should all bear a strong resemblance to their original "Source." If they are all unique parts of a common global spirituality, their interpretation of Ultimate Reality should be identical, or at least run parallel. As you read the views on the nature of God contained in this section, you will discover this is certainly not the case.[2]

Religions that acknowledge a Supreme Being portray him as transcendent (existing above and beyond the material world), as immanent (present within the material world) or various mixtures of these two views. Some of the most recognized characterizations of God (or of supernatural realities) are as follows:

⌣ **Animism** is the belief in a multitude of spiritual beings that either bless or curse, help or harm man's condition of existence. These spirits have limited powers and localized dwelling places, such as rivers, trees, and mountains. Some can also function on other planes of existence, above or beneath the earth. Appeasing these spirits and appealing to each spirit's unique abilities or powers is very much a part of primal religions.

- **Deism** is the belief that after creating the universe God transcended creation, leaving it to function on its own, in accordance with certain rational laws. Understanding of God takes place through reason, not revelation. God does not involve himself in the affairs of men or the shaping of history.

- **Dualism** is a belief in two supreme gods or powers that are in opposition to each other.

- **Henotheism** accepts the existence of many gods, but exalts one to a position of greater prominence.

- **Monotheism** is the belief that there is just one God. Normally, monotheistic traditions, such as Christianity, Islam and Judaism, do not subscribe to either pantheism or panentheism. In worldviews such as these, God is immanent because he is omnipresent, but he is not actually "manifested" *as* the material universe. He is still distinct from creation. Sikhism is an exception, definitely standing for monotheism, yet embracing not a pantheistic, but a panentheistic stance on creation.

- **Pantheism** is the belief that the universe, with its substances, laws and forces, is an emanation of God. In absolute pantheism God does not exist apart from these. In ordinary pantheism, though God is expressed *as* the universe, God is not confined *to* the universe. By identifying the universe with its Maker, pantheism carries the concept of the immanence of God to its furthest extreme. "All is God, and God is All."

- **Panentheism** is a modification of pantheism, insisting that God is the principle behind nature, the essence of life *within* creation, yet he has not manifested himself *as* creation. God is not only immanent; he is also transcendent. He is both in the world, yet beyond it. "All is in God, and God is in All."

- **Polytheism** is a belief in the existence of many gods. Each god is usually unique in some personality trait or in the care of a specific facet of nature or a specific condition of human existence.

- **Theism** is the belief in a Supreme Being that highlights divine transcendence, yet believes in his immanence and his care for those who are in this world. God is omnipotent, omniscient, and omnipresent in theism. He is perfect, even though evil exists in the world. He is a personal God and often intervenes in the affairs of men. The life of creation is a gift *from* God, but is not a manifestation *of* God.

THE ELEVEN MAIN LIVING RELIGIONS

Buddhism: There are diverse opinions within the Buddhist camp concerning the nature of Ultimate Reality. The oldest sect, **Theravada Buddhism** (called the Lesser Vehicle), is often labeled atheistic because Buddha did not train his disciples to worship any deity. However, "ancient Buddhist doctrines do not deny the existence of gods." On the contrary, Buddha acknowledged the existence of gods inhabiting the cosmos, yet he insisted that they are "impermanent like all other living beings. Thus, they too must escape rebirth through nirvana."[3] It is possible that Buddha had contempt for the Indian concept of gods and goddesses because they indulged in sensual behavior or exhibited human frailties. Some Buddhists go a step further, explaining like Reginald Ray—"that while they [deities] appear to exist on a relative level, they have no final reality. Instead they are projections of the deepest qualities of our own human nature."[4] Unlike some other branches of Buddhism, Theravada Buddhists do not revere Buddha as a god. He is considered merely a teacher, an enlightened master. Most of them would agree that even speculating about the nature of God is useless, a hindrance to achieving enlightenment.

Mahayana Buddhism (called the Greater Vehicle) contains many different schools, such as the following groups. **Zen Buddhism** professes that there is no god who can assist a seeker in achieving enlightenment *(satori)* or final extinction *(paranirvana)*. Yet other Mahayana schools emphasize that Gautama Buddha was a mere earthly manifestation of a transcendent, celestial Buddha, who is the highest deity. Ultimate Reality is *sunyata* (the void)—an impersonal cosmic force that expresses itself through various gods, Buddhas and bodhisattvas who are worshipped.

Pure Land Buddhists worship Amida Buddha (different than the Gautama Buddha) as a personal savior god. He is also called Amitabha. He was originally a monk, Dharmakara, who attained Buddhahood. **Nichiren Buddhists** place their faith in Nichiren, a thirteenth century Japanese monk, who is believed to be a reincarnation of Jogyo Bosatsu. According to this sect, Jogyo was a bodhisattva (one who attains Buddhahood but delays passing into Nirvana in order to bring spiritual assistance to others through his boundless supply of good merits).

Tibetan Buddhism promotes worshipful devotion to a long line of Dalai Lamas. The most recent one, Tenzin Gyatso, is the fourteenth and is presently exiled from Tibet. All Dalai Lamas are considered to be bodhisattvas, as well as incarnations of their predecessors. Tibetan Buddhists worship a pantheon of innumerable Buddhas, bodhisattvas, gods, goddesses and divine beings. Image worship is spurned in some branches of Buddhism, yet promoted in others.

THE NATURE OF GOD

Christianity: Christian doctrine teaches there is one God to the exclusion of all others, and that he has a triune nature. The Godhead is comprised of the Father, the Son, and the Holy Spirit. These three are one. They are distinct from one another, yet not divided. They work in perfect unison and they are never in conflict with each other. Jesus Christ is revealed in John's writings as the Word who was "with God" in the beginning and yet "was God." *(John 1:1)* He has no beginning and no end, existing "from everlasting to everlasting." *(Micah 5:2 KJV, Psalms 90:2)* Whenever God appeared in any form during the Old Testament era (such as the "Pillar of Fire" leading the Israelites through the desert) that was a manifestation of the pre-incarnate Christ. *(See 1 Corinthians 10:4.)* In his incarnation, Jesus is described as being "God manifested in the flesh." *(1 Timothy 3:16)*

The personal God of Christianity is the personal God of Judaism: the God of Abraham, Isaac and Jacob. He is so holy and flawless he cannot be tempted with evil, neither does he tempt any person. *(See James 1:13–14.)* There is no negative, evil or dark side to his nature. *(See 1 John 1:5.)* He is transcendent: existing above and beyond this material world. Yet he is also immanent, actively manifesting himself in this world and making himself accessible to men. *(See Jeremiah 23:23–24, Ephesians 3:17.)*

Through the example and teachings of Jesus, the Creator was especially revealed as the "heavenly Father" who is motivated by a deep concern for mankind. The apostle John explained, "God so loved the world that he gave his only begotten Son." *(John 3:16)*

Idolatry is prohibited in Christianity. Some branches of Christianity use statues and icons, though not in the same sense as idols. Other Christian sects speak against this practice as being non-biblical and idolatrous.

Confucianism: In this worldview, more a philosophy of life than a religion, Ultimate Reality is primarily described as a universal law, a moral principle, omnipresent, invisible and eternal. Confucius contended, "There is no place in the highest heavens above or in the deepest waters below where the moral law is not to be found." *(Doctrine of the Mean 12)* However, popular Confucianism has been mixed with other beliefs, becoming polytheistic and animistic. Numerous deities and divine beings are worshiped. Some adherents promoted the worship of Confucius himself, though this practice was never popular. In recent years, the temples of Confucius have fallen into great neglect. Ancestor worship is also encouraged, conducted at special altars erected in the home or temple.

Hinduism: Hinduism accepts the existence of many gods. However, most Hindus believe that all gods are emanations of the One God who pervades everything. Consequently, some might describe this worldview as monotheistic polytheism. In the Upanishads, Ultimate Reality is described as the impersonal Brahman. Brahman is described as possessing two aspects: transcendent (unmanifested) and immanent (manifested). According to the Sankhya School, Ultimate Reality manifests in two main ways: as consciousness *(purusha)* and as material form *(prakriti)*. Upon manifesting, "It" (the word "Brahman" is neuter gender) is expressed in a multitude of ways, including lesser gods and demigods. Ultimate Reality, which is impersonal ("without attributes"—*nirguna*), manifests in numerous deities who are personal ("with attributes"—*saguna*). "Nirguna Brahman is not an object of prayer, but of meditation and knowledge."[5]

According to the Puranas, the most important manifestations of Brahman make up the Hindu triad (or Trimurti)—Brahma (the Creator), Vishnu (the Preserver), and Shiva (the Destroyer). It should be noted, though, that in the Vedas (the most revered and ancient sacred texts) Vishnu is seldom mentioned and Shiva is left out altogether.

Some Bhakti sects (devotional sects) in Hinduism are henotheistic, exalting a singular god, such as Vishnu, Shiva or Krishna, to a place of superiority or prominence above all others. Multiplied thousands of gods are worshipped (the traditional figure is 330 million). Hindu Scripture encourages, "O gods! All your names [and forms] are to be revered, saluted and adored." *(Rig-Veda 10.63.2)* Some gods are associated with nature, like Surya the sun god; others with animals, such as Ganesha the elephant-god and Hanuman the monkey-god. Brahman is the underlying Self, the essence of life common to all things. This equates the creation with the Creator—the former is an emanation of the latter. Some Hindus profess a pantheistic view of the relationship between the Creator and the creation; while others hold a panentheistic view.

Though most Hindus are quite tolerant and quick to declare that all religions are one, historical Hinduism is still somewhat exclusive in its claims to correct revelation. Their Scripture states, "In the beginning this [universe] was Brahman alone...whoever reveres any other deity... does not rightly understand." *(Brhadaranyaka Upanishad 1.4.10)* In other words, worshipping any personal deity as Ultimate Reality is an unenlightened view of the supreme essence of God. Some Hindus even propose that those who make this error are kept in the cycle of rebirth.

For those who subscribe to Brahman being "the origin, the cause and basis of all existence," the same is an infinitely inexhaustible reservoir of (1) Pure being *(sat)*; (2) Pure intelligence *(cit)*; (3) Pure delight *(ananda)*.[6] However, this Ultimate Expression of Divinity is beyond the comprehension of the human mind. The essence of the Kena Upanishad communicates, "He who thinks he knows Brahman, knows not." Image worship is accepted and cultivated in Hinduism, though some claim it is only an aid in worship for the spiritually immature.

Islam: Islam is strongly monotheistic, teaching that Allah is the only true God. This name for the Creator probably stems from *al illah*, meaning *"the God."* To associate God with any created thing is the most abominable of sins and is called *shirk*. Because of this, Islam does not accept the pantheon of Hindu gods, the Trinity of Christianity, or the deification of any religious leader. God has no partner nor equal. The word "Allah" in Arabic cannot be plural and is actually neither male nor female.

Though Allah is a personal God, most Muslims consider him so lofty as to be incomprehensible to the minds of finite men. God never speaks directly to men; he always sends a messenger: either an angel or a prophet (Mohammed being the last). However, for those who are truly devoted God grants *noor hidayah*—the "light of guidance." This is the "opening of a person's heart" to understand Allah's nature and ways. Sufism, an offshoot of Islam, teaches differently: that Allah is personally accessible, and that ecstatic, mystical experiences with God are obtainable, especially through a whirling kind of sacred dance.

Allah has 99 names, all of which describe various divine attributes (e.g., the Living, the Eternal, the Supreme, the Tremendous, the Merciful and the Compassionate). He is transcendent, independent of the material universe and perfect in all his ways. Muslims believe strongly in the sovereignty of God, to the point that all events in life are traceable to his will. A byword often heard among Muslims is, "if Allah wills." A great emphasis is placed on Allah's justice and mercy. Idolatry or image worship is strictly prohibited in Islam.

Jainism: The founder, Mahavira, taught no separate existence of God. Everyone can attain godhood by making supreme efforts in the right direction. Later deified by his followers, Mahavira is described in Jainist Scripture as descending from heaven, living a sinless life and worthy of worship as the "Omniscient." He is revered as the twenty-fourth Tirthankara (meaning Ford-maker, a great teacher who guides his followers across the river of transmigration).

Five different types of "Supreme Beings" are venerated in the Jainist religion. Dedicated Jainists participate daily in certain rituals aimed at invoking these "Supreme Beings": (1) Arhats—also known as Jinas (conquerors, great teachers) or Tirthankaras (Ford-makers). Because they have been liberated from the world and its affairs, though they are worshipped, Tirthankaras cannot intervene personally in the lives of their devotees; (2) Siddhas—perfected saints, those who have attained liberation and dwell in eternal ecstasy at the uppermost part of the universe; (3) Archaryas—spiritual teachers who lead monastic orders; (4) Upadhyayas—teaching monks who train other monks and nuns; (5) Monks—devotees who live the life of a monk (necessary for salvation, according to some Jains).[7]

Though Mahavira initially refused the multiplicity of gods found in Hinduism, modern Jainism has developed into a polytheistic belief system. For instance, along with superior deities, "there are in heaven and hell ninety-nine kinds of gods who are regarded as menial because they serve."[8] Image worship is presently accepted among some Jains, though originally Mahavira taught against this practice. Two principal sects reject the use of temples and idols.

Judaism: Passionately monotheistic, Judaism teaches that there is only one God to the exclusion of all others. He is omnipotent, omniscient and omnipresent: the sole Creator and Sustainer of the universe. In Isaiah 44:6 God declares, "I am the first and I am the last; apart from me there is no God." A greatly revered passage in Scripture is Deuteronomy 6:4 (the *Shema*): "Hear, O Israel: The Lord our God is one Lord." *(KJV)* God is transcendent (independent of the material universe), holy and perfect in all his ways. Idolatry and any representation of God are strictly prohibited. The first two commandments of the Decalogue declare, "I am the Lord your God, who brought you out of the land of Egypt, out of the house of bondage. You shall have no other gods before me. You shall not make for yourself a carved image, or any likeness of anything that is in heaven above, or that is in the earth beneath, or that is in the water under the earth; you shall not bow down to them nor serve them." *(Exodus 20:2-4)* God is formless. Anthropomorphisms found in Scripture are merely symbolic, a literary device used to emphasize some aspect of God's character.

The ineffable name of God is considered so holy it is not even written in common writing. In the original Hebrew it is represented by the Tetragrammaton: transliterated YHWH. Later translators erroneously rendered this Jehovah (an impossibility because there is no "J" in Hebrew). The more correct pronunciation is most likely Yahweh, or Yahovah or something similar. None of these is fully accepted by all Jews. When the Tetragrammaton appears in Scripture, those reading in Hebrew usually insert the word "Adonai" meaning "Lord" (the word used in most English versions). The knowledge of the correct pronunciation of the name of God is something else the Messiah will restore when he comes.

Shinto: The word *Shinto* means "the way of the *kami*." This stems from two Chinese words: *shen* meaning "divine being" and *tao* meaning "way." The word *kami* refers primarily to the various gods or deities worshipped in this religion. However, it also relates to the sacred essence abiding in both animate and inanimate objects (such as oceans, mountains, waterfalls, trees, plants, and animals). Specifically, it alludes to the spirits that dwell in the numerous shrines dedicated to them. Generally speaking, the word *kami* can be used in reference to anything awe-inspiring, mysterious or impressive—including that which is evil. On the highest level this term speaks of the Divine Consciousness that flows through all things, the vital force of the universe.

Originally, almost all Shinto gods were identified with forces or objects in nature, such as: Tsuki-yomi, the moon god, and Kagase-wo, the star god. Different *kami* fulfill different functions, such as: Fudo, who guards against danger or misfortune; Yakushi, who imparts healing for the mind and the body; or Inari, the rice god who brings an abundant harvest. Some *kami* are righteous in character, while others are wicked, like the evil god Susa-no-wo, and a whole group of "lying deities." *(Nihon-gi 1:20, Ko-ji-ki, 229)* There are at least 3,700 gods who have shrines dedicated to their worship, though a common declaration is that there are 800 myriads of deities.

Shinto emphasizes the worship of ancestors as divine beings, because all eventually become *kami* (thirty-three years after death). Worship of emperors as direct, divine descendants of Ama-terasu, the sun goddess, has also been a dominant theme until recent years.

Sikhism: Sikhs believe in a monotheistic view of God, as revealed to the founder, Guru Nanak. God is described as being "timeless and without form," the Creator, Sustainer and Director of the universe. Sikhism emerged in the early 1500s in a culture and geographical area dominated by Hinduism, yet it does not accept the pantheon of Hindu gods, nor Hindu concepts like pantheism, monism and the caste system. Yet this religion is very syncretistic, teaching that all religions and sects are merely using different names for the same God. "There is but One though your forms be unnumbered, Guru of gurus, Creator of all."[9] Another scripture adds, "From nothingness the Formless One assumes a form, the Attribute-free becomes full of attributes."*(Adi Granth, p. 940)*

The main name attributed to the Ultimate Deity in Sikhism is Sat Nam ("True Name"). Other important designations are: Sat ("Truth"), Sat Guru ("True Guru"), Karta Purakh ("Creator"), Akal Purakh ("Timeless Being") and Wahi-Guru ("Wondrous Guru"). The God of Sikhism is a God of grace (unmerited love). God is the Eternal Guru or Teacher. Sikhs consider God to be both Father and Mother; they do not attribute a specific gender to the Creator.

THE NATURE OF GOD

The doctrine of Brahma, the Creator god in Hinduism, dying and then being reborn in a new era of manifestation is refuted in Sikhism. (See "Hinduism" under *Cycles, Ages, and the Ultimate State of the Universe.*) In the *Mool Mantra,* Sikhs make a confession of their faith. In it is the statement, "There is One God...the Omnipresent, pervades the universe...is not born, nor dies to be born again." He is also described as being "without fear" and "without hate." The concept of Avatars, or God incarnating in human form, is a contested doctrine among Sikhs. Idolatry or image worship is outlawed.

Taoism: Lao-Tzu, founder of Taoism (pronounced "Dowism") explained his interpretation of Ultimate Reality in the following terms: "There was something undifferentiated and yet complete, which existed before heaven and earth. Soundless and formless, *it* depends on nothing and does not change. *It* operates everywhere and is free from danger. *It* may be considered the mother of the universe. I do not know *its* name; I call *it* Tao." (*Tao-te Ching 25,* emphasis by author)

Five times the governing principle of the universe is described in this passage, not as a *he*, but as an *it*. So Ultimate Reality in Taoism is not *someone* personal, but rather *something* impersonal, an existing order that guides all things. One source declares this to be simply the "rhythm of the universe."[10] This Universal Principle is both *yin* and *yang*, negative and positive, passive and active, darkness and light. Though *yin* is not always synonymous with evil, the existence of evil would be assigned to the *yin* principle in creation. In contrast, good would be assigned to *yang*, its complementary opposite. (See the explanation of the *yin-yang* symbol on page 5.)

The word "Tao" means *the Way*. It speaks of "*the way*" all things function in harmony, from the smallest atom to the largest swirling galaxy. Beyond human comprehension, "The cosmic Tao is invisible, inaudible, unnameable, undiscussable, inexpressible."[11] The cosmic Tao is not a personal Creator and Lord to whom men are accountable or by whom men are ruled—"It [the Tao] creates them but never tries to own them...It raises them but never tries to control them. Herein lies its mysterious virtue." (*Tao-te Ching 51*) *Wu* (Being) and *Yu* (Not-Being) are terms for the two aspects of the eternal Tao (the Seen and the Unseen, the Manifested and the Unmanifested). *Yu* (Not-Being) is not a reference to nothingness, but rather, an absence of observable characteristics.

Taoism is pluralistic. Many personal gods are worshipped. The founder of this religion, Lao-Tzu, is considered by many Taoists to be the highest of all deities. In this exalted role he is known as T'ai-shang Laochün. Viewed as the original personification or emanation of the Tao, he is sometimes revered as the Emperor of the Undifferentiated

Realm (Hun-yuan Huang-ti). Out of Lao-chün were emanated the Three Pure Ones (the Celestial Lords of the Three Pure Realms). Next come "the Jade Emperor, who passes judgment on mortals and decides their fate," and the Mother Empress of the West, the goddess who "decides who attains immortality."[12]

And there are many other deities worshipped in Taoism. Some have existed from various stages in creation, while many others are individuals who attained immortality or expressed great goodness during their earthly sojourn, thus obtaining a high place of recognition in the celestial world. To these personal gods Taoists pray hoping for divine intervention. Especially emphasized are the "Three Star Gods" (Shou Hsing, God of Longevity: Tsai Shen, God of Wealth; and Fu Shen, God of Happiness) and the "Eight Immortals."

Zoroastrianism: Teaches a dualistic view of God, that there are two eternally existent gods. Ahura Mazda (meaning "Wise Lord," also called Ohrmazd) is the god of light who is assisted by *ahuras*, which are good spirits or angels. He is counterbalanced and opposed by Angra Mainyu (also called Ahriman, "the bad spirit"), the evil prince of darkness who is assisted by evil spirits called *daevas*. At one point these two gods were believed to be twin brothers born of the god Zurvan (a name meaning "Infinite Time")—the Ultimate Essence of deity in Zoroastrianism. However, worship of Zurvan (the unified aspect of a dualistic Godhead) is now considered by most Zoroastrians an erroneous concept and a heretical practice.

Ahura Mazda and Angra Mainyu have always been, from the beginning of time, self-existent, co-equal, and able to create. Yielding to one or the other determines whether a person is participating in the Kingdom of Light, Wisdom and Justice, or the Kingdom of the Darkness, Falsehood and Evil. These will continue to struggle against each other for a position of supremacy until the end of the age when Ahura Mazda finally overcomes. Because of this prophesied ultimate triumph, most Zoroastrians consider themselves, not dualistic, but monotheistic.

Ahura Mazda created Spenta Mainyu (meaning Bounteous Spirit, similar to the Holy Spirit) to oppose the Destructive Spirit, Angra Mainyu. Six other divine beings (three male and three female) are also individually worshipped. They are called the "Beneficent Immortals" *(Amesha Spentas)*. They are Asha Vahishta (Justice, Truth), Vohu Manah (Righteous Thinking), Armaiti (Devotion), Khshathra Vairya (Desirable Dominion), Haurvatat (Wholeness) and Ameretat (Immortality). These archangel-like entities were created by Ahura Mazda to help govern his creation. Their golden thrones surround his throne in the celestial world. Fire is especially sacred in Zoroastrian worship, being representative of divine emanation.

THE NATURE OF GOD

OTHER RELIGIONS, SECTS OR TEACHERS

Bahá'í: God cannot be known or experienced directly. All created things reflect qualities or attributes of God. So, a seeker can gain knowledge of God by observing nature, saintly human beings, or most perfectly, by studying the lives of those select messengers known as "Manifestations of God."[13] Shoghi Effendi (guardian and leader of the Bahá'í faith from 1921-1957) described God as "one, personal, unknowable, inaccessible, eternal, omniscient, omnipresent and almighty...a supreme reality." He firmly "rejected incarnationist, pantheistic and anthropomorphic conceptions of God," insisting that "human conceptions of God are mere imaginations, which some individuals mistake for reality." However, since God's attributes are best expressed in human beings, Bahá'ís are encouraged to "turn their gaze to their own selves" in order to find God.[14] Mystical experiences also grant insight into the divine nature. The greatest name of God is Bahá.[15]

Brahma Kumaris World Spiritual Organization (Raja Yoga): God is the Supreme Soul, the Father—a personal God (one having a "personality"). The correct name for God is Shiva, which basically means "benefactor father, the seed of creation and point-source and implies that there can be no other creator above Him."[16] He is "the supreme teacher, guide, liberator, friend and purifier of human souls." Usually the word "Baba," meaning "father," is joined to the name Shiva by true devotees.

Though omniscient and omnipotent, God is not omnipresent. To describe him this way would mean that God permeates all things. Therefore, "if God were omnipresent He would be responsible for good and evil."[17] The doctrinal explanation of the relationship between God and the universe is this: "Human souls created the present human systems, not God...If God had really created everything, then my woes would also be His will—and we know that cannot be the case."[18] So the pantheistic union of the Creator with the creation is not accepted in this worldview.

God does not possess a subtle body, neither is he formless. He is light, an infinitesimal point of radiant light residing in one location. However, God is not light-years away from human beings. He can be contacted as quickly as a prayerful thought passing through the mind of a worshipper. Only in a figurative sense does God dwell in the heart of human beings—through love. His real home is in the Soul World. What human beings perceive as "God within" is really only their collective impressions of him. God is changeless and his attributes are constant and perfect.

ECKANKAR: The founder of this sect, Paul Twitchell, describes Ultimate Reality as a "cosmic current," existent everywhere and in all things (a pantheistic, monistic view). God is detached and unconcerned about man and the universe. Paul Twitchell's main name for God is SUGMAD (pronounced SOOG'MAHD). The manifestation of the Absolute is called ECK—a word also used as an abbreviated form of the word ECKANKAR. The most ancient, secret name for God is HU (pronounced HYOO).

Gnosticism: The Supreme God, the Highest of All, "interposes between himself and finite creatures a long chain of aeons or middle beings, emanations from the divine, which together constitute the Pleroma or fullness of the divine essence. It is only through these intermediate beings that the highest God can enter into various relations with created beings."[19]

ISKCON (International Society for Krishna Consciousness): Ancient Vedic teachings, transferred through disciplic succession to Swami Prabhupada, declare Krishna to be the principal expression of the Godhead, exceeding even the impersonal Brahman. He admits, "There is a common controversy over whether the Supreme Absolute Truth is personal or impersonal. As far as Bhagavad-Gita is concerned, the Absolute Truth is the Personality of Godhead, Sri Krishna…the primeval Lord, the reservoir of all pleasure…the eternal form of complete bliss and knowledge."[20]

This is an altogether different view than traditional Hindu doctrine, which normally promotes the impersonal Brahman as the Ultimate Expression and Absolute Essence of Deity. However, references in revered Scriptures support this approach. In the Bhagavad-Gita, Krishna asserts, "I am the origin of all this world and its dissolution as well. There is nothing higher than I." *(Bhagavad-Gita 7.6-8)* In another Scripture source (the *Hari-vamsa*), Brahman is relegated to a somewhat inferior status. Krishna explains, "The glaring effulgence of the impersonal Brahman [the impersonal Absolute] illuminates all existences, both material and spiritual. But…you must understand that this Brahman illumination is the effulgence of My body."[21]

Deity-forms are accepted and encouraged in ISKCON facilities (the term "idols," having a negative connotation, is not used). Images of Krishna are bathed, clothed, and "fed." Followers drink the water used to bathe the deity-forms. The devotees also eat food offerings. This practice is called *prasada*—a method used to purify the consciousness.

Kabbala (Mystical Judaism): God or Ultimate Reality, is called Ein Sof (meaning "Infinite" or "Without End"). Ein Sof is not personal, but rather, an impersonal principle, a supreme divine will beyond human reasoning. Ten emanations stream forth from Ein Sof, called *Sefirot*, that personify ten different aspects of the divine nature. As seekers come back into union with God, the Sefirot are "ten stages…by which God the

Creator can be discerned."[22] The generally accepted order and naming of the *Sefirot* are: (1) *Keter Elyon* ("Supreme Crown"); (2) *Hokhmah* ("Wisdom"); (3) *Binah* ("Understanding"); (4) *Hesed* ("Lovingkindness") or *Gedullah* ("Greatness"); (5) *Gevurah* ("Power") or *Din* ("Judgment"); (6) *Tiferet* ("Beauty"); (7) *Nezah* ("Victory" or "Lasting Endurance"); (8) *Hod* ("Splendor" or "Majesty"); (9) *Zaddick* ("Righteous One") or *Yesod Olam* ("Foundation of the World"); (10) *Malkhut* ("Kingdom") or *Atarah* ("Diadem").[23] A series of three-letter sequences in Hebrew provide the celebrated "72 Names of God." Each of these names is believed to contain a unique energy that can be used as a mystical means of connecting with certain desirable blessings, like health and prosperity.

There is a female aspect of God as expressed in the third and tenth *Sefirot*. Referred to as the Shekinah, she is considered the bride of God. She is a demiurge, a lesser deity who manifests creative powers. She is also considered the daughter of God and mother of man. Normally, Kabbalists do not embrace pantheism. "Nature may be the garment of God, as the Zohar teaches, but it is not the body of God."[24]

Though omniscient, omnipotent, omnipresent, and genderless, Ein Sof has surrendered some sovereign power over the world to allow humans to function with "free will." This is called *tzimtzum* ("self-limitation").

Kriya Yoga (Paramahansa Yogananda): Though on the highest level of reality God is impersonal, he can be persuaded to take a personal form by intense devotion being generated toward him. Confining God to just the role of an impersonal Being is "a philosophical error, because God is everything: personal as well as impersonal."[25] Because he created humans as personal beings, "their Originator could not be wholly impersonal."[26] "The Lord is Spirit; the Impersonal is invisible. But when He created the physical world He became God the Father. As soon as He assumed the role of Creator, He became personal. He became visible: this whole universe is the body of God."[27] "In forming for Himself a physical body of planetary systems, God manifested three aspects: cosmic consciousness, cosmic energy and cosmic mass or matter."[28]

Yogananda especially promoted the idea of addressing God either as the "Heavenly Father" or the "Divine Mother." He insisted that if a person approaches God in this latter role, his prayers are especially efficacious. He also taught that a seeker can approach God in any form and by any name, and God will respond.

In interpreting the concept of the Trinity, Yogananda offered, "The Father *(Sat)* is God as the Creator existing beyond creation. The Son *(Tat)* is God's omnipresent intelligence existing in creation. The Holy Ghost *(Aum)* is the vibratory power of God that objectifies or becomes creation."[29]

Kundalini Yoga (Yogi Bhajan): Offered a monistic and pantheistic view of God. "We have never realized what God is. On the other hand, we say,

'God is omnipresent, omniscient and omnipotent.' We say it. We know it. We all agree to it. We expect to find him in a church, in a temple; we find him here, we find him there. God is a stick, God is a cup, God is a man, God is a woman; God is everything and God is nothing—anything which exists in any totality...that dance goes on...Hindus call it *anhat*, Christians call it communion, Buddhists call it light, Confucians call it wisdom, a Sikh knows it as ecstasy. All is one and one is all."[30]

Meher Baba: God is beyond all distinction and thought, the one Reality at the heart of all religions. God is both an Impersonal Absolute and personal in manifestation. Creation is an emanation of God himself. "God has three Infinite aspects: Knowledge, Power, Bliss."[31] There are "Ten Principal States of God:" (1) God in Beyond Beyond State; (2) God in Beyond; (3) God as Emanator, Sustainer and Dissolver; (4) God as an Embodied Soul; (5) God as a Soul in the State of Evolution; (6) God as a Human Soul in the State of Reincarnation; (7) God in the State of Spiritually Advanced Souls; (8) God as the Divinely Absorbed; (9) God as a Liberated Incarnate Soul; (10) God as a Man-God and God-Man.[32] A Man-God is a Spiritually Perfect Master. A God-Man is the Avatar, the Christ. God in his original state existed in "infinite unconsciousness."[33] (See *The Origin and Nature of the Universe.*) The first two states mentioned above are descriptions of God in an Impersonal State. The third is a semi-personal state, while the other seven states concern God manifesting in creation. The evolution of creation is actually the process of God discovering himself, or becoming fully conscious of his own divinity and nature.

Scientology: The Church of Scientology has "no set dogma concerning God that it imposes on its members."[34] Such a practice is not meant to imply an atheistic, agnostic or non-caring attitude about this vital subject. Quite the contrary, L. Ron Hubbard taught that men "without a strong and lasting faith in a Supreme Being are less capable, less ethical, and less valuable to themselves and society... A man without an abiding faith is, by observation alone, more a thing than a man."[35] As adherents expand their spirituality and awareness, they will come to their own realizations concerning the "Allness of all," a common designation for God. The Supreme Being or Creator is more correctly and simply defined as "infinity."

Sufism (Mystical Islam): In the beginning, the only thing existing was *Dhat* (the essence of Being). It existed as nothing, a formless Being. Then "a consciousness arose out of the Absolute, a consciousness of existence... This stage is called *Wahdah*." From this original consciousness a sense developed...which formed the Ego, the Logos, which is termed *Wahdani-yyah* by the Sufis...the all-pervading radiance formed its center...the divine Spirit, or the *Nur*, in Sufi terminology—*Arwah*."[36]

God is utterly transcendent, for he cannot be compared to any created thing. Even so, he is to be discovered within the heart. Ibn al-Arabi, an early leader, implied a somewhat pluralistic view with the statement, "in every object of worship there is a reflection of Reality." He also asserted, "We ourselves are the attributes by which we describe God; our existence is merely an objectification of His existence."[37] In Sufism is found a synthesis of an impersonal view of Ultimate Reality (as found in the Eastern traditions) and a personal and relational view of God (as found in the Western traditions). The pronoun "Hu" is recognized by Sufis to mean the indwelling Presence of the Divine. The ninety-nine names of God as found in the Qur'an are an emphasis in Sufi worship and doctrine. These especially reveal the nature and attributes of Allah.

Theosophy: Presents a monistic and pantheistic view of God (All is One and All is God). Ultimate Reality is an impersonal "Life Force." "We reject the idea of a personal...God."[38] "God and man are the two phases of the one eternal life and consciousness that constitutes our universe! The idea of the immanence of God is that he is the universe; although he is also more than it is; that the solar system is an emanation of the Supreme Being as clouds are an emanation of the sea...It is the idea that nothing exists except God, and that humanity is one portion of him—one phase of his Being."[39]

Transcendental Meditation (Maharishi Mahesh Yogi): "God has two aspects, the personal and the impersonal...The impersonal aspect of God is formless, supreme; It is eternal and absolute Being. It is without attributes, qualities, or features, because all attributes, qualities, and features belong to the relative field of life, whereas the impersonal God is of an absolute nature."[40] "God is one; It appears as many, however, the appearance of the one as many is only phenomenal. The reality of the one impersonal God is still eternal and absolute."[41] A pantheistic view of God is promoted: "Everything in creation is a manifestation of the unmanifested absolute impersonal being, the omnipresent God."[42]

United Church of Religious Science (Dr. Ernest Holmes): Taught that God is "the Neutral Force," yet personal to those who believe in "the Infinite." He redefined the Christian concept of the Trinity using the following descriptions: "The Father [is] the supreme creative Principle... [and] means Absolute Being."[43] Furthermore, "the entire manifestation of the Infinite in any and all planes, levels, states of consciousness, or manifestations, constitutes the Son."[44] Finally, "the Holy Ghost signifies the feminine aspect of the Divine Trinity. It represents the divine activity of the higher mental plane."[45] Ernest Holmes' concept of God was pantheistic, promoting the idea that the cosmos is the "entire manifestation of Spirit"[46] and that "God is in everything."[47]

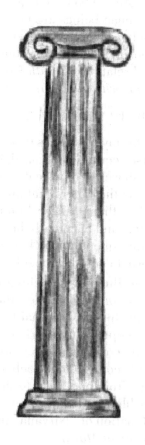

3

The Origin and Nature of Man

✳ **The Origin of Man**—Numerous theories, legends, and stories exist concerning the beginning of mankind. Usually there is an initial individual or a pair who fill the role of progenitors of the human race.

✳ **The Nature of Man**—Concerning the nature of man, there are a wide variety of beliefs, from bipartite (consisting of a body and a soul), to tripartite (consisting of body, soul, and spirit, or body, soul, and higher Self), to ideas that human beings are made up of four, five or seven elemental parts. Some believe that the highest essence of man *is* God; others believe that men are not divine in essence, but their highest calling is to experience a vital and real relationship *with* God. *The majority of the information in this section deals with the nature of man, not his origin.*

THE ELEVEN MAIN LIVING RELIGIONS

Buddhism: One myth explains that at the end of each cyclical dissolution of the universe, certain brahma deities from *Rupa-dhatu* (the "realm of form" just above the physical world) are attracted by the recreation of the earth. "As the waters that are left from the old cataclysm start to coagulate below them...these brahma deities gradually descend into the lower realms and eventually become the first inhabitants of the new earth."[1] All subsequent human beings then descend from them, giving to all mankind what could be considered a divine-like origin.

Unique to Buddha's teaching is the idea that men have no souls (the doctrine of *anatta*). Rather, there are five aggregates *(skandhas)* that make up the human personality—the physical form *(rupa)*, feelings *(vedana)*, perception *(sanna)*, dispositions or mental formations *(sankhara)*, and consciousness *(vinnana)*. These are impermanent and only temporarily connected to each other. In the process of reincarnation, no soul passes from one body to the next. Rather, these "aggregates" are disassemsbled and others reformed to make a new living being. (See the explanation of "Nirvana" under *The Spiritual Journey and the Ultimate Destiny of Man.*)

Buddhism teaches four major chakras, or energy centers, within human beings. Every man, actually every living thing, is a potential Buddha. All have a Buddha nature that will be awakened after completing the full cycle of necessary incarnations.

Christianity: The Bible teaches that on the sixth day of creation, God created the first man, Adam, out of the dust and breathed into him the breath of life. He then placed Adam in a deep sleep, removed one of his ribs and made Eve, the first woman. Apparently, the man and woman were created last because they are the highest expression of God's creative genius—being in the "image" and "likeness" of God—and all other created things were merely preparations for them. *(Genesis 1-2)* Adam and Eve were placed in the Garden of Eden where there were two significant trees: the Tree of Life and the Tree of the Knowledge of Good and Evil. The foreparents of the human race fell when the Serpent (Satan) seduced them to ignore God's commandment and partake of the "Tree of the Knowledge of Good and Evil." They were then exiled from the Garden of Eden and denied access to the Tree of Life. The calamity of death, both natural and spiritual, came on the whole human race as a result. *(See Romans 5:12-21.)*

Concerning the nature of man, he is a tripartite being consisting of body, soul, and spirit. *(See 1 Thessalonians 5:23.)* The body is the abode of the senses and natural passions. The soul is the abode of the mind, will and emotions. The spirit, in its original perfect state, was the abode of conscience, intuition and communion with God. However, prior to the experience of being born again, human beings are described as being "dead in trespasses and sins." *(Ephesians 2:1)* Because of this inherited state of spiritual death and separation from God, the functions of the spirit have been drastically reduced or eliminated altogether. Communion with God is no longer possible (unless initiated by the Creator himself). Intuition is restricted primarily to lesser, non-spiritual insights (intellectual, scientific, artistic, literary, etc.). True intuitive knowledge about God is rare, especially in any kind of depth. Conscience is the primary part of the spirit that remained functional after the fall of man, though it, too, has been defiled by sin and is, therefore, undependable. *(See Titus 1:15.)* The conscience is the guardian of the soul. It is not the presence of God within a person, but an inward sense of what is morally wrong and morally right, normally influencing a person toward what is morally right.

Once regenerated, through the entrance of God's Spirit, a saved person's spirit has the capacity of experiencing restored communion with God, the higher levels of intuition and a cleansed conscience. Spirituality then manifests in a person according to the level of consecration. The flesh enables men to be "world-conscious." The soul enables men to be "self-conscious." The spirit enables men to be "God-conscious" (conscious of the reality of God).[2] Christianity does not teach that man has a higher universal "Self." Man is a separate entity from God; he is not God in expression, nor does he ever become God. Man is born into this world with a sinful nature, having inherited the same from Adam (termed by some theologians as the doctrine of "Original Sin"—*Psalms 51:5, Romans 5:19*). Although man has been greatly distanced from the full glory of his identity in the dawn of creation, he is still, to a limited degree, in the "image" and "likeness" of God. *(Genesis 1:26-27)* Some Christian theologians insist that man is bipartite, possessing only a body and a soul.

THE ORIGIN AND NATURE OF MAN

Confucianism: Teaches that man is innately good and noble. "The nature of man is good." "The tendency of man's nature to good is like the tendency of water to run downwards." *(Mencius 6.1.1.2)*[3] "All are good at first. But few prove themselves to be so at the last."*(Shi King 3.3.1.1.7–8)*[4] Confucius taught that there is more to man than just his physical body. He insisted, "Such is the evidence of things invisible that it is impossible to doubt the spiritual nature of man." *(Doctrine of the Mean 16)*

Hinduism: Concerning the origin of man, the Bhagavatam shares the following explanation: "Brahma's first human creations were saints, who, immediately upon being created fell into deep meditation, finding no interest in the things of the world. Thus, through them, Brahma saw no possibility of propagation of their species. While he was meditating upon what course he should pursue, his own form divided itself, one half became man and the other half became woman. The man was called Manu, and the woman Shatarupa, and from them have sprung all mankind."[5] So man is considered, not a creation of God, but an emanation of God. At the beginning of every secondary cycle another Manu appears to become the father of the human race.

Concerning the nature of man, numerous theories are found in Hinduism. The following seems to be the most dominant and accepted. Man is made up of three primary bodies or "sheaths" *(sharira)* that surround the *atman* (the real Self): (1) The gross body—*sthula-sharira*, also called *annamaya kosha*; (2) The subtle body—*sukshma-sharira*, also called *linga-sharira*, and; (3) The causal body—*karana-sharira*, identical with *anandamaya-kosha*.[6] The subtle body is subdivided further into three parts: the vital sheath *(pranamaya-kosha)*, the mental sheath *(manomaya-kosha)*, and the intellectual sheath *(vijnanamaya-kosha)*. So altogether there are five "sheaths" or bodies in which the *atman* is contained (a viewpoint expressed in the Taittiriya Upanishad). The subtle body is the means by which the *atman* passes from one life to the next on its journey toward perfection. The causal body contains the "idea template"—the spiritual blueprint for the subtle and gross bodies. Some sources say that the causal body is also divided into three parts, bringing the total number of "bodies" to seven.

The *atman* (Sanskrit meaning "God within") is the true Self, the higher Self. It is eternal, uncreated, without gender, pure, unchanging, indestructible, omniscient, omnipotent, and omnipresent. It cannot feel pain, and it does not evolve. This divine essence is within every living thing: plant, animal, and human. These variations are not differences in the *atman* itself, but in the degree it manifests in a physical form.

When dwelling in a human body, it erroneously identifies itself with the flesh body, the mind, and the intellect, until a person's consciousness is awakened. Then the *atman* rules a person's existence.

A primary doctrine that pervades much of Hinduism is the perception that *atman*, the individual soul, is actually *Brahman*, the universal Soul. Often quoted is the passage out of the Chandogya Upanishad in which Uddalaka admonishes his son, Svetaketu: "The subtle essence is universally diffused in all things wherever found. It is the true Self; and, Svetaketu, *that thou art (tat twam asi)*!"

Conflicting interpretations of this passage exist within the camp of Hinduism itself. Sankara, an eighth century Hindu philosopher, believed this statement indicates *atman* and *Brahman* are identical. Ramanuja, an eleventh century Hindu teacher, insisted it infers *atman* and *Brahman* are inseparable, but not identical.

When the *atman* becomes personalized and individualized, it is referred to as the *jiva* (pronounced jee´va, meaning "that which lives"). This is the embodied *atman*, the individual personality that wrongly identifies with the physical form and the mind. As the human ego, it imparts a fallacious sense of duality (distinction between God and man) that keeps the *jiva* bound to the cycle of birth and death. The *atman* transcends time, space, causality, name, and form, but these five things bind the *jiva*. This condition is only a temporary illusion on the way to the final destiny of *atman* (the true Self) merging into oneness with Brahman. *Jivas* are infinite in number.

Everything in the manifest world is comprised of the three *gunas*: *sattva, rajas*, and *tamas*. When it relates to the evolutionary development of human beings, *sattva* concerns that part of our inherent nature that is veiled and must be realized; *tamas* is what hinders that realization; *rajas* is the energy or force that overcomes *tamas*. *Tamas* is laziness, unconcern, and the dullness of the sense-bound human mind; *rajas* is passion, zeal, and holy action that overcomes *tamas* to attain the *sattva* of serenity and understanding. *Sattva* is goodness and harmony. It is not cosmic consciousness, but it leads a person to the boundary of this ultimate state of being.

Final liberation happens after many incarnations, with the circumstances of each incarnation determined by karma from previous lives. Karma attaches itself to the subtle body. Karma is comprised of merits *(punya)* or demerits *(papa)* that result from every action. There are sixteen basic elements of the physical body and nineteen elements of the subtle body, which correspond to thirty-five basic idea-elements of the causal body.

• **Note on the caste system of Hinduism:** In discussing various beliefs concerning the nature of man, this subject should not be overlooked. In the Laws of Manu (an ancient Hindu text) society is divided into four main castes *(varnas)—Brahmins* (priests), *Kshatriyas* (nobles), *Vaisyas* (merchants and farmers) and *Sudras* (manual laborers, peasants and servants). These originated from four parts of the body of Brahma. *(See Rig Veda 10:90,12.)* The *Brahmin* priestly caste proceeded from Brahma's head, the *Kshatriyas* from his arms, the *Vaisyas* from his thighs and the *Sudras* from his feet. Far beneath the *Sudras* are the "untouchables" *(Harijans)* who were rejects from the social order altogether. (Mahatma Ghandi preferred to call them the "Children of God.") These four main castes are divided into various sub-castes (around 3,000). Each of these divisions determines a certain status and duty in life.

When this social order is strictly observed, the castes do not intermarry or even eat with each other. In 1949 Ghandi and others persuaded the Indian Parliament to make this practice illegal. Nevertheless, some still live according to this standard, believing it to be divinely inspired. (In Hindu Scripture Krishna declares, "The four castes were created by me." *Bhagavad-Gita 4:13)*

The caste system has been a matter of great controversy, even within the camp of Far Eastern religions. Buddha was appalled at this doctrine. Mahavira, the founder of Jainism, and Guru Nanak, founder of Sikhism, were both born in the second caste, yet they arose to become noted spiritual leaders. Both of them repudiated this concept, teaching that society should be casteless and that all people have equal value. Some Hindus compromise the unyielding imposition of this doctrine, teaching that a person's caste is determined, not by the social status inherited at birth, but by personal choice or personal accomplishment. Thus, any person can be positioned in any caste according to his own intellectual, emotional, spiritual and/or social development.

• **Note on the Yoga School within Hinduism:** Yoga is one of the main schools of thought within Hinduism. In many groups that promote the practice of yoga, human beings are described as possessing spiritual energy centers called chakras. Though there are some different views promoted by various yogis and swamis, it is generally believed that there are seven main chakras, five of which are positioned along the spinal column. The sixth is the "third eye" and the seventh, the "crown chakra" located at the crown of the skull. The third eye (in the middle of the forehead) is described as one of the main gateways out of the body into the astral realm. Each chakra is associated with a different deity. When the kundalini (the latent deposit of divine energy at the base of the spine) is "awakened," this energy travels upward through the chakras. Upon reaching the crown chakra, God consciousness is attained. According to the Sankhya Yoga School, there are two main aspects to man: the self *(purusha)* bound inside of a body of matter *(prakriti)*.

Islam: Though accepting a slightly altered version of the biblical story of Adam and Eve, Islam does not teach that their fall caused a transfer of the "Original Sin" to Adam's seed. Human beings become sinners by sinful acts only, not because of a sinful, fallen nature. Satan, the tempter, is called Iblis. He was rejected by God in the beginning because when the angels did obeisance to Adam, he refused to do so.

Man, though admittedly frail, is believed to be the noblest of God's creatures. He is commanded to serve God, to honor God, but is too distanced from God to experience the indwelling of his personal presence. One belief, quite unique to Islam, is the story of God, not only creating the first man, Adam, out of clay, but also out of a blood-clot. *(Sura 96, ayat 1–2)* Also unique is the belief that the original man and woman were created from a single soul. *(Qur'an 4:1)* Islam teaches man is bipartite: possessing a body and soul.

Jainism: Mahavira, the founder of Jainism, "strongly asserted the independence or autonomy of the individual soul" as opposed to the monistic view from Hinduism that "souls do not remain individualized in eternity, but become absorbed in Brahman."[7] The life essence or soul of any living thing is termed a *jiva*. The *jiva*, in its original state, possesses absolute knowledge. After numerous existences in various forms (such as earth, water, vegetables, worms, bugs, and animals) the *jiva* eventually evolves to the level of a human being. It then reincarnates many times as a human being until liberation takes place. Man is bipartite, with all matter and the physical body being essentially evil, and the soul, essentially good. The *jiva* is indestructible, invisible, and without shape.

Judaism: The origin of man is the same as that related under Christianity being drawn from Genesis, the first book of the Bible. However, Jews do not identify the Serpent as Satan, nor do they believe that Adam and Eve's transgression constituted a "fall" for the entire human race. Concerning the nature of man, it is taught that man is not a mere "dichotomy of body and soul...and certainly not a trichotomy" (as found in Christianity) but a "multifaceted unitary being."[8] The first man, Adam, became a "living soul" when God breathed into him the "breath of life." *(Genesis 2:7)* In a godly person, the soul should dominate the body. The soul is compared "in similes that go back to antiquity, to the rider of a steed, the captain of a ship and the governor of a state. Yet paradoxically, the soul is also often considered as a stranger on the earth, an alien yearning for its supernal home."[9]

God creates the soul from nothing, coincidental with the formation of the body in the womb. "The soul requires the good acts of the body to perfect its peculiarly immaterial, celestial-like substance, even as the body needs the faculties of sensation and reason which the soul provides."[10] Man has a *nephesh* (something also possessed by animals). This is the natural life (life-force) of a human being. Unique to man is the possession of a *neshemah* (the soul that entered Adam with the breath of God). According to Kabbalistic legend, on the Sabbath, every Jew "acquires an extra soul, a *neshema yeterah*" in order to experience the joy, peace and blessedness of this holy day to the fullest.[11]

Man is a free agent, able to choose between good and evil. Judaism does not promote the idea that human beings are born into this world under the burden of "Original Sin" inherited from Adam, as taught in Christianity. However, some Jewish theologians would explain that "man's moral ambivalence derives from the two inclinations within him: the good inclination *(yezer tov)* and the evil inclination *(yezer ra)*."[12]

The body is not denigrated as in some religions, but valued, along with the soul, as being in the image and likeness of God. While some religions discourage marital union in order to achieve enlightenment, conversely, in Judaism marriage is a blessed, divine institution, and a holy mandate. Members of the Jewish community are normally expected to marry in order to participate in the revealed purpose for mankind and to perpetuate the human species, specifically those who are in covenant with the God of Abraham, Isaac, and Jacob.

Shinto: In this Japanese religious worldview, human beings are considered children of the *kami* ("gods"). Therefore, they have an inborn nature of goodness that can dominate their lives if the defilement of evil is removed.

Sikhism: Man is the noblest of all creatures. He is not born with a sinful nature, but with a divine potential. "The inaccessible illimitable God dwelleth in man's heart. The body is the palace, the temple, the house of God. Into it he putteth his eternal light."[13] There are "Nine Abodes [of sensation]; in the Tenth [the superconscious mind] is lodged the Lord, unknowable, limitless." *(Adi Granth, Maru Sohale, M.1., pp. 1035–1037)* These "nine abodes" are a reference to the nine openings in the human body. The tenth is a "spiritual" opening.

The idea of a caste system as found in classical Hinduism is rejected, "All are equal before the Creator; none exalted and none abased." *(Japji 33)* Man's goal is to create God's Kingdom on earth by manifesting the divine nature. The main hindrance to this is something Guru Nanak referred to as *haumai*, meaning "self-centeredness." Because of *haumai* the soul becomes lost in a maze of worldly pleasures and pursuits that prevent it from reaching its divine potential.

Taoism: During the creation process, the Tao brought forth the first man, Pangu. After his death, various parts of his body became different parts of creation. The germs in his body were distributed by the wind throughout the world and became the masses of people. (See "Taoism" under *The Origin and Nature of the Universe*.) Because the various aspects of creation were originally made from the body of Pangu, in Taoism, each person's body is compared to, and related to, various aspects of creation. This creates a sense of "connectedness" between the creature and the creation. The vital essence of creation is called *ch'i* (pronounced both "chee" and "key"). As the *ch'i* flows through creation in diverse expressions, so it flows through the body in varied ways, by means of numerous invisible "meridians."

At birth, "this internal energy is separated into three components: generative *(ching)*, vital *(ch'i)* and spirit energy *(shen)*."[14] These are called "the Three Treasures," "the Three Flowers and the Three Herbs."[15] There are three "cauldrons" in the body in which these three types of energy are stored: lower, middle and upper. Associated with these "cauldrons" in human beings are three "Tan-t'iens" (Elixer Fields). Gates to these Elixer Fields are located along the spine.

Ch'i is expressed in creation and in humanity two main ways: in the complementary opposites of *yin ch'i* and *yang ch'i*. Because of this, each individual is described as possessing two kinds of souls: three *hun* souls, made up of *yang ch'i* (representing the superior spiritual and intellectual essence of a person); and seven *po* souls, made up of *yin ch'i* (the inferior, lower aspect of the human nature). So a total of ten souls reside in each human being. "The three spirit [*yang*] souls are located beneath the liver. They look like human beings and all wear green robes with yellow inner garments" [royal, courtly attire].[16] Their names are Spiritual Guidance, Inner Radiance and Dark Essence. If these dominate a person's character and actions, demonic activity is restrained, and troubles, misfortunes and suffering are averted.

"The seven material souls consist of the energy of yin and of evil. They are basically demons. They can make a person commit deadly evils...Through them people will completely lose all original purity and simplicity. These souls, far from looking like human beings are strangely formed devils...Their names are accordingly Corpse Dog, Arrow in

Ambush, Bird Darkness, Devouring Robber, Flying Poison, Massive Pollution, and Stinky Lungs."[17] Though these material souls draw men toward defilement and depravity, they are necessary for physical survival. If these souls dominate a person, the ultimate end is illness and death. The only remedy is responding to the influence of the higher souls and striving toward those things that lead to immortality.

In Taoism, the human body is a microcosm, a small reflection of the cosmos as a whole. Therefore, just as there are three major divinities who rule the universe (the Celestial Emperor, the Cinnabar Sovereign and the Primordial King), so these three divinities reside in every human being's body (respectively, in the head, the heart and the abdomen). "Together they supervise the twenty-four energies of the body and bring them in accord with the twenty-four deities of Great Tenuity."[18] These three *yang*-type divinities are "powerful good forces of the Dao, divine powers of longevity, good fortune, and immortality that can be called upon and utilized toward perfecting one's inherent heavenly nature. They…assist the practitioner in his ascent to the divine."[19] There are also five spirits that protect the five internal organs of the body: the liver, lungs, heart, spleen and kidneys. "In the liver is the human spirit, in the lungs is the soul, in the heart is the seed of the immortal spirit, in the spleen is the intention, and in the kidneys is the generative energy."[20]

Numerous "palaces" are in the body that provide dwelling places for various deities, such as the nine palaces in the head.[21] There are also *yin*-type beings that dwell in the body of every person: primarily the "three deathbringers." These are "a cross between demons and souls, who reside in the head, torso and lower body of the individual… Assisted by a group of parasites known as the nine worms."[22] Together, these make every attempt to bring a person under the influence of evil, lust, sickness, mental and emotional stress, aging, and death. The name of the upper deathbringer is Peng Ju (also called Shouter); the middle deathbringer is Peng Zhi (also called Maker); the lower deathbringer is Peng Qiao (also called Junior).

The "nine worms," on the other hand, are not spiritual, but literal. They are physical parasites, who act as "minions of the three deathbringers" to bring about the destruction of the individual. The nine worms are driven to accomplish this, knowing that they will actually feed on the corpses of those persons they successfully conquer. Virtuous behavior, meditation on the Three Major Divinities, and certain ritualistic vigils will counteract the three deathbringers and the nine worms, freeing humans from their influence and propelling them toward the desirable goal of immortality.[23]

Zoroastrianism: Ahura Mazda, the righteous God in this worldview, fashioned the first man, naming him Gayomart. "Gayomart's spirit…lived for 3,000 years during the period in which creation was only spiritual. His mere existence immobilized the evil spirit [Angra Mainyu] who wanted to invade creation. Then Ahura Mazda created Gayomart incarnate—white and brilliant, shining like the sun."[24] After thirty years of conflict with Angra Mainyu, Gayomart (the first man and the first fire-priest) was killed. His body became the minerals and metals of the earth. Gold was the seed of Gayomart, bringing forth the human race.

Man is seen as basically good. He is a triune being. As promoted in many worldviews, a human being has a soul and a body. However, Zoroastrianism also emphasizes that each person possesses a preexistent divine essence called a *fravashi*. This is the "higher Self," which is in union with Ahura Mazda, the God of righteousness in Zoroastrianism. The *fravashi* is actually "the presence of Ahura Mazda in every human being. It is the Divinity in Humanity. It is the conscience. The *fravashi* is immortal and…is ever present to guide and protect the person."[25] In making choices between right and wrong, good and evil, each person is obligated to consult with his *fravashi*.

OTHER RELIGIONS, SECTS OR TEACHERS

Bahá'í: Adam is considered the father of humankind and a "Manifestation of God." (See explanation under Question #9 in Part 4.) The biblical story of Adam and Eve is taught to be symbolic, not literal, with Eve serving as a type of Adam's own soul and the serpent, an emblem of attachment to the world.

Man is bi-partite, comprised of a "physical body and a non-material, rational soul (or human spirit)."[26] He is made in the image of God and is capable of reflecting all of God's names and attributes. Man is basically good, not in a state of depravity because of an inherited sin status (Original Sin). He possesses both an angelic and an animal nature, and can yield to one or the other. "Self-love is 'kneaded' into the human clay," so human beings must be trained, especially through religion, to reach for higher ideals.[27] The body is subject to limitations and death, but the soul is unlimited and immortal.

Benjamin Creme (Share International Foundation): Based on the concept of reincarnation, Benjamin Creme instructs that all human beings are governed basically by five ray forces: (1) The ray of the soul (which is the same for countless aeons); (2) The ray of the personality (which changes from life to life "until all qualities are developed"); (3) The ray governing the mental body; (4) The ray governing the astral-emotional equipment; (5) The ray of the physical body, including the brain. These rays "predispose us to certain attitudes of mind and certain strengths and weaknesses, which we call the virtues and vices of the rays... The evolutionary aim is to transmute the vice of the ray into its higher (virtue) aspect."[28]

Brahma Kumaris World Spiritual Organization (Raja Yoga): Man has a body and a soul. The soul enters the body sometime around the fourth or fifth month of pregnancy. The physical body is temporary and perishable. The soul is permanent and imperishable. It is uncreated and eternal, and has neither race nor gender. It is weightless, possessing no physical size. It is not an invisible duplicate of the body. The soul is indestructible because only that which is created can be destroyed. There is a fixed, eternally unchanging number of existent souls. In deep contemplation the soul is seen as an "infinitesimal point of non-physical light surrounded by an oval-shaped aura."[29] The "seat of the soul" is the third eye (approximately in the center of the forehead, where the pituitary and pineal glands are located).

The soul has three subtle organs: the mind, the intellect, and the subconscious. The Conscious Mind is made up of thoughts, emotions, and desires. The Intellect part of the soul uses judgment, discrimination, and decision-making power. The Sub-Conscious is made up of memories, impressions, instincts, and habits. These are called *sanskaras*. They take the form of "habits, talents, emotional temperaments, personality traits, beliefs, values or instincts." Together these are the "basis of the soul's individuality."[30] Suffering is the result of negative actions due to negative *sanskaras*. Suffering is a "punishment for...wrongful acts" committed in previous lives during a state of body-consciousness.[31]

There are three basic functions that the soul executes: "to give and maintain life, to express and experience its role, and to receive the rewards or fruits of past actions performed in previous existences."[32] The Darwinian concept of evolution is rejected.

ECKANKAR (Sri Harold Klemp): The present leader of this religious group explains, "Soul is an individual; It retains its individuality throughout all time, beyond time, in all universes, beyond all universes."[33] **(Paul Twitchell)** The founder of ECKANKAR states, "We are gods of course, but gods of our own universe, and gods among other gods. Every man, woman and child is God! No one can dispute this basic fact of cosmic wisdom!"[34] "The individual is truth Itself."[35] Paul Twitchell also taught the eternal existence of the Soul: "We have lived for eternity whether in this universe or another, because eternity has no beginning or ending."[36] Man is made up of four parts: "Spirit, Soul, mind, and body."[37] The physical body is referred to as *Nuri Sarup*; the soul body that can travel through the astral plane is called *Atma Sarup*.

Gnosticism: Through the error of a lesser god referred to as a demiurge (usually identified as Yahweh or Jehovah, the God of the Jewish people) the material world was created and man's soul became trapped. However, there is a spark of divine nature within every human being. Because of its illegitimate beginning, matter is considered evil. It prevents man from realizing his celestial origin.

ISKCON (International Society of Krishna Consciousness): According to exact karmic predictions, the *jiva-atma* (soul) enters the semen of the man as it unites with the ovum in conception. Its measurement is "one ten thousandth part of the tip of a hair. This is very small; in fact, it is atomic."[38] "The soul is a small God."[39] Krishna, as a personal manifestation of Deity, resides within the heart of every living thing, but must be discovered in order for a relationship to be established. The soul is part of God, but it is not God. Human beings possess three bodies: (1) The gross body (made of the five basic elements: earth, water, fire, air, and ether); (2) The subtle body (comprised of the mind, intelligence, and the false ego); and, (3) The spiritual body (made up of *sat-chit-ananda*, meaning "eternal-knowledge-bliss"). The *atma* (the soul) is not created; it is eternal and therefore, indestructible.

Kabbala (Mystical Judaism): Man has a body and a soul. Some Kabbalistic schools teach that the soul consists of five "levels" or "dimensions of awareness." These correspond to the five levels of consciousness in creation. (See "Kabbala" under *The Origin and Nature of the Universe*.) The two higher aspects of the soul are identified in Kabbalistic teachings as *hayyah* and *yehidah*. These relate to the fourth and fifth levels of creation, the "world of the spirit" and the "primordial source" (also known as the "world of emanation" and the "world of will"). These "represent the sublimest levels of intuitive apprehension and to be within the grasp only of a few chosen individuals."[40] *Hayyah* (or *chayah)* means "living essence." *Yehidah* means "unity," and speaks of the highest state of "unity" or communion with God available. *Yehidah* is described as the "center point of the soul, and as such it disappears into the infinitude of creation."[41]

The first three parts of the soul consist of "a vital spirit, an intellectual spirit and the soul proper."[42] The Hebrew terms are *nefesh*, *ru'ah*, and *neshamah*. The *nefesh* is found in every man, entering at birth, and is the source of all his psychological and physical functions as a human being. It relates to the "world of physicality" (the "world of action"). The *ru'ah* or *anima* is "aroused at an unspecified time when a man succeeds in rising above his purely vitalistic side. This relates to the "world of emotions" (the "world of formation"). It is the third part of the soul, the *neshamah* or *spiritus*, which excels in importance. It is aroused in a man when he occupies himself with the Torah and its commandments, and it opens his higher powers of apprehension, especially his ability to mystically apprehend the Godhead and the secrets of the universe."[43] *Neshemah* relates to the "world of the intellect" (the "world of creation").

These three lower soul-parts, collectively referred to as *naran*, originate from three different sources (three of the ten emanations from the Godhead called *Sefirot*): "the *nefesh* originates in the *Sefirah Malkhut*, the *ru'ah* in the *Sefirah Tiferet*, and the *neshamah* in the *Sefirah Binah*."[44]

There is also an aspect of man called the *zelem* (the "image" mentioned in Genesis 1:26 when God said, "Let us make man in our image, after our likeness"). The *zelem* is the essence of individuality bestowed upon every human being. It is also man's "ethereal garment" or "ethereal body which serves as an intermediary between his material body and his soul." "It is the garment with which the souls clothe themselves in the celestial paradise before descending to the lower world and which they don once again after their reascent following physical death." "Unlike the soul, the *zelem* grows and develops in accordance with the biological processes of its possessor."[45]

So apparently there are seven divisions that comprise the whole of man: the physical body, the ethereal body, and the five aspects of the soul. In the Encyclopedia Judaica, Gershom Scholem explains the Kabbalistic view of the "Nature of Man," "At opposite poles, both man and God encompass within their being the entire cosmos...man's role is to complete this process by being the agent through whom all the powers of creation are fully activated and made manifest...Man is the perfecting agent in the structure of the cosmos: like all the other created beings, only even more so, he is composed of all ten *Sefirot* and "of all spiritual things," that is, of the supernal principles that constitute the attributes of the Godhead."[46] By this last statement and on the basis of the concept of the shattering of the Vessel, it is apparent that in Kabbalism a divine essence is believed to be resident within every human being.

An extremely unique idea, basic to Kabbalistic teaching, concerns the origin of the lower order of angels. They are described as either negative or positive "concentrations of energy that are constantly flitting in and out of existence." Human beings actually bring them into existence by deeds, thoughts and feelings and can eliminate them by the same method. These angels are "a direct expression of what is in our hearts and minds."[47]

Kriya Yoga (Swami Sri Yukteswar): In his book titled *The Holy Science*, he asserts that each person is a son of God *(purusha)*. Each *purusha* is covered by five sheaths *(koshas)*: (1) The heart *(chitta)*, that which experiences bliss *(anandamaya kosha)*; (2) The intelligence or *buddhi*: the seat of knowledge *(jnanamaya kosha)*; (3) The mind *(manomaya kosha)*, composed of the sense organs; (4) The body of energy, life-force or prana *(pranayama kosha)*; (5) The body of gross matter *(annamaya kosha)*. **(Paramahansa Yogananda)** Human beings have three bodies (from which Consciousness must be delivered): (1) A physical body of sixteen elements; (2) An astral body of nineteen elements (composed of life-force and mind); (3) A causal body of thirty-five elemental ideas (the combination of the sixteen God-thoughts that produced the physical body and the nineteen God-thoughts that produced the astral body). The "consciousness, or soul, is a spark of the cosmic consciousness of God."[48] "God is the essence of our own being."[49] "He is your Self...He exists equally and impartially in all beings."[50]

Kundalini Yoga (Yogi Bhajan): Human beings possess ten bodies: a spiritual body (the soul), three mental bodies (the negative mind, the positive mind and the neutral mind), the physical body, the arc body, the auric body, the subtle body, the pranic body and the radiant body.[51] There are eight main chakras (energy centers): the seven chakras traditionally taught in Yoga, and an eighth (the aura or magnetic energy field around a person). Of the three functional minds there are nine aspects, twenty-seven projections and eighty-one facets.[52]

Meher Baba: An ordinary human being possesses four main parts: (1) A gross body (the physical body); (2) A subtle body *(pran)*; (3) A mental body *(mana)*; (4) A "higher Self" *(Atma)*. As a person evolves spiritually, other parts are developed or 'awakened.' A God-realized person is comprised of seven parts: (1) A gross body; (2) A subtle body; (3) A mental body; (4) A universal body; (5) A universal mind; (6) An unlimited divine ego; (7) Infinite consciousness. The soul is formless and eternal.

There are 18,000 worlds inhabited by human beings, but only those born in this world can transcend into the higher spheres. Souls from the other worlds will be reincarnated here when it is time for their spiritual development. When this earth ceases to be, another planet will be chosen to fill this special role. "After a billion years, man will only be five inches in height at the most, but will be very brainy. In the beginning of this cycle man was fourteen feet tall and would live up to 300 years."[53] The Son of God or divine nature is in every man, but needs to be manifested.

Scientology: Teaches that man is innately good. He is made up of three main parts: the body, the mind and the *thetan* (pronounced thay'-ten). This term, unique to this religion, is drawn from the Greek letter *theta*, used traditionally to represent "thought" or "life." *Theta* is the spiritual essence or life-force of all living things. Human beings are *thetans*, possessing a mind and inhabiting a body. *Thetans* originally existed in a pre-creation, supernatural state with unhindered, godlike abilities and attributes. Through a long association with the physical universe these beings became trapped in MEST (Material-Energy-Space-Time), descending from a spiritual, divine-like state to the present limitations of human existence. Because of this tragic "fall from perfection," men and women, in their earthly state, normally fail to realize both their former estate and their present potential. So the *thetan* is the "higher Self," and, though often neglected, it is the seniormost, spiritual essence of a person. The body and the mind are only temporary vehicles used by the *thetan* in the "handling of life and the physical universe." It is described as "the source of all creation and life itself."[54]

Very important to the Scientologist worldview is the belief that each person possesses two distinctly different minds: the reactive mind (which is negative) and the analytical mind (which is positive). The reactive mind works on a "stimulus-response basis," is not under the control of human will, and subconsciously exerts adverse influence over a person's "awareness, purposes, thoughts, body and actions."[55] This mind is full of negative data resulting from the emotionally and mentally damaging experiences of all earthly existences, both past and present. The analytical mind is "the mind which thinks, observes data, remembers it and resolves problems."[56] Conquering the reactive mind frees the analytical mind, enabling a person to make positive choices about how he or she will act and react in life.

Sufism (Mystical Islam): Sufis accept the creation story as found in the Qur'an. The early mystic, Suhrawardi, also taught that souls preexist in the realm of angels. As they enter the body, they separate. One part remains in a heavenly sphere while the other descends into its fleshly "prison." Helminski concludes, "That is why the soul is unhappy in this world; it searches for its other half and must be reunited with its heavenly prototype in order to become perfected and to become itself again."[57]

According to the thirteenth century Sufi Master of the Kubrawi order in Central Asia, "Ala" al-Dawla Simnani, there are "Seven Subtle Substances" in the human makeup: (1) body *(qalab)*; (2) soul *(nafs)*; (3) heart *(qalb)*; (4) conscience *(sirr)*; (5) spirit *(ruh)*; (6) mystery *(khafi)*; (7) reality *(haqq)*.[58] Tightly embraced is Mohammed's teaching—"the heart of the believer is the house of God."[59] Overcoming the "lower self" to manifestly become this "house" is the path to union with the Divine. In other words, Sufis strive to become God's eyes, ears, speech, will and life expressed in the world.

Orthodox Muslims have often misinterpreted such lofty aspirations. For instance, one of the recognized leaders of early Sufism, Ibn al-Arabi, was martyred for what some construed to be a declaration of his own divinity, "I am He Whom I love. He Whom I love is I; we are two souls co-inhabiting one body. If you see me you see Him and if you see Him you see me." Another controversial Sufi leader, Hallaj, was martyred for saying, "I am the truth." Strict Islamic doctrine does not allow for any man claiming oneness with God. Most notable is the ecstatic outburst of Bayazid Bistami, "Glory be to me, how great is my majesty."[60] Other Sufis, who appreciate and share the mystical ideas of these men, defend their assertions—insisting they were not heretical claims of personal Divinity. Rather, they were enlightened claims of spiritually mature "friends of God" who succeeded in experiencing union with God and "reflecting" his attributes. "The standard explanation of these sayings was that the ego of the individual is annihilated during an ecstatic state, and so it is really God speaking and not the human being."[61]

Hazarat Inayat Khan (1882-1927 A.D.) was a modernistic Sufi, an Indian mystic, who taught a universalistic brand of Sufism. On some issues, his ideas are extreme and quite distanced from mainstream Sufism. One example is his unique concept concerning the nature of man: that the "soul, born on earth, contains three beings: the angel, the jinn and the human."[62] Each has its own body, the angelic body being larger than the jinn body, which is itself somewhat larger than the physical body—yet these three bodies blend together in oneness. Traditional Sufis distinguish angels, jinn and humans from each other as separate, unrelated entities.

Theosophy: Teaches that man has a "Septenary Nature," one consisting of seven aspects: (1) The physical body *(rupa or Sthula-Sarira)*; (2) Life or vital principle *(prana)*; (3) Astral body *(linga sharira)*; (4) Animal soul *(kama rupa)*; (5) Mind or intelligence—the human soul *(manas)*; (6) Spiritual soul *(buddhi)*; and (7) Spirit *(atma)*. The first four make up the discardable and perishable "Lower *Quarternary*." The last three make up the "Upper Imperishable *Triad*."[63]

The "animal soul" *(kama rupa)* is the temporary personality associated with a single incarnation. It is even referred to as the "false personality." The "human soul" *(manas)* is the "permanent individuality or reincarnating ego." The "spiritual soul" *(buddhi)* is "the divine Ego," the "vehicle of pure universal spirit." The "spirit" *(atma)* is the highest essence of God above a person. It is one with the Divine or Brahma.[64]

A unique aspect of Helena Blavatsky's teaching is the idea that the astral body (also called the "phantom body" or *"eidolon"*) is that which appears to spiritualists in their attempts to contact those who have died. This "part" of the "Lower Quarternary" has already been disposed of in the realm called "Kama-loka." It is in the process of disintegration, and, because it is disconnected from the eternal "Self," it actually grants deceptive, false experiences to spiritualists. The true "Self" (the "manas" or "ego") has, in most cases, already passed into the higher realm called "Devachan," awaiting the next reincarnation.

Man is also spoken of as being divine, God in expression..."For Christ—the true esoteric savior—is no man but the DIVINE PRINCIPLE in every human being."[65] One theosophist offers, "If the idea of the immanence of God is sound, then man is a literal fragment of the consciousness of the Supreme Being...an embryo god...destined to ultimately evolve his latent powers into perfect expression."[66]

Transcendental Meditation (Maharishi Mahesh Yogi): "The impersonal God is that Being which dwells in the heart of everyone. Each individual in his true nature is the impersonal God."[67]

United Church of Religious Science (Dr. Ernest Holmes): "There is something Divine about us that we have overlooked. There is more to us than we realize. Man is an eternal destiny, a forever-expanding principle of conscious intelligence...the ocean in the drop of water, the sun in its rays. Man, the real man, is birthless, deathless, changeless; and God, as man, in man, is man!"[68] "Man is the Self-Knowingness of God; the Consciousness of God in execution; the Action of God moving into fulfillment; the Thought of God seeking self-expression."[69]

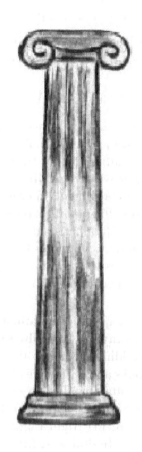

4

THE NATURE OF
SALVATION, LIBERATION,
OR ENLIGHTENMENT

There are a wide variety of ideas in world religions concerning the correct methods or means to be used in achieving deliverance from, dominion over, or ascendancy above the lower nature, this world, and physical mortality. Greatly simplified, they usually fall under one of the following three categories—salvation, liberation, or enlightenment by:

(1) Religious works or self-effort;

(2) Acquired spiritual knowledge;

(3) The grace, favor or merits of a mediatorial savior.

THE ELEVEN MAIN LIVING RELIGIONS

Buddhism: There are differences of opinion within the various Buddhist sects on this subject. Originally, the Buddha taught that salvation or liberation is attained, not by prayer, or grace or sacrifice, but by knowledge. **Theravada Buddhism** (the "Lesser Vehicle") proposes that it is necessary to be a monk in order to attain salvation (liberation from rebirth). The Buddhist monk is required to affirm his trust in the "Three Refuges": (1) the Buddha; (2) the *Dharma* (the doctrine); (3) the *Sangha* (the monastic order). Buddha's teaching, called "The Middle Way," encourages adherents to avoid two extremes: on the one hand, sensuality and self-indulgence—and on the other hand, extreme asceticism and self-mortification.

The great majority of Buddhists belong to a school that developed later called **Mahayana Buddhism** (the "Greater Vehicle"). This expression of Buddhism teaches that enlightenment is available for all Buddhists: monks and lay people alike. In both Theravada and Mahayana Buddhism, the attainment of an enlightened status comes primarily by following "The Eightfold Path": (1) Right Knowledge; (2) Right Thought; (3) Right Speech; (4) Right Conduct; (5) Right Livelihood; (6) Right Effort; (7) Right Mindfulness; (8) Right Meditation. So, for the majority of Buddhists, salvation is a product of self-effort. Buddha warned of five mental hazards and ten fetters which must be conquered before liberation from karma (*kamma*) and the cycle of rebirths can be achieved. Some of these include: "belief in a self, belief in the efficacy of good works, desire for a future life in heaven, pride and ignorance."[1]

Pure Land Buddhism (a sect of Mahayana Buddhism, a.k.a. Jodo-Shinshu) instructs its followers that they must place their trust in the power, compassion and overflowing merits of Amida Buddha (the Buddha of infinite light, different than Gautama Buddha) in order to be saved. **Nichiren Buddhism** obligates its adherents to chant an incantation from the Lotus Sutra in order to achieve liberation. (Sutras are the record of the discourses of the Buddha.) **Zen Buddhism** promotes the perfecting of certain meditation techniques in order to achieve *satori* (enlightenment—a sudden realization of one's true nature—a necessary step on the journey toward Nirvana). A number of methods are used, including: "*zazen* (seated meditation) and *sanzen* (interviews with a Zen master). During meditation, Zen Buddhists use *koans* (irrational phrases) to cut through rational thinking and discriminating thought to attain non-thinking."[2]

Final liberation for any Buddhist is Nirvana. This could be described as non-being—the extinction of personal existence by absorption into pure Being. Nirvana is passionless peace, detached serenity, cessation of desire, freedom from both pain and pleasure. Most Buddhists resist the idea that Nirvana means the annihilation of the soul; for they do not believe there is a soul to annihilate. One popular Vietnamese Buddhist writer, Thich Nhat Hanh, explains Nirvana to be "the extinction of ideas and concepts and suffering based on ideas and concepts; the ultimate dimension of reality."[3] In order to attain Nirvana a person must overcome the "three unwholesome roots—desire, hatred and delusion."[4]

Thich Nhat Hanh also offers that there are 84,000 dharma doors ("entries into the stream of the Buddha's teaching and realization"). He also advises "monks and laypersons who practice well always observe the Five Wonderful Precepts, the Thirty-eight Bodhisattva Precepts, or the 250 Pratimoksa Precepts."[5] Contrary to Jainism, Buddha taught that women are just as capable of enlightenment as men.

One unique feature of Mahayana and Tibetan Buddhism is the idea of **bodhisattvas** (a word meaning "enlightened beings"). These are spiritually advanced persons who are ready for Nirvana, but choose to postpone entrance, in order to assist others as they strive to attain liberation from this realm. Through their accumulation of spiritual merit, they can speed the spiritual advance of devotees. There are six transcendental activities that happen spontaneously to the one who walks the bodhisattva path: "transcendental generosity, discipline, patience, energy, meditation and knowledge. These virtues are called the six *paramitas*, meaning "arriving at the other side or shore."[6] In other words, leaving the ego behind, the bodhisattva arrives at the "other shore" of enlightenment and unselfishness. One can attain the status of a bodhisattva while in a physical body, but once released from this world, they still continue this role in the spiritual realms. Their "tenure of office" can continue for three, seven, or thirty-three eons, before achieving the status of a Buddha.

Tibetan Buddhism promotes the use of various esoteric methods to achieve enlightenment including; *yantras* (visual representations of the cosmos); *mudras* (bodily motions used during meditation); and *prayer*

THE NATURE OF SALVATION, LIBERATION, OR ENLIGHTENMENT

wheels (cylinders inscribed with sacred phrases and often containing many rolled up sacred phrases spun mechanically by hand, air, or water to accumulate merit for the individual). The veneration of certain Divine Beings is also essential, especially devotion to the Dalai Lama.

Christianity: Salvation is provided through the crucifixion of Jesus Christ, his resurrection, calling upon his name in prayer, true repentance, faith and the experience of being "born again." *(John 3:3)* The Bible teaches that the Lord Jesus Christ, though perfect himself, became one with transgression on the cross, assuming the sin-debt of the entire human race. *(See 2 Corinthians 5:21.)* He also tasted "death for every man." *(Hebrews 2:9)* The Christian view is that all human beings deserve death, not only physically, but also spiritually and eternally, as a result of their sins. But Jesus, by identifying with sinners on the cross, paid the ultimate price to deliver his people from the failures of their past.

Several things work together to produce a salvation experience. The main steps are described in the epistle to the Romans: "That if you confess with your mouth the Lord Jesus and believe in your heart that God has raised him from the dead, you will be saved. For with the heart one believes unto righteousness, and with the mouth confession is made unto salvation." Three verses later, another essential feature is added, "Whoever calls on the name of the Lord shall be saved." This involves more than just intellectual assent concerning the historical existence of Jesus. When repentant, believing persons call on the name of Jesus, accepting him into their hearts as Lord of their lives, they are "born again." This is more than just a moral reformation. It is a supernatural regeneration of the human spirit. *(See Ephesians 3:17, Titus 3:5.)* The blood of Jesus washes away all sin. *(See Revelation 1:5; 7:14.)* This cleanses the heart, rendering it suitable for the indwelling of the Spirit of God. This spiritual rebirth is necessary to enter the kingdom of God. *(See John 3:1–16.)*

All this takes place because of God's grace (unmerited love and divinely imparted ability). *(See Ephesians 2:8–9.)* Water baptism (immersion) is a required New Covenant ritual representing the old person being buried with Christ and a new person emerging from the waters, resurrected in Christ, to live a new life under the Lordship of Jesus. *(See Matthew 28:19, Acts 2:38, Romans 6:4, Colossians 2:12.)*

Confucianism: Although Confucius originally deemphasized prayer, attentiveness to the supernatural or devotion to spiritual beings, numerous deities have traditionally been worshipped in Confucianism (especially as advocates mixed this worldview with other religious beliefs). *(See Analects 3:13, 7:34, 6:20.)* Even so, this philosophy of life promotes essentially a self-dependent scheme of salvation: "What the superior man seeks is in himself." *(Analects 15:20)* This striving for excellence, however, must be prompted by sensitivity to spiritual knowledge, for "Without recognizing the ordinances of Heaven it is impossible to be a superior man." *(Analects 20:3.1)* There are three hundred rules of ceremony and three thousand rules of demeanor to which men should conform. *(Doctrine of the Mean 27:3)*

Confucius' instructions revolved around *jen*, a Chinese word rendered "love," "goodness" and "human-heartedness." *Jen* primarily concerns the development of moral excellence. It is taught in conjunction with *li* (proper conduct and ritual harmony), *shu* (the concept of reciprocity), *chung* (faithful devotion to one's true nature), *yi* (righteousness) and *hsiao* (obedience to, and care of, parents and elder family members).

Hinduism: In Hinduism there are three main paths *(marga)* to salvation or liberation: (1) The Way of Knowledge *(jnana-marga*—study of the sacred texts and contemplation of the soul's oneness with Brahman); (2) The Way of Devotion *(bhakti-marga*—loving surrender of the self to God, often in the form of worshipful service of an individual deity); (3) The Way of Works *(karma-marga*—the way of good deeds, as well as properly following religious ceremonies, traditions and ethical duties).

These three paths could also be otherwise identified as Jnana Yoga, Bhakti Yoga and Karma Yoga. Many teachers, including Ramakrishna, identify a fourth main path as Raja Yoga, differentiating between the pursuit of knowledge (Jnana Yoga) and the psychophysical techniques aimed at subduing the mind and experiencing the super-conscious state (Raja Yoga).

These methods include body postures, breath control and concentration or contemplation: all aimed at the ultimate goal of achieving *samadhi*. Following one or all of these paths can finally deliver a person from *samsara* (the cycle of rebirths). Many Hindus would say that total liberation *(moksha)* comes when the soul achieves undifferentiated union with Brahman.

In contrast, the **Sankhya Yoga School** within Hinduism teaches that final liberation is not signified by an absolute, monistic oneness with Brahman: a perception of everything being in the Self and the Self in everything. Instead, it involves the freeing of the individual soul from the cycle of rebirth, yet simultaneously, an isolation from all other 'Selves' within the sphere of its own personal, omnipresent, omniscient, divine, eternal existence. In this viewpoint, absorption into Brahman does not mean the absolute loss of individuality.

—THE NATURE OF SALVATION, LIBERATION, OR ENLIGHTENMENT—

A Hindu sage named Patanjali (app. 200-150 B.C.) codified the practice of yoga titling the stages as "The Eight Limbs of Yoga": (1) Self-control—*yama*; (2) Religious observance—*niyama*; (3) Postures—*asanas*; (4) Breath and life-force control—*pranayama*; (5) Withdrawal from control of the senses—*pratyahara*; (6) Concentration, steadying of the mind—*dharana*; (7) Meditation—*dhyana*; (8) Profound contemplation—*samadhi*—which ultimately ends in complete absorption in God. Though not emphasized today, in historical Hinduism animal sacrifices were cited as a means of atonement and an answer for the human dilemma.

Islam: The primary path to salvation centers around submission to Allah, submission to the Qur'an, and submission to the "Five Pillars" of Islam: (1) *Shahada*—The daily profession of faith, "There is no God but Allah and Mohammed is his prophet"; (2) *Salat*—Prayer must be made toward Mecca five times a day; (3) *Ramadan*—This is the month of fasting. During the month of Ramadan Muslims cannot eat, drink, smoke or have sexual relations between dawn and sunset; (4) *Zakat*—Almsgiving: two-and-a-half percent (1/40th) of the annual savings must be donated to charity; (5) *Hajj*—Pilgrimage: a Muslim is expected to make a journey to Mecca once in his lifetime. Another major emphasis is repentance. It is always possible to repent (*tawbah*) and those who do are restored to a state of sinlessness.

Adherence to the teachings of all the prophets of Allah is a major expectation in Islam. Twenty-eight prophets are mentioned in the Qur'an. Twenty-two of these are found in the Old Testament, including: Adam, Enoch, Methusaleh, Noah, Abraham, Lot, Ishmael, Isaac, Jacob, Moses, David, Solomon, Elijah, Elisha and Jonah. Three are discovered in the New Testament: Zechariah, John the Baptist and Jesus. Mohammed is presented as the final prophet, surpassing all others in greatness. God's prophetic spokesmen are honored, but none are considered divine.

An interesting offshoot of Islam is Sufism. This is the esoteric branch of Islam. For most Muslims, Allah is so far above this material world that, to finite men, he is incomprehensible and unattainable. Sufis, on the other hand, claim mystical experiences with God are available through meditation and a whirling kind of dance that brings on an ecstatic experience.

Jainism: According to the teachings of the founder, Vardharmana Jnatiputra (later named Mahavira, meaning "great hero"), liberation is attained, not only by following a regimen of meditation, but also by strict ascetic practices. These include adhering to the 'Five Great Vows'—a renunciation of (1) Killing any living thing; (2) Lying; (3) Greed; (4) Sexual pleasure and, (5) Worldly attachments. The 'Three Jewels' are Right Faith, Right Knowledge and Right Living.

Jains believe in *Anekantavada,* the concept that "there is no single reality and there are many perspectives on the truth."[7] Also greatly emphasized among Jainists is *Ahimsa* (non-violence). A true Jainist refuses to kill any living thing. Deeply respectful of life, Jainists even strain the water they drink to avoid killing small organisms. Monks often sweep the path in front of them to avoid accidentally stepping on insects. Even farming is discouraged for fear of killing creatures in the soil.

Because of their passion to transcend the natural realm, Jainist monks often go to extreme measures of self-denial, such as: refraining from taking baths, brushing their teeth or sleeping on a bed. These rules of asceticism have been modified for Jainist laymen. However, laymen are expected to take upon themselves twelve vows, and as they progress, to fulfill the eleven promises, and develop the twenty-one qualities which mark a true Jain. These vows and promises include commitments to non-violence, truthfulness, meditation, abstinence, times of temporary celibacy, non-attachment or limitation of possessions and the worship of a true *deva* (Tirthankara). Certain days are set aside for layman to voluntarily live a monastic type of life.

Altogether, there are fourteen steps to liberation from accumulated karma. Full salvation is unattainable by laymen unless, as the end of life draws near, they take the vow of old age, which includes voluntary starvation (*sellekhana*). Monks (ascetics) are instructed to abandon love as well as hate, because both are forms of attachment. Final liberation comes when one is delivered from the cycle of rebirths. Jainist monks believe that ideally nudity should be a part of their discipline, after the pattern of their founder (as a wandering ascetic, he went without clothes). However, a major schism exists between the Svetambaras ("white-clad") and the Digambaras ("sky-clad"). The former believe that owing to the present degeneration of the universe nudity is no longer advisable. The latter believe nudity is appropriate and correct when its practice is feasible. In the Digambara sect of Jainism, a woman cannot hope for salvation until, because of a virtuous life, she is reborn as a man. The highest level of consciousness attainable is *keval-jnana,* which is perfect perception, knowledge, and bliss.

Judaism: Personal salvation in Judaism is based on repentance, good deeds and adherence to the Torah (the Law). However, these three ingredients are mixed with a strong trust, not in self-achieved righteousness, but in the mercy of God. Actually, in Judaism, the concept of salvation is more national than personal. It differs significantly from Christianity, which promotes the concept of a 'fallen nature,' which a person must be 'saved from.' The Jewish belief is that a person is born good and can remain good by observing God's commandments.

Rightness with God, though always available, is especially obtainable once a year on Yom Kippur, the Day of Atonement. "The capstone of the Jewish view of man is his ever-present opportunity for repentance and forgiveness...If he repents in sincerity he is immediately forgiven...Thus the Rabbis suggested that *t'shuvah* or penitence was created even before the world itself was formed. In fact, they project the thought that *t'shuvah* is the cement which keeps the world from falling apart."[8] Such respect for this concept gives rise to comments like R. Jacob's, "One moment of repentance and good deeds in this world is better than the entire life of the world to come." (*Mishnah, Ethics of the Fathers 4:17*) The age of accountability is thirteen for boys (*Bar Mitzvah*) and twelve for girls (*Bat Mitzvah*). At these ages, children become legally responsible for keeping God's commandments.

Prior to the destruction of the Temple in Jerusalem in 70 A.D. and subsequent exile of the Jewish people, atonement for sin was represented by animal sacrifices. Since sacrifices could only be performed in the Temple, after its destruction, the sacrifices ceased. Many Jews consider the non-observance of these sacred rites an indication of God's punishment for the collective sins of the Jewish people. However, ancient Jewish prophets predicted that this deprived condition would last only for a season—that in the "latter days" there would be a restoration of the Jewish people to their homeland, a rebuilding of the Temple and a continuation of their original methods of sacrifice (finalized apparently, when the Messiah comes). The full benefits of salvation will then be available once again to the sons and daughters of Abraham. *(See Jeremiah 32:37-42, Ezekiel 37-48, Hosea 3:4.)*

It is believed in Judaism that only those who embrace the belief in one God (monotheism) can inherit an eternal reward. (In Isaiah 45:21-22 God declares, "There is no other God besides Me...I am God; there is no other."). One rabbi, Moses Luzatto, insists, "The Torah is the only remedy for the evil impulse. Whoever thinks that he can be helped without it is mistaken and will realize his error when he dies for his sins."[9] However, this does not exclude non-Jews from having hope for the future. Many Jewish teachers open wide the door of opportunity. In his code, Moses Maimonides proposes "the pious of the nations of the world have a portion in the world to come." *(Yad. Teshuvah 3:5)*[10] And Rabbi Yohanan ben Zakkai said, "Just as the sin-offering atones for Israel, so righteousness atones for the peoples of the world." *(Babylonian Talmud, Baba Batra 10b)*[11]

The "Noachide Laws" are the seven laws considered by rabbinic tradition as the minimal moral duties enjoined by the Bible upon all humankind. Jews are obligated to observe the whole Torah, while every non-Jew is a "son of the covenant of Noah." *(See Genesis 9:1-17.)* Hence, they are duty-bound to keep the laws revealed to this ancient patriarch and receive them as being divinely inspired. Traditionally, there are seven "Noachide Laws." The first six are negative laws, involving the prohibition of (1) Idolatry; (2) Blasphemy; (3) Bloodshed; (4) Sexual sins; (5) Theft; and (6) Eating from a living animal. (7) The seventh is a positive law, the demand for the establishment of a legal system.[12] Those non-Jews who abide by these rules qualify for acceptance by God eternally in the world to come. So there is a general covenant between God and humanity (the Adamic and Noahic Covenants), and a specific covenant between God and the Jews (beginning with the Abrahamic Covenant).

The primary emphasis in Judaism is abiding in "covenant" *(berith)* with the God of Abraham, Isaac and Jacob by observing his "commandments" *(mitzvoth—613* are found in the Torah). Traditional Orthodox Judaism has defined the commandments through *Halakhah* (lit. "the way"—the way in which to live according to Jewish law, custom and practice). Modern reformed Judaism considers *Halakhah* non-obligatory, while the Conservative Movement has redefined it with a more modernistic view. Circumcision for males is practiced by all Jews, being a major facet of the original covenant God made with the patriarch, Abraham. *(See Genesis 17.)*

Shinto: Salvation is secured by appeasing the gods, by worshipful reverence toward departed ancestors and by obeying the numerous social, religious and physical regulations, codes, and taboos that have been interwoven into the Japanese lifestyle. Every true Shinto home contains a *Kami-dana,* or 'god-shelf.' On this miniature shrine are placed emblems and names of various gods and ancestors, along with offerings. There is no fully defined concept of sin or of human beings being born under the burden of a fallen nature. Since adherents feel they are the offspring of the gods, they consider themselves heirs of a nature that is basically good and potentially divine. Most forms of this religion teach a person must be Japanese to be a Shintoist. However, of the approximately

150 sects, some are quite zealous about converting those who are not Japanese into their ranks.

Sikhism: Guru Nanak, founder of Sikhism, taught liberation *(mukti)* could be obtained through four progressive steps. They are the Name *(nam)*, the Word *(sabad)*, the Teacher *(guru)* and Harmony *(hukam)*. *Nam*, the divine Name, and *sabad*, the divine Word, reveal the essence and character of God. Man, however, is subject to the bondage of his fleshly, ignorant state. He fails to recognize God's presence in his Name and Word, so he needs a *guru*, one who leads from darkness *(gu)* to enlightenment *(ru)*. Through the guru's influence, the seeker is 'awakened.' He can then perceive *hukam*, the Divine Order, or Harmony.

A seeker harmonizes his life with the Divine through acceptance of, and obedience to the Word (the *Adi Granth*) and meditation on the divine Name *(nam simaran)*. In all reality, though, these can only lead a person into a godly lifestyle. Ultimate salvation or liberation (release from the cycle of rebirths) can only be attained through God's grace. It is stated in the Japji (a basic Credal Statement) that—"The body takes its birth because of karma. But salvation is attained because of the grace (of the Lord)." *(Japji, Pauri 4)* Though many Sikhs do believe in reincarnation, some feel this doctrine is not definitely indicated in their holy writings and that 'liberation' *(mukti)* is primarily freedom from an egoistic existence. Personal salvation, escape from suffering, or remaining absorbed in spiritual bliss is not the Sikh ideal. For many Sikhs, striving for moral, spiritual progress is not an end in itself; it is a preparation to equip oneself for the better service of humanity.

Internal attitudes, as opposed to outward religiosity, are emphasized in yet another verse *(Japji 21)*, "Pilgrimage, austerities, charity and alms earn no more merit than a paltry sesame. Hear, believe, nurture love in your heart, for thus one is cleansed by the waters within." Also, renouncing the flesh and withdrawing from the world are not requirements, as in the asceticism of Hinduism. Instead, Sikhs are expected to work toward liberation through their day-to-day living—and not only for their own sake, but for others. Because of this, some would describe it as a 'whole life religion.'

Also emphasized for orthodox Sikhs are the outward symbols referred to as the "Five K's": the *kesh* (uncut hair), the *kangha* (a comb that fastens the hair in place), the *kirpan* (a dagger), the *kara* (steel bangle) and the *kachh* (undertrousers). These articles of faith represent various values that Sikhs attempt to live by, such as: fulfilling God's will, living in purity and courage, and defending the weak and oppressed. Prohibitions include refraining from the use of alcohol, tobacco and all intoxicants.

Taoism: Because the *Tao* (the Principle that rules the universe) "never acts, yet nothing is left undone," a passive life of creative inaction (quiet non-striving) is advocated for those seeking spiritual maturity. The model Taoist is calm and peaceful, like the Source of all things, the underlying flow of life. This ideal standard of living is called *wu-wei.*

Viewing the human family in its unity and expressing kindness and goodness impartially toward all is also encouraged, for "to know the eternal is enlightenment; not to know the eternal means to run blindly to disaster. He who knows the eternal is all-embracing. He who is all-embracing is impartial. To be impartial is to be kingly. To be kingly is to be heavenly. To be heavenly is to be one with the Tao. To be one with the Tao is to endure forever." *(Tao-te Ching 16)*

A person achieves immortality when he rises above a sense-controlled existence, when he lives a virtuous life, when he abides by the standard of the Tao and is in harmony with his body. Such an individual is titled *chen jen*—a perfected person. In order to accomplish this, there are many ceremonies, magical rites, traditions, meditation practices and religious disciplines that a devoted Taoist will normally pursue. Different sects emphasize different means. For instance, Celestial Teachers Taoism emphasizes the use of talismans and incantations, especially to cure illnesses and ward off evil spirits.

Shang-ch'ing Taoism emphasizes "Keeping the One" (staying in harmony with the Tao) and "holding the guardian deities" (the *San-yuan,* the gods who live in the body).[13] Meditating on these deities—named the Three Pure Ones or the Three Primal Ones—replaces "the three deathbringers in the major energy centers of the body and make the person immortal."[14] Once every two months the "deathbringers" have to "ascend to the heavens to make their report to the celestial administration" (the Jade Emperor).[15] If a Taoist successfully keeps nightly vigils during at least seven such times, the "deathbringers" become emaciated and die, thus freeing a person from their influence. Fasting, abstinence from grains, stilling the mind and eliminating craving are also offered as means of overcoming these 'monsters' in the body.

Other unique esoteric practices promoting physical and spiritual well being include: (1) Absorbing the essence of the sun, moon, stars, and vapor—and their related deities—through various meditative practices, in order to bring the microcosms of the body into harmony with the macrocosms of the universe; (2) Pursuing spiritual transformation through the gathering of, and preservation of, generative energy. Different sects claim this is accomplished by one of two approaches: either by the restraint or regulation of sexual practices (called "the Singular Path") or by the absorbing of generative energy through involvement with multiple sexual partners (called "the Paired Path"). For the latter to be effective there must be "no love, no pleasure, and no desire" and the sexual act must be halted before orgasm occurs for the one seeking to accumulate generative energy.[16] The energy gained by this procedure is of a lower nature and must be refined and transmuted into a higher form of vital energy to be physically and spiritually useful to the practitioner.

Zoroastrianism: Because this religion emphasizes 'salvation by works,' adherents tend to display a greater tolerance toward people of other religions. Zoroastrians must have a dominance of good works to be saved. The three most honorable and desirable virtues are good thoughts, good words and good deeds. Man's chief duty is to offer his body as a habitation for the Beneficent Immortals. (See "Zoroastrianism" under *The Nature of God.*) Hell is considered merely a temporary abode for the correction of the wicked, because all souls will be saved in the end (the doctrine of universalism). The practice of imbibing a hallucinogenic drink called *haoma* has become an emphasized rite. Also, instead of burying or cremating the dead, corpses are placed above the ground in a *daxma* (a 'tower of silence') where the remains are eaten by vultures and insects. Disposing of human remains in any other way is considered a serious sin.

OTHER RELIGIONS, SECTS OR TEACHERS

Bahá'í: This faith teaches the unification of all religions. However, it emphasizes, not "salvation" (as Christianity, Islam and others) or "enlightenment" (as most Eastern traditions), but "transformation" of the individual into a spiritual, godly person. Two main things are necessary for this 'spiritual transformation' to take place: (1) "Faith in the current Manifestation of God (at present, Bahá'u'lláh)"—the founder of Bahá'í, and; (2) "Good deeds."[17]

Also emphasized are meditation on the Word of God, serving others and teaching the faith to others (through both explanation and example). Bahá'ís do not seek to know or experience God directly, since he can only be known through his messengers. Members of the Bahá'í community are "under the obligation to pray daily; to abstain from narcotics, alcohol, or any substances that affect the mind" and "to practice monogamy." They are also urged to "attend the Nineteen Day Feast on the first day of each month of the Bahá'í calendar."[18] Asceticism is forbidden.

Brahma Kumaris World Spiritual Organization (Raja Yoga): "Soul consciousness" is spoken of as being "the Gateway to God," as opposed to body consciousness. When a person maintains the attitude, "I am a body," he or she becomes "trapped in a world of temporary illusions, likes and dislikes."[19] Relating to oneself as a soul is, therefore, the first main step in achieving higher levels of consciousness. When this happens the truth-seeker tends to realize: "the soul is the driver; the body is the car. The soul is the guest; the body is the hotel. The soul is the actor; the body is the costume. The soul is the musician; the body is the instrument."[20]

Furthermore, when seeking persons realize their union with the Ultimate Reality and begin burning with love toward the 'Supreme Soul,' "sin can be rapidly incinerated. To this end the soul need only increase its love for God. Blind faith, penance, worship or despair will not help."[21] Loving communion with the most holy Supreme Soul purifies the individual soul and moves it toward its original state of purity and bliss.

"The belief that we have inherited sin from the time of Adam is not true. Each soul has become impure by its own actions during its births. We ourselves became impure and peaceless through losing our self-awareness, so it is useless to blame anyone else...The soul itself creates its accounts, good and bad, so the soul itself must balance them. No human soul, whether Christ or Buddha, or even some guru or spiritual guide can settle someone else's account of sins. In this respect many souls are being misled by those who claim to be able to alter or interfere with the workings of the laws of karma...The account of impure actions can only be balanced by pure actions on the part of the 'doer': the soul."[22]

Five steps are given to release a person from this spiritual bondage: (1) "Acceptance of personal responsibility"; (2) Recognition of the impressions *(sanskaras)* that promote soul-consciousness and God-consciousness, as opposed to the impressions *(sanskaras)* that promote body-consciousness; (3) Attentiveness to thought-life, and a commitment to stop the development of thoughts that tend toward body-consciousness; (4) Elimination of negative karma, that manifests in negative *sanskaras*, by developing "deep communion with the Supreme Soul"; (5) "Accrual of credit through pure and God-inspired actions for the spiritual welfare of others."[23]

The "Four Pillars" of Raja Yoga are: (1) Sattvic Diet: Vegetarianism is mandatory. Also, food to be eaten must be prepared by a pure person who maintains loving remembrance of God; (2) Good Company, the development of godly virtues by being in daily contact with spiritual-minded persons; (3) Study of Raja Yoga; (4) Celibacy. These four things are required in order to reach a fully enlightened state of soul-consciousness. It is also necessary to walk in: faith, renunciation *(Tiag)*, intense meditation *(Tapasya)*, and service of others *(Seva)*. Renunciation means primarily renunciation of negativity, not necessarily material things. Those who reach the depth of meditation can visit and experience the spiritual world above this natural plane. The primary emphasis is love generated constantly toward the Father, rendering rituals and ceremonial religious acts inferior and unnecessary.

A follower of this worldview believes that the destruction of this world is imminent (to take place at the end of the Diamond Age), and that the duty of every enlightened person is to warn others to prepare for this pivotal change.

ECKANKAR: Enlightenment comes through the experience of the cosmic "Light and Sound" of God, a revelation said to be most perfectly unveiled through the teachings of this sect. Great emphasis is also placed on the interpretation of dreams and on "soul travel," which is called "the secret path to God." Through this experience a person can ultimately achieve omniscience. It can only be taught by a Living ECK Master.

Students of ECKANKAR are also trained to meditate on the current "Mahanta" (the ECK master) until he appears to them in a radiant form. Being in the presence of the "Mahanta" burns away negative karma and grants followers of this path a quicker entry into God-realization. What constitutes moral behavior is an individual discovery and decision, established by a person's inner authority. Souls can never be lost, but they can forget who they are.

Paul Twitchell, the founder of this sect, taught that it is not possible to enter the Kingdom of God except through the teachings of ECKANKAR.

Gnosticism: Salvation is a process of achieving enlightenment through the acquisition of esoteric knowledge *(gnosis)*. The eating of the forbidden fruit by Adam and Eve in Genesis resulted in their eyes being 'opened.' In Gnosticism this does not indicate a 'fall' but a state of *gnosis*— enlightenment concerning their own divine essence. Ultimate "salvation consists in the separation of the immortal spirit from the mortal psyche and from physical creation. The consummation of salvation will be when the whole Sonship (the emanated sparks in humanity) ascends and passes beyond the Great Limit."[24]

Helen Schucman (*A Course in Miracles*): "Salvation is nothing more than right-mindedness."[25] "Never forget that the Sonship is your salvation, for the Sonship is your Self...Your Self does not need salvation, but your mind needs to learn what salvation is. You are not saved *from* anything, but you are saved *for* glory."[26] "When you realize that all guilt is solely an invention of your mind, you also realize that guilt and salvation must be in the same place. In understanding this you are saved."[27] "My salvation comes from me. It cannot come from anywhere else...Within me is the world's salvation and my own."[28]

Referencing Christian doctrine, Schucman insists "the crucifixion had no part in the Atonement."[29] Instead, when we forgive ourselves, when we receive forgiveness from fellow human beings, or when we extend forgiveness to others, we are participating in, and perpetuating, 'the Atonement.' "Forgiveness is for God and toward God, but not of Him. It is impossible to think of anything He created that could need forgiveness. Forgiveness then is an illusion…a kind of happy fiction, a way in which the unknowing bridge the gap between their perception and the truth."[30]

ISKCON (International Society of Krishna Consciousness): The world is now in a lengthy era of degeneration called the *Kali Yuga* ("the dark age"). Liberation of the soul at this time can only be accomplished by *kirtana*—communing with the Lord by singing, dancing and chanting his name (advised to be "Hare Krishna"). Most dedicated adherents chant this mantra on each of 108 japa beads, sixteen times a day.

Numerous rules govern the life of Krishna's followers, such as: purification of desire, mandatory vegetarianism (including exclusion of onion and garlic from the diet), and abstinence from drugs, alcohol and caffeine. Devotees place thirteen symbolic marks on their bodies daily using special clay. Men are encouraged to shave their heads leaving a *sikha* (similar to a 'pony tail') by which Krishna can pull them up to heaven if he chooses. According to Swami Prabhupada, "To the perfect devotee, everything is spiritual *(sarvam khalv idam brahma)*. So, we have to train our eyes to see Krsna everywhere. And this training is devotional service to Krsna, which is a process of purification."[31]

"The preliminary qualification for going back to Godhead is given in the Bhagavad-Gita [15.5]: "One who is free from illusion, false prestige, and false association, who understands the eternal, who is done with material lust and is free from the duality of happiness and distress, and who knows how to surrender unto the Supreme Person attains that eternal kingdom.""[32] Echoing Caitanya, an earlier and greatly revered leader in this movement, Swami Prabhupada asserted, "The actual identity of every living creature is that he is the eternal servant of God. If one thinks like that—"I am no one else's servant; my business is to serve God"—then he is liberated."[33]

Kabbala (Mystical Judaism): Salvation consists of the ascent of the soul, through various religious disciplines, from the material world *(Asiyyah)* to the supernal world *(Atzilut)*. According to the *Sefer Yezeriah* (the Book of Creation) the goal is to reach the realm of God *(Ein Sof)* by meditating on the thirty-two paths. These are made up of the ten *Sefirot* (emanations of God) plus the twenty-two connections between the *Sefirot*. Originally, "ten" merely related to the foundational numbers and "twenty-two" to the letters in the Hebrew alphabet. Later, these came to be interpreted as "divine potencies." The Kabbala also teaches fifty gates of understanding through which a person must pass in order to achieve enlightenment. Transmigration of the soul is not accepted in all Kabbalistic schools. However, among those who do, a belief is sometimes embraced that a person's predestined mission in life must be fulfilled in order to avoid rebirth. A primary goal in life is to receive for the purpose of sharing, thus becoming one with the God who is motivated this way.

Kriya Yoga (Paramahansa Yogananda): Taught that man has three bodies from which Consciousness must be delivered, the physical body, the astral body and the causal body. "When all desires are conquered by meditation, the three body-prisons are dissolved; the soul becomes Spirit."[34] He taught that it is very rare that a soul regresses to an animal state. Final liberation is achieved when a person becomes Self-realized. This is only accomplished by unceasing devotion to God.

Kundalini Yoga (Yogi Bhajan): "If you want to get out of your karma there is only one way, vibrate the Nam. The Nam is the vibration of the praise of infinity."[35] This quote is an echo of Sikh doctrine. The word *Nam*, meaning "name," is usually combined with *Sat*, meaning "true." *Sat Nam* or "True Name" is the main designation for God in Sikhism. Yogi Bhajan also taught, "Who is the savior? It is your own higher consciousness which can save you from your own lower consciousness."[36]

Meher Baba: "Do not search for God outside of you. God can only be found within you, for his only abode is the heart."[37] In his book, *God Speaks*, Baba declares that there are as many ways to God as there are souls. In another book, he explains, "Your own religion, if put into practice, is sufficient to bring salvation to you. It is a mistake to change one's own religion for that of another. The surroundings and circumstances in which you find yourself are best suited to work out your destiny or to exhaust your past karma."[38] Salvation or liberation is attained when the reincarnation process ends and the soul experiences oneness with God. Baba was adamant in insisting that except for the very first soul, in order to reach Enlightenment (God-Consciousness, Self-Realization), all souls must have the help of a God-realized Perfect Master or the Avatar. So it is vitally important in life to find that Master and to serve him or her in love and obedience.

Scientology: Promotes the belief that man is basically good, and that his spiritual salvation is dependent upon: (1) Himself, (2) Relationships with others (family, friends, co-workers, other church members, etc.), and (3) Relationship to the universe as a whole.

"The road to spiritual freedom" is that process by which an adherent becomes a "Clear." This is the objective of every Scientologist, accomplished by the removal of "engrams" (pronounced en'-grahams). This last term refers to the negative, subconscious perceptions, held in the memory bank of the reactive mind, that continually prevent a person from making healthy, right, good decisions in the analytical mind. (See "Scientology" under *The Origin and Nature of Man*.) By removing these "engrams," these repressed negative memories that create emotional and mental blocks, a person can live a more fulfilling, happy, stable, creative, powerful life. The thetan (the 'higher Self') is then in a place of ascendancy and control.

Very precise techniques have been developed, called "Dianetics" (lit. through the soul), aimed at accomplishing this goal. It involves aspirants participating in "auditing sessions" in which the "auditor" analyzes the reactions of the preclear to various questions that are posed while the latter is holding an "electropsychometer" or E-meter. Once areas of "charge" or upset are located and examined, the auditor and the preclear work together to "erase" those engrams, thus lifting the preclear to a higher state of awareness. During the auditing sessions, preclears experience many realizations about life called "cognitions." Once cleared of engrams, a person can embark on a spiritual journey of increased awareness and enlightenment, the ultimate goal of which is freedom from the endless chain of physical birth-death and personal, spiritual immortality.

A further defining of existence by the "Eight Dynamics" brings order and harmony in life. These "dynamics" concern man's passion to survive as and through: (1) Self, (2) Family, (3) Groups, (4) Mankind, (5) All living things, (6) The physical universe, (7) The spiritual universe, and (8) God (Infinity). Scientologists seek optimum survival along all eight of these dynamic urges. Evil can be defined as that which is destructive to the "Eight Dynamics"; good can be defined as that which is constructive to the "Eight Dynamics." Scientologists believe that the spiritual freedom attainable through this approach has been "sought throughout history but never attainable before Dianetics."[39]

Sufism (Mystical Islam): Salvation or liberation comes by overcoming the false ego *(nafs)* and achieving oneness with God. A foundational, dual goal of a Sufi is *fana* (dying or melting into God by eradicating the human self and its attributes) and *baqa* (living in God and attaining divine attributes).[40] When *fana* is achieved, the worshipper is absorbed into God. The present-day author, Kabir Helminski, emphasizes the Sufi gateway to this state: "Only Love can tame the ego and bring it into the service of Love…In order to really love, our ego structure has to dissolve and re-form on a new basis…Love then re-creates the self."[41]

There are three main aspects of spiritual life: *fikr*—meditation, *tawakkul*—total reliance on God, and *dhikr*—perpetual remembrance of God. Sufis recommend beginning this spiritual journey by worshipping God as the "Beloved" or "Friend." Final enlightenment comes when "there is no longer that difference which a worshipper makes between himself and God; as Khusrau the Persian poet says, 'When I have become Thee and Thou hast become me…Beloved, there is no difference between I and Thou.'"[42] The revered Sufi poet, Rumi, often drew attention to this concept. He disclosed, "I've spent my life, my heart and my eyes this way. I used to think that love and beloved are different. I know now they are the same. I was seeing two in one."[43]

Various means of achieving this state are utilized, including the whirling dance of the dervishes and the practice of the "remembrance of God." The latter is especially accomplished by chanting and repeating the ninety-nine names for God found in the Qur'an. Yet even though paradise is the longing of every Sufi, they seek to be motivated not by fear of hell or love of paradise, but by an overwhelming love of God.

"There are four stages of practice and understanding in Sufism— *shariah* (religious law), *tariqah* (the mystical path), *haqiqah* (Truth), and *Marifah* (Gnosis). Each is built upon the stages that go before."[44] *Shariah* is a term for the teachings of Islam, the moral and ethical rules that have already been spoken. *Tariqah* means, in essence, the path in the desert that leads to the oasis (the experience of truth and reality). *Haqiqah* is the experience of the mystical states of Sufism, an inward experience of the presence of God. *Marifah* (Gnosis) is the highest state of revelation knowledge and wisdom, even beyond *Haqiqah*. During this earthly sojourn, there are "three great blessings given to those who are lovers of God. They are *islam* (submission), *iman* (faith), and *ihsan* (awareness of God)… *Ihsan* means "to act beautifully." The essence of the word is "to worship God as if you see Him. The person who fully develops *ihsan* is aware of God at all times and has reached the goal of Sufism."[45]

Theosophy: Liberation comes by overcoming negative karma and achieving release from the cycle of reincarnation. It is salvation by self-effort. Similar to the Buddhist idea of bodhisattvas, Theosophists believe in *Nirmanakayas*, highly evolved beings who have a right to enter Nirvana, but renounce such a privilege out of compassion for the human race. These "have no right to interfere with karma, and can only advise and inspire mortals for the general good."[46]

Annie Besant, a principal leader, taught that seekers after truth should "surrender all the fallacious ideas of forgiveness, vicarious atonement, divine mercy, and the rest of the opiates which superstition offers to the sinner."[47] Co-founder Helena Blavatsky also insisted such beliefs are "dangerous dogma"[48] and that in all reality, "every Ego…becomes its own Saviour."[49] When asked if God can forgive sin, Blavatsky responded, "This is what Christianity teaches, and what we combat." She also rejected the notion that "God's mercy is boundless and unfathomable."[50] Human beings do not need mercy; they need enlightenment. The promise is also given that, "Every noble thought and every unselfish deed are stepping-stones to the higher and more glorious planes of being."[51]

Transcendental Meditation (Maharishi Mahesh Yogi): This worldview teaches there are seven states of consciousness: (1) Waking—*Jagrat Chetana*; (2) Dreaming—*Swapn Chetana*; (3) Sleeping—*Sushupti Chetana*; (4) Transcendental Consciousness—*Turiya Chetana*; (5) Cosmic Consciousness—*Turiyatit Chetana*; (6) God Consciousness—*Bhagavat Chetana*; (7) Unity Consciousness—*Brahmi Chetana*.[52] Complete liberation comes when the highest states of consciousness are achieved.

Maharishi Mahesh Yogi counters the traditional belief that extreme renunciation and detachment are necessary for the attaining of enlightenment. In his commentary on the Bhagavad-Gita, he claims this view is a "complete distortion of Indian philosophy."[53] Some TM advocates may practice a life of strict renunciation, while others may function in a secular world. Both paths are acceptable, being a matter of personal choice.

Another unique point of view concerns the attaining of the state of Samadhi. While many Far Eastern worldviews maintain that Samadhi is the end result of adhering to all the various stages of yogic self-discipline, Maharishi insists, "The practice of yoga should start with Samadhi."[54] In other words, seekers of God should begin with a consciousness of their separateness from a world of action and their oneness with God, then all other disciplines and all other strivings toward virtuous character become an automatic and simultaneous outgrowth of this high awareness level.

United Church of Religious Science (Dr. Ernest Holmes): "We have tried to show that there is no sin but a mistake and no punishment but a consequence. The Law of cause and effect. Sin is merely missing the mark. God does not punish sin. As we correct our mistakes, we forgive our own sins."[55] "True salvation comes only through true enlightenment, through a more conscious and more complete union of our lives with the Invisible."[56] Dr. Holmes also offered, "When any individual recognizes his true union with the Infinite, he automatically becomes the Christ."[57]

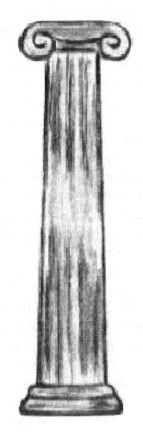

5

<u>DIMENSIONS OR PLANES</u>
<u>OF EXISTENCE</u>

All religions promote ideas concerning unseen, transcendent 'dimensions' beyond this natural realm. The beliefs are quite varied. Usually various types of spirit-beings either inhabit, or are confined to, these realms.

THE ELEVEN MAIN LIVING RELIGIONS

Buddhism: Modern Buddhism (especially Western Buddhism) tends to de-emphasize subjects like this, placing greater emphasis on pursuits like mindfulness, meditation, ethics, and compassion. Consequently, some groups might not agree with the concepts listed below, or they may interpret them differently. Buddha himself discouraged speculation on cosmological issues. Over a period of time, however, Buddhists developed what has become a traditional belief involving thirty-one planes of existence. These spheres provide paradise-like dwelling places for the highest of spiritual beings, this natural world for animals and living humans, and purgatory-like, hellish existences for the lowest entities.

Three main divisions exist within the portion of the universe affected by *samsara* (the cycle of rebirths). *Arupa-dhatu* ("the sphere of formlessness") is the highest plane of existence. It is totally non-material, populated by highly evolved, formless brahma-deities occupied in the deepest states of contemplation. One source explains that this plane of existence is at the "summit" of the universe, consisting of "four realms of purely mental rebirth, without form."[1]

Next comes *Rupa-dhatu* ("the sphere of form"). It contains only the subtlest type of material substance. In this realm there are numerous deities many of whom are recognized personalities in Buddhist mythology. From this sphere certain brahma-deities descend, assuming human form, to repopulate the earth after it passes through the cycle of destruction and recreation.

The lowest sphere is called *Kama-dhatu* ("the sphere of desire"). In *Kama-dhatu* there are six principal divisions of rebirth called *gatis* ("destinies"): those of (1) gods; (2) demi-gods (*asuras*, rebel gods, demonic beings); (3) humans; (4) animals; (5) hungry ghosts (*pretas*, beings who are tortured with continual hunger and thirst) or (6) hell-beings (those confined to various hells). *Kama-dhatu* contains the *Tushita* Heaven (the abode of all Buddhas who need to be reborn on earth one more time) In this sphere, the next Buddha *(Maitreya)* awaits his appointed time to come to earth. It also contains the Heaven of the Thirty-Three Gods and the Heaven of the Four Guardian Kings.

It should be mentioned that some Buddhists, especially advanced contemplatives, deny the existence of gods and demons, identifying them merely as parts of an illusory, phenomenal world. Furthermore, many people who call themselves Buddhists have mixed their belief system with various regional or cultural traditions that are not necessarily Buddhist. So the ideas presented here may not be universally true for all those claiming to be part of this religion.

Christianity: The Bible teaches at least seven planes or realms of existence: three heavens, the earth and three locations in "the underworld."

Though the Bible does not explicitly define the characteristics of the three "heavens," most likely their order is as follows: (1) The First Heaven—the earth's atmosphere and physical universe beyond; (2) The Second Heaven—an intermediate, spiritual sphere filed with both demonic and angelic activity; (3) The Third Heaven (also called Paradise)—the highest sphere, filled with the manifest presence of God, the abode of righteous angels and departed saints. *(Luke 23:43, 2 Corinthians 12:2-4, Revelation 2:7)* These three realms are concentric (having a common center)—similar to the triune blending of body, soul and spirit in human beings. It is evident that both angels and demons have the power to infiltrate the natural world and influence those who dwell in the earth.

Concerning the underworld, the Bible also speaks of a spiritual, subterranean abyss called the "bottomless pit" where certain evil spirits are imprisoned, and a place of torment called "hell," reserved for the unsaved. Ultimately, hell will be cast into "the lake of fire," which is the ultimate, eternal place of confinement for Satan, evil spirits and all who are eternally separated from God. Some theologians teach this pivotal event will take place immediately after the Millennial Reign of Christ on earth. *(See Revelation 20:1-10.)*

Roman Catholicism promotes the idea of other realms, specifically "limbo" and "purgatory." "Limbo" is described as a somewhat peaceful, blissful realm, situated on the edge of hell, where unbaptized infants and others free from personal sin (like the mentally impaired) are sent at death. Though not worthy of the tortures of hell or purgatory, still, they have not qualified for the supreme beatitude of heaven. "Purgatory" is sometimes described as a temporary hell-like state that exists for the punishment of certain souls that are not so wicked as to deserve hell, yet not so righteous as to inherit heaven immediate upon death. So God requires a time of 'purging' before these souls are released into the ultimate heavenly state. Protestant sects in Christianity, generally speaking, do

DIMENSIONS OR PLANES OF EXISTENCE

not embrace these two concepts, believing them to be non-biblical. The concept of purgatory is in direct conflict especially with the belief that salvation comes through grace and through Jesus' death on the cross, not through "works of righteousness." Contrary to popular misconceptions, Satan and his underlings do not presently 'rule' in hell, nor will they do so in the Lake of Fire, but will instead be tormented. *(Titus 3:5, See 2 Chronicles 6:18, Psalms 102:19; 115:16, Luke 8:30–31, 1 Corinthians 15:47, 2 Corinthians 12:2–4, Revelation 9:1, 2, 11; 20:1–3.)*

Confucianism: This philosophy of life primarily speaks of heaven and earth. Though modern Confucianism may have enhanced views of this topic, having been mixed with other belief systems, historically, it emphasizes only two planes of existence.

Hinduism: On a fundamental level, Hinduism defines existence as being comprised of three worlds. (1) The First World *(Bhuloka)* is the material universe, the physical plane. (2) The Second World *(Antarloka)* is the subtle, astral plane, the mental and emotional sphere, occupied by angels, spirits and *devas* (divine beings). (3) The Third World *(Brahmaloka)* is the causal plane, the spiritual universe of the Mahadevas, 'great radiant entities,' the gods and highly evolved souls spoken of in Hinduism. This superior, superconscious realm has also been referred to as *Karanaloka* or *Sivaloka* (by Saivites who believe Shiva is the Creator). The philosophy of Hinduism revolves around the harmonizing and interaction of these three worlds. In Hindu Scripture is found the prayer, "Make me immortal in that realm where movement is accordant to wish, in the third region, the third heaven of heavens, where the worlds are resplendent." *(Rig Veda 9.1113)* Some Hindus would list the three worlds as: (1) Heaven *(Svarga)*; (2) Earth *(Bhumi)* and; (3) The Underworld *(Patala)*.

More specific categorization speaks of "seven underworlds" (known collectively as *Patala* and *Sapta Adholoka)* and "seven upperworlds" (known collectively as *Sapta Urdhvaloka).*[2] The seven "upper worlds" are a more detailed breakdown of the "three worlds" already mentioned. First there is *Bhuloka*, the physical, material plane. Then the second, third and fourth planes *(Bhuvarloka, Svarloka, and Maharloka)* make up the subtle plane, *Antarloka*. The fifth, sixth and seventh *(Janaloka, Tapoloka and Satyaloka)* make up the highest realm of the gods, the causal plane.[3]

Another reference speaks of "twenty-one hells beneath the netherworld."[4] Hordes of snakes inhabit all of these "hells." They are considered only temporary planes of existence for disembodied souls who deserve such negative treatment because of their karmic debt. Such persons must go through a preparatory purging as they await the next reincarnation on their journey toward ultimate perfection and liberation.

DIMENSIONS OR PLANES OF EXISTENCE

Islam: "The seven heavens declare his glory and the earth (too)." *(Surah 17.44)* "Allah is He who created seven firmaments and of the earth a similar number. Through the midst of them (all) descends His command: that ye may know that Allah has power over all things, and that Allah comprehends all things in (His) Knowledge." *(Qur'an 65:12)*

The wicked, as well as Satan *(Shaitan)* and his demons, will be confined to an eternal hell. A realm of hell called *Djahannam* (Heb. *Gehenna)* is said by some Qur'anic theologians to be reserved for those Muslims who have committed "grave sins" and have not repented. They are punished only for a season before they are finally accepted into the presence of God. Paradise *(Djanna)* is the ultimate goal of the righteous. Its location is directly under the Throne of God and just above the highest heaven.

Jainism: Five regional subdivisions make up the Jain universe: (1) The Supreme Abode *(Siddha-silla)*; (2) The Upper World *(Urdhavalok)*; (3) The Middle World *(Madhyalok)*; (4) The Nether World *(Adholoka)*; (5) The Base *(Nigoda)*.

"The Supreme Abode" is a celestial sphere at the top of the universe to which perfected souls ascend. "The Upper World" contains thirty heavens: sixteen heavens for superior celestial entities and fourteen for ordinary celestial entities. "The Middle World" contains the earth, planets and stars. "The Nether World" is made up of seven hells, with each successive level becoming darker, more threatening and more torturous. "The Base," located just beneath the Nether World, is the dwelling place for the lowest forms of life called *nigodas*. There is little or no activity in this sphere of existence. It is a 'storage space' for an infinite number of bonded souls. Every time that a soul ascends to *Siddha-silla*, one is freed from *Nigoda*.

Numerous concentric continents separated by large bodies of water make up the middle world *(madhyaloka)*. The centermost continent is called *Jambudvipa*. Though human beings are said to exist on two other continents, liberation of the soul can only take place for those inhabiting *Jambudvipa* (a name for our world).

Jainist Scripture states, "Men who commit sins will go to hell. But those who have walked the road of righteousness will obtain a place in heaven." *(Uttara-Dhyayana Sutra 18.25)* The region referred to as hell *(bhumis)* is only a temporary abode on the karmic journey toward perfection. Souls confined to hell are tormented by demonic beings until the accumulation of evil karma is depleted. Beyond the cosmos (the *loka*) three levels of wind exist, before reaching the *aloka*, the non-universe, which is utter emptiness.

Judaism: The average Jew has little opinion on concepts like this since normal Judaism de-emphasizes the afterlife and cosmological issues. Such mystical insights are found primarily in Kabbalistic writings, which promote ideas such as the following—"the Bible has seven different designations for heaven; therefore there must be seven heavens. There are seven heavens, named respectively *Vilon, Rakia, Shechakim, Zebul, Maon, Machon, and Araboth.*"[5] In the highest heaven (called the "heaven of heavens" in Scripture) resides "righteousness and judgment; the treasuries of life and peace and blessing; the souls of the righteous dead; the souls and spirits that are yet to be created; the dew with which God will revive the dead; there are the *ofanim* and *seraphim*, the holy beasts ('living creatures') and the ministering angels."[6]

"Corresponding to the seven heavens, the earth was also pictured as consisting of seven strata, since there are seven different words for it in the Bible."[7] The realm of the dead is called *She'ol.*[8] Other names are given to *She'ol* such as: *eretz* ("earth," "netherworld"); *qever* ("grave"); *afar* ("dust"); *bor* or *shahat* ("pit"); *dumah* ("the place of abiding" or "the abode of silence"); *'avadon* ("Abaddon"); *mahalei beliyya'al* ("the torrents of Belial"); "the depths of the pit" (*Lamentations 3:55)* and "the land of darkness." *(Job 10:21)* Some commentators feel that *She'ol* is located "at the bottoms of the mountains *(Jonah 2:6)*, or under the waters—the cosmic ocean *(Job 26:5)*."[9]

The area reserved for the souls of the wicked is *Gehenna* (also called *Gehinnom*). This term is derived from a valley on the south side of Jerusalem where, at one time, children were caused to walk through fire as they were sacrificed to the god Moloch. Traditionally "this accursed valley, designated for suffering, became identified with the place of retribution for the wicked after their death."[10] There are seven names applied to *Gehenna*, "seven departments, one beneath the other," and "seven kinds of pains."[11] This "prison" for evildoers is described as both a place of fire and darkness.

Paradise, the ultimate realm of the righteous, is also referred to as *Gan Eden* (the "Garden of Eden"). It is described as having "at least three levels...one higher than the other, the uppermost being nearest to God's abode in heaven."[12]

Sikhism: The Guru Granth (the holy book of Sikhism) seems to imply that there are "many millions" of realms or planes of existence—"thousands of worlds and underworlds." *(Adi Granth 276:11–12, Japji 22)*

Taoism: On a basic level, there are nine layers of heaven and nine underworlds. An additional tenth level in the underworld serves as a final court (thus, a total of ten hell courts). The dead must pass through all of these levels in the underworld in order to progress to higher levels. The underworld, though acknowledged as a place of punishment, is also seen as a place of learning and rehabilitation. Its inhabitants are under the oversight and tutelage of Celestial Beings (Underworld Governors), who are aided by a staff of Good and Radiant Demons. The Lords of the Five Mountains are some of the most important underworld deities. They are the gatekeepers, who must be petitioned to open the gates that the souls of the deceased might enter.

Concerning the upper, celestial realms, a more detailed and expanded view of Taoist beliefs reveals thirty-six levels. These higher spheres are divided according to the Buddhist tradition of Three Worlds: (six heavens in the World of Desire, eighteen heavens in the World of Form and four heavens in the World of Formlessness—twenty-eight in all). Those who inhabit these twenty-eight heavens are still subject to reincarnation.

There are also four Brahma-Heavens for the spiritually advanced (gods and the members of the Celestial Administration). Then further above are the Three Clarities (in ascending order: Jade Clarity, Great Clarity and Highest Clarity—also called the Three Pure Realms). These are the dwelling place of the immortals, which are divided into twenty-seven ranks. Finally, the highest sphere is referred to as the Galaxy of Grand Network, where the Tao exists in its purest form and where the sacred celestial Scriptures reside. In this ultimate heaven of heavens is found the Jade Capital of Mystery Metropolis from which the Three Venerables rule the universe. Added together, these heavenly realms total thirty-six.

Zoroastrianism: The cosmos has three levels: heaven, earth and the underworld. Ahura Mazda, the righteous god, rules in heaven. Angra Mainyu, god of evil, rules in hell.

OTHER RELIGIONS, SECTS AND TEACHERS

Bahá'í: Bahá'u'lláh taught a "cosmological framework, which was traditional in certain schools of Islamic metaphysical thought." This included a belief in five dimensions or planes of existence:

(1) *"hahut:* the realm of the unknowable, unmanifested essence of God." Even God's prophets cannot penetrate or experience this realm.

(2) *"lahut*: the realm in which the divine names and attributes become defined within the divine consciousness as the archetypal forms of all created things. This is the 'All-Glorious Horizon' of the primal will, the active means by which God has created the heavens and the earth.

(3) *"jabarut*: the realm of the revealed God acting within creation, the 'All-Highest Paradise' of divine decrees in which reside the imagery forms of the archangels;

(4) *"malakut*: the angelic realm, 'world of similitudes' *('alam-i-mithal)*.

(5) *"nasut*: the physical world, subdivided into animal, vegetable and mineral kingdoms."

God is expressed or manifested only in the second through the fifth level. "Human beings exist at the interface between the angelic and physical realms, and are able to choose in which to live."[13]

Heaven and hell are "states of the soul, which may be entered both in the present life and the afterlife." Because the soul is immaterial, "heaven and hell are not physical planes."[14]

Brahma Kumaris World Spiritual Organization (Raja Yoga): There are three realms: (1) The Corporeal World (Physical Plane); (2) The Subtle World (Astral), and (3) The Soul World *(Brahmlok)*. There are three separate regions in the Subtle World *(Brahmapuri, Vishnupuri* and *Shankarpuri)* named after the "Trimurti" or the three highest gods beneath Shiva: Brahma, Vishnu and Shankar. In the Subtle World, bodies are made of light, not of matter. The highest realm, the Soul World, is pervaded by the golden-red, divine light, which is the sixth element called "Brahm." In the Soul World, souls have neither bodies of matter nor of light. Prior to descending into this world, "Souls abide there as star-like points of light."[15]

ECKANKAR: Paul Twitchell, the founder, taught the Kingdom of heaven is divided into eleven different realms: the upper six are heavenly, the lower five are ruled by the devil (who is given the name Kal Niranjan). They are, from lower to higher: (1) The Physical Plane; (2) The Astral Plane; (3) The Causal Plane; (4) The Mental Plane; (5) The Etheric Plane; (6) *Atma Lok*; (7) *Alakh Lok*; (8) *Alaya Lok*; (9) *Hukikat Lok*; (10) *Agam Lok*; (11) *Anami Lok*. The true heaven where God dwells is called *Anami Lok*. The hub of the spirit world is a spiritual, capital city named *Sahasra-dal-Kanwal*.

DIMENSIONS OR PLANES OF EXISTENCE

ISKCON (International Society of Krishna Consciousness): "There are different *lokas*, or planetary systems, and you can go to the higher planetary systems where the demigods live and take a body there, or you can go where the Pitas, or ancestors, live. You can take a body here in Bhuloka, the earthly planetary system, or you can go to the planet of God, Krsnaloka."[16]

Kabbala (Mystical Judaism): There are five levels or planes of existence. From the lowest to the highest, they are known as: (1) *Assiyah* (the "world of physicality," the "material world," the "world of action"); (2) *Yetzirah* (the "world of emotions," the "world of formation"); (3) *Beriyah* (the "world of the intellect," the "world of creation"); (4) *Atzilut* (the "world of the spirit," the "world of emanations"); and (5) *Adam kadmon* (the "world of will," the primordial source).[17] Some Kabbalists believe hell is not a physical location, but rather an 'inner distance': being estranged from the truth and from God. Others believe it to be an actual place.

Kriya Yoga (Swami Sri Yukteswar): Proceeding from the highest substance, the Absolute, to the lowest, gross matter, there are seven spheres of existence: (1) *Satyaloka*, the Sphere of God; (2) *Tapoloka*, the Sphere of the Holy Spirit, a normally inaccessible realm; (3) *Janaloka*, the Sphere of Spiritual Reflection; (4) *Maharloka*, the Sphere of the Atom, the beginning of maya, the door and the link between the spiritual and material creation; (5) *Swarloka*, the Sphere of Magnetic Aura; (6) *Bhuvarloka*, the Sphere of Electric Attributes; (7) *Bhuloka*, the Sphere of Gross Material, visible to everyone.[18] The first three comprise the spiritual creation, the last three comprise the material creation and the fourth is the door between the two. (**Paramahansa Yogananda**) emphasized three main planes: Physical, Astral and Causal.

Meher Baba: There are seven planes that the soul can experience above the physical or gross plane. The soul exists apart from these planes, experiencing them according to the level of spiritual maturity: (1) The subtle world of energy (the gross world on the threshold of the energy world); (2) The subtle world of infinite energy (minor miracles); (3) The subtle world of infinite energy (grand miracles); (4) The subtle world on the threshold of the mental world (the dark night of the soul); (5) The mental world: inquiring or reflective thought; (6) The mental world: impressions or sympathetic feelings; (7) Reality: the experience of Infinite Knowledge, Power and Bliss. The first six planes are in the realm of duality and thus, can afford false or delusional experiences. The seventh plane alone provides an experience of the Absolute or the Real.

DIMENSIONS OR PLANES OF EXISTENCE

There are "seven subdivisions of the first Subtle plane (the Astral), seven stages of evolution, seven planes and seven heavens in involution."[19] Heaven and hell do have an existence in the Subtle World, but they are actually "states of mind; they should not be looked upon as being places. And though subjectively they mean a great deal to the individualized soul, they are both illusions within the greater illusion."[20] Heaven and hell states provide temporary, transient experiences to the soul between incarnations.

Scientology: Offers no set doctrinal stance on dimensions of existence after death (heavens and/or hells). Scientology is primarily concerned with the betterment of life here and now, as well as helping to produce a more sane civilization worldwide.

Sufism (Mystical Islam): Planes or dimensions of being, categorized from the highest to the lowest: (1) *lahut*: the realm of the Absolute where the divine nature reveals itself; (2) *jabarut*: spiritual existence, beyond form where decrees and spiritual powers are located; (3) *malakut*: the angelic world; (4) *nasut*: the place of humanity, the natural world.[21]

Theosophy: Teaches seven planes of existence: the physical plane, emotional (astral) plane, mental plane and four higher planes that are beyond the present state of human evolutionary development. Theosophists do not believe in "hell or paradise as localities" but "a postmortem state or mental condition such as we are in during a vivid dream."[22]

United Church of Religious Science (Dr. Ernest Holmes): Teaches the following concerning heaven and hell. Heaven is defined as "Harmony—Wholeness—Health—Physical Well-being—Happiness—Mental peace, poise, and well-being."[23] Hell (Hades or Sheol) is defined as "Symbolic of the lower plane of consciousness. The torment of experiencing that which contradicts Truth."[24] It is "the underworld," the "drama of the soul in its conflict with opposing desires and state of consciousness before the transition from the lower to the higher plane of perception."[25]

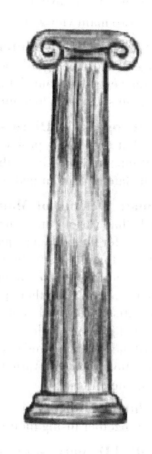

6

THE SPIRITUAL JOURNEY AND ULTIMATE DESTINY OF MAN

✳ **The Spiritual Journey of Man**—Concerning this aspect, some religions teach one life in this world; others teach numerous incarnations. Some reincarnationists teach that karma *must* have its ultimate effect. Retributions for negative karma and rewards for positive karma are both inescapable. Others teach various means by which negative karma can be cancelled or avoided.

There are two main views among reincarnationists:

⌣' **The "Progressive Evolutionary View"**—the belief that the soul or essence of being *only* progresses through successive stages (mineral, vegetable, animal, then human); it never digresses from the human stage back to animal, plant or mineral form.

⌣' **The "Progressive/Digressive Evolutionary View"**—the belief that the soul is progressing toward perfection and final liberation, but sometimes this involves shuttling between a human state and an animal, vegetable, or inanimate form.

✳ **The Ultimate Destiny of Man**—Concerning this aspect, some religions teach that various heavens, hells and purgatories are only temporary abodes for the soul on its journey to Absolute Consciousness; while others teach that these spiritual sites are ultimate and permanent. Some religions teach that these are only 'states of mind.' Others teach these are actual 'locations' (either spiritual or physical, or both).

A universalistic view (all souls eventually achieving union with God) is embraced in some worldviews; while others assign to the righteous an inheritance in some kind of paradise, but to the wicked, a state of eternal separation from God. Varied beliefs can usually be categorized under one of six headings:

(1) **Absolute Divinity**—Ultimately, all human beings become God, altogether losing their own individual identity.

(2) **Qualified Divinity**—Ultimately, all souls will merge with God, becoming omnipresent, omniscient and divine, yet retain their own individual identities.

(3) **Sub-Divinity: Independent Eternal Existence**—Though enjoying ultimate, infinite communion and oneness with God, the souls of those who are 'saved' or 'liberated' are, in a sense, 'sub-divine' (submitted to God, and as such, partakers of his divine nature). However, such persons never actually 'become' God. They possess a unique, independent and personal existence eternally.

(4) **No Association with Divinity**—In some worldviews, at death, the wicked are cut off from the Creator eternally. Their potential of oneness with the divine nature is forever lost. Some believe in an eternal consciousness in this state of separation; others believe in the annihilation of the souls of the wicked.

(5) **Cessation of Personal Existence**—A few religions teach there is no continuation of personal existence after death or after the cycle of reincarnation is over.

(6) **Little or No Speculation**—A few religious groups de-emphasize, while others avoid altogether, any speculation concerning the afterlife of human beings.

THE ELEVEN MAIN LIVING RELIGIONS

Buddhism: Buddhists do not believe in a soul. They believe in five aggregates that unite to make a human being. These aggregates do not pass from one life to the next. Instead, a certain 'unconscious disposition,' with its attached karma accumulated from past existences, is transferred at each incarnation.

All forms of Buddhism teach numerous reincarnations until Nirvana is attained (a word meaning "to blow out"). So the final destiny of man is like the *blowing out* of a candle. Such terminology does not imply the annihilation of 'self,' because according to Buddhist doctrine there is no 'self' to annihilate. Rather, it is end of karma, the final annihilation of desire and absorption into pure Being.

Karma (or *kamma)* is a foundational doctrine in Buddhism: the idea that every deed is a "cause" that will result in an "effect." These make rebirth necessary. To avoid this, one must be certain that deeds are not the result of desire, hatred or delusion. Buddha taught his disciples that there are twelve karma formations from which men must be freed to escape the wheel of rebirth. Nirvana can be attained during a person's earthly life; Parinirvana is that final, complete liberation that takes place at the death of those who have attained this ultimate state.

A dominant teaching in Buddhism concerns thirty-one planes of existence. Emphasized are the six principal realms of rebirth called *gatis* ("destinies"): the realm of (1) gods; (2) demi-gods (*asuras*, rebel gods); (3) humans; (4) animals; (5) hungry ghosts (*pretas*, beings who are tortured with continual hunger and thirst) or (6) hell-beings (those confined to various hells). At the "summit" of the universe there are also "four realms of purely mental rebirth, without form."[1] Buddha said, "Just as there are few pleasant parks and lakes, but many dense thickets and inaccessible mountains, so are there few beings who will be reborn among men. More numerous are those who will be reborn in purgatory [hell]." *(Anguttara Nikaya 1.19)*

Theravada Buddhism emphasizes the primary goal of becoming an *arhat* ("one who is worthy"). These are Buddhist monks who have achieved a state of enlightenment and will, therefore, not experience rebirth. **Mahayana Buddhism** argues that the goal of a good Buddhist should be attaining the status of a bodhisattva. This is a spiritually evolved person who is ready to enter Nirvana, but declines, choosing rather to remain in the cycle of rebirths in order to aid others in their spiritual development. Rebirth for a bodhisattva does not have to take place in the material sphere; it can continue on in higher realms of existence. (See "Buddhism" under *The Nature of Salvation, Liberation or Enlightenment*.)

Pure Land Buddhism teaches that after death, Amida Buddha (different than Gautama Buddha) will take good Buddhists to a paradise-like place called "the Pure Land." They will abide there until they attain Nirvana. Traditional Buddhism does not accept this idea, probably because it implies a 'self' that survives the death of the body.

Tibetan Buddhism: According to "The Tibetan Book of the Dead" *(Bardo Thodrol)* there is an interval of forty-nine days between death and rebirth. After seven days in this intermediate "bardo" state, forty-two Peaceful Deities surround the deceased in a circular pattern referred to as a mandala. After another seven days, this mandala dissolves and is replaced by fifty-eight Wrathful Deities with hideous appearances (blood-drinking, flesh-eating, demonic beings). Some Buddhists believe these deities are merely aspects of the deceased person's own mind or symbolic expressions of past karma.

The Tibetans believe that the consciousness of the deceased person can be contacted during this interim. So normally a Lama (a spiritual leader, a guru) performs special ceremonies to provide guidance through a maze of bewildering, and at times, horrifying spiritual experiences awaiting beyond the grave. If these images are correctly identified, the deceased person will merge with the state of enlightened consciousness represented by them. If, because of ignorance or fear, this proves impossible, the disembodied individual will plunge deeper into the bardo realms.

Eventually, the Peaceful and Wrathful Deities fade from view. As the wheel of *samsara* turns, the deceased person enters the third and final bardo state: the "Bardo of Becoming." A mental body complete with all five senses is formed and a descent toward rebirth begins.[2] Some forty-nine days after death the condition of the soul is judged by an entity named Emma-O or Yama, the "Overlord of Hell," who determines which of the six realms the deceased will enter upon rebirth. So it is of high importance that at the climax of the funeral ceremony, a picture of the deceased (either a block print or drawing on white paper) is burned as the Lama pronounces that the sins of that person have been absolved.

Concerning the "reincarnation" process, primitive Buddhists tend to believe humans can digress into non-human life forms, while modern Buddhists do not believe this can happen.

Christianity: The Bible teaches just one earthly existence. "It is appointed for men to die once." *(Hebrews 9:27)* At death, the soul of a born-again believer is immediately received into heaven. The promise is given that to be "absent from the body" is to be "present with the Lord." *(2 Corinthians 5:8)* When Jesus returns at the end of this age, the souls of all departed saints will return with him. The resurrection of the dead will take place (with souls and new bodies rejoined), as well as the translation of living believers.

Diverse opinions exist concerning the exact timing of this grand, pivotal event. All theories revolve around a proposed seven-year period of time at the end of this age usually termed the "Tribulation Period" and/or "Daniel's Seventieth Week" (made up of three parts: the first thee-and-a-half years, called the "beginning of sorrows," then a very dark time called the "great tribulation," followed by a terribly catastrophic time known as the final outpouring of God's wrath). *(See Daniel 9:24-27, Matthew 24:1-44, Luke 21:5-38, 2 Thessalonians 2:1-10, Revelation 6-16.)* According to different schools of thought, the coming of the Lord and subsequent glorification of God's saints will take place either pre-tribulation, mid-tribulation, pre-wrath or post-tribulation (the author's view). According to this last view, the saints will rise to meet the Lord in the air, then victoriously usher Him back into this world to rule from Jerusalem over all the earth. The other views believe that after an initial 'rapture' of the church, God's people will abide in a heavenly realm until the end of the age, when they will return with the Lord Jesus Christ.

Whenever this wonderful event finally transpires, all redeemed, saved persons will then be given eternal forms, glorified bodies, that will shine with the radiance of the heavenly world. Glorified saints may retain male or female characteristics (according to their gender while on earth). However, Jesus taught they will not marry (being "as the angels of God in heaven"). *(Matthew 22:30)* Though enjoying oneness with God, and an infilling of the divine nature, God's offspring will ever maintain their unique, individual soul and identity. Children of God never actually become God, nor is their destiny formless absorption into the Godhead.

Those who are saved will enjoy the status of being both "kings and priests," reigning with the Messiah in this world, when God's Kingdom comes in its fullness. (See "Christianity" under *Cycles, Ages, and the Ultimate State of the Universe* for the comparison of differing views on this subject.) Many teach that this era, called the Millennial Reign, will last a literal thousand years—an era of heaven-on-earth conditions when the natural and supernatural worlds will blend. There are several other interpretations of this unique concept in Scripture. *(Revelation 20:1–6)*

Then the renovation by fire will take place and the flawless and glorious New Creation will emerge. Ultimately, God's glorified king/priests will be located in New Jerusalem, the capital city of this New Creation, the bridal city of the Most High God. Those who are unsaved will spend eternity separated from God. *(See Matthew 13:43; 25:34, 41, 1 Corinthians 15:51–58, Philippians 3:20–21, 1 Thessalonians 4:14–18, 1 John 3:2, Revelation 1:5–6; 20:1-6.)*

Confucianism: "Following the moral principles means to conform oneself to the will of heaven, but more metaphysical speculations about heaven and afterlife are useless." *(Analects 7, 20)* When questioned about the afterlife Confucius responded, "Why do you ask me about death when you do not know how to live?" However, he did offer, "Heaven means to be one with God."[3]

Hinduism: Adherents are directed toward four successive goals in life: *dharma* (moral law), *artha* (wealth), *kama* (pleasure) and *moksha* (liberation of the soul, ultimate God-consciousness). These bring satisfaction to the four divisions of a person: the physical body *(sharira)*, the mind *(manas)*, the intellect *(buddhi)*, and the self *(atman)*. Individuals are also described as owing 'three debts': first, to God, second, to the sages and saints who have gone before, and third, to ancestors. Generally speaking, there are four stages *(ashramas)* in life: that of a student, a householder, an ascetic and the final stage of fully renouncing all worldly ties and pursuing the depth of contemplation.

Reincarnation is a foundational belief in Hinduism, the idea that the soul passes through numerous incarnations (mineral, plant, animal and human) on its journey toward perfection. According to some Hindu commentators, a *jiva* (life-force) is granted a human life only after going through 8,400,000 previous incarnations as lower forms of life.

Conditions in each human life are determined by past karma. Any negative thoughts, attitudes or deeds cause proportional, negative results in the future, either in the same life or a future one. Any positive thoughts, attitudes and deeds are likewise reaped in a positive way. It is important to understand "Hindus hold that God...does not punish or reward anyone. We create our own destinies by our own thoughts and deeds."[4]

Numerous means are offered within Hinduism enabling spiritually inclined persons to escape negative karma. Not only do wicked deeds produce binding karma; righteous deeds performed with the desire of obtaining a sense of fulfillment or recognition from others also bind a soul to rebirth. Non-attachment to both good and evil are, therefore, promoted in the Hindu scheme of salvation. *Moksha* (liberation) cannot be achieved until the soul is rid of all worldly desire, including the desire for *moksha* itself.

There is a certain soul or 'self' that is transferred from one incarnation to the next on its journey toward perfection. One source explains, "The two sheaths, *vijnanamaya kosha* (the intellectual sheath) and *anandamaya kosha* (the causal body), are the bodies that go from birth to birth; the other three sheaths are grown again in each life."[5] (See "Hinduism" under *The Origin and Nature of Man*.) In between incarnations, the soul (in the form of a subtle or astral body) lives in the subtle or astral realm. In this plane, the soul experiences an existence very similar in some ways to its previous earthly sojourn. Sometimes, unrealized hopes and unfulfilled dreams may even be brought to realization and fulfillment.

Though a variety of beliefs exist in Hinduism concerning the soul's ultimate state, two main veins of thought seem to dominate. Sankara, an eighth century teacher, believed that when souls *(atman* or *jiva)* are finally released from the cycle of rebirths *(samsara)* they do not retain their individual personality. Instead they are absorbed into God. They actually become God. Ramanuja, an eleventh century philosopher, argued that souls retain their individuality in the ultimate state and instead have eternal communion with God. Sankara's system of thought was based on the idea that God is impersonal; Ramanuja's view was based on the premise that God is personal.

Yama, the first person to die in the world, is considered the Lord of the dead. He reigns over the dead, determines the retribution for deeds done in the previous life and the conditions of the soul's next incarnation. He bears a noose, by which he catches the 'dead,' who must rush past his four-eyed guard dogs that guard the gate to his kingdom.

Islam: The Muslim faith teaches two judgments. First, all human beings will face a personal judgment after death. Two angels, Munkar and Nakir, will scrutinize their earthly existences. After this initial determination is made, the soul remains in the grave until the resurrection of all humanity and the final Day of Judgment. There will be a preliminary experience of the misery of hell or the bliss of heaven even in the grave.

Second, there will be a final judgment at the end of this age. At the first blast of the trumpet, all living things will die. At the second blast of the trumpet, the resurrection *(al-kiyama)* will take place. All who have ever lived will be brought to the "place of gathering" *(al-mashar)*. Allah will personally question each individual. All deeds will be reviewed from God's book, as well as the individual book written on each person's life. Evil and righteous deeds will be weighed in God's balances, to see which is dominant. An appropriate reward or judgment will then be meted out.

The judgment that God brings upon men and women will hinge primarily on their response to the teachings of Mohammed and, to a lesser degree, those recognized prophetic voices preceding him (twenty-eight are named in the Qur'an). If they have been disobedient to the divine will their destiny is hell. If they have been obedient, paradise *(al-jannah)* is promised. Paradise (also called heaven) is a beautiful garden where those who have eternal life can dwell near to Allah. It is also depicted as a place of sensual pleasure (where wine is consumed and men may marry as many wives as they desire). Some Muslim theologians feel these descriptions are allegorical, not to be taken literally.

Submission to the Muslim worldview is normally emphasized in order for a believer to be saved. However, there are "several verses in the Qur'an that speak of the resurrection of distinct communities that will be judged" by the standard of "their own book." *(See Qur'an 45:27–29.)*[6]

Jainism: Though believing in the reincarnation, Jainism strongly asserts the independence, uniqueness and autonomy of the soul during this process. According to the philosophical Hindu worldview, "the individual soul and all matter" are merely a "phase of the world soul." Contrasted to this, Jainism is a dualistic philosophy, declaring "the reality of the individual soul and all matter."[7]

There are eight kinds of karma that keep the soul trapped in the cycle of births and fourteen steps to liberation from this inexorable law. Acquired karma can be canceled through *nirjara*. This process includes self-denial, service toward others, renunciation of the world, mortification of the body, various atonements for sin, and meditation.

There are four states of existence *(gatis)* into which souls can be reincarnated (determined by accumulated karmic merits or demerits): (1) Heavenly beings; (2) Human beings; (3) Tiryancha beings (animals, plants, lower life forms); (4) Infernal beings (those tormented in hell).[8]

There are five levels in which souls can be incarnated in this physical plane. Each level directly relates to the number of senses active in the creature after incarnation. (For instance, worms are on the second level because they possess only two senses: touch and taste; human beings are on the fifth level because they possess five senses: touch, taste, smell, sight and hearing.) After numerous existences in various forms (such as earth, water, vegetables, worms, bugs, and animals) the *jiva* eventually evolves to the level of a human being. It then reincarnates many times as a human being until liberation takes place. Liberated souls rise to the top of the universe. The number of souls *(jivas)* is infinite. Jains believe human souls can revert spiritually and be reincarnated in non-human life forms. Once Absolute Consciousness is attained, this state is eternal and irreversible.

Judaism: Definitely teaches an afterlife, but offers a wide variety of interpretations concerning the state of existence following the demise of the body. In early Judaism, it was generally accepted that after death, both the evil and the righteous descend into *She'ol*, the underworld, "a shadowy, ghostlike existence...a region of darkness and silence deep within the recesses of the earth."[9] There the soul sleeps, in a realm of "neither pain, nor pleasure, punishment nor reward," awaiting the resurrection.[10]

Later on, Judaism gravitated toward two similar projections concerning the afterlife: (1) The soul of a righteous Jew, immediate upon death, enters Paradise, also known as the celestial Garden of Eden, or (2) The soul of a righteous Jew ascends to a heavenly "treasury" beneath "the throne of glory," an "upper heaven called *Aravot*"[11] (spelled *Araboth* in a previous section). As opposed to being trapped in the grave, Scripture does seem supportive of views such as these two. For instance, Ecclesiastes 12:7 states, "Then the dust will return to the earth as it was, and the spirit will return to God who gave it."

Though not central to Jewish belief, in some of their literature, the righteous enter Paradise and the wicked enter *Gehenna* immediately after death. In other references, this only happens after the resurrection takes place. *Gehenna* (also called *Gehinnom*) is the netherworld region reserved for the wicked. "There is difference of opinion between Bet Shammai and Bet Hillel [two schools of thought during the first century] as to the duration of the punishment in *Gehenna*...according to the former, the thoroughly wicked remain there for everlasting disgrace; the intermediate ones (between the wicked and the good) descend to *Gehenna* to be purged and ascend after purification. According to the latter, the intermediate ones do not go there at all...and whereas transgressors (both Jewish and Gentile) are punished in *Gehenna* for only twelve months, only special categories of sinners...are punished there for all time."[12] The pained prisoners of this place of torment suffer six days a week, "but on the Sabbath are given rest."[13] Some believe that after twelve months in *Gehenna*, the wicked are "annihilated, to suffer no more"; while others believe that after twelve months, the wicked "having atoned for their sins...will join the righteous in Gan Eden" (the Garden of Eden).[14]

Conflicting views are also found in Judaism concerning the relation of the soul to the body after it expires. Beliefs exist such as—the soul hovering "over the body for three days hoping to return to it," the soul sorrowing over the body for "seven days of mourning," or the soul even repeatedly revisiting the body for twelve months following death until the physical body is decomposed and "the soul ascends nevermore to descend."[15]

At the culmination of creation, there will be a resurrection and a Final Judgment. The visionary Daniel predicted, "those who sleep in the dust of the earth shall awake, some to everlasting life, some to shame and everlasting contempt." *(Daniel 12:2, See Ecclesiastes 12:5-7, Isaiah 25:8; 26:19.)* Many believe these final events will coincide with the coming of the Messiah, who will usher in a utopian era when Israel will once again be exalted to a place of spiritual, political and material prominence in the world. "It is somewhat unclear whether the resurrection is for the righteous alone, or whether the wicked too will be temporarily resurrected only to be judged and destroyed."[16]

Though historically, the resurrection is a "cornerstone of rabbinic eschatology" some sects and teachers in Judaism have denied a literal 'raising of the dead,' spiritualizing scriptures that refer to this event. It was especially a matter of contention between the "Pharisees and the Sadducees, the latter asserting that the soul died together with the body."[17] Many literal references to this event exist in the Talmud, as well as a warning that disbelievers of this doctrine ("the resurrection") will have no part in the world to come. Nevertheless, in modernistic versions of Judaism, a belief in the resurrection is often discarded, in favor of a belief in the immortality of the soul.

Shinto: It is believed that after thirty-three years, the *tama* (the spirit of a deceased person) loses its distinctive personality and blends in with the "collective body of family ancestral spirits or *kami*."[18] So ultimately, each human being is destined to become a *kami* (a divine being) after the loss of the mortal body. Because of this belief, the *kami* of the ancestral family line are worshipped at shrines in the home. Departed ancestors watch over their living descendants to bless and protect. There is no developed theology concerning 'final things': no standard teaching concerning the future state, whether it be hell or purgatory for the wicked, or heaven for the righteous. Shintoists, however, do maintain a basic belief in the immortality of the soul.

Sikhism: Most Sikhs believe in the linked doctrines of karma *(karam)* and reincarnation (though some feel the latter is not clearly indicated in their holy writings). Once souls are released from the cycle of rebirths, they become one with God. Guru Nanak taught five successive levels of attainment ending in *Sach Khand* or the Realm of Truth, the mystical union of the soul with eternal bliss and serenity. These five levels enable a person to pass from the state of being a *manmukh* (an "evil-doer") to *gurmukh* ("absorption into God"). The main hindrance is something called *maya*. In Hinduism *maya* is delusion, the Godhead's ability to make Itself 'appear' as the world. In Sikhism the world is real, so the word means something different. *Maya* is the self-deceived state of mind that results from placing too much emphasis on the material world and too little focus on spiritual values.

Five ascending levels on the spiritual path are (1) *Dharam Khand*—Living by God's law; (2) *Saram Khand*—Living a self-disciplined life; (3) *Karam Khand*—Living in God's grace; (4) *Gian Khand*—Living in the revelation and knowledge of God; (5) *Sach Khand*—Attaining Ultimate Truth. Those who achieve this absolute state arrive at the final objective of every Sikh: *sahaj*, the rapturous peace of blending with the Divine (which many would say results in final liberation from the painful sequence of death and rebirth).

Taoism: Each human being has two souls (actually two groups of souls—three *hun* souls and seven *po* souls). At death, the *hun* soul ascends upward toward heaven, being the positive *yang* aspect of a person. According to popular belief, this aspect of a person can be accessed through the ancestral tablets found on the altar of a traditional Chinese home. However, after five to seven generations of ancestor worship, this *hun* soul (ancestral spirit—*shen*) reverts back to its original state, 'dissolving' into the cosmos. On the contrary, the *po* soul, being the negative *yin* aspect of a person, descends to the earth to abide with the dead physical body.

Neither of these soulish destinations will be reached, though, if the prescribed burial rites and associated offerings have not been properly implemented. Instead, the disembodied spirit will haunt the living until the necessary rituals are satisfactorily performed. For instance, according to Chinese folklore, the spirit cannot pass over the river of death without money to pay the boatman. So money and clothes are burned during funeral ceremonies in order to translate these items, in a spiritual form, into the spirit realm. Food offerings are also supplied to the deceased as necessary sustenance for the continuation of existence.

It is also believed that the *po* soul descends into the lower regions or hells, to be judged for all misdeeds and appropriately punished. Once arriving in the underworld, souls are brought before the Ten Magistrates who officiate over the Ten Tribunals of Hell. Each of these Underworld Courtrooms deals with different types of crimes or sins. Once judgment is administered, the necessary punishment is meted out. This involves passing through successive regions or layers of hell, according to the degree of guiltiness pronounced over the deceased person. No matter how long the punishment seems to last to the suffering soul, the time lapse per hell is seven earthly days. The deceased can only be contacted through various rituals for seven weeks (a total of forty-nine days in the first seven hells). In the remaining hells they are unreachable. Religious rites are performed to carry the deceased successfully through this difficult transitional experience. The final stage is entrance into the "Palace of Rebirth, where bridges lead to the five forms of rebirth—gods, human, animals, hungry ghosts, and hell-dwellers—and where all past memories are cleansed."[19]

At this climactic point, if the proper ceremonies have been performed and sins have been successfully expiated, it is possible that the soul can instead achieve permanent residence in a celestial state. Some philosophical Taoists speculate that the life or *ch'i* essence in a person can even go through a supernatural metamorphosis that transforms it into some other aspect of creation altogether.

The primary goals of the serious, mystical Taoist are longevity and immortality. The disciplines that promote longevity (such as meditation, trance training, extreme diet regulations, etc.) aid a person in achieving immortality as well. Attaining immortality allows the devotee to escape the usual pattern of rebirth and the descent of the soul into the hell-realms after death.

As a person matures spiritually, the three energies—generative, vital, and spirit—return to the original undifferentiated state of the Tao. "This undifferentiated vapor descends to the abdomen to form the immortal fetus."[20] This initial stage of the sacred, spiritual 'fetus' incubating and developing lasts ten months and is called *lien-hsu-ho-Tao*. Then, if the process is not interrupted, the immortal fetus emerges from the 'womb' to become "the original spirit" *(yuan-shen)*. It changes locations, rising from the abdominal area to the chest, to be further nourished and developed. Eventually the *yuan-shen* locates in the head, at times leaving the body from the top of the head on excursions into the spiritual world. This is all a preparation for the day when the physical body dies and the "*yuan-shen* is liberated and is once again merged with the undifferentiated energy of the Tao."[21]

"Ascension, flight, and travel in the celestial realm" are some of the means by which mystical Taoists achieve "union with the Tao in the external universe." It is believed that ultimately "immortals of the highest caliber ascend to the sky in the physical body and in broad daylight, often in the presence of witnesses." "In the case of immortals of secondary caliber, only the spirit ascends: at death, the immortal spirit within rises to the celestial realm. This is called "shedding the shell." Often, the shell, or body, disappears after the spirit has ascended."[22] Though able to move at will through the entire universe, the "Immortals" are said to reside at either the awe-inspiring paradise of Mount Kunlun in the Western Mountains or the mysterious, enchanted island of Penglai in the Eastern Sea. Both of these are 'other worldly' sites.

Zoroastrianism: In the beginning of creation, God presented the choice to preexistent beings *(fravashis)* to either stay in an embryonic spiritual state or be born in the material world. Their purpose would be to war against Angra Mainyu, the god of evil and darkness, until victory could be obtained in this natural realm. These soulish beings opted to be born and face the inevitable conflict. Now the fate of every person is determined by whether he or she yields to Ahura Mazda, the god of life and light, or Angra Mainyu, the god of evil and darkness.

On the fourth day after death, "the soul is led by *daena* (conscience portrayed as a maiden) to the Chinvat Bridge, the Bridge of Judgment. Those whose good deeds predominate are led to paradise. Each righteous soul is reunited with its *fravashi* (the preexistent higher Self). Those whose evil deeds predominate fall off into the House of the Lie, a place of torment."[23] This latter abode is synonymous with hell. There is also a place for those whose good deeds and evil deeds are evenly balanced. Its name is *hamestagan* meaning "the place of the mixed," where the inhabitants experience suffering from both heat and cold.

Two judgments take place: the first is after the physical death of each individual. The second is after the resurrection of all men, who will be gathered together from heaven and hell. Zoroastrians explain that there are two judgments because the first judgment deals with the soul; the second judgment deals with the body. The second judgment will determine if the wicked need further correction before they are allowed entrance into paradise.

Hell is considered only a temporary place of suffering. At the end of time, Saoshyant Astvatereta, the final Savior, will make his appearance. He will be a son of Zoroaster, miraculously conceived by a virgin who swims in a lake where Zoroaster's seed has been preserved. When Saoshyant arrives to establish the Kingdom of Righteousness, after a cosmic year (approximately 12,000 earthly years) there will be a general resurrection of both the good and the evil.

Gayomart, the first man, will be given the honor of coming forth first in the resurrection, then Mashya and Mashyoi, humanity's foreparents, then all others. Saoshyant will purify both the wicked and the righteous by causing all to pass through a river of molten metal (obtained through the melting of the mountains). This experience will be pleasant for the righteous (like being bathed in warm milk) but agonizing for the wicked (until all sins are purged away). After this Saoshyant will grant all the sons and daughters of this world the drink of immortality *(haoma)*, transforming their bodies into eternal perfection. Those who expired during childhood will experience renewed existence at the age of fifteen; those who passed away as adults will be brought back to life at the mature age of forty.

OTHER RELIGIONS, SECTS AND TEACHERS

Bahá'í: The opposing concepts of "resurrection" and "reincarnation" are both rejected. With regard to the latter, some Bahá'ís feel that claims of past-life experiences are mere fabrications of the imagination, while others avoid speculation on this matter. After death, souls retain their individuality and consciousness. "The soul is immortal. After the death of the body it continues to progress until it attains God's presence and manifests divine attributes."[24] After death, the soul recognizes the good or evil accomplished during the previous life, resulting in joy or grief, faith or fear, contentment or consternation.

"The actual nature of the afterlife is beyond the understanding of those who are still living."[25] However, Bahá'u'lláh explained that heavenly angels were those people who experienced the fire of the love of God purging them of all human traits and limitations. These are "blessed beings" who have "been released from the chains of self, and become the revealers of God's abounding grace."[26]

Brahma Kumaris World Spiritual Organization (Raja Yoga): All souls exist in a preincarnate state in the "Soul World." In this upper world there is "neither thought, word nor action; just complete stillness, silence and peace."[27] Souls born into this world during the first age (the Golden Age) are all soul-conscious human beings, or deities, who take birth by thought, not through sexual urge. This latter method of taking on a physical body does not begin until the third age (the Copper Age) when the consciousness level of human beings sinks very low, into the deep mire of evil and ignorance.

Perfection is achievable in this world. As long as body-consciousness rules a soul's existence, it remains trapped in the cycle of rebirth. The soul creates its own destiny. No teacher or highly developed soul can interfere with, or cancel, negative karma for another person. Souls can be reincarnated up to a maximum of eighty-four times during a complete cycle (5,000 years). Souls that incarnate to this degree spend very little time in the "Soul World." Some souls may only incarnate the minimum of one time in a full cycle, spending most of their time in the "Soul World."

Every thought, attitude and action has karmic consequences. "*Vikarmas* are those actions performed in body-consciousness. *Sukarmas* are those actions performed in soul and God-consciousness."[28] No human soul ever transmigrates to an animal state. Human souls only reincarnate as humans.

Egyptian Mythology: The *ka* is the superior spiritual aspect of a person that survives the death of the body to enter the kingdom of the dead. It is identical to the flesh body in appearance. Because the *ka* cannot exist without the physical body, the Egyptians took great pains to embalm and mummify the corpses of the dead (a tradition supposedly initiated by the goddess, Isis, who mummified her deity-husband, Osiris, when he perished). For this reason, stone or wood statuettes of the deceased were also placed in the tomb to be substituted for the body in case the mummy suffered severe damage or ruin. The deceased descend to a realm called Duat, to be judged in the throne room of Osiris, Lord of the underworld. Their deeds must be weighed in the scales and assessed by the gods to determine if the person lived a good or evil life.

ISKCON (International Society for Krishna Consciousness): This belief system promotes the idea of a conscious preexistence of human beings: that all were formerly "in the spiritual world as transcendental loving servants of God."[29] Swami Prabhupada taught that according to "the Vedas...there are 8,400,000 species of life, from amoebas to humans and demigods."[30] Accepting a human form is quite uncommon and only takes place after "evolving through millions of lower species."[31] Liberated souls go back to the Godhead, becoming one with the Divine. Though achieving oneness of consciousness, they do not become one in substance. The identity of the individual is maintained eternally.

Kabbala (Mystical Judaism): Transmigration of the soul is a basic tenet of Kabbalistic doctrine even though it does not play a central role in all Kabbalistic schools. It became most prominent in the Luranic school in the 16th century. All subsequent schools were influenced greatly by Luria and his teachings. Some teach there is a conscious preexistence of the soul before its incarnation. It passes before God in the "Room of Love" before descending into this world. "God makes the soul swear to fulfill its earthly mission and attain to the 'knowledge of the mysteries of the faith' which will purify it for its return to its homeland."[32] If a soul fulfills its mission in one life, it can return to dwell near to God. If its mission is not accomplished, the soul must go through as many incarnations as neces-sary for this purpose to be achieved (a concept called metempsychosis). Some extremely wicked souls are "denied even hell or reincarnation... exiled without the possibility of finding rest."[33] Though reincarnation is one of their basic beliefs, Kabbalists also cling to the concept of the "resurrection of the dead, which will take place at the end of the days of redemption, 'on the great Day of Judgment.'"[34]

"In its root every soul is a composite of male and female, and only in the course of their descent do the souls separate into masculine souls and feminine souls."[35] The Zohar states "these souls are rejoined by God at the right time into one body and one soul." This doctrine suggests the existence of 'soul-mates' in the world.[36]

As mentioned under *The Origin and Nature of Man,* Kabbalists believe in five main soul-parts. The lower three of these five parts originate from three distinctly different sources (three of the ten emanations from the Godhead called *Sefirot*): "the *nefesh* originates in the *Sefirah Malkhut,* the *ru'ah* in the *Sefirah Tiferet,* and the *neshamah* in the *Sefirah Binah.*"[37]

At death, these three soul-parts also depart to different destinations: "the *nefesh* remains for a while in the grave, brooding over the body; the *ru'ah* ascends to the terrestrial paradise in accordance with its merits; and the *neshamah* flies directly back to its native home. Punishment and retribution are the lot of the *nefesh* and *ru'ah* alone."[38]

Kabbalistic doctrine yields a great deal of eschatological viewpoints concerning the "fate of the soul after death, and its ascent up a river of fire, which resembles a kind of purgatory, to the terrestrial paradise and from there to the still sublimer pleasures of the celestial paradise and the realm referred to by the early kabbalists as 'eternal life.'"[39]

The upper two levels of the soulish part of a person—*chayah, and yehidah*—along with the third part—the *neshamah*—always remain pure, regardless of the life of the individual. The lowest level of the soul—*nefesh*—is that part of the human makeup most involved with "the process of purification after death."[40] Following death, the upper levels of the soul go back to their original 'home,' but they must delay a state of final rest until the *nefesh* is redeemed. For the first week after a person passes away, the *nefesh* searches from the new grave to the old earthly dwelling of the deceased, looking for its living body. Then after being purified in *Gehinnom* (hell) it "wanders the world until it has a garment (signifying an awareness level)." *(See Zohar 1:226a-b.)* This purification process lasts for twelve months. Once clothed, the *nefesh* is admitted to "the lower Garden of Eden where it joins the *ruach*. The *ruach* then gets crowned, the *neshamah* unites with the Throne, and all is well."[41]

There is disagreement among some Kabbalists, and Jews in general, concerning *Gehinnom.* For instance, though not a kabbalist fraternity, early rabbinic teaching from the House of Shammai offers there are three types of people: the righteous who go immediately to paradise, the wicked who are doomed to spend a tortured eternity in *Gehinnom*, and the intermediate who are penalized for a season but then released. However, another rabbinic source, the House of Hillel, announces that in the messianic era *Gehinnom* will be consumed and destroyed, but not its inhabitants. All its inhabitants will be released by the mercy of God.

The Kabbalistic experience of union or merging with God is called *devekut*—a term also used by non-kabbalistic Jews (such as Mamonides) who may interpret the experience differently. Some broad-based Kabbalists might liken this ecstatic occurrence to the non-dual Buddhist experience of "Nirvana" or the Hindu experience of "Samadhi." However, the majority of Kabbalists would never propose such an absolute stage of oneness with God as promoted in Far Eastern religions. With traditional Kabbalists, 'separateness' is ever maintained between the Creator and his devoted ones. Though the depth of divine 'communion' is possible, there can never be a complete, undifferentiated 'union' of the soul with God.

"Five stages" are spoken of in the "Kabbalist's journey through his soul: (1) Animal Nature; (2) Spiritual Nature; (3) Breath; (4) Living Essence; (5) Unique Essence, or Union."[42] Final perfection and completion are only possible by passing through this earthly existence.

Because two judgments, one at death and the other at the end of days, seemed illogical to some Kabbalists, the final great Day of Judgment is assigned to the nations of the world. In their estimation, the souls of Israelites are judged only once, after the death of the body. Some Kabbalists believe that any 'Final Judgment' is primarily a self-judgment, not a Divine review of a person's life, as individuals see what they actually did as compared to what they could have done. There is also a distinction made between "the domain of pleasure after death *olam ha-neshamot* ("the world of souls"), and...*olam ha-ba* ("the world to come").[43]

Kriya Yoga (Paramahansa Yogananda): Promoted a scheme of reincarnation in which the soul always progresses to higher lives, though it can be retarded by negative actions. Full cosmic union with God is the ultimate goal.

Kundalini Yoga (Yogi Bhajan): Reincarnation ultimately liberates the soul into oneness with God. At the end of each incarnation, when a person dies, the Spiritual Body (the Soul) and the Subtle Body leave the other eight bodies (See "Kundalini Yoga" under *The Origin and Nature of Man*.) to begin the spiritual journey to the next karmically determined destination. The ultimate goal of the soul is absorption into

God. However, becoming one with the Universal Consciousness is not considered a "loss of identity," but rather, a "loss of limitation," the "discovery and experience of one's greater identity which is infinite... Succinctly put: Sat Nam: Truth is your identity."[44]

Meher Baba: Though born in a Zoroastrian family (a worldview that teaches just one life), Meher Baba taught reincarnation. He instructed that "in pursuit of consciousness, evolution of forms occurs in seven stages: stone or metal, vegetable, worm, fish, bird, animal and human."[45] Every individualized soul ordinarily experiences all of these forms in order to gain full consciousness. "After attaining the human form, as a rule there is no reversion to animal forms; cases of retrogression to subhuman forms are special and rare exceptions."[46] Also, the soul must pass through 504,000,000 pre-human forms "and 8,400,000 human forms on its way to enlightenment."[47] In its utmost essence, the soul is formless and eternal.

After the evolutionary journey brings the soul to human form, the remainder of the journey consists of progress through the seven planes of existence (a process called "involution"). Though the soul may exist on these planes between incarnations, all evolutionary progress through these planes is made while actually living in the physical world. The highest plane is Consciousness of Absolute, Infinite Oneness. If a soul advances to the fourth plane, but misuses its power, the result can be extremely detrimental, involving possible reversion in the next incarnation to the lowest form, starting the process of evolution all over again.

"The way to divinity lies through the renunciation of evil in favor of good...The good *sanskaras* [accumulated imprints of positive, past experiences that determine a person's desires and actions] deposited by the manifestations of these qualities overlap and balance the opposite, bad *sanskaras* of lust, greed, and anger. When there is an exact balancing and overlapping of good and bad *sanskaras*, there is at once a termination of both types and the precipitation of consciousness from a state of bondage to a state of Freedom. The credit and debit sides must be exactly equal to each other if the account is to be closed...The limited self can linger through good as well as bad *sanskaras*. What is required for its final extinction is an exact balancing and overlapping of the bad and good *sanskaras*."[48]

Scientology: Accepts the idea of past lives, recurring embodiments that determine a person's spiritual evolution. They do not subscribe to some beliefs that are sometimes associated with reincarnation, such as regression into a life form other than human. Man must progress spiritually in order to achieve his own salvation.

Sufism (Mystical Islam): Many teachers in Sufism instruct that there are seven levels the soul passes through on its journey to spirituality and wholeness: (1) *The Commanding Self*—compulsive and obsessive, this is the self active in all human beings that is given over to evil and seeks to dominate the life; (2) *The Regretful Self*—this self is still somewhat controlled by vices, but repentant over its choices to commit evil; (3) *The Inspired Self*—motivated by high ideals, desirous of moral boundaries and one who takes pleasure in the things of God; (4) *The Contented Self*—at peace adoring God and serving others. This is a period of transition in which the old self, with its selfishness and sensuality, is significantly losing its control. (5) *The Pleased Self*—this person is not only contented with his lot in life, but pleased with both blessings and difficulties, with both pleasure and pain, for all comes from the hand of God. (6) *The Self Pleasing to God*—one who has attained wholeness in God, oneness with him and total submission to him. (7) *The Pure Self*—ego is dissolved; those reaching this highest level have transcended the lower self altogether, realizing that only God exists and that "any sense of individuality or separateness is an illusion."[49]

"Sufis believe that before the material universe was created, we were all souls in the world of souls": close to God and conversing with him.[50] "God made a pact with the unborn souls of humanity, prior to the creation." Those who responded negatively were predestined to walk as rebels in the world. Those who responded submissively and lovingly to him received the 'sealing' of their destiny to be obedient servants of God. It was the first "tying of the bond and covenant of love."[51]

At the Day of Resurrection, God will review the deeds, evil and good, of every individual. Paradise, as taught in the Qur'an, is the ultimate destiny of lovers of God, a place of "gardens with flowing rivers and beautiful youths and maidens who serve the souls of the blessed."[52] Though hell is a major theme in the Qur'an and in Sufism, ultimately, through the power of the Resurrection, all who have lived will, in some sense, be embodied again in a purified way.

Theosophy: Teaches that all men, as emanations of God, originally "possessed all the powers of our divine Father."[53] The purpose of reincarnation is to reawaken this latent, divine potential. Theosophists reject the idea that reincarnation can involve a digression into subhuman states of existence. One writer warns of the inexorable law of karma, "We as immortal souls are the molders and masters of our own destiny...No one is to blame except ourselves for our birth conditions, our character, our opportunities, our abilities, for all these things are due to the working out of forces we have set going either in this life or in former lives."[54]

Mankind as a whole is described passing through the evolution of seven stages. According to Helena Blavatsky, there were two spiritual races and then the first physical "root race" was the Lemurian race. Their history goes back millions of years. After the Lemurians came the Atlanteans. This next "root race" was destroyed during a catastrophic end to the island of Atlantis. It was followed by the present human race. Each "root race" has a number of subraces. At the beginning of each new subrace, the spirit of the Supreme World Teacher (the Christ) enters the body of a human disciple to share new divine insights and aid the human race in its spiritual evolution. For example, Jesus of Nazareth was chosen as this vessel at the beginning of the fifth subrace (the race of intellectual man).

A paradigm shift is taking place now, because the sixth subrace is presently emerging (the race of the spiritual man) and the sixth 'Messiah' is soon to appear to take the human race to the next level of revelation. This sixth subrace will develop until it envelops the globe and replaces the present subrace. Life on earth will come to an end after the seventh "root race" is established and brought to completion. Then evolution will continue in other worlds (a later Theosophical writer suggested the planet Mercury as being one location).

The hope and purpose of every Theosophist is to progress spiritually through the seven planes of existence. As already mentioned under *The Origin and Nature of Man*, there are seven aspects to every person: (1) The physical body *(rupa or sthula-sarira)*; (2) Life or vital principle *(prana)*; (3) Astral body *(linga sharira)*; (4) Animal soul *(kama rupa)*; (5) Mind or intelligence—the human soul *(manas)*; (6) Spiritual soul *(buddhi)*; and (7) Spirit *(atma)*. The first four make up the discardable and perishable "Lower *Quarternary*." The last three make up the "Upper Imperishable *Triad*."[55]

After death, the lower three aspects depart from a person forever, remaining on earth. The higher four aspects (the "Animal Soul" and the "Atma-Buddhi-Manas Upper Triad") enter the "astral world" or "auric sphere" called *Kamaloka*. This post-mortem destination has "neither a definite area nor boundary, but exists within subjective space...beyond our sensuous perceptions." It is there that "the astral *eidolons*" (the disembodied astral aspect) of all living beings, including animals, abide awaiting their "second death."[56]

Once in *Kamaloka*, the "Upper Triad" separates from the "Animal Soul" (the *Kama rupa*). The "Animal Soul," after languishing for a season, collapses and begins disintegrating, having no more connection to the enduring part of a person. The "Upper Triad" merges into oneness, passing into the *Devachanic* state where its bliss is complete. There it experiences "absolute oblivion of all that gave it pain or sorrow in the past incarnation, and even oblivion of the fact that such things as pain or sorrow exist at all."[57]

The *Devachanee* experiences this transitional cycle between two earthly existences as "the ideal reflection of the human being it was when last on earth." It is surrounded by "everything it had aspired to in vain, and in the companionship of everyone it loved on earth. It has reached the fulfillment of all its soul-yearnings. And thus it lives throughout long centuries an existence of unalloyed happiness, which is the reward for its sufferings in earth-life."[58] The average time the Ego spends in the *Devachanic* state between incarnations is ten to fifteen centuries. In the case of an extremely wicked person, there is no *Devachanic* state prior to the next incarnation, indicative of a wasted life.

Escape to the highest level of oneness with the Absolute is the ultimate goal of all evolving souls. The "Adepts" and "Initiates" who pass beyond the veil of *maya*, who perfect themselves through the process of reincarnation, do not enter Devachan (which is an illusionary experience anyway, similar to a 'happy dream'). They ascend to Nirvana, to higher spheres, joining the other members of the Hierarchy of Masters, who have gone on to that advanced spiritual state. The purpose of these highly-evolved beings is to aid the progress of lesser-evolved souls. The absolute goal for all is godhood, that is, conscious union with the divine nature within.

United Church of Religious Science (Dr. Ernest Holmes): Taught immortality: a continuation of existence beyond death. "Our place hereafter will be what we have made it. We certainly cannot take anything with us but our character. If we have lived in accordance with the law of harmony, we shall continue to live after this Divine Law. If we have lived any other way, we shall continue to live that way until we wake up to the facts of Being."[59] There are no rewards or punishments from God awaiting those who die. If we make mistakes, the consequence is personal suffering. If we do well, the consequence is peace, enlightenment and personal fulfillment. "We are our own reward and our own punishment."[60] "Every man is an incarnation of God. The soul can no more be lost than God could be lost."[61]

THE SPIRITUAL JOURNEY AND ULTIMATE DESTINY OF MAN

Physical resurrection of the body is not a part of man's destiny; instead 'resurrection' is simply an overcoming of death by believing in the perpetuation of personal immortality. The concept of reincarnation is also rejected. Holmes said, "I do not believe in the return of the soul to another life on this plane. The spiral of life is upward. Evolution carries us forward, not backward."[62] "Everyone is a budding genius, a becoming God, an unfolding soul, an eternal destiny."[63] Souls will have spiritual bodies in the spiritual state. "Form is necessary to self-expression...there can be no consciousness without something of which to be conscious. It is one of the first laws of consciousness to clothe itself in form."[64]

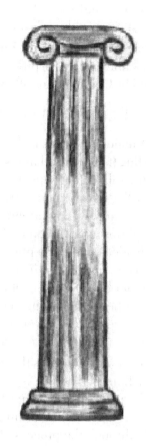

7

Cycles, Ages, and the Ultimate State of the Universe

Generally speaking, there are two main beliefs explored in this section concerning *Cycles, Ages, and the Ultimate State of the Universe*:

(1) **Endless Cycles (Cyclical)**—The future of the universe is a series of infinitely repeating cycles. Normally, this involves endless dissolutions and recreations, periods of manifestation and non-manifestation, with no ultimate or climactic end.

(2) **A Final New Creation (Linear)**—The future of the universe (usually after a series of progressive ages) is a climactic recreation, effected by God, bringing all things to final, unchanging perfection.

THE ELEVEN MAIN LIVING RELIGIONS

Buddhism: A major emphasis is the doctrine of "Emptiness" *(sunyata)*: the understanding that nothing has lasting value or significance. Buddhists also promote the related concept of "Impermanence" *(anicca)*: the belief that nothing will exist permanently. "Along with "suffering" *(dukkha)* and "no-soul" *(anatta)*, "impermanence" *(anicca)* is the third pillar of the Buddhist philosophy...People should not be attached to anything, including their ideas and perceptions of themselves because nothing is permanent."[1] The unique identity of a person is only a temporary condition brought about by the illusion of this realm. Ultimately all things will dissolve into non-being, including the universe in which we live. However, after each dissolution of the universe, another cycle of manifestation takes place, a condition that persists for eternity.

On the cover of this book is the dharma wheel symbol for Buddhism, surrounded by flames. The fire is symbolic of Buddha's first sermon to his ascetic colleagues. It has been titled "The Fire Sermon," a message that stressed how "insubstantial things in this world are, how like a fire they exist only through the process of burning."[2]

A cyclical view of the future is also promoted in Buddhism (the details of which may not be accepted by all Buddhists). The word *kalpa* signifies an extremely lengthy period of time. A *kalpa* is "divided into four parts: the arising of a universe, the continuation of the arisen universe, the demise of that universe, the continuation of chaos."[3] These four phases constitute a *"great kalpa" (mahakalpa)*. It is further divided into twenty small kalpas. The small *kalpa* is then subdivided into four ages: iron, copper, silver and gold.

"During the generational period of a small *kalpa*, human life-span increases by one year every hundred years until it has reached eighty-four thousand years...In the period of decline of a small *kalpa*, which is divided into phases of plague, war, and famine, human lifespan decreases to ten years."[4]

Japanese Buddhism (comprised of six major sects, including: Pure Land, Nichiren and Zen) divides the period following Buddha's death into three ages: the age of the "true law," the age of the "counterfeit law," and the age of the "degeneration of the law." The world is presently in the third age, an epoch of increasing evil and chaos named *mappo*. Each of the first two ages was 1,000 years long; the third age is 10,000 years long. It is generally believed that Buddha died around 480 B.C. Adding 2,000 years for the first two ages; this would place the third age beginning around 1520 A.D. and continuing for ten millennia.

Christianity: Some teachers of the Bible insist that the earth has gone through at least six major stages spiritually (some of which overlap in their influence) and that two more are yet to come:

(1) The Age of Innocence (prior to the fall of Adam and Eve in the Garden of Eden);

(2) The Age of Conscience (the era following the fall in which God dealt with men primarily by means of this 'inner witness');

(3) The Age of Human Government (beginning with Noah and the revelation he received);

(4) The Age of the Promise (from Abraham to Moses);

(5) The Age of the Law (following the giving of the Law to Moses);

(6) The Age of Grace (in place since Jesus' death, burial and resurrection and the coming of the Holy Spirit into the hearts of believers on the day of Pentecost).

(7) The Kingdom Age (possibly a literal, thousand-year-long reign of the Messiah on earth, initiated at his Second Coming, if that is the correct interpretation of Revelation 20:1–6).

(8) The New Creation (the eternal state following a renovation of the universe by fire).

The seventh era will immediately follow the Second Coming of the Messiah. After returning in glory, the Lord Jesus will restore this world to paradise beauty. He and his glorified saints (those resurrected from the dead or translated at his return) will then reign on earth. *(See Revelation 21.)* Other schools of thought exist concerning the seventh and eighth phases. The author has emphasized the Premillenial view; there are two other primary views: (1) Postmillenial (the belief that the preaching of the Gospel will have such an all-pervasive effect that Christ will, in a spiritual sense, reign over the earth for a thousand years. After this, the literal, physical coming of Christ will initiate the time of Final Judgment and the end of the present order); (2) Amillennial (the view that there is no Millennial Era at all, just the expectation of a final New Creation. Amillennialists believe that Satan and his demons are presently bound, which is difficult to accept, considering the rampant evil in this world).

According to the Premillenial view, during the Kingdom Age, wars will cease, harmony will be restored in nature (for instance, lambs will coexist peacefully with lions), sickness will be non-existent, the curse will be lifted, peace will be established and God will personally dwell among men. All of the problems that plague humanity will be solved. Satan and all his demonic underlings will be incarcerated in a spiritual prison called "the bottomless pit." *(Revelation 20:1,3)* Glorified saints will rule as God's representatives over the natural people who will repopulate the earth after the devastating effects of the last days' holocaust. *(See Isaiah 2:3–4; 33:24; 65:25, Psalms 46, Zechariah 14, 1 Corinthians 6:2, Revelation 12.)*

Immediately following this Kingdom Age, there will be a renovation by fire of the entire cosmos. "The heavens will pass away with a great noise, and the elements will melt with fervent heat; both the earth and the works that are in it will be burned up." *(2 Peter 3:10)* Out of this cosmic conflagration will emerge a New Heaven and a New Earth both of which will be permanent and perfect.

In this New Creation, all negativity will cease forever. "God will wipe away all tears from their eyes; there shall be no more death, nor sorrow, nor crying. There shall be no more pain, for the former things have passed away." God also promises, "Behold, I make all things new." *(Revelation 21:4–5)* The dwelling place of God's people will be an eternal, celestial city called New Jerusalem. The light of the sun and moon will not be needed in this city, for the glory of God will radiate out of this capital city of the New Creation. This will be a state of existence far beyond this present, natural, physical world.

Hinduism: Vedanta cosmology (a view based on the Vedas) speaks of the manifestation and the non-manifestation of the universe. In the former state things are seen in their tangible form, and in the latter, they go dormant as seed. These two universal states are called the "day of Brahma" and the "night of Brahma" (Brahma being the creator-god in traditional Hinduism).

The period of manifestation is called a *kalpa,* or cycle. One *kalpa* consists of 4,320,000,000 years. Two *kalpas* make a day and night of

Brahma—a total of 8,640,000,000 years. 360 such days and nights make one year of Brahma. One hundred such years constitute Brahma's lifetime of 311,040,000,000,000 years. Brahma then dies and another Brahma is reborn, a process infinitely repeated.[5]

When Brahma dies everything dissolves, returning back to the primordial substance *(prakriti)*. Some sources say that even the highest divine beings, gods and demigods, are subjected to this process. If this is the belief held, those who experience release *(moksha)* from the cycle of rebirths will eventually be recaptured by the merciless turn of the wheel...again and again...*ad infinitum*. Other sources say that liberated souls are not affected by this final dissolution and 'night of non-manifestation'—*Mahapralaya*—but rather, remain in the highest state of oneness with Brahman.

Each *kalpa* is made up of 1000 *maha-yugas*. A *maha-yuga* is 4,320,000 years long, comprised of four *yugas* or world ages: *Krita (or Satya) Yuga* (1,728,000 years), *Treta Yuga* (1,296,000 years), *Dvapara Yuga* (864,000 years) and *Kali Yuga* (432,000 years). These four *yugas* are named after the four throws in a dice game, progressing from the best to the worst. Added together, they make up a *Mahayuga ("great yuga")*. Notice that each age is a multiple of 432,000. The reasoning behind this is as follows: the *Krita Yuga* is the golden age of perfection when *dharma*, the moral order of the world, is one hundred percent manifested. There is a progressive degeneration in every age, with twenty-five percent of *dharma* being lost with each age. The *Kali Yuga*, being a fourth as long as the *Krita Yuga*, is the darkest of all ages subsisting "on twenty-five percent of the full strength of *dharma*. Egoistic, devouring, blind and reckless elements now are triumphant and rule the day. *Kali* means the worst of anything... During the *Kali Yuga*, man and his world are at their very worst."[6] The general consensus is that this dark period began in 3102 B.C. and will, therefore, end approximately 426,898 years from now.[7] Conditions will increasingly worsen until virtue and religion disappear, chaos reigns and the destruction of the world takes place. Then the cyclical process begins all over again, beginning with another *Krita Yuga*.

In breaking down this cyclical view even further, there are three levels at which partial or complete dissolution of the universe takes place: (1) *laya*—at the completion of a *mahayuga* the material world is destroyed; (2) *pralaya*—at the close of a *kalpa*, both the material world and the subtle worlds are destroyed; (3) *mahapralaya*—after the full cycle of a *mahakalpa* takes place, all three worlds (physical, subtle, and causal) are re-absorbed (some say into Brahman, others say into Shiva).

Islam: This present age will continue until the Final Judgment takes place and all human beings stand before Allah. They will either be allowed entrance into paradise or condemned to hell. These two locations, paradise for the righteous and hell for the wicked, are actual, permanent and eternal.

Muslims who commit grave sins and do not repent will go to hell only temporarily. After a sufficient punishment they will be allowed to enter paradise. Some Muslims, who believe in the Imam Mahdi, teach that this messianic leader will usher in a golden era of justice, goodness and true religion in the earth, but it will only last seven to nine years before the end of the world at the Final Judgment. There is also a belief that sometime in the future there will be an emerging of the Antichrist (*al-Dajjal*) who will suffer destruction when Isa (Jesus) returns just prior to the judgment.

Jainism: The universe has no beginning or end and is subject to infinitely revolving stages of growth and decline. Each cosmic cycle involves six phases of 'ascent' and six phases of 'descent' in the condition of civilization (beginning with the very best and ending with the very worst).

The symbol of this is a wheel with twelve spokes that are referred to as *aras* ("ages"). One full rotation of this 'wheel of time' is called a *kalpa*. This world is presently going through the fifth period of a cosmic phase of 'descent' (*Dukham Kal*). It is believed that this age began 2,500 years ago and will last for a total of 21,000 years. Degenerative spiritual conditions will increase more and more in this age until the teachings of Mahavira are lost altogether. The next age (*Dukham Dukham Kal*) will be totally irreligious and full of misery. Then another upswing of positive ascending cycles will begin.

Judaism: "Jewish eschatology deals primarily and principally with the final destiny of the Jewish nation and the world in general, and only secondarily with the future of the individual."[8] Traditional Jews believe in a coming "Day of the Lord" in which divine judgments and wrath will be poured out on the heathen world. They also believe that with the subsequent coming of the Messiah (*yemot ha-mashi'ah*) there will be a restoration of godliness and paradise perfection throughout the earth. The restored nation of Israel will then be the political and spiritual 'head' of all nations.

Most sources position this 'golden era' of messianic majesty as a "transitional stage" to a final, spectacular, infinite state, simply referred to as the "Kingdom of Heaven" (*malkut shamayim*) or the "world to come" *(olam ha-ba)*. Other interpretations exist that blend the Messianic Age and *olam ha-ba* together, insisting that these two descriptive phrases are actually referring to the same era.

Various projections are given for the length of the Messianic Age: "40, 70…365…and 400 years."[9] Some even project that the Messiah's reign will last "1,000, 2,000, 4,000 or 7,000 years."[10] Kabbalists believe "the Messianic Age will last approximately a thousand years."[11] A late *baraita* (a teaching from a source other than the Mishnah) postulates that this world will exist for "6,000 years, of which the first 2,000 will be a period of desolation, 2,000 of Torah, and the last 2,000 the messianic era." Another teaching exists that "the Holy One Blessed be He will renew His world only after 7,000 years." *(Babylonian Talmud, Sanhedrin 97b)*[12] This renewal will involve a final, fiery transformation and the manifestation of "new heavens and a new earth." *(Isaiah 65:17-25)* By these references it is clear that much latitude is allowed in forecasting the future in Judaism.

"It is said that the Sabbath is a taste from God of *olam ha-ba / the World to Come*, of paradise, a time in which it will always be Shabbat" [the Sabbath].[13] Speculation about the final state beyond the Messianic Age is sparse. One rabbinic description, though, that is often quoted, "In the world to come…the righteous will sit with their crowns on their heads and enjoy the splendor of the Shekinah" [the Divine Presence].[14]

Sikhism: The universe is destined to pass through a limitless number of emanations and dissolutions. The Adi Granth (the Sikh sacred Scripture) also mentions and verifies various, recurring ages *(yugas)*. *(See Adi Granth 275:10, 276:12–13.)*

Taoism: Taoism embraces the concept of an unending number of *kalpas* (ages) and an infinite number of creations *(yang)* and dissolutions *(yin)* of the universe. Furthermore, there are four primary cycles associated with the Chinese calendar: the Sexagenary Cycle (sixty years), the Three Eras (each era is sixty years long), the Nine Cycles (twenty years each), and the twenty-four seasonal markers (two to each month). Note that in 180 years there are, therefore, Three Eras (sixty years each) or Nine Cycles (twenty years each).

Zoroastrianism: Teaches that history is divided into four ages, each of which is 3,000 years in length. In the beginning there existed light and darkness and a Void separating the two. Ahura Mazda, the righteous Lord, lived in the light; Angra Mainyu, the god of evil, lived in the darkness. At the end of the first tri-millennium, Angra Mainyu (also called Ahriman) passed over the Void of separation and attacked Ahura Mazda.

Ahura Mazda defeated him by reciting the most sacred of all prayers, the Ahuna Vairya. Overpowered and ousted, Ahriman fell back into the abyss to remain there for another 3,000 years. During this period Ahura Mazda fashioned the spiritual creation, the Beneficent Immortals, and the physical creation. Simultaneously, Angra Mainyu created six demons and a rival material creation.

At the end of the second tri-millennium, Angra Mainyu killed Gayomart, the primeval man. From Gayomart's body the earth's metals and minerals were produced. Gold was Gayomart's seed and from it the human race was generated. In the third tri-millennium, Angra Mainyu conquered the material world, but became trapped in it.

In the beginning of the fourth and last tri-millennium, Zoroaster was born. Every thousand years following, a new savior and posthumous son of Zoroaster was predicted to appear on the world scene. The third and final savior, Saoshyant, will usher in the final judgment, the destruction of Angra Mainyu and the closing stage of the four-step cycle. He will set up the Kingdom of Righteousness for one cosmic year (12,000 earthly years). At the end of this era, the resurrection of both the good and evil will take place and all will be granted eternal life with Ahura Mazda. The final act of divine intervention will be a world-consuming fire that dissolves all things and brings to birth a permanent New World.

OTHER RELIGIONS, SECTS AND TEACHERS

Astrology: There are various branches of astrological thought (Egyptian, Chinese, Hindu, etc.) with many differing opinions, sometimes concerning key astrological issues. The most widely accepted zodiac contains twelve signs (houses) through which the sun passes. Different schools of thought believe in eight, ten, fourteen or twenty-four signs or houses. However, all forms of astrology agree on a cyclical view of human history and destiny.

Theoretically, a new era begins worldwide whenever the sun enters a new sign of the zodiac on the day of the vernal equinox (one of two days a year when the sun is directly above the equator). This solar event occurs approximately every 2,200 years, heralding the entrance of a new age. After the completion of twelve astrological ages (if the twelve house theory is embraced), the process is finished. This takes approximately 26,000 years. Then the whole process repeats itself indefinitely. In astrology, no ultimate, dramatic, permanent change ever comes to this world or the universe as a whole. Rather, there is an endless repetition of astrological ages that never fully solve the problems of the human race.

Though no one can pinpoint the exact time of transition, most astrologers believe the world is presently in the process of entering a glorious new era titled, "The Age of Aquarius." This desirable period is predicted to be a time of enlightenment, perfection, harmony and spiritual intensification in the world: a time when wars will cease, many earthly problems will be solved (hunger, poverty, pollution, etc.) and the human race will walk in God-consciousness. Many astrologers believe it will also involve a New Age Messiah who will usher in many of these changes. It is in reference to this "Aquarian Age" that we get the popular term, "The New Age Movement." Of course, this 'age of enlightenment' will only last 2,200 years and then another astrological era will unfold, bringing in a new phase on this planet.

Bahá'í: Spiritual dispensations are marked by the entrance into this world of select religious leaders referred to as "Manifestations of God." These choice individuals are "theophanies: mirrors who reflect God's glory and reveal his attributes"…they are the "means of approach to God," being his "messengers," "bringers of divine revelation." However, they "are not incarnations of God; they do not embody the divine essence."[15]

With each "Manifestation of God" there is a new spiritual era in which a new religion is born, gradually matures and then declines, necessitating another "Manifestation" with fresh insight. Each of these eras is an independent dispensation, occurring within one of the two primary cycles promoted in the Bahá'í faith. This present cycle is titled "the Bahá'í Cycle." It began with the Bab (founder of the Babi faith and forerunner of Bahá'u'lláh) and Bahá'u'lláh (founder of the Bahá'í faith). Both these individuals are considered "Manifestations."

(1) **The Adamic Cycle**—This cycle was initiated by the prophet, Adam (considered a "Manifestation"), and lasted approximately 6,000 years. It ended in 1844 when the Bab (the Iranian founder of the Babi faith) began promulgating his revelations;

(2) **The Bahá'í Cycle**—This began with the declaration of the Bab and will include the future establishment of the Kingdom of God on earth. It will last some half-a-million years, during which there will be a succession of future Manifestations of God, all appearing "under Bahá'u'lláh's shadow."[16] According to the Universal House of Justice (the governing body of the Bahá'í faith) the next Manifestation will appear after one thousand years from the date of Bahá'u'lláh's imprisonment in Tehran in 1852. So the next great Era heralded by a new World Teacher is expected to begin some time after 2852 A.D.

The human race will reach the desirable goal of a one-world, global society in two stages yet to come: (1) the Lesser Peace (a stage during which governments will end war and establish minimal international standards for economic and social interaction); then (2) the Most Great

Peace (the ultimate establishment of the Kingdom of God on earth). The transition to the Lesser Peace, which is already occurring, has been marked by the development of a global consciousness and infrastructure, as well as calamities that continue to engulf the planet. This could possibly escalate to something as severe as a nuclear war. However, there will be no literal, personal, supernatural intervention by God. Change will take place within society and within the hearts of humankind. Ultimately, there will be a unification of all people, bringing harmony to this planet— with characteristics like "a universal language, a single currency and a uniform judicial and police system," established by a "universal executive and legislative body."[17] In anticipation of this future "Golden Age," Bahá'u'lláh exhorted the nations of the world, "You are the fruits of one tree, and the leaves of one branch."

Benjamin Creme (Share International Foundation): There are seven rays or streams of energy that created the Cosmos. "Like everything in Cosmos, the rays have periods of activity and inactivity, ebb and flow. In the case of the rays, these cycles cover thousands of years and are determined by the Plan of the Logos.

The 7th ray of Ceremonial Order or Ritual is (since 1675) coming into manifestation. The 6th ray of Abstract Idealism or Devotion is (since 1625) gradually passing out. Our present problems are the result of the fact that these two highly potent energies are functioning simultaneously and in roughly equal potency. As a consequence, the world is divided..."[18] The struggle politically, economically, religiously and socially traces back to the resistance of those who cling to the 6th-ray energies to the increasing acceptance and manifestation of the "new incoming 7th-ray energies."[19]

Brahma Kumaris World Spiritual Organization (Raja Yoga): The drama of human history is spoken of in cyclical terms. There is a continual, eternal reoccurrence of five world ages, the first being an age of perfect beauty, purity and truth called the Golden Age. In this age, the law of love rules all the activities of human beings. From its inception, however, there is a continuing loss of perfection until the end of the Iron Age, when truth is hidden and evil abounds. After the Golden Age *(Sat Yuga*—the Age of Perfection), come the Silver Age *(Treta Yuga*—the Three-Quarters Age, an Age of Decline), the Copper Age *(Dwapur Yuga*—the Age of Duality), the Iron Age *(Kali Yuga*—the Age of Death), and finally, the Diamond Age *(Sangam Yuga*—the Confluence Age, the Age of Illumination). Each of the first four ages lasts 1,250 years. The Diamond Age only lasts 100 years. Therefore, a complete cycle is 5,000 years long. The Diamond Age is called an Age of Confluence (which means a "convergence" or a "coming together") because in this final age, there is a meeting of God and all mankind, as well as a meeting of the old world and soon-to-be-recreated world.

Human beings who start incarnating with the beginning of the Golden Age can experience a maximum of eighty-four births during the completion of all five cycles (Golden Age—eight births, Silver Age—twelve births, Copper Age—twenty-one births, Iron Age—forty-two births, Diamond Age—one birth). Its level of purity, power and spirituality determines the number of births that an individual soul experiences.

The Diamond Age is a crucially important era. At its onset, God Shiva descends, entering a human form. Because the world is in a state of great darkness and wickedness, he comes to purify and liberate souls taking them back to their original abode. According to this worldview, such a notable happening took place in 1937, when Shiva descended into the body of Lekh Raj (later to be known as Prajapita Brahma) the founder of this religious group. God visits the earth in this manner to demonstrate his teachings through the example of the one in whom he dwells. Those who acknowledge Shiva Baba and follow the teachings of Brahma are referred to as Brahmins, the "twice-born." "Through Brahma the Supreme Soul gives human souls a spiritual birth...through the 'breath' of God's knowledge the soul experiences total spiritual rebirth: a new mind, a new vision, a new dimension of living."[20]

So we are presently over halfway through the Diamond Age, that critical time of spiritual transition, that pivotal era bridging the totally degenerate Iron Age and the perfection of the next Golden Age. Finding the truth and living in it is crucial at this time. Those who strive for spirituality and sensitivity to God during this era are preparing for the next cycle, for an important, individual role during the next Golden Age.

ISKCON (International Society for Krishna Consciousness): A cyclical view identical with traditional Hinduism is taught with four different *yugas* (ages) of varying length totaling 4,320,000 years. The life span during these four *yugas* is: (1) The *Satya-yuga*—approximate life expectancy for human beings during this most perfect of all ages, 100,000 years. (2) The *Treta-yuga*—an average life expectancy of 10,000 years. (3) The *Dvapara-yuga*—a potential life expectancy of 1,000 years. (4) The *Kali-yuga*, this "present age of quarrel and hypocrisy"—a maximum life expectancy significantly reduced to 100 years. This has since been lowered to seventy years. "It will eventually decrease to the point where if a man lives for twenty to thirty years, he will be considered a very old man." This *yuga* began about 5,000 years ago.[21]

The four *yugas* make up a *kalpa*. After seventy-one *kalpas*, the disintegration of all things is described reverting back into Krishna instead of Brahma. Krishna is quoted as saying; "At the end of an era *(kalpa)* all creatures disintegrate into my nature and at the beginning of another era I manifest them again. It is my nature to manifest all potentials, sustain them, and disintegrate them back into myself and then to begin again the process of manifesting, sustaining and disintegrating. Such it is my nature to follow the pattern of the infinite manifestations and disintegrations." *(Bhagavad-Gita 9, 7–8)*

Kabbala (Mystical Judaism): [Please note: these cyclical concepts do not play a major role in classical kabbalistic tradition. They were first promoted by one eccentric school of Temunah and ignored altogether by the writer of the Zohar (Kabbala's main sacred text). However, it seemed proper to include this category for the reader's sake.]

According to the Kabbalah of Gerona, in the *Sefer ha-Temunah* (anonymously written about 1250 A.D.) the following cyclical view is presented. "The first three *Sefirot* remain concealed and do not activate 'worlds' outside themselves…From the Sefirot Binah, also called 'the mother of the worlds,' the seven apprehendable and outgoing Sefirot are emanated." (See "Kabbalah" under *The Origin and Nature of the Universe.*)

"Each one of these *Sefirot* has a special role in one creation-cycle. Each such cosmic cycle [historical aeon], bound to one of the Sefirot, is called a shemittah or sabbatical year—a term taken from Deuteronomy 15—and has an active life of 6,000 years. In the seventh millennium, which is the *shemittah* period, the Sabbath-day of the cycle, the sefirotic forces cease to function and the world returns to chaos. Subsequently, the world is renewed through the power of the following *Sefirah* and is active for a new cycle. At the end of all the shemittot there is the "great jubilee," when not only all the lower worlds, but the seven supporting *Sefirot* themselves are reabsorbed into *Binah.* The basic unit of world history is therefore the 50,000-year jubilee."[22]

A 13th century Jewish writer (Babya b. Asher) proposed "the world-process lasts for no less than 18,000 jubilees."[23] This time-span is not calculable by present standards, though, because with each seventh millennium "measurements of time change," being affected by a gradual slowing of universal bodies. Though some assert that at the conclusion of each "great jubilee," God begins a new creation out of nothing *(ex nihilo),* no Kabbalist writings imply an infinite stream of jubilees yet to unfold.

There are diverse opinions concerning which *shemittah* in the jubilee period we are participating in presently. The generally accepted view is that we are in the *shemittah of Din* (judgment), ruled by the *Sefirah Gevurah,* and the principle of strict justice. The previous era was the *shemittah of Hesed* (lovingkindness) an "aeon of Grace...entirely bathed in light...[in which] there existed no evil inclination and no tempting serpent."[24] This age of judgment and justice began with the giving of the Torah. Other projections include the posture that we are in the last *shemittah* of the present jubilee period. The world will ultimately, at the coming of the Messiah, return to the bosom of its Infinite Source. Then hell will disappear and endless bliss will begin.

Kriya Yoga (Swami Sri Yukteswar): This patriarch of the Kriya Yoga worldview redefined the cyclical view espoused in Hinduism. Drawing from Oriental astronomical beliefs, Swami Sri Yukteswar proposed that our solar system as a whole (the sun and its planets and their moons) makes a revolution around a certain universal focal point every 24,000 years. This involves an Ascending Arc of 12,000 years and a Descending Arc of 12,000 years.

The development of dharma is divided into four stages: *Kali Yuga* (1,200 years); *Dwapara Yuga* (2,400 years); *Treta Yuga* (3,600 years); and *Satya Yuga* (4,800 years). Altogether these four yugas make up the Ascending Arc. Notice that each Yuga is a multiple of 1,200 years. Each *yuga* increases, not only in time span, but in spirituality. In the final *yuga (Satya Yuga) dharma* (mental virtue) is fully developed and "the human intellect can comprehend all, even God the Spirit beyond this visible world." The fourfold cycle altogether is called a *"Daiva Yuga,"* also referred to as "the Age of the Gods." One thousand of these ages constitute "one day of Brahma," with a "night of Brahma" of equal length (12,000,000 years each).

According to certain cosmic calculations, around the year 500 A.D. the *Kali Yuga* (in the Descending Arc) reached its darkest moment. The next stage became the *Kali Yuga* (in the Ascending Arc) ending around 1700 A.D. Then the ascending *Dwapara Yuga* began, destined to continue for 2,400 years, bringing with it an increase of mental awareness in the human race. In 4,100 A.D. the *Treta Yuga* will begin. In 7,700 A.D. the Satya Yuga will begin. According to Yogananda, in that final age of the Ascending Arc "men will work in harmony with the divine plan."[25]

Swami Yukteswar insists that the Hindu calculations are wrong which predict a continuance of the dark *Kali Age* for approximately another 427,000 years, and calls such scenario, "A dark prospect! And fortunately one not true." Because this is an ascending age, and humanity has been freed long ago from the *Kali Yuga*, the human race is "reaching out for spiritual knowledge, and men require loving help one from the other." These alternating cycles continue throughout the ceaseless ages to come.[26]

(Paramahansa Yogananda): "The universal cycle of the scriptures is 4,300,560,000 years in extent and measures out a 'Day of Creation.'... The life span for a whole universe, according to the ancient seers is 314,159,000,000,000 solar years, or "One Age of Brahma."[27]

Meher Baba: Unique to Meher Baba's teaching is the concept that "in each cycle of time, which ranges from 700 to 1400 years, there are eleven ages of 65 to 125 years each."[28] Each cycle brings an Avataric manifestation (an Avatar such as: Rama, Krishna, Buddha, Jesus, Mohammed, Meher Baba). He also claimed "the evolution of creation has seven stages," and that a major cycle of cycles "is twelve thousand million (12,000,000,000) years" long.[29]

Scientology: Promotes, first, an objective of helping individuals attain and maintain a state of spiritual freedom. This, in turn, should lead to the ultimate objective of "clearing the planet"—in other words, ridding the earth of negative things like: selfishness, dishonesty, violence, crime, insanity and war. Thus, a more enduring civilization results.

Sufism (Mystical Islam): One of the most succinct, simple, yet potent descriptions of Sufi doctrine in this area comes from the 'pen' of Carl W. Ernst, Ph.D.: "For the Sufi tradition, the Qur'an frames all of time and eternity into three days. Yesterday is the dawn of creation, when God created the universe and sealed the destiny of his lovers. Today is this world when all are called upon to live according to God's wishes. Tomorrow is the resurrection and the judgment day, when souls will testify against themselves and be held to account, and God's mercy will be displayed."[30]

Theosophy: Theosophists believe that the earth is presently in its fourth cycle, and the human race is now experiencing the third "root race" and the beginnings of the sixth subrace. (See "Theosophy" under *The Spiritual Journey and Ultimate Destiny of Man*.) Similar to Hinduism, Theosophy teaches that the universe is eternal, existing without end in great cosmic cycles of the evolution of matter, intelligence, and spirit. Life on earth will come to an end after the seventh "root race" is established and brought to completion. Then this evolution will continue on in other worlds.

United Church of Religious Science (Dr. Ernest Holmes): The biblical phrase, "world without end" *(Ephesians 3:21)* is interpreted as referring to "the endless creation of the Almighty. Particular worlds will always begin and end...but creation itself—the necessity of God manifesting Himself in time and in space—will never end. If creation could end, then God would end."[31]

ACKNOWLEDGING
THE
CONTRADICTIONS

ACKNOWLEDGING THE CONTRADICTIONS

After contrasting the beliefs of various religions and sects, it is easy to see that they often exhibit irreconcilable differences on major doctrinal issues. In the mind of any studious, sincere and reflective person, questions such as the following will inevitably surface:

> ### The Origin and Nature of the Universe

Was the universe created by God, the view of Christianity, Islam and Judaism, emanated out of God, the view of Hinduism, or is it eternal and uncreated, as believed in Raja Yoga and Jainism?

Was the universe created out of nothing, as believed in Christianity, Islam and Judaism, or was it formed from some kind of preexisting substance, as promoted in Hinduism?

Did the universe result from causal actions, as promoted in Buddhism, a series of verbal commands from God, as declared in Judaism, or from Brahma opening his eyes, as taught in Hinduism? Did it manifest from the emanation of ten *Sefirot*, as believed in Kabbala, seven rays of energy, as promoted by Benjamin Creme, four primal thoughts, as indicated in Kriya Yoga, or nine Energies and two kinds of Primordial Breath, as stated in Taoism?

Is the material world an illusion, as taught in Hinduism and Theosophy, a terrible error perpetrated by an evil, subordinate god, as indicated in Gnosticism, or is the material world an unquestionable reality, a good act of a good God, yet defiled through the entrance of sin, as believed in Christianity, Sikhism and Judaism?

Is the correct view of Ultimate Reality the impersonal Brahman of Hinduism, the Universal Principle of Taoism, Krishna of ISKCON, or Jesus Christ of Christianity?

> ### The Nature of God

Is God a singular Being, as believed in Islam, a Triune God (one God, yet three expressions of the Godhead), as taught in Christianity, or are there two eternally existent gods that oppose one another, as promoted by Zoroastrianism? Does God have ten emanations, as taught in Kabbalism, or countless millions of manifestations, as believed in Hinduism? Is he omnipresent, as embraced by most religions, or is he confined to an infinitesimal point of light, the doctrine promoted in the Brahma Kumaris World Spiritual Organization?

Is nature (the natural creation) the body of God, as expressed in Hinduism, the garment of God, as taught in Kabbalism, or just a declaration of the glory of God, as promoted in Judaism? Did the Godhead manifest 'Itself' *as* creation, the view of philosophic Hinduism, or is God the essence of life *within* creation, as believed by most Sikhs and Sufis?

Or does God exist apart from creation altogether, the belief of Christianity, orthodox Islam and Judaism? Is God so transcendent, so aloof and distant, that he does not interact with the affairs of men, the view of Deists, or is he both transcendent and immanent, manifesting himself personally to those who come into a relationship with him, as believed in Christianity?

Is the greatest, most excellent name of God "Bahá," as taught in the Bahá'í faith, "SUGMAD," as believed in ECKANKAR, "Krishna," as declared in ISKCON, "Ein Sof," as promoted in Kabbala, "Sat Nam," as unveiled in Sikhism, "Tao" as taught in Taoism, "Ahura Mazda," as expressed in Zoroastrianism, Yahweh, as found in Judaism, or something altogether different than any of these?

Does Ultimate Reality contain the *yin-yang* duality of darkness and light, evil and good, the doctrine of Taoism and most pantheistic world-views, or is God light and goodness, with no darkness or evil resident in him at all, the belief common to theistic religions?

Was the first human being a man named Manu, as alleged in Hinduism, Adam, as taught in Judaism, Pangu, as told in Taoism, or Gayomart, as promoted in Zoroastrianism? Was this progenitor of the human race fashioned from the dust, as taught in Judaism, or from Brahma dividing his own form, as explained in Hinduism?

The Origin and Nature of Man

Did the human race descend from Adam and Eve, as taught in Christianity, Islam and Judaism, or from the germs of Pangu's body, dispersed by the wind, the doctrine of Taoism? Or was the gold of the earth actually the seed of Gayomart (the first man) bringing forth the human race, according to Zoroastrianism?

Is the Buddhist doctrine of no-self *(anatman)* correct, or the Hindu belief in a permanent self *(atman)*? Are human beings innately good and divine, as believed in Shintoism, or have they inherited a fallen nature, as taught in Christianity?

Is man a triune being, the doctrine of Christianity; is he made up of four parts, as promoted in ECKANKAR, or seven parts, as taught in Theosophy and Kabbala? Is a human being comprised of ten bodies as taught by Yogi Bhajan, five aggregates, as believed in Buddhism, or five sheaths covering the 'self,' as explained in Kriya Yoga?

Does the soul consciously exist prior to embodiment, as believed in Sufism, or is the soul created from nothing, coincidental with the formation of the body, as normally accepted in Judaism? Did God predetermine a 'covenant of love' with preincarnate souls who agreed to serve him during their earthly sojourn, as conceptualized in Sufism, or do all men have an opportunity to repent and enter a covenant relationship with God, as declared in many branches of Christianity?

Is the caste system promoted by historical Hinduism a correct order for society, or are Buddhists, Jainists and Sikhs justified in their rejection of this concept and their declaration that all men have equal value?

Is it impossible for a woman to reach enlightenment unless she is reincarnated as a man, as some Jainists teach, or are women just as capable of enlightenment or salvation as men, as Buddhism and most other religions declare?

Is "salvation" or "enlightenment" effected in human beings by erasing engrams (repressed negative memories) in the reactive mind, which is Scientology's position, or must we be awakened to God-consciousness through meditation, as promoted in various Yoga sects? Is it necessary for salvation-seekers to chant the Hare Krishna mantra, as expected in ISKCON, or meditate upon the living ECK master, as taught in ECKANKAR?

The Nature of Salvation, Liberation, or Enlightenment

Is salvation or enlightenment accomplished primarily by living a righteous life, as taught in Islam, Judaism, and Zoroastrianism, by meditating on the thirty-two paths to Ein Sof and the fifty gates of understanding, as held by some Kabbalists, by granting our ancestors proper recognition and worship, as promoted in Shintoism, by yielding to the Beneficent Immortals, as commanded in Zoroastrianism, by repentance and cleansing from sin through the blood of Jesus, as taught in Christianity, by faith in Bahá'u'lláh and good deeds, as declared in Bahá'í, or by devotion to Amida Buddha, as commanded in the Jodo-Shinshu sect of Buddhism?

Are there eight kinds of karma that must be overcome, as Mahavira declared, twelve karma foundations from which men must be freed, as Buddha instructed, or is it the sin nature, and not karma, that must be overcome in order to inherit salvation, as Jesus promoted in his scheme of deliverance from this world?

How can the Jainist belief of *Ahimsa* (non-violence) be an achievable goal (and a prerequisite for salvation) since millions of microorganisms are constantly being killed through our daily activity?

Is salvation finalized by the survival and perfecting of a unique personality in a heavenly state or by the eradicating of that personality in order to obtain an undifferentiated, cosmic oneness with all things?

Is sexual involvement with multiple partners an aid to achieving immortality, as believed by some Taoists, or is sexual intercourse outside of marriage a sin requiring repentance, as taught in the Bible?

**Dimensions
or Planes
of Existence**

Are there three heavens, as taught in Christianity, seven heavens, as taught in Hinduism, Islam and Judaism, nine layers of heaven, the belief of Taoism, thirty heavens in the "Upper World," as taught in Jainism?

Are there nine underworlds, as Taoism instructs, seven, as declared in Jainism and Hinduism, or three, as indicated in Christianity?

Are there thirty-one planes of existence altogether, as embraced in Buddhism, eleven, as accepted in ECKANKAR, four, as revealed in Kabbalism, or seven, as promoted in Theosophy, Kriya Yoga and the teachings of Meher Baba?

Are "heavens" and "hells" actual localities, as believed in many religions, or just a 'state of mind,' as presented in Theosophy?

Is the highest dwelling place of God "Anami Lok (ECKANKAR), "Hahut" (Bahá'í), "Araboth" (Judaism), "Brahmaloka" (Hinduism), "Djanna" (Islam), "Krsnaloka" (ISKCON), "Adam kadmon" (Kabbala), "Satyaloka" (Kriya Yoga) or "Paradise" (Christianity)?

At a person's demise, does the soul remain in the grave awaiting the resurrection, as taught in Islam, or is the soul of a saved person immediately taken to paradise, as taught in Christianity and modern Judaism?

**The
Spiritual
Journey
and
Ultimate
Destiny
of Man**

Which is true—the Tibetan Buddhist belief that forty-nine days after death human beings face an entity named Emma-O who dictates the next step in their evolution, or the Muslim belief that the deceased are scrutinized by two angels, Munkar and Nakir, in order to determine their final destiny, or the Hindu belief that Yama, the Lord of death, determines the details of the next incarnation, or the Christian belief that at death, every person is assessed by the Lord Jesus Christ, and assigned to an everlasting location?

Which is correct—the Shinto belief that after thirty-three years a deceased person loses his or her individual personality and enters forever into the ranks of the *kami* (the gods), or the Theosophist belief that every evolving soul normally waits ten to fifteen centuries before reincarnating?

How can the universalist belief that all souls will eventually reach perfection be fused with the idea that there is a final judgment out of which only righteous sons and daughters of God will emerge with eternal life?

How can the doctrine of reincarnation, espoused by Hinduism, Buddhism, Jainism and others, be united with the idea that the soul has only one existence in this world, as embraced by Christianity, Judaism, Islam and Zoroastrianism? Is reincarnation the true journey of every soul, or is resurrection the ultimate outcome? Or is the Bahá'í faith right in saying that neither reincarnation nor resurrection are correct doctrines?

Will all souls ultimately become formless spirits, merging with the Godhead, or will the heirs of eternal life receive definite, visible, celestial forms: eternal glorified bodies?

Is the soul, as a separate entity, destined to enjoy eternal communion with God, as advocated in the teachings of Christianity, Judaism and Islam, or will the liberated soul forever lose its individuality and be absorbed into God, as promoted in certain branches of Hinduism?

Are we entering, as astrologers claim, the glorious Age of Aquarius (a golden age of enlightenment and peace in the earth), or are we caught, as Hinduism asserts, in the ever-deepening quicksand of the *Kali Yuga* (an age of increasing darkness and evil)?

Is this present age, the soon-to-climax New Covenant Age of Christianity, the ascending *Dwapara Yuga*, as believed in Kriya Yoga, the corrupt *Mappo Age* of Japanese Buddhism, the fourth tri-millennium of Zoroastrianism, the *shemittah* of judgment, as believed in Kabbala, the transitional Diamond Age of the Brahma Kumaris World Spiritual Organization, or the fifth period of a cosmic phase of descent, as promoted in Jainism?

Cycles, Ages, and the Ultimate State of the Universe

Will this present wicked age end in 425,000 years, as Hinduism foretells, about 9,500 years, as Japanese Buddhism predicts, about 400 years, as implied in Zoroastrianism, or will it continue until at least 2892 A.D. after which a new Manifestation of God will arrive in this world, ushering in a new cyclical era, as taught in the Bahá'í faith?

Will the universe go through endless cycles of creation, dissolution and recreation, as taught in Buddhism and Hinduism, or will there be, as Christianity, Judaism, Zoroastrianism declare, one permanent renovation by fire resulting in a New Heaven and a New Earth?

And the inescapable questions keep surfacing, again and again—?????

These are certainly not trifling issues, of negligible importance. These are matters of deep concern for all of us. The validity and the dependability of the doctrines we embrace determine whether or not the "seven pillars of wisdom" we choose crumble or stand forever.

CHOOSING BETWEEN THREE OPTIONS

So what are we going to do with all of this conflicting data?

At this pivotal point, we are constrained to choose one of the following three options:

(1) **Ignore**—We can ignore the contradictions and refuse to deal with them.

(2) **Synthesize**—We can make a supreme, philosophical effort to force all these views into syncretistic, monistic harmony.

(3) **Distinguish Right from Wrong**—We can carefully review all of these concepts in order to discern that which is correct: retaining what is right and discarding what is wrong.

Normally, only those who passionately love the truth find it. Because ordinarily, only lovers of truth are willing to pay the price that truth demands. And what is that price? First, it often involves becoming intensely focused on transcendental things, at the expense of sacrificing, neglecting or rising above things which are temporal. Second, it often involves a willingness to sacrifice beliefs that are dear or comfortable to us, culturally, intellectually and religiously. This is certainly not easy, but necessary at times.

So pause for a moment. Recommit yourself to the role of a truth seeker. Dare to scrutinize your own heart—then release it to explore possibilities—without the restraint of preset doctrinal biases. Purpose in your heart of hearts that whatever cost is involved in knowing the mysteries of God, you are more than willing to pay it. My hope and prayer is that your love for the truth will undergird you with strength, put the fire of discernment in your eyes, and guide you like a knowledgeable boatman in this journey of all journeys—from the dark shore of spiritual uncertainty to the bright shore of absolute assurance.

IS TRUTH REALLY RELATIVE?

As a yoga teacher, I taught that all world religions were just different paths to the same God. I firmly believed that part of walking in the "True Light" involved accepting the monistic view that "All is One." However, I could not hide my eyes, nor my heart, from the evident contradictions that kept rising to the surface of my worldview. The more I studied, the more I wondered, "Was I trying to mix oil and water?" (These two liquids, when vigorously shaken, seem to blend, but within a few moments they always separate. Philosophically, was I doing the same thing: 'forcing' a merging of all religions, which given to themselves would automatically separate?)

During this pivotal phase, I poured over numerous books and pamphlets dealing with the human condition. Comments similar to the following from S. Radhakrishnan seemed to prop open the door of understanding:

> *"The truth, which is the kernel of every religion,*
> *is one and the same; doctrines, however, differ*
> *considerably since they are the applications of the*
> *truth to the human situation...Rites, ceremonies,*
> *systems and dogmas lead beyond themselves to a*
> *region of utter clarity and so have only* **relative**
> **truth***...Every work, every concept is a pointer*
> *which points beyond itself. The sign should not be*
> *mistaken for the thing signified. The sign-post is not*
> *the destination."*[1]

Statements like this temporarily stilled my concerns. They seemed to exude compassion and wisdom. Yet this idea of '*relativism*' increasingly left me with an uncomfortable feeling. I pondered, "How can anything be correctly labeled 'Truth' if it is true only for those who can *relate* to it because of their culture, tradition or era? If it is untrue for others, how can it be substantive at all?"

Convincing myself that truth is *relative* felt like cutting a boat free from its moorings—with no sails, no oars, no steering mechanism, and no fuel for the engine—to drift on an ocean of human speculation. If *relativism* is correct, why should the 'truth-seeker' confine himself to any religion? If none of them has a verifiable belief system that is universally acceptable and eternally dependable, why adhere to any religious dogma?

Why should a Buddhist believe in Buddhism, a Christian in Christianity, a Hindu in Hinduism, a Muslim in Islam or a Jainist in Jainism—if the doctrinal base of all these religions, as well as their ceremonial traditions, are filled with erroneous assumptions, wrong beliefs and false conclusions? If God is beyond human reasoning, and if differences of opinion concerning his nature are simply the by-product of human imagination (as relativism suggests), why should we even bother investigating the recorded explanations of various religions concerning his character and being?

Eventually I realized that I had to make a choice. I had to choose between two possible scenarios. Either truth is vague, all-inclusive, fully syncretistic and doctrinal differences have no real relevance. Or truth is precise, definable and exclusive, and doctrinal differences have extreme relevance—demanding the discarding of certain beliefs in order to embrace others. If the former is true, then it matters little what any religion promotes as truth. Words and concepts are just symbolic. Wrong concepts and warped views will all blend into one Ultimate Reality anyway, like muddy rivers emptying into the ocean, to be purified in the process. However, if truth is definable and exclusive, words and concepts are of absolute importance.

Something drastic happened when I dared to entertain the latter of these two conclusions as the probable scenario. Inspiration, like a mother eagle, flapped its wings without warning and threw my soul like a baby eaglet into the air, so it could learn how to fly. It wasn't long before I caught...

THE WIND UNDER MY WINGS

Nicolaus Copernicus quipped:

> *"To know that we know what we know, and that we do not know what we do not know, that is true knowledge."*[2]

In other words, those who are wise concerning the mysteries of life are not prideful and protective of things that can only be labeled 'speculation' or 'personal opinion.' They are completely honest with themselves. They boldly declare certainties; yet are equally willing to humbly concede areas of uncertainty.

The controversial philosopher Rene Descartes commented, "If you would be a real seeker after truth, it is necessary that at least once in your life you doubt, as far as possible, all things."[3] Only the brave explore this region of thought. So desiring to be brave, I left my 'comfort zone.' I flexed my 'wings,' and caught the wind, rising to a higher vantage point.

Allowing my heart to be pliable in the sculpting hands of the Eternal Potter, I once again scrutinized my own belief system. Like a prosecuting attorney, I put my worldview on the witness stand and subjected it to an intense cross-examination—"How can truth be self-contradictory?"—"How can beliefs so opposite coexist harmoniously?"

In *The Great Learning* Confucius implied in similar words:

> *There is never a case where the root is in disorder and yet the branches are in order.*[4]

It seemed my 'roots' were in disorder. How could my 'branches' truly be in order? Then the dam broke and a flood of questions rushed in. Is there a right way to God and a wrong way to God, or is every 'path' equally effective? Are some religious practices and beliefs based more on myths, traditions and ceremonialism than the truth? How do we discern the difference between what is correct and what is incorrect?

Can verifiable concepts be extracted out of every religion to create some new, unflawed, composite belief system? Is truth really subjective? Can each person 'create' his or her own spiritual reality? Or is truth objective? Is it the same for every person, regardless of whether or not it is acknowledged and accepted?

If 'God is one,' should we embrace all religious practices and beliefs as having equal legitimacy without examining them to either prove or disprove their claims? Are all the religions of the world just a huge combination of personal opinions and private interpretations concerning the nature of spirituality? Or are there absolutes, spiritual parameters that are the same for everyone?

Is there a solid rock of inspired truth, a firm foundation on which we can build our future hopes?

Of course, these are not only questions I needed to ask myself. These are questions that have eternal importance for all of us, questions that surely led you to this book, questions that will continue to occupy our attention as we continue our journey into the next three sections.

PART 3

MY SPIRITUAL JOURNEY

"The unexamined life is not worth living."
Socrates[1]

"Religion alive...calls the soul to the highest adventure it can undertake."
Huston Smith[2]
(*See special note: p. 329)

Monumental moments are significant turning points in our lives. For the remainder of our days we can look back to these moments—decisions, events, experiences—and feel their worth and their warmth all over again. It's as if a monument is erected in our souls that we can visit to have our vision and zeal renewed.

According to Buddhist tradition, Siddhartha Gautama encountered such a 'monumental moment' around the age of twenty-nine. Modern thinkers might even term it a 'personal paradigm shift' (a private transformation in lifestyle and beliefs that effected a societal change). Though sheltered all his life within the confines of a royal palace, he dared to venture into the outside world. According to legend, it was then that Siddhartha viewed what has since been titled "The Four Sights"—a sick man, an old man, a corpse and an ascetic.

No longer could he remain spiritually asleep on a bed of princely ease. Having witnessed the suffering that abounds in this world, he was shaken, jarred from a self-serving mentality. The resulting desperation to find answers became the raw building material necessary for constructing a new life.

The palace protege made a radically unorthodox decision. Walking away from the opulent surroundings to which he had grown accustomed, he turned instead down the narrow path of renunciation. Hoping to transcend the natural world, he subjected himself to intense ascetic disciplines. Then after a number of years, while meditating under the Bodhi tree, he claimed to receive an experience of Ultimate Reality. At that point, according to those who subscribe to his philosophy, he became the "Buddha," the "Awakened One," the "Enlightened One."

Even if we do not agree with Buddha's conclusions, most of us can definitely relate to him—for we can isolate certain heart-touching incidents as defining moments in our lives. A near-death experience in my freshman year of college proved to be a pivotal point for me.

That almost-tragic night, I had the distinct impression that my soul was actually leaving my body and passing into a very frightening and dark void. I felt totally unprepared. I have heard it said that those who desire to die well, must first learn to live well. I certainly had not been living well, so I wasn't ready to die well either.

> *"Those who desire to die well, must first learn to live well."*

There was nothing pleasant about my encounter with this ever-present stalker of the human race. Yet it proved to be extremely beneficial. What looked like nothing more than a negative experience became a positive one, because I emerged with a new set of values. My former life was no longer attractive or fulfilling to me. Quite the contrary, it seemed overwhelmingly senseless, selfish and vain. The pursuit of pleasure left my heart empty. Temporal goals that had been all-consuming seemed frustratingly unimportant.

Earn a college degree? Pursue a career? Become financially secure? For what—if ultimately a grave was waiting somewhere in my future? That inward voice kept probing and prodding with admonitions similar to the one given to Horatio in the Shakespearean play, "Hamlet": *"There are more things in heaven and earth…than are dreamt of in your philosophy." (Hamlet 1.5.167-8)*

Like a blind man I stumbled through the darkness, grasping for something of substance. I was desperate to go beyond my self-imposed boundaries and find lasting answers. Once again, an inward sense of desperation became "the raw building material necessary for constructing a new life."

Religion took on a renewed importance. I was raised a Roman Catholic. Until my early teens I was very devoted, but the idea that Christianity was the only way to God, to the exclusion of all other religions, just seemed too narrow-minded, too unreasonable. Besides, I decided I could no longer embrace something just because it was part of my cultural or family belief system. I purposed to 'wipe the slate clean' and start from a pure and unbiased beginning point.

For many years I served as an altar boy in the Catholic Church. (second from left)

Socrates said, "The unexamined life is not worth living." I resolved that beliefs left unexamined might not be worth much either...at least, to me personally. Intending to explore various religions of the world with an open mind, I set out on a quest for "True Light." Even though I recognized I was studying the revelations, theories and opinions of others, my primary goal was to experience God for myself. I had faith that

> *"The unexamined life is not worth living."*
> Socrates

something somewhere would prove to be my connection with Ultimate Reality.

Elizabeth Barrett Browning's words well describe my mindset at that time:

> *Earth's crammed with heaven;*
> *And every common bush afire with God;*
> *But only he who sees takes off his shoes,*
> *The rest sit round it and pluck blackberries.*[3]

'Blackberries' held no interest for me any longer. I was willing to 'take off my shoes' and look at things differently. I was definitely searching for my 'burning bush.' All of this was definitely progress in the right direction. Little did I anticipate the unique turns my life would take before reaching this goal. The first main milestone in the road was...

AN ENCOUNTER WITH FAR EASTERN RELIGIONS

I began reading a lot of literature on Far Eastern religions and related subjects. The new phraseology filled up my mind: yoga, astral projection, mantras, chakras, the third eye, Nirvana, God-consciousness—all of these things sounded very intriguing and appealing.

Then in the fall of 1969 I went to hear Yogi Bhajan: a guru from India who claimed he came to North America to help the 'flower child,' 'peace' generation find their way spiritually. He taught us about yoga (a word literally meaning 'to be yoked,' the inference being that the goal of the devotee is to be 'yoked with God'). He explained that this 'union' could be achieved through various means, especially prolonged meditation. With his full beard, long black hair and intense dark eyes, this teacher of Far Eastern mysticism was somewhat imposing and quite convincing.

However, it was much more than the mystique surrounding this tall, muscular, turban-clad Sikh that attracted me. It was more than the passion he displayed concerning his beliefs. It was more than just the stimulus of a new approach to spirituality. It was the promise that I could actually experience God and penetrate the supernatural realm for myself.

This drew me to Yogi Bhajan's words and to the system of yogic discipline he was propagating (Kundalini Yoga, also called the 'yoga of awareness').

Attaining my 'higher Self' soon became the primary focus of my day-to-day existence. In between and after college classes, I used every available hour to pursue the goal of 'reaching enlightenment.'

"Without devotion to God, you will make yourself into a stale crumb to be eaten by the tiger of time."
Surdas

The Hindu Bhakti poet, Surdas, warned, "Without devotion to God, you will make yourself into a stale crumb to be eaten by the tiger of Time."[4] Appalled at the thought of becoming a 'stale crumb,' the following spring, I made the decision to use my time more wisely. Along with another college friend, I quit school to 'escape the jaws of the tiger.'

Packing up my belongings, I left the campus of Florida State University in Tallahassee, Florida, to help start an ashram in Daytona Beach (a commune where yoga devotees live together to more effectively practice their religious disciplines). Every day involved hours of meditation and Mantra Yoga (the chanting of certain Hindu words and phrases, called mantras, designed to carry a person to higher levels of consciousness). We also set aside time for the study of Hatha Yoga. This centered on physical exercises *(asanas)* and breathing exercises *(pranayama)*, both of which were aimed toward opening up something called *chakras* (supposed spiritual centers of energy in the body).

Our daily routine also included what could be termed Jnana Yoga (the study of sacred texts and other religious writings). Central to our attention were the Bhagavad-Gita, the Vedas (ancient Hindu Scriptures) and the writings of mystics and teachers like Edgar Cayce, Helena Blavatsky and Yogananda. Then, of course, there was participation in yoga classes several nights a week. Every waking hour and every activity, even bathing and eating meals, was controlled by a prearranged discipline. We were motivated by the supreme goal of all ashram devotees—our souls *(atman)* consciously awakened to oneness with the Oversoul *(Brahman)*. We were totally committed to the process.

Peculiar things began happening to me: a sense of peace and detachment from the world, what seemed to be occasional out-of-body excursions into some kind of higher realm, vivid spiritual dreams. The suffocating control of the natural realm seemed to be easing its grip. A kind of spiritual adrenaline surged through me daily—the prospect that I was wrenching myself free from what my teachers called *maya*, the illusion of this present world. I felt encouraged that transcendent love would prevail for me—that I, in an Adam-like sense, would one day awake out of spiritual sleep to find myself gazing into the face of my Maker. What could be better?

So I pursued. I followed hard after God, until every waking moment was pulsating with the heartbeat of a sacred quest. Nothing can express the cry of my heart at that time better than the following quote from the "Sayings of Shri Ramakrishna" (a teacher I respected at that stage of my life):

> *"If you fill an earthen vessel with water and set it apart upon a shelf, the water in it will dry up in a few days; but if you place the same vessel immersed in water, it will remain filled as long as it is kept there. Even so is the case of your love for the Lord God...if you keep your heart immersed always in the ocean of divine love, your heart is sure to remain ever full to overflowing with the water of the divine love."*[5]

"Full to overflowing"...to be *full*: that spoke of my own spiritual needs being met. With every passing hour, I yearned for such a state of intimate communion with God. But to *overflow*: that spoke of satisfying the thirst of others for spiritual truth. Though my chief, initial desire was to be *full* myself, day by day I began sensing even greater concern for the parched state of others. I needed to *overflow*. I concluded that such an unselfish state of existence was, and will always be—the high calling. I could no longer ignore the plight of a human race draped in spiritual ignorance. So after conferring with those in leadership, I left the ashram to go to another city and start teaching classes myself.

Feeling strongly compelled, I moved to the thriving city of Tampa, Florida. Four universities in that area (the University of South Florida, the University of Tampa, Florida Presbyterian and New College) opened their doors, allowing me to use their facilities for extra curricular classes. Several hundred students began attending. It was fulfilling. Touching other hearts with my 'touched heart,' changing other lives with my changed life—this was the continuation of a cycle, the evolution of true spirituality. Desiring to devote themselves more completely, a number of my students requested that I rent a suitable facility and form a small ashram. Gladly, I complied.

One night, during that time, I experienced what some have termed 'white light.' I had the distinct impression that my soul exited my body and was drawn into a very intense and timeless radiance. Though now I have a different interpretation of what really happened to me, at the time, I felt I was passing into the highest state of meditation. More assured than ever that I was truly on my 'path,' I intensified my efforts.

Then it happened! Very abruptly...very unexpectedly...a divine appointment interrupted what had become a predictable pattern of life. I wasn't even seeking for a new direction, but God knew my heart. He knew my love for him and my sincerity of purpose. So he intervened for me by orchestrating some very significant events that brought about...

A DRAMATIC CHANGE

Several key happenings took place within a few weeks that caused the most important 'turning point' in my life. First, the Tampa Tribune newspaper published a half-page interview with me. The reporter questioned me concerning my beliefs as a teacher of Kundalini Yoga and reported all that I was doing in the Tampa area. I was thankful for the exposure, certain that this free publicity would increase the attendance in my classes.

Little did I know that it would also alert a
local Christian prayer group to begin praying for me.

'Ong Namo Guru Dev Namo'
... *Michael Shreve begins the asanas*

The article from the "Tampa Tribune"

A member of the prayer group cut the article out of the paper and pinned it to their prayer board. From that point on, various members of the group committed to fast and pray for me—every hour of every day—until my conversion took place. During this same period, I received a letter from my college friend who left school at the same time I did, for the same reason. The content of Larry's letter was quite a surprise. It described an abrupt change that had just taken place in his life. Though he had been devoted to Far Eastern religions and certain yoga disciplines, something had radically transformed his whole approach to the things of God. Larry explained how he had received a blessed, supernatural experience with Jesus called being "born again."

Larry also claimed this experience was different than any experience acquired through yoga and that it validated Jesus' claim of being the only way to salvation. Larry's words were emphatic, "Mike, you'll never find ultimate peace through yoga and meditation. You have to go through the cross. You have to be born again. Jesus is the way to eternal life."

I wrote my college comrade back, explaining how happy I was that he had found 'the path of Christianity' to be right for him. However, I stated unequivocally that the claims of Christianity were too exclusive for me. My beliefs encompassed all the religions of the world. All were different 'paths' to the same God: that was my firm conviction. Strangely, though, I could not get Larry's letter off of my mind. His words kept echoing inside of me, even though their logic escaped me.

After several weeks, I decided I needed to deal with this issue. Dismissing Christianity without fully exploring its claims would be unfair—unfair to me and unfair to the One who claimed to be the Savior of the world. I realized I had never really given Jesus an opportunity to prove himself. So I concluded, "If he really was who he claimed to be, and if I don't test his teachings, I might miss the very thing I've been searching for…Besides, if Jesus allowed himself to be crucified for the salvation of the human race, I owe it to him to at least open my heart to the possibility of his claims being true." So one morning, though it involved an inward struggle, instead of following my usual yoga routine, I decided to…

Dedicate One Day to the Lord Jesus Christ!

I got up, as usual, about 3:15 a.m. That was our normal time of rising in the ashram. Beginning at 3:30, we would spend about an hour doing various postures and breathing exercises. Then from 4:30 to 6:30 we would sit cross-legged and motionless, in what is called the "lotus position," doing various kinds of meditation. Usually we practiced Mantra Yoga. That pivotal morning, though, I decided to break away from the ordinary.

Purposefully, I went into a room by myself and sat down. Though it seemed spiritually incorrect, I prayerfully dedicated the entire day to this One Larry claimed was the only "Mediator between God and men." *(1 Timothy 2:5)* Several times I confessed, "Lord Jesus, I commit this day to you. I believe, if you are real and if you are the Savior of the world, you will show me today." Then I began reading the Bible, spending most of my time immersed in the Gospel of John and the book of the Revelation. I was especially stirred by this latter book, with its powerful, prophetic imagery, especially those verses foretelling that final conflict between the forces of good and evil at a battleground in Israel called Armageddon (the valley of Megiddo).

As I read, I kept praying. Even though I was fully expecting some kind of powerful, supernatural visitation (a vision, an audible voice) initially, it didn't happen that way. For about ten hours that day I persisted, reading the Bible and seeking after the Lord Jesus. Then, right when I was about to give up and dismiss the claims of the Bible, God intervened, and I arrived at my...

MOMENT OF DESTINY!

Kent Sullivan was a senior at the University of South Florida. He was an accomplished student, but his educational pursuits had not brought him the answers to life or the peace of mind he desired. A few months before, he had been studying Far Eastern mysticism. Specifically, he was following the teachings of Yogananda, a well-known Indian guru who authored a popular book titled *The Autobiography of a Yogi*. Abruptly, though, Kent had switched from Kriya Yoga to Christianity.

Kent Sullivan

Though I had never met Kent personally, I was well aware of his unexpected 'conversion.' It was the 'talk of the town' among those involved in yoga and meditation. All of us were wondering, "How could he do it? He was recognized as one of the most advanced students of yoga in the Tampa area. How could he get involved with people who teach that Jesus is the only path to salvation?" Not only were we stunned over Kent's 'departure from the faith,' our assessment was that he had opted for a lesser path. I mused, "How could anyone who understands the concept of 'all religions being one' ever depart from it? What changed his mind?" Of course, as I pondered these things, I had no idea that....

Kent belonged to the very prayer group that was praying for me.

That divinely appointed day, Kent decided to wash his dirty clothes. He had a free hour between classes. It was a perfect time to take care of a boring, but necessary task. With an armful of clothes up to his chin, he got about halfway through the door of the laundromat when the Spirit of God stopped him. He heard that still, small voice in his spirit say, "Don't go in there. I have something else for you to do. Get back in your van and drive where I lead you." It all seemed impractical and illogical. Besides, being a new Christian, Kent was not used to having his plans interrupted by the Holy Spirit. He submitted to God's design, though, thinking it quite peculiar that for some reason God did not want him to wash his laundry. Of course, he had no idea that about two miles away...

The yoga teacher who had been the object of his prayers for several weeks was hitchhiking, trying to catch a ride to the University of South Florida.

Even though I had spent the day focusing on the claims of Christianity, I was on my way that afternoon to conduct one of my yoga classes. (Because I had renounced ownership of all unnecessary material possessions, I usually had to walk or hitchhike everywhere.) While standing on the side of the road, I was still praying that if Jesus was 'the Way,' he would somehow reveal himself.

As Kent drove, the Spirit of God impressed him to make several definite turns, eventually leading him down a road directly behind Busch Gardens. He was still wondering why he was doing all of this when he noticed a unique-looking, young man 'thumbing' for a ride. With long, curly, brown hair, a long beard and loose-fitting Indian-style clothing, I definitely looked the part of a Western devotee to Far Eastern religions. Kent never picked up hitchhikers, but felt strangely 'led' to pull over. As I opened the door and stepped in the van, my heart started racing in my chest, because...

Taped to the ceiling of Kent's van was a large picture of Jesus.

I knew this was no mere coincidence; I knew this was my answer.

My mind and heart felt charged with anticipation. After a few minutes of silence, Kent blurted out, "Friend, can I ask you a question?" Without hesitation, I responded, "Yes!" He immediately asked, "Have you ever experienced Jesus coming into your heart?" I quickly answered, "No, but when can I? I've been praying about the experience all day long."

Kent's face broke into a look of surprise. He certainly did not expect me to respond so quickly. He offered, "You can come to our prayer meeting tonight." I replied, "I don't want to wait for a prayer meeting. I've been praying all day. If this is a valid approach to God, I want to experience Jesus right now." Thrilled over my eagerness, Kent pulled out of the traffic into the first parking lot he could find. After turning the engine off, he invited me to sit with him on the floor of the van. Pulling the curtains behind the front seats so we would have privacy, he began carefully explaining the way of salvation. Then, right when I was on the verge of embracing the Christian approach to salvation, my own intellect became....

A Very Difficult Stumbling Block!

A compelling thought gripped my mind. If I was going to be sincere during this time of prayer, I had to first deal with some disturbing doctrinal issues. One by one, I brought up traditional biblical concepts that were very perplexing to me. With each question or comment Kent would calmly reassure me with the words, "Don't worry about that. JUST TRY JESUS!" As I pinpointed certain Far Eastern beliefs I felt I could never give up, Kent kept emphasizing, "Don't concern yourself with those things, JUST TRY JESUS!"

Being a former student of yoga himself, Kent understood my apprehension. He could relate to the protectiveness I felt toward my belief system. He showed tremendous wisdom. He knew that if we got involved in some deep discussion over doctrine, I might turn my heart away from the experience of Jesus altogether. So he kept emphasizing the essential thing. Repeating Jesus' words, he explained, "Except a man be born again, he cannot see the kingdom of God." *(John 3:3 KJV)*

Kent understood something I am very convinced of now. It takes a spiritual rebirth before anyone can see or comprehend the mysteries of God's kingdom. Because Jesus is "the truth," once he comes into a person's heart, he sets in motion a process of leading that person, by the Holy Spirit, into all truth. *(See John 14:6.)* So the most important thing is for seekers to first experience the reality of Jesus' personal presence. Then they can far more easily sort out all the related truths that surround this central theme of true Christianity.

"It takes a spiritual rebirth before anyone can see or comprehend the mysteries of God's kingdom."

Kent finally persuaded me. His logic was strong enough to nudge me into the unknown.

Besides, I was so hungry to know God; temporarily setting my intellect aside wasn't too much to ask. Just repeating a single petition seemed much too simple—but again, I was willing to try. We bowed our heads and this newfound friend led me in a prayer for salvation:

> *"Lord Jesus, come into my heart. Wash me in your blood. Forgive me of my sins. By faith, I receive the gift of eternal life. Fill me with your presence and your love. I acknowledge that you died for the sins of the world and that you arose from the dead. I accept you now as Lord of my life."*

I felt a warm sensation in the deepest part of my heart. Something different was taking place, much different than anything I had ever experienced. As a child, I attended mass regularly at various Catholic churches. I served for years as an altar boy and attended parochial school. The nuns and priests who influenced me during that formative stage of my life inspired me with their humility, sincerity and commitment. But still, in all those years—filled with numerous rituals, traditions, and ceremonies—I had never received such a real encounter with God.

Paul, the apostle, called this experience "the washing of regeneration and the renewing of the Holy Spirit." *(Titus 3:5)* Though I still had many questions stirring in my heart, the inner 'knowing' that I had finally been restored to a right relationship with God filled me up. I was confident that if I died, I would spend eternity in heaven. The indescribable peace of God settled like fresh dew on my soul. I was changed—and I knew it.

Vietnamese Buddhist, Thich Nhat Hanh, writes, "If we touch the Holy Spirit, we touch God, not as a concept, but as a living reality."[6] This was definitely my mindset as a yoga teacher and I still believe it to this day. However, I now understand that experiencing something 'supernatural' may or may not indicate an actual experience of God. I sincerely *thought* (just as Thich Nhat Hanh) that I was experiencing the "living reality" of the Holy Spirit during my yogic disciplines, but after being born again, I realized this was definitely not the case.

For several days following this life-changing experience, I announced to all my students that I had finally encountered this "living reality." I confessed that I had been wrong in my previous assessment of Ultimate Reality, that I never encountered the true Spirit of God until I went through Jesus, and that consequently, all of my yoga classes

> *"If we touch the Holy Spirit, we touch God, not as a concept, but as a living reality."*
>
> Thich Nhat Hanh

would be cancelled. Though such an abrupt change was shocking to my students, many trusted my newfound insights and readily accepted Jesus as Lord of their lives.

I knew from the beginning it was impossible, doctrinally, spiritually, and logically, to blend yoga with Christiannity. So, I closed the ashram and moved to a Christian commune in Central Florida. For about four months, I spent many hours studying the Bible and seeking God in prayer, in order to know God's will for the next phase of my life and to develop a more intimate relationship with the Savior of the world.

"God is truth and light his shadow."

Plato

In the early Spring, I was baptized in water (an important symbolic ritual in Christianity). Properly administered, it involves full immersion, because it represents identifying with Jesus in his death and burial. Emerging from the water symbolizes partaking of the power of Jesus' resurrection and walking in newness of life. *(See Matthew 28:19, Acts 2:38, Romans 6:4, Colossians 2:12.)*

It was a pivotal time, a blessed season of radical transition. As Plato observed, "God is truth and light his shadow."[7] Because the God of heaven was finally overshadowing me with his personal gracious influence, the light of truth began to shine more and more with every passing day.

(A more detailed version of my transformation story is available in over 10 languages as a free download on www.thetruelight.net *The Highest Adventure: Encountering God.)*

PART 4

STRIKING THE TOUCHSTONE

30 Relevant Questions and Answers

> *"Part of finding the 'True Light' involves discerning correct doctrine from that which is the product of man's propensity for inventiveness in spiritual matters, his impressionable nature, and his passion for religious tradition."*
>
> Mike Shreve

> *"Any doctrine that will not bear investigation is not a fit tenant for the mind of an honest man."*
>
> Robert Green Ingersoll: *Intellectual Development*[1]

A touchstone is a hard, black stone that can be used to determine the quality of gold. The test involves striking a piece of gold against the touchstone. The color of the resulting streak indicates the purity of the precious metal. In a similar sense, seekers after "True Light" must take all personally held theories about the nature of God, man and the universe, and 'strike' them against the 'touchstone' of irrefutable, eternal truth.

After experiencing salvation through Jesus, in a spiritual sense, I subjected every belief in my worldview to such a test. Though I had absolutely no doubts concerning the reality and exclusivity of Jesus, in all honesty, at first, I was not fully convinced of the infallibility of biblical revelation. Yet I realized that it was biblical instruction concerning salvation that alone ushered me into the true experience of God. So it seemed logical to assume that the rest of the Bible was also inspired and dependable. I wasn't sure—but I was willing to perform what could be termed an 'objective, spiritual experiment.'

Beginning with the premise that the Bible is the source of irrefutable, eternal truth, I took each doctrine I previously embraced as a yoga teacher and struck it against the 'touchstone' of the Word of God. I surmised that I might be able to 'rescue' some of my Far Eastern beliefs and export them into the framework of Christianity. Almost always, this proved to be impossible.

Then one day, all the data I 'computed' fell into place. Ironically, I recalled a singular comment from a certain guru that helped me view my former beliefs from a totally different perspective. It all hinged on the Far Eastern concept of "Avatars" (incarnations or physical manifestations of God on earth).

I distinctly remembered this guru sharing that because Jesus was an Avatar, he could only speak the truth. Reflecting on this comment, I felt almost suspended in time and space. It suddenly dawned on me, "If merely in the role of an enlightened Avatar (one of many), Jesus could only speak the truth, what about the biblically assigned role of being the *only* incarnation of God? If he were 'just another Avatar,' why did so many of his teachings contradict the Far Eastern religious views I promoted as a yoga teacher?" Why did he teach one life as opposed to reincarnation? Why did he teach about an external, personal God who would enter the hearts of believers when I taught that an impersonal spark of divinity already resided within every human being? Why did Jesus teach a final, spectacular, permanent emergence of a new creation, when my yoga teachers taught the endless continuation of recurring cycles universally?

As many adherents of my former mindset tend to do, I mused over the possibility that the early disciples or later translators may have distorted Jesus' teachings, removing any references to oriental mystical ideas. But what if that was not the case? What if the Bible was and is the correct record of the words of the Messiah—what then?

Purposing to maintain scholarly precision, I began pinpointing the areas of doctrinal conflict and carefully examining the biblical viewpoint, especially the teachings of Jesus. Topics like those discussed in the second section of this book occupied my thinking for months—the nature of God, the nature of the human condition, the nature of true salvation and the ultimate destiny of man, this world and the universe as a whole.

My conclusions were not only revelatory; they were revolutionary to me personally. In an incredibly beneficial way, they shook my world and lifted me to a new level of understanding. The unchanging touchstone of eternal truth prevailed and my worldview had to be adjusted accordingly. I emerged from the 'darkroom' of introspection with a new, fully developed belief system.

> *"Faith is the daring of the soul to go further than it can see."*
>
> William Newton Clark

William Newton Clark defined faith as "the daring of the soul to go further than it can see."[2] My first uncertain steps of faith toward the Lord Jesus definitely did take me much further than I ever envisioned at the start. The same thing can happen for you, if you are hungry for spiritual realities.

So let us proceed together. Like spiritual metallurgists, let us strike each one of the following issues against the 'touchstone' of logic—and then, against the 'touchstone' of biblical truth—to discern that gold which is pure and that which contains doctrinal 'alloys' that must be purged from our thinking. Throughout the process, may we always keep in mind—

Truth is everlasting. It endures forever and cannot be amended or modified. Those who receive it are transformed forever.

"STRIKING THE TOUCHSTONE"
30 RELEVANT QUESTIONS AND ANSWERS

In the remainder of this section, you will find thirty of the most relevant and essential "Questions and Answers" for anyone seeking after "True Light," especially those who have been pursuing or exploring the nature of truth as presented in various Far Eastern religions or New Age spiritualities.

#1 Is there one God with one name (the view of Christianity, Islam and Judaism), or one God with many names (the view of Sikhism), or many gods with many names, all springing from one eternal essence called God (the view of Hinduism)?

#2 Are adherents of all world religions actually worshipping the same God?

#3 Is Ultimate Reality an impersonal 'Life Force' or a personal Creator?

#4 Does Ultimate Reality have a 'dual nature': both negative and positive, both darkness and light, both evil and good?

#5 Is the character of the Godhead perfection and unity, or imperfection and disunity?

#6 Is the use of deity forms (idols) a legitimate method of worship?

#7 Was Jesus the product of a sexual union between a man and a woman, or was he born of a virgin, the product of a supernatural conception?

#8 Where was Jesus during his hidden years?

#9 Was Jesus just one of many Avatars, or was he the only incarnation of God?

#10 What is the true meaning of this celebrated title: "the Christ"?

#11 Was the cross merely an example of "at-one-ment," or did it provide "atonement" for the sins of mankind?

#12 Are human beings divine in essence, destined to eventually become God?

#13 Prior to salvation, is the Creator internal or external?

#14 What does it mean to be "one with God"?

#15 What really is "the kundalini"?

#16 Which view is right: reincarnation or resurrection?

#17 Is our future really determined by past "karma"?

#18 Does salvation come by human effort or by the grace of God?

#19 What is the correct view of "desire" and "suffering"?

#20 Do we have a "sin-problem" or an "ignorance-problem"?

#21 Maya or deception: which influence is clouding the minds of men?

#22 What is the origin of evil?

#23 Mantras: are these repetitious phrases a valid tool in reaching God?

#24 Was Jesus 'a' Door or 'the' Door to eternal life?

#25 Are all human beings "children of God," or is this status only granted to those who fulfill certain conditions?

#26 What did Jesus mean when he said, "You are gods"?

#27 Are there any other quotes of Jesus that some interpret as being supportive of the New Age or Far Eastern doctrinal stance?

#28 How will this present age end, and what is the meaning of the "Second Coming of Christ"?

#29 Which is the correct view of the future: endless cycles of creation and destruction (the view of Hinduism and other Far Eastern worldviews), or one ultimate universal change (the view of Christianity)?

#30 Do doctrinal differences between various sects have any relevance since, according to some belief systems, we are all headed for the same ultimate destiny anyway?

The answers to these questions are vitally important!

> **1** **Is there one God with one name (the view of Christianity, Islam, and Judaism), or one God with many names (the view of Sikhism), or many gods with many names, all springing from one eternal essence called God (the view of Hinduism)?**

Dealing with this question is first an issue of semantics. Three people can say, *"There is only one God!"* yet mean three different things by the same statement. The first two concepts are inclusive; the third is exclusive.

One religionist might be suggesting, *"There is only one God* that people of all religions worship. However, they use different names for him, and they possess different interpretations of his character and being" (the view of Sikhism). Another might mean, "There is one underlying, impersonal essence behind all personal gods that are worshipped. These gods are not actually the same, but they spring from the same source" (the view of philosophic Hinduism).

The final concept would be, *"There is only one God* to the exclusion of all others, identified by the correct name or names which are associated with the correct interpretation of his character and being" (the view of Christianity, as well as other monotheistic traditions). The first two viewpoints could be described as inclusive (including all religions and all gods). The third view is exclusive (excluding all other religions and all other gods).

Though I am deeply moved by the compassion and tolerance that normally motivates those who choose an all-inclusive view, may I offer the following observation? If God were to accept, and respond to, all of the names assigned to him in various worldviews, he would be making a confusing and contradictory statement about his own character.

For instance, if God responded to the name Zeus, he would automatically be indicating divine approval of the pantheon of gods promoted in Greek mythology. If the name Brahman (Hinduism) or SUGMAD (ECKANKAR) brought a response, it would be an immediate disclosure that the Ultimate Source of all things is actually an impersonal cosmic energy. If the name Krishna connected a worshipper with God, he would simultaneously be acknowledging that he had 16,108 literal wives while on earth.

If God responded to the name Ein Sof, he would be verifying the Kabbalist claim that the Godhead has ten emanations. If he responded to the entitlement Sat Nam (the Sikh designation for God, meaning "True Name") he would be verifying Guru Nanak's claim that the God of the Muslims and Hindus is actually the same God. If he responded to the name Allah, God would automatically be characterizing himself as an omnipresent, omnipotent Spirit who has no Son (a basic doctrine of Islam) and that "there is no God but Allah" (a primary confession of faith in Islam). However, if God responds to the name Yahweh (the Old Testament revealed name) or Jesus (Heb. *Yeshua*, the New Testament revealed name) then he is showing approval of Christianity's claims: that he is a triune being, comprised of the Father, the Son, and the Holy Spirit, that he is a personal God, omnipotent, omniscient, omnipresent, transcendent, perfect in all his ways, and accessible only through the redemptive work of the cross.

Just suppose that the Bible is right: that Jesus really is the only "image of the invisible God" and that there really is "no unrighteousness in him": no error in his judgments and no flaw in his character. *(Colossians 1:15, Psalms 92:15)* If he responded in prayer to the name Indra (an ancient Hindu god) he would automatically be characterizing himself as a seducer of a sage's wife, who was cursed with a thousand *yonis* on his body (symbols of the female sex organ) as a result of his evil deed. I personally would not take on another man's name, especially if the true possessor of that name was a person of criminal or immoral behavior. Why should I expect God to be pleased with an arrangement just as undesirable?

The problem is this—through the millennia, certain persons, in an attempt to define the unseen spiritual realms, have attributed to numerous deities a great number of humanly-created titles, names, myths, and legends. Most likely, many have possessed a genuine love for God—yet, there is a vast difference between loving God and knowing God. I can personally testify that I loved God intensely long before I actually knew him. It was only after I met the Lord in a personal relationship that I came to understand his true nature.

I admit that some names or titles given to God in various religions do correctly define his character and attributes, such as the majority of the ninety-nine names Muslims attribute to God (e.g., the Living, the Eternal, the Supreme, the Tremendous, the Merciful, and the Compassionate). Undeniably, these are all actual personality traits of the true God, but not one is a personal name for him. Correct character titles for God can be discovered in many religions, but names that identify his actual person are another matter. So, the essential thing is correctly distinguishing this personal name of God.

With the exception of the one true God, I propose that all other 'gods' are humanly manufactured. They are the product of man's often sincere, yet erring attempt, to interpret the realm of the supernatural. Again, because the various characters assigned to these deities are in many ways a misrepresentation of the true character of God, he does not accept these names, nor does he respond to them. Furthermore, if seeking persons use these wrongly assigned divine names, they automatically associate them with the rest of the doctrinal base of the religion being referenced. In so many cases, if God allowed this, it would be counterproductive to the promotion of truth.[1]

Hindu Scripture strongly declares "nothing is more purifying than the holy name of God." *(Srimad Bhagavatam 6:1)* If this is true—and it is—then one of the chief pursuits of life should be a holy quest to know the true name of God (which is only discoverable in the Bible). The legendary founder of Taoism, Lao-Tzu, taught that 'Ultimate Reality' is an impersonal, cosmic energy force. He admitted, "I do not know *its* name; I call *it* Tao." *(Tao-te Ching 25,* emphasis by author) How heartbreaking it is that a person, longing to know 'Ultimate Reality,' is unaware of the correct name to use, and so invents one! Yet how often this happens![2]

Another very fitting example is Guru Nanak, founder of Sikhism. He was most likely a very sincere, pure-hearted man. His heartfelt prayers exude genuine love for God and passionate devotion to righteous principles. His life story is intriguing, especially the supreme effort he made to unite Hindus and Muslims. Guru Nanak insisted that repeating the wonder of the Creator's Name "is a stairway which leads to the Maker, an ascent to the bliss of mystical union." Another version of this same passage says, "the way to perfection, the stairs leading to honor." *(Japji 32)* There is great truth in this statement. Guru Nanak taught that the right designation for God is "Sat Nam" meaning "True Name." Yet those words are only descriptive of the very thing we all long to know. Yes, I agree with Guru Nanak. God does have a "True Name" and worshipfully uttering that name will usher us into his bliss-filled presence. But what actually is that "True Name"? Certainly this is something Guru Nanak longed to know, just as any seeker after "True Light," and something I believe he would have readily received had he been exposed to the correct revelation.

I believe with all my heart that I now have the answer. At certain pivotal, historic moments, God revealed different facets of his "True Name" to certain key biblical figures who then recorded this insight for others. Just as a human name is usually made up of several names, and some-times a title, so God's true name is a combination of all the names and titles that he has assigned to himself. God responds to those names and titles revealed in the Bible, because the character and doctrine attached to those names and titles correctly represent who he is, how he acts toward men, and the doctrinal base that is truly inspired.

In the Old Testament God assigned to himself various names that were then transferred to us in the Hebrew language, such as: Elohim ("God"), El Shaddai ("the Almighty God"), Yahweh-Rapha ("the Lord our Healer"), Yahweh-M'Kaddesh ("the God who Sanctifies"), and so on. Later on, when the incarnation took place, God sent an angel to Mary announcing what the name of the Son of God should be. Gabriel rejoiced to proclaim, "You shall call His name JESUS [Heb. YESHUA, meaning "salvation"] for He will save His people from their sins." *(Matthew 1:21)* This heaven-conferred name perfectly describes what Jesus was born in this world to accomplish (for he was God manifested in a human body, sent from heaven to bring *salvation* to the world). The promise given later in the New Testament is very plain—"Whoever shall call on the *name* of the Lord shall be saved." *(Acts 2:21, See Luke 1:31, Deuteronomy 6:4, 1 Kings 18:24.)* Notice this passage of Scripture does not say to call upon "*a name* for the Lord," but "*the* name of the Lord." (Of course, this includes the pronunciation and spelling of the name JESUS in other languages as well.)

I personally used a number of humanly assigned names for God unsuccessfully before I used the name of Jesus. I was sincerely wor-shipping God from my heart of hearts, but I was not "connecting" with God. Only when I called on the "True Name" of the true Savior did I experience true salvation and the true Spirit of God. I understand the logic of those who claim we are all worshipping the same God, however, this cannot be the case. Furthermore, some religions are atheistic and not even concerned with adoring the Almighty. Still others promote devotion to lesser deities who occupy subordinate roles in some huge pantheon of gods. I acknowledge that some worshippers are actually expressing heart-felt devotion to the Supreme Creator of heaven and earth, whoever they conceive him to be. In such cases, there is definitely a similarity of intent—a desire to love the Everlasting Father and contact him in prayer—but the fulfillment of this desire is only possible by going through "the door" *(John 10:9)*.

There are many ways this 'connection' between God and man has been conceptualized, but only one way it can be actualized. The Bible explains that the "Lord Jesus Christ" is a name "above every name" and there is "no other name under heaven given among men by which we must be saved." *(Philippians 2:9, Acts 4:12)* It is the triune name of the Triune God (the Lord=Father, Jesus=the Son, Christ=meaning anointed one, a reference to the anointing of the Holy Spirit). God honors this name because it identifies his true character and his present mode of working in this world. This is an essential point.

2   Are adherents of all world religions actually worshipping the same God?

First of all, not all world religions acknowledge a "Supreme Being." Some consider the universe to merely be the outcome of "cause and effect." Others misconstrue Ultimate Reality to be an impersonal force or level of consciousness, which does not interact with worshippers, instead of a personal Creator who does. But what about those who believe in a personal Creator? Are they all worshipping the same God? No, not really. In a very broad sense, they may all be casting worship upward toward the Source of all things, without actually connecting with that Source. The American Indian who praises the Great Spirit, the Hindu who acknowledges Brahma, the Muslim who worships Allah, the Sikh who sings songs of devotion to Akal Purakh (Timeless Being), and the Zoroastrian who honors Ahura Mazda (the Wise Lord) are all generating devotion toward the One they consider to be the Supreme Power of the universe. At times, they may even "generically" cry out, "O God, help me!" or "O God, I adore you," inclining their hearts toward the Almighty without using some name for him assigned in their religion. However, in cases like this, in their minds, they are still associating their prayerful cry with interpretations of the Godhead found in their worldviews. This in itself would block them from a real connection with the true and living God.

It is very important to note that all of these supposed 'Supreme Beings' are not *literally* and *specifically* the same God, since their personalities, attributes, and names are often quite different. Here is the fundamental truth that must be grasped. True Christians are worshipping God with understanding; others are worshipping without understanding, but in many cases, all are worshipping. I believe that even when a person is ignorant of the true nature of Ultimate Reality, genuine love toward God still does not go unnoticed in heaven.

The essentially important difference is this: even though the devotees and believers of these various religions are all generating worship *toward* God, except for the Christian believer, they cannot be in actual communion *with* God. In Acts 10, we find Cornelius, a centurion, who worshipped God in sincerity, but apparently, he was unaware of how to be in true communion with God—so God sent an angel to him instructing him to call for Peter. The apostle came and preached, and the Holy Spirit fell from heaven on those who gathered. God did not affirm that Cornelius' previous approach was sufficient, but because he had true love for God, the Lord revealed to him the correct means of salvation.

In a similar way, I was a sincere lover of God before I knew him and experienced union with him. I was a "worshipper" of God long before I became a "true worshipper." Jesus explained this mystery to a Samaritan woman many years ago in words that are still profound. He bluntly pointed out, "You worship what you do not know," then he added:

> *"But the hour is coming, and now is, when the*
> *true worshippers will worship the Father in spirit and*
> *truth; for the Father is seeking such to worship Him."*
> *(John 4:22–23)*

Worshipping in spirit—In this era, to be a true worshipper of God, a person must first have a regenerated spirit. The biblical view is that man is a triune being: body, soul, and spirit. *(See 1 Thessalonians 5:23.)* The body and soul are the primary functioning parts in ordinary human beings who have not been "saved." Human beings are "dead in trespasses and sins"—rendering the spirit nearly non-functional. *(Ephesians 2:1)* (See "Christianity" under *The Origin and Nature of Man*.)

The human spirit is saved or regenerated only through the experience of being washed in the blood of Jesus and born again. Only after this rebirth of the inner man can a worshipper truly contact the true and living God, for only then does the Spirit of God dwell within. The Holy Spirit that flows into born-again believers, then flows out of them, back to the Father, in the form of worship. Devotees of other religions may be very religious, saintly, loving, humble, and even powerful in supernatural ways, but this necessary facet of true salvation is still missing.

Worshipping in truth—There are five main aspects to fulfilling this requirement. Worshipping God "in truth" involves worshipping the Most High: (1) in sincerity; (2) in honesty; (3) with correct methods; (4) by embracing the true revelation of his name and nature; (5) by walking in the truth of the Bible and applying the truth to our day-to-day lives.

As a yoga teacher I passed on the first two points but missed the last three. I was sincere. I was honest with God. But I used non-biblical methods in trying to reach God. I loved God intensely. But I never experienced true communion with the Father—until I approached him using those methods endorsed in the Bible and until I came to him with the true revelation of his name and nature. When I fulfilled these requirements, I was granted access into his presence. It is not enough to be worshippers; we must be *"true* worshippers"—if we are to know the true God and enjoy a true relationship with him

---

3   **Is Ultimate Reality an impersonal 'Life Force' or a personal Creator?**

Pantheism—Many Far Eastern religions embrace some kind of pantheistic worldview: the belief that the universe is an emanation of God.

Pantheism identifies the Creator with the creation: all substances, forces and laws in this universe are essentially God in manifestation. "God is All and All is God." Ultimate Reality is an impersonal 'Presence' permeating all things—from the smallest atom to the largest, swirling galaxy. This is not a personal Creator who delights to interact with his creation, but a mere 'cosmic energy' (a supreme level of consciousness) expressing 'Itself' as minerals, plants, animals and human beings. In absolute pantheism, God does not exist apart from these things.

Modified pantheism, also called panentheism (pronounced pan'-en-the-ism), declares God to be the principle behind nature, the essence of life within all of creation. "God is in All and All is in God." He is both immanent and transcendent; he is in the world, yet beyond it.

Causal principle—Some religions and teachers reduce the Source of all things to nothing more than an underlying "Causal Principle." The Dalai Lama of Tibetan Buddhism expressed this opinion in a recent interview, claiming that "there is not an autonomous being [God] 'out there' who arbitrates what you should experience and what you should know; instead, there is the truth contained in the causal principle itself."[3]

Personal versus impersonal God—Contrary to the idea of a causal principle, the Bible teaches that there is a God 'out there.' He is a personal God (one who thinks, remembers, hears, speaks, plans, expresses emotion, demonstrates character, exercises will, and makes choices and judgments based on reason). Biblical revelation declares the universe to be a creative act of God, not an emanation of his own being. It also indicates that God is not contained by his own creation; rather, he transcends it. Yet this

External God' promises to manifest himself to those who call upon his name and indwell their hearts. So, a personal relationship with him can be received and experienced. He is also personally involved in the affairs of this world.

As some interpret it, an impersonal 'Life Force' would have to be a non-thinking, non-emotional, non-volitional cosmic Presence, incapable of hearing, seeing, communicating, or interacting with human beings. Challenging this concept, the Bible questions, "He who planted the ear, shall he not hear? He who formed the eye, shall he not see?" *(Psalms 94:9)* A cosmic energy force requires an elaborate system of magic formulas, incantations, symbolic rituals and other manipulative, esoteric methods to operate its power. A personal God is more interested in relationship than rituals—he desires from his offspring sincere love, adoring worship and submission to his Word and will.

In the Old Testament, we discover the God of Judaism to be a very personal God that cared for his people in a very personal way. He powerfully opened the Red Sea before them as they fled from Egypt. He audibly declared his Ten Commandments from trembling Mount Sinai to the entire camp of Israel. In their wilderness journey, he compassionately fed them with manna out of heaven and supernaturally produced water out of a rock to quench their thirst. An impersonal cosmic energy could never intervene in such ways for "Its" followers.

The incarnation—Then it happened, a pivotal event that would forever change the human race. The God of Abraham, in an attempt to communicate his true and personal nature even more effectively, visited the earth in a bodily form and walked among men. By angelic revelation, this incarnation of Deity was given the name Jesus (in Hebrew, Yeshua meaning "salvation"). This unique "man" was such a complete and perfect personification of God that he even asserted, "He who has seen Me has seen the Father." *(John 14:9)* Of course, not only did he image the Everlasting Father during his earthly existence; Jesus always has been and always will be "the image of the invisible God." *(Colossians 1:15)*

Two kinds of life—Far Eastern, pantheistic worldviews teach that the life of creation *is* the life of God, that the former is actually an emanation of the latter. In opposition to this view, the Bible teaches that there are two kinds of life—natural life (the life in the plants, animals and every human being) and divine life (the supernatural life of God). Natural life is not the same as divine life. The Bible differentiates between these two by using two different Greek words for the word "life." Generally speaking, when the natural life (temporal life) of a human being is being described, it is *psuche* (pronounced psoo-khay'). When divine life (everlasting life) is being described, the Greek word is *zoe* (pronounced zo-ay').

The breath of God—The existence of two kinds of life is excellently illustrated by what took place in the creation and fall of Adam (the person identified in the Bible as the first human being). After God shaped Adam from the dust, he breathed into his nostrils the "breath of life." *(Genesis 2:7)* What actually entered into Adam? Maybe we should first ask what God breathes. Does he inhale oxygen, hydrogen, and nitrogen? Does he have to breathe the gases that fill our atmosphere in order to live? Of course not! When God breathes, surely he breathes his own divine essence. When he breathed into Adam's nostrils, he breathed himself, his very own being, into this progenitor of the human race and Adam became a "living soul" (a Holy Spirit infused soul—*Genesis 2:7*).

When Adam fell, he lost this vital principle, this divine breath. The life-imparting Holy Spirit that enabled him to constantly commune with the Father in a personal way exited from his soul. Adam was still alive physically, but because of sin's entrance, he was dead spiritually. Though he still possessed natural breath, he no longer possessed divine breath. Though he still possessed natural, physical life and a fallen soul, he no longer possessed divine life. All of Adam's offspring have since been born into a similar state of spiritual death. We have natural life *(psuche)*, which is a gift from God, but until salvation takes place, we are devoid of divine life *(zoe)*.

The Bible records a very significant happening that took place after Jesus arose from the dead. After appearing to his disciples in the upper room, he breathed on them, saying, "Receive the Holy Spirit." *(John 20:22)* In essence, he was restoring to them what Adam lost—the breath of divine life. This could not happen until the blood of Jesus was shed, to cleanse the hearts of his disciples and qualify them for the indwelling of the presence of God.

Conclusions—It is important to note that when Christians are filled with this divine life of God, they do not *become* God any more than water becomes lemon juice when the two are mixed to become lemonade. Rather, they merge into oneness. The Spirit of God blends with the spirits of those persons he redeems, enabling them to have communion with him and to yield to the influence of his indwelling personality. However, both God and those he indwells maintain their separate and distinct identities.

We need to focus our attention also on God's initial statement concerning the creation of man. He said, "Let us make man in our image, after our likeness." *(Genesis 1:26 KJV)* This was fulfilled a number of ways, but one primary point needs to be emphasized. A basic law of nature is the fact that any living thing reproduces after its likeness. The genetic blueprint is passed on to the offspring to perpetuate any given species. Giraffes do not reproduce elephant-like offspring, neither do mice produce horses. Giraffes produce giraffes and mice produce mice. There is a perpetuation of like physical characteristics and like nature. On the basis of this observation, the following two logical conclusions can be reached:

⌣· If the highest expression of God is impersonal, then we who have been made in his image should also, on the highest level, be impersonal. But if God is a personal Being, on the highest level, we also should be personal beings. Christian doctrine pronounces this latter view the correct one.

⌣· We know that it is possible for a personal being, a human, to produce a force or energy source that is impersonal, but theoretically, it does not seem possible or logical that an impersonal force could actually produce personal beings. Even Hazarat Inayat Khan, the Sufi Universalist, insisted, "If God has no personality, how can a human being have a per-sonali-ty—we human beings who come out of His own Being."[4] Can an inanimate object like a rock produce an animate object like a tree? Of course not! Can a flow of electricity give birth to a host of angels? Absolutely not! Then the question must be asked, "Can an impersonal God produce personal beings?" Logic would dictate that our answer be in the negative.

---

4   Does Ultimate Reality have a 'dual nature': both negative and positive, both darkness and light, both evil and good?

In his teachings, Yogi Bhajan explained, "What is God? Is he six hands? Ten heads? Is he matter? Is he a body? No. He is cosmic energy: it prevails through everybody. All that we can feel, can know, or can imagine is God. His identity is Nam because he is Truth; that is why we call him *Sat Nam* [meaning either "True Name" or "Truth is his name"]. He is Yin-Yang; he is positive and negative. He is male, female. He is the Creator and his creation."[5]

In describing God as *yin-yang*, Yogi Bhajan was drawing from Taoism, the ancient religion of China. *Tao* means "way," "path" or "eternal principle." This religious system does not promote the concept of a personal Creator. It teaches that there is a creative principle, an impersonal energy force that rules the universe. This 'force' contains both negative and positive attributes. It is both darkness and light, evil and good.

Someone can yield to the negative side of this 'cosmic force' and become an evil person, filled with 'darkness,' who may exhibit destructive, occult powers. Another person can yield to the positive side of this 'cosmic force' and become a powerful, saintly person, filled with 'light,' who may even manifest constructive, supernatural powers, for the sake of accomplishing good. The source of the power remains the same. Both can be traced back to that formless, impersonal, cosmic energy identified in Taoism as Ultimate Reality.

Congruent with this worldview, Yogi Bhajan taught that "in all darkness there is a light and in all light there is a darkness."[6] There are valid applications of this principle, which could be reworded and made acceptable within the framework of any religion. For instance, in every good person there is potential for evil and in every evil person there is potential for good, just as the *yin-yang* symbol portrays. However, in some ways, especially its extreme application, the Taoist worldview departs from the biblical one.

For instance, Yogi Bhajan taught "spirituality has three dimensions": black, red or white (a reference to magic or witchcraft). Black witchcraft involves utilizing 'cosmic energy' for evil purposes; red witchcraft involves utilizing 'cosmic energy' to manifest the miraculous, yet it draws attention to itself in an egotistical way. White witchcraft, or white magic, is the highest expression of the 'universal energy force,' causing a yielded person to "live humbly, universally, radiantly, truthfully, so that when one sees you, one sees God through you."[7] Again, the source of all three 'dimensions of spirituality' is the same basic essence of life. It is referred to as *prana* in Hindu philosophy. It is called *ch'i* in Taoism. The modern day movie "Star Wars" and its sequels have popularized this view of duality in the Godhead—with Darth Vader, the chief villain, using the 'Force' to manifest very dark, negative, occultic powers and Luke Skywalker, the hero, using the 'Force' to produce positive, noble powers and achieve righteous goals.

The opposite, yet complementary forces of *yin* and *yang* are represented in the T'ai Ch'i diagram that follows. Evidence of this all-pervasive duality permeates the natural world. These words identify the polarity of energies, *yin* being the negative and *yang* being the positive. Yet these opposites counterbalance one another. These two terms literally mean the "dark side" or the "sunny side" of a hill. When the *yin-yang* symbol below is spun or rotated it appears to blend together into oneness at the center, illustrating the union of these opposites.

YIN	*YANG*
Negative	Positive
Female	Male
Darkness	Light
Passive	Active
Earth	Heaven
Winter	Summer
Cold	Heat
Death	Life

Since evidence for the *yin-yang* principle permeates the natural universe, it is often assumed in certain Far Eastern religions that this same duality exists within the Highest Principle that governs the universe. In God, therefore, characteristics must exist that are at opposite ends of the spectrum.

The Judeo-Christian view of God is quite different. An Old Testament passage announces, "The Lord is upright...and there is no unrighteousness in him." *(Psalms 92:15)* The New Testament verse, 1 John 1:5, explains, "God is light and in him is no darkness at all." In the Lord Jesus Christ is "life, and the life was the light of men." *(John 1:4)*

Satan is directly the opposite. His very name means "hater" or "accuser." This fallen angelic being is "the destroyer," "the prince of darkness" "the prince of the devils,"—the one who wielded the "power of death" in this realm until Jesus' great victory over the grave. *(Matthew 12:24, Hebrews 2:15)* Satan is NOT a negative emanation of the divine Oversoul. Neither did God author the evil resident in him. Rather, he is an individual entity who willfully rebelled against God, who is an outcast from God's presence, and who is recognizably the adversary of the human race. He is the "thief" who comes to "kill, steal and destroy." As "the great Deceiver," he and his associate demons have succeeded in deceiving every person entering this world. *(See Isaiah 14:12–19, Ezekiel 28:12–19, John 10:10, 1 Peter 5:8, Revelation 12:9.)*

Thankfully, through his death on the cross, Jesus cast Satan out of his position as "the prince of this world" and reclaimed this exalted position for himself. As the resurrected Savior, Jesus is now titled the "Prince of life." *(John 12:31, Acts 3:15)* He commissions his representatives in this world to turn others from "darkness to light, and from the power of Satan to God, that they might receive forgiveness of sins." *(Acts 26:18)* The wording of this passage of Scripture makes it clear that the "power of Satan" is totally different from the "power of God," and that human beings are delivered from the former when they embrace the latter. The power of Satan accompanies deception in this world and the perpetration of evil. The power of God works in conjunction with the truth and the perpetration of righteousness. They do not come from the same source.

The related Far Eastern doctrines of pantheism (All is God) and monism (All is One) give birth to this notion of God's nature being a blend of darkness and light. If God is the essence expressed in all of creation and if all things are one, then evil and death must spring from him, as well as goodness and life. But if God is a transcendent Being who exists apart from the physical universe, the dark and evil things that abound in this world cannot be ascribed to him.

---

5   **Is the character of the Godhead perfection and unity, or imperfection and disunity?**

According to traditional Hindu theology, the highest expression of God is the impersonal Brahman, the Source of perfect awareness and perfect bliss. However, this perfect, original Source has expressed 'Itself' in numerous gods and goddesses who are often found to be much less than perfect. Invariably, all of these deities have character flaws and areas of weakness or vulnerability (as is the case in all polytheistic religions). Major conflicts are recorded even among the highest gods. I realize that many Hindu people revere these gods deeply. However, I plead with such persons to prayerfully consider the following observations concerning certain deities worshipped in that worldview:

Brahma, Vishnu, and Shiva—Brahma, Vishnu, and Shiva make up the Hindu triad (Trimurti). Brahma (the Creator god) initially possessed five heads. This came about because his female companion, Saraswati, being timid, was always trying to avoid his gaze. So, he created five heads, allowing him to see her at all times, no matter where she moved. Later on, his head count was reduced to four. The god Shiva irately destroyed one of his heads just because Brahma offended him.

Krishna—Krishna is described in the Bhagavad-Gita as an Avatar, the eighth incarnation of Vishnu, entering this world "for the protection of good men, for the destruction of evil-doers, for the re-establishment of piety." *(Bhagavad-Gita 4:8)* His exhortations seem to answer many questions concerning life, suffering, purpose, and eternal destiny—for those who subscribe to Hinduism and some related Far Eastern or New Age worldviews. Yet this Hindu deity seems to exhibit, at times, what many would interpret as human frailties. For instance, as a child he is described lying and stealing butter. Devotees have logical explanations for these things. It is perfectly acceptable for Krishna to lie, in order to provide protection or pleasure to his people. And because Krishna made all things, the butter belonged to him anyway, so it was not actually 'stealing.'

Another inclination that 'outsiders' might label 'peculiar' is Krishna's habit of hiding the clothes of women who are river bathing. Devotees simply interpret this to mean Krishna's power to remove shame. Krishna is also portrayed luring women, some the wives of other men, to dance with him in the moonlight. They become so caught up in this romantic adventure that each woman feels he is making love to her alone. This, too, is often interpreted symbolically—representing Krishna's power to woo devotees away from human ties and worldly attachments by his overpowering love.

Though Krishna does have a preferred mistress named Radha, while he was on the earth he married 16,108 women making them his queens. Eight were married individually; the remaining 16,100 were married all at once after Krishna delivered them from the Demon King, Bhaumasura. Swami Prabhupada of ISKCON interprets this information quite literally, explaining that Krishna "expanded himself in 16,108 forms" so he could be personally and simultaneously present in a palace with each of these 16,108 wives.[8] In the Srimad Bhagavatam Krishna is described fathering ten sons by each of these women over a span of 125 years.

By the standards of most religions, such a large number of sexual relationships would be unacceptable behavior for any man pursuing godliness, especially one claiming to be a manifestation of God. A Krishna devotee, Romapada Swami, elucidated the ISKCON viewpoint, "Krishna's activities are not subject to judgment by ordinary morality for he is the creator, maintainer and destroyer and thus the owner of everything in existence…Everyone…is an energy of Lord Krishna. So, it is only proper for him to enjoy his own energies."

Ganesha—One of the more popular Hindu gods is Ganesha, depicted as having a human body, but the head of an elephant. He is worshipped as the 'overcomer of obstacles.' The legend goes like this. Parvati, Shiva's female companion, created Ganesha to guard her while she bathed. When Shiva returned home, Ganesha did not know him and consequently, refused to grant him entrance. Enraged, Shiva responded with violence, unaware that Ganesha was Parvati's 'son.' The result? Ganesha's head was sliced off. Upon learning his error, Shiva sent forth his servants into the forest, directing them to cut off the head of the first creature they encountered. They found an elephant. Upon their return, Shiva replaced Ganesha's severed head with the elephant's.

Indra—Though he was originally chief of the Vedic gods, Indra is now given very little regard. Maybe it has something to do with the disappointing behavior and resulting appearance of this ancient, though neglected deity. He is often depicted with a thousand marks on his body that look like eyes. These are actually *yonis*, symbols of the female sex organ. Hindu tradition states that this abnormal appearance resulted from a curse pronounced upon this god by a sage, whose wife Indra seduced. The *Ramayana 7,30,20-45* actually blames Indra with bringing adultery into the world.

Soma—This Hindu moon god, in a boastful gesture over his own strength, abducted Tara, the wife of Brihaspati, chaplain of the gods. Because he refused to restore Tara to her husband, a war erupted. The demons *(asuras)* assisted Soma in this conflict until Brahma intervened, compelling Soma to set Tara free.

Attributes of the True God

Contrasted to these myths, the God of the Bible is perfect in all his ways. *(See Psalms 18:30, Matthew 5:48.)* The following list describes his most glorious and praiseworthy attributes.

He is omnipotent—the all-powerful Creator of heaven and earth. Unlike Brahma, who lost one of his heads, the true God is not vulnerable; he cannot be damaged by an attack from any foe. Furthermore, he is the Lord of hosts, which in essence means, "the God of an army of angels who do his bidding." He would never degrade himself by enlisting an army of demons, as Soma did, to execute his rescue. *(See Isaiah 40:28, Jeremiah 32:7, Revelation 19:6.)* Being omnipotent, he is also tireless. Psalm 121:3–4 declares that God neither slumbers nor sleeps. On the contrary, Hindu mythology explains that when Vishnu sleeps, creation recedes into seed form, to be re-manifested when he awakes.

He is omniscient—a God of perfect knowledge. Unlike Shiva, who mistakenly decapitated Ganesha, the true God does not make terrible mistakes through ignorance. The Bible reveals that "his understanding is infinite" and that he "knows all things." *(Psalms 147:5, 1 John 3:20, See Isaiah 46:9–10.)*

He is omnipresent—Had Shiva been omnipresent, nothing could have escaped his scrutiny. He would have been fully aware of the creation of Ganesha. The true God's omnipresence is interconnected with his omnipotence and omniscience. Because he is everywhere, he can be completely cognizant of all that is happening in his universal domain and exercise his power as he sees fit. As Proverbs 15:3 states, "The eyes of the Lord are in every place, keeping watch on the evil and the good." *(See Psalms 139:6–16.)*

He is holy—a word meaning pure and separate from the world. He would never give moral standards to mankind and then fail to live up to those standards himself. He would never be found indulging in the kind of lustful, adulterous behavior associated with Indra. The Scripture plainly states God, in his transcendent state, is so holy he "cannot be tempted by evil, neither does He tempt any man." *(James 1:13, See Psalms 92:15, Isaiah 57:15, John 7:18.)* In his incarnate state, Jesus still remained perfect and sinless. Even as a child, he was never involved in lying or stealing, as Krishna. Furthermore, he did not participate in human procreative actions; he was never involved sexually with any woman and he never married, after the manner of this Hindu deity. As God, he remained totally separate from such temporal, fleshly activities.

He is everlasting—Some believe that except for Brahman (the impersonal Oversoul) and possibly Krishna (for those who consider him to be 'Ultimate Reality') all gods mentioned above have only temporary existences. According to the *Mundaka Upanishad 2,1,1* and the *Taittiriyaka Upanishad 3,10,4*—all deities will cease to exist when Brahman reverts back to an unmanifested state. They will be absorbed back into Brahman to be remanifested or reborn in the next era of cyclical manifestation. (See "Hinduism" under *Worldviews Contrasted: Cycles, Ages, and the Ultimate State of the Universe.)* On the contrary, the God of the Bible is everlasting. Psalm 90:2 proclaims, "From everlasting to everlasting, you are God."

He has a triune nature—The true God is a triune God. There is only one God, but he has manifested himself in three ways: the Father, the Son and the Holy Spirit. *(See Deuteronomy 6:4.)* The Father is the essence of the Godhead, the Holy Spirit is the emanation of the Godhead, and the Son is the "form of God," the "image of the invisible God." *(Philippians 2:6, Colossians 1:15)* All are co-equal, eternally existent, and one in substance. Though the Godhead is made up of three distinct 'centers of consciousness,' they are not divided. "These three are one," according to 1 John 5:7. This concept is not tri-theistic (three separate gods manifested from one source) such as the Hindu triad of Brahma, Vishnu and Shiva springing out of Brahman, who is described as the Supreme Source and Origin of all things. In Christianity, there is no Ultimate Reality above the triune Godhead. Neither is the Christian concept of God modalistic (a mono-personal God consecutively assuming three distinct forms during different eras of manifestation). He always has been, he is, and he always will be—a triune God.

He is personal, yet perfect—Ultimate Reality in Hinduism is an 'It,' an impersonal, cosmic energy—perfect, yet possessing no attributes. On the contrary, all lesser deities have personalities, but they are flawed, containing both negative and positive attributes. In Christianity, God is personal, but he possesses only positive and perfect attributes. He is not without personality (as Brahman); neither does he have a flawed personality (as all other Hindu gods). So, we find the true interpretation of God's nature exactly in the middle of the two erroneous extremes discovered in Hinduism.

The Godhead is in perfect unity—The composition of the triune Godhead is comparable to the composition of those human beings who are made in his image. Human beings are triune in nature, possessing a body, soul and spirit. If human beings were in a perfect state, these three parts would work together in perfect unity. In a similar way, though each member in the Godhead has his own individual mind, will and center of consciousness, there has never been a time when they worked in competition with, or in opposition to, each other.

When Jesus was baptized in the river Jordan, the audible voice of the Father spoke over him saying, "This is My beloved Son in whom I am well pleased." *(Matthew 3:17)* Simultaneously, the Holy Spirit came upon him in the form of a dove. After that notable event, Jesus boasted, "I do nothing of Myself; but as My Father taught me, I speak these things. And He who sent Me is with Me. The Father has not left Me alone, for I *always* do those things that please Him." *(John 8:28–29,* emphasis by author)

Even Jesus' crucifixion took place because of his submission to the Father's will. When the Son of God intercedes over His people, he searches the "mind of the Spirit" so intercession is made "according to the will of God." *(Romans 8:27)* The Holy Spirit is then sent forth from the Father to accomplish God's purposes in this world. Jesus explained, "When He, the Spirit of truth, has come, He will guide you into all truth; for He will not speak on His own authority, but whatever He hears He will speak; and He will tell you things to come." *(John 16:13)* These few passages illustrate the perfect harmony and common purpose that always has and always will exist, unbroken and unchanged, in the eternal Godhead. This is far different than the internal strife, jealousy, and division that is often evidenced in the various pantheons of gods in other religions.

He is a Father—In none of the other main living religions is the Fatherhood of God emphasized as in Christianity. To those who accept him as their Savior, Jesus especially came to exemplify and reveal the Father. *(See Luke 10:22, John 14:8–9.)* Some 175 times in the Gospels alone, Jesus makes reference to the "Father." Over 250 times, God is titled this way in the entire New Testament. Furthermore, when the Spirit of Christ enters the hearts of repentant sinners, he automatically establishes them in a son or daughter relationship with the Everlasting Creator. The Scripture reveals that once the Spirit of God's Son enters the hearts of believers, they gain the legal, spiritual right to refer to God as "Abba, Father," meaning "dear Father." *(See Romans 8:15, Galatians 4:4–7.)* In other words, born-again believers inherit Jesus' relationship with the Father and his accepted and blameless status in the Father's presence.

---

6   **Is the use of deity-forms (idols) a legitimate method of worship?**

[Important note: worshippers who use deity-forms as objects of devotion normally do not describe this practice as idolatry. I would ask such persons to tolerate my use of the term and seriously consider my arguments against this religious tradition.]

What is idolatry? Basically, it means ascribing divinity and granting worship to something created: either created by God or fashioned by man. It is usually an attempt on the part of human beings to relate to the infinite, invisible God by identifying him with something finite and visible. Often this involves some kind of statue, image, or picture representing a being thought to be divine.

In the broadest sense, the term "idolatry" can be divided into at least eleven categories: (1) Worship of inanimate objects like stones, mountains, or rivers; (2) Worship of animate things such as animals, trees, or plants; (3) Worship of heavenly bodies like the sun, moon, or stars; (4) Worship of the forces of nature like wind, rain, or fire; (5) Worship of deceased ancestors; (6) Worship of humanly-authored, mythological deities by means of pictures, statues, or images; (7) Worship of angels, demons, or spirit-beings of any kind; (8) Worship of a process of life, specifically sexual reproduction; (9) Worship of any ordinary human being who claims to be divine; (10) Worship of an ideal or some philosophical view instead of the Creator; (11) Allowing anything other than God to become the highest priority of life, demanding one's full devotion and attention.

Several of the main living religions prohibit idolatry altogether— Judaism, Christianity, and Islam. Hinduism encourages and cultivates this custom. Three primary Far Eastern religions—Buddhism, Sikhism, and Jainism—began as reform movements teaching against the idolatry so prevalent in the predominantly Hindu culture of the day (though Jainism and certain Buddhist sects now promote the use of idols).

The Hindu people as a whole are probably some of the most intensely religious people in the world. (I have grown to respect and love them deeply for this.) In India and other areas with a large Hindu populace, idolatry abounds. Many shrines, both large and small, contain pictures and images adoringly viewed by a daily stream of worshippers. Often the gods portrayed in pictures or statuary are shown to have multiple human parts (four heads, six hands, etc.) or they bear an animal-like resemblance. Consider the popular Hindu god, Hanuman, who has the appearance of a monkey, or Ganesha, who has the head of an elephant, but the body of a human. At Hindu temples and private altars in homes, idol-gods are sometimes bathed, dressed, adorned with jewelry and flowers, 'fed,' and even tucked into bed at night.

Though many educated Hindus do not participate in these traditions, they usually react with kindness and tolerance. According to the Far Eastern worldview, every expression of worship, no matter how primitive, is a steppingstone toward Ultimate Reality. The Hindu mystic Ramakrishna explained this perspective with the following analogy: "We see little girls with their dolls, but how long do they play with them? Only so long as they are not married...Similarly, one needs images and symbols so long as God is not realized in his true form. It is God himself who has provided these various forms of worship...to suit...different stages of spiritual growth and knowledge."[9] Even though teachers of Far Eastern doctrine considered more mature admit idolatry is an inferior approach based on myths and false assumptions, yet they infer that it is an elementary step in the right direction. The stories of the activities of the Hindu gods may be fictitious, but on the level of the common people, they illustrate valuable spiritual truths.

Again, I must admit that I admire the spiritual passion that dominates the Hindu culture. Their evident hunger for spiritual realities has warmed my heart every time I have visited the land of India. In some ways it exceeds that which I have witnessed in a predominantly materialistic, and often hedonistic Western world. Yet, as I have said before, sincerity is not always an indication of veracity. Should idols be used in worship? Let me answer that question with a series of questions especially directed toward those religious leaders who promote the practice of idolatry, though they recognize its falseness:

> *Is it not unethical to promote something that is spiritually false as if it were absolutely true and valid? Does this not constitute a spiritual kind of coercion, a manipulation of the simpleminded multitudes who unquestionably believe? Moreover, how can false methods in seeking God, and false interpretations of the nature of God, ever lead to a true understanding of his attributes?*

Directly opposite to any tolerant view is the strong and unmistakable mandate spoken by the personal God of the Israelites from the top of Mount Sinai. The thunderclap of his voice declared, "You shall have no other gods before me. You shall not make for yourself an idol in the form of anything in heaven above or on the earth beneath or in the waters below." *(Exodus 20:3–4 NIV)* Such a blunt, divine edict leaves no room for discussion. God was very plain in instructing his people never to participate in this method of worship. He never said, "It may be wrong, but it is a step in the right direction, so I will allow it for a season."

Isaiah, God's prophet to the Jews, urged his listeners to be awakened to the falsehood of this practice. He revealed, "they have no knowledge, who carry the wood of their carved image, and pray to a god that cannot save." *(Isaiah 45:20)* A god who cannot hear, see or walk cannot intervene in the lives of 'his' or 'her' devotees.

Of course, most advocates of this practice would argue that the inanimate idol is only a crude representation of an existent spiritual entity, a literal god. The idol, though lifeless, is actually inhabited by the spirit of a god who *is* alive and who *can* hear, see and walk. Just suppose, though—if a particular god is the product of human imagination and doesn't actually exist—and if there is a spirit inhabiting a wood, stone or metal image of that god—what kind of spirit is it? The New Testament writer, Paul, explained that these spirit-beings are actually demons impersonating those 'gods' being sought. This was one of the main reasons he commanded Christians to "flee from idolatry." *(1 Corinthians 10:14, 20)*

Such prohibition of idolatry makes many customs and traditions in Far Eastern religious groups unacceptable to a Christian who embraces the biblical worldview. A good example is the initiation ceremony for those making a commitment to practice TM (Transcendental Meditation—the organization founded by Maharishi Mahesh Yogi). The opening ceremony of worship, called a *puja*, involves a Hindu hymn being sung before a picture of Maharishi's mentor, Guru Dev. The favor and presence of the Hindu gods are invoked and various offerings, including fruits and flowers, are presented to Guru Dev, celebrating his revered status in the spiritual lineage of this movement. The final prayer begins with a statement of faith concerning this world-famous promoter of TM:

> *"Guru in the glory of Brahma, guru in the glory*
> *of Vishnu, guru in the glory of the great Lord Shiva,*
> *guru in the glory of the personified transcendental*
> *fullness of Brahman, to him Shri Guru Dev, adorned*
> *with glory, I bow down."*

Advocates of Transcendental Meditation do not consider Guru Dev an Avatar. In Far Eastern religions, though, each person is said to possess a divine essence, so such worshipful actions toward a human being would not be considered wrong. This is not acceptable for a Christian, especially considering the invocation of those Hindu gods who according to the Bible are false gods and do not exist. *(See Acts 14:1–18.)*

---

7   **Was Jesus the product of a sexual union between a man and a woman, or was he born of a virgin, the product of a supernatural conception?**

As a yoga devotee I was introduced to the theory that Jesus was most likely an illegitimate child, conceived outside of marriage by an illicit sexual union between Mary and some unidentified man, probably Joseph.

My teachers insisted that because God was an impersonal 'Life Force,' he (or 'It') could never manifest himself (or 'Itself') in such a personal way: overshadowing a virgin and placing a seed of life within her womb. The Bible plainly teaches otherwise—that the Holy Spirit actually descended upon the Virgin Mary causing her to conceive. The resulting child was therefore titled "the Son of God." *(Luke 1:35)* This supernatural origin sets Jesus apart from every human being born into this world, before or since. It presents Jesus as being uniquely God, not just divine in the general sense promoted by a pantheistic, monistic worldview.

Altogether, five of the eleven main living religions—Buddhism, Christianity, Jainism, Taoism and Zoroastrianism—claim supernatural events surrounding the birth of the founder. Buddha was supposedly a preexistent heavenly being who was born in connection with his mother receiving a prophetic dream. Jainism teaches that its founder, Mahavira, was supernaturally placed in the womb of his royal mother and that he lived a sinless life. The most remarkable story concerns Lao-Tzu of Taoism, who, according to legend, was born a fully mature, wise, old philosopher after being carried seventy-two years in his mother's womb. Zoroaster, and all subsequent saviors in Zoroastrianism, are described being born of a virgin. So, this kind of doctrine is certainly not confined to Christianity.

Islam seems to oppose Christianity's claim, strongly disputing the thought that God could ever 'beget' a son, but the argument is really semantical. A passage from the Qur'an firmly declares, "Say, he is God, the One! God, the eternally Besought of all! *He neither begets nor was begotten* and there is none comparable unto him." *(Qur'an 112,* emphasis by the author, See *Qur'an 3:42–47, 19:22–36.)* This definitely is true in a natural, physical sense: God would never 'beget' a son through an actual conjugal relationship with a woman. However, in terms quite similar to Christianity's claim, the Qur'an reveals Jesus was born of the Virgin Mary by the 'inbreathing of the Holy Spirit.' It also declares that he lived a sinless life. Jesus is even called "the Spirit of God" seven different times.[10] Yet he is strangely placed in a position inferior to the prophet Mohammed, who was born of the normal reproductive process.

According to the Bible, virgin birth was a necessary characteristic of the true Messiah. Isaiah 7:14 prophesied that "a virgin shall conceive and bear a Son, and shall call his name Immanuel" (meaning "God with us"). Jesus was that holy child called Immanuel. He was *God with us*, born of a virgin. John 1:14 and John 3:18 even title him "the *only* begotten of the Father" and "the *only* begotten Son of God." This makes it clear that all other claims to this holy status are false claims.

Why was such an exclusive, spiritual status essential? In order to provide forgiveness for a sinful human race, there had to be a sinless, substitutionary sacrifice. Jesus could not have filled this role had he been conceived naturally, for the Bible teaches all human beings are conceived in sin. *(See Psalms 51:5.)* In other words, because of the sinfulness of all parents, a sinful status is imparted by conception. This results in a sinful nature being resident in children even before they are old enough to make conscious choices between resisting or yielding to evil impulses. The correct line of logic is this: that we human beings are not sinners because we sin, we sin because we are sinners. The sin nature of the first man, Adam, has been passed to all his offspring. *(See Romans 5:12.)*

Being conceived by the sinless Holy Spirit, Jesus was born with a sinless nature. He could, therefore, succeed in living a sinless life, something no other human being has ever accomplished. This understanding is basic to Christianity, a doctrinal hinge on which it turns. *(See Hebrews 4:15; 7:26–27, 1 Peter 1:19; 2:22, 1 John 3:5.)*

---

8   Where was Jesus during his hidden years?

As a yoga teacher I believed and taught that Jesus spent a great portion of the years between twelve and thirty studying under gurus in the Far East who taught him how to awaken his Christ nature. I based this view on the general opinion that prevailed among my peers, but even more so, on *The Aquarian Gospel of Jesus Christ* written by Levi Dowling and the teachings of Edgar Cayce.

Both of these individuals claimed to receive insight on this matter from the Akashic Records. This is supposedly an immense field of knowledge surrounding the earth containing a complete record of every thought, emotion, or action in this world since its inception. After becoming a Christian, I realized that the accounts given by Dowling and Cayce actually contradict each other. If they got their inspiration from the same source, why did this happen?

According to Edgar Cayce, Jesus was discipled by an Essene teacher named Judy. She later instructed him to travel to Persia and India in order to learn astrology and other yogic and spiritual disciplines. It should be noted that this is highly unlikely because the Essenes traditionally did not regard women as capable of filling such positions of prophetic influence.

Levi Dowling shares an altogether different version. He explains that an Indian prince named Ravanna obtained permission from Jesus' parents to take him to India in order to learn from the wisdom of the Indian sages. Dowling offers that Jesus studied under Brahmic masters for a season, then went on to Benares of the Ganges where he was mentored by Hindu healers who taught him their art, then on to Tibet. Finally, he journeyed to Egypt where he allegedly became part of a "Secret Brotherhood" in Heliopolis. There he advanced through seven degrees of initiation to become the Christ.

The Bible is largely silent about Jesus' hidden years. However, it does shed some light on what probably happened. When Jesus was twelve years old, he purposefully remained in Jerusalem after attending the Passover Feast with his family. Joseph and Mary, who thought he had been lost from their caravan, finally found him in the temple area discussing vital spiritual concepts with the teachers of the Word of God. Seeing their concern and responding to their request, the Bible explains, "he went down with them, and came to Nazareth, and was subject unto them." *(See Luke 2:41-51.)* The wording is very plain.

Years later, when Jesus announced his ministry in Nazareth at the age of thirty, "*as his custom was*, he went into the synagogue on the Sabbath day, and stood up to read." This wording suggests that this practice had been a pattern in his life for some time. When he announced his claim to Messiahship by quoting Isaiah 61, the awed listeners "marveled at the gracious words that proceeded out of his mouth" and questioned, "Is this not Joseph's son?" *(Luke 4:16, 22,* emphasis by author) Obviously, this unique Nazarene was a familiar figure to them all. Because of these and other pertinent arguments, I now contend that Jesus never departed from the land of Israel during his 'hidden years.'

The popular Christian author, Ron Rhodes, offers an informed and insightful observation:

> *"Among those who became angriest at Jesus were the Jewish leaders. They accused him of many offenses, including breaking the Sabbath, blasphemy and doing miracles in Satan's power. But they never accused him of teaching or practicing anything learned in the East. The Jews considered such teachings and practices to be idolatry and sorcery. Had Jesus actually gone to India to study under " the great Buddhas," this would have been excellent grounds for discrediting and disqualifying him regarding his claim to be the promised Jewish Messiah. If the Jewish leaders could have accused Jesus of this, they certainly would have."* [11]

---

9   Was Jesus just one of many Avatars, or was he the only incarnation of God?

The definition of an Avatar is an incarnation of God, or a god, into a fleshly form, usually human. In Hinduism, it normally refers to an incarnation of Vishnu. However, it has also come to include the reincarnation of any enlightened soul who has achieved final and absolute oneness with the Oversoul. Though delivered from all negative karma and released from the cycle of rebirths, the Avatar instead chooses to return to earth again for the duration of a human life. His purpose is to counteract evil and bring about change for good. We will inspect what the Bahá'í faith, Buddhism, Christianity, Hinduism, Jainism and others have to say about this subject.

Bahá'í—This faith does not accept the idea of Avatars, but they do believe in "Manifestations of God." This concept differs from the Hindu belief in Avatars in one main respect. Bahá'ís believe that these advanced and exalted individuals are infallible and "protected from sin." They are "theophanies: mirrors who reflect God's glory and reveal his attributes"... they are the "means of approach to God," being his "messengers": "bringers of divine revelation." However, they "are not incarnations of God; they do not embody the divine essence." [12]

There is no definitive list of recognized "Manifestations of God" available. However, Bahá'í authoritative texts do appear to verify fourteen: Adam, Noah, Salih, Hud, the Sabaean Manifestation (whose name is lost), Abraham, Moses, Krishna, Buddha, Zoroaster, Jesus, Mohammed, the Bab and Bahá'u'lláh. The Bab, whose name means "the gate," was, in essence, the 'initiator' of the Bahá'í religion, for he announced that he was the forerunner of the 'Promised One' (the Messiah). After he was killed, one of the Bab's followers, Mírzá Husayn-'Alí, claimed to be this Messiah (or Mahdi) who was to come. He assumed the name Bahá'u'lláh, meaning "the glory of God."

Buddhism—Buddha originally denied being a god. However, some of his followers eventually deified him. Though he preached a non-theistic worldview (it has been described as 'atheistic monism'), different branches of Buddhism include in their belief system worshipful devotion to numerous Buddhas (enlightened ones who have attained Nirvana) and bodhisattvas (saints or semi-divine beings who have renounced Nirvana and Buddhahood in order to help others achieve enlightenment). Both of these are considered worthy of worship and are somewhat similar to the Hindu concept of Avatars.

Hinduism—There are four main sects within Hinduism. Surprisingly, each sect has a different opinion concerning this important issue:

(1) **Vaishnavism** (devotees of Vishnu) insists that only Vishnu can incarnate.

(2) **Saivism** (worshippers of Shiva) asserts that God does not incarnate on earth.

(3) **Saktism** (followers of the goddess Sakti, or a wide variety of goddesses) maintains that Sakti, the Divine Mother, can manifest as an Avatar.

(4) **Smartism** teaches that all gods can have Avataric incarnations.

Hinduism has conflicting references in its sacred writings concerning the number of Avatars who have descended into this world. The *Mahabharata* gives three lists of Vishnu's Avatars: first, there are four mentioned, then six, and finally, a list of ten. The *Garuda Purana* lists nineteen Avatars of Vishnu, while the *Bhagavata Purana* lists twenty-two in one place and twenty-three in another. Since the time of the *Bhagavata Purana* the number of Avatars has been uniformly recognized as ten. They are: (1) The fish Matsya; (2) The tortoise Kurma; (3) The boar Varaha; (4) The man-lion Narasinha; (5) The dwarf Vamana; (6) Parasurama, also called Rama with the ax; (7) Ramachandra, called Rama; (8) Krishna; (9) Buddha, and; (10) Kalki (also called Kalkin) the last Avatar, who allegedly is still to come.

The stories associated with these various incarnations of deity stretch the imagination. For instance, the related stories of the first and second Avatars (the fish Matsya, and the tortoise Kurma) go like this. A demon stole the Vedas from Brahma. Consequently, a deluge was sent on the earth by the gods in order to drown the demon and recover the holy writ. Vishnu assumed the form of a fish, prophesied of the coming flood to Manu (the progenitor of the human race) and rescued him and his family by guiding his ship to safety. During this watery destruction of the earth, the cream of the milk-ocean (*amrita*) was lost. This was the 'elixir' that enabled the gods to reclaim their youthfulness and escape death. Working together, the gods and the demons succeeded in producing *amrita* by churning the ocean of milk. They utilized a mountain as a churning stick and Kurma (the tortoise Avatar) as a pivot on which the stick rested.

Like these two examples, most of the stories of Hindu Avatars contain no historical proof of the Avatar's existence. The animal-like incarnations are evidently mythological, which some Hindu teachers readily admit. Some proponents of Hinduism feel Rama and Krishna may have had an actual earthly existence. In later Hindu Scripture, Buddha is included as an Avatar, and he was most certainly a historical figure. However, in what could have been an attempt to invalidate his teachings, sacred writings explain that when Vishnu incarnated as Buddha, he "deluded the *assuras* [demons] and flouted the Vedas." *(Garuda Purana 3.15.26)* To "flout" is to disregard, to defy, to disobey or to ignore. How curious it is that God would visit the earth only to disregard and disobey, his own declaration of truth! Would it not seem much more logical that an incarnation of God would uphold and defend the truth in the sight of men?

One of the most peculiar aspects of Hindu teaching on this subject is one Avatar, Parasu-Rama (Rama with an axe) being in conflict with the next Avatar, Rama-chandra, because he broke Shiva's bow. Parasu-Rama was defeated in the clash and was, therefore, denied a place in heaven. If both Avatars are expressions of the Godhead, why would they strive against one another? God does not oppose himself. It seems unthinkable as well that a manifestation of God would actually be excluded from heaven. Christian apologist Ernest Valea challenges this myth, also asking, "Why didn't the first Rama leave in time? Or why couldn't he solve the problem for which the next Avatar came?"[13]

With regard to this doctrine, there are definitely projections for the future. Rabi Maharaj, author of *The Death of a Guru* explains, "Many orthodox Hindus believe that Kalki, the next Avatar after Christ, is due to appear on earth in about 425,000 years."[14] Kalki will put an end to corruption in this world. He will accomplish the final destruction of the wicked and usher in the renewal of creation and the resurgence of virtue in the next *mahayuga*. (See "Hinduism" under *Cycles, Ages, and the Ultimate State of the Universe* in Part 2.) Considering many Hindus embrace this belief (that the next Avatar will not arrive for many millennia), it is paradoxical that many Indian gurus and swamis in this era have themselves claimed to be Avatars.

One explanation of this paradox is the Hindu belief that there are both 'partial Avatars' and 'full Avatars.' Those labeled 'full Avatars' are the greatest spiritual teachers who have influenced the human race in profound ways. 'Partial Avatars' do not have this kind of impact. Of course, some of those who have claimed Avatarship might be quite unwilling to accept only a 'partial' status. And some of those who have appointed their leaders to such a position might readily reject such a demeaning proposition.

ISKCON—Lord Caitanya (1485–1533 A.D.) is considered one of the greatest leaders and promoters of devotion to Krishna. Adherents claim that he was a dual incarnation of both Krishna and his lover, Radha. This movement insists that there are two broad, primary categories of Avatars: (1) Direct forms of God (*Vishnu-tattva*). Krishna and Rama would be included under this heading. (2) Individual souls (*jiva-tattva*) who are empowered by God to manifest one or more of the following: knowledge, devotion, creative ability, personal service of God, authority over the material world, ability to support planets, or power to destroy evildoers and troublemakers. Jesus and Mohammed would be placed in this category.

Islam—To associate God with any human being or any material thing is an extremely serious sin, according to the tenets of this religion, and is called *shirk*. According to their traditional, doctrinal foundation, this concept of Avatars is absolutely unacceptable.

Jainism—Though its founder, Mahavira, denied the existence of any God or gods, he was eventually deified by his followers. They profess that he descended from heaven, that he was supernaturally placed in the womb of his mother, that he was sinless, that he possessed unlimited knowledge, and that he was the twenty-fourth Tirthankara (meaning "Ford-maker—a great teacher who guides his followers across the river of transmigration"). Mahavira is believed to be the final and greatest of all savior beings to make an appearance during this age. This notion seems to preclude the possibility of any other person occupying such an Avatar-like role since the death of the founder of this religion in 527 B.C. He and the other Tirthankaras are offered worship by Jainists.

Shinto—According to Shinto Scripture, all the Mikado (emperors) are considered divine descendants, tracing their ancestry back to the Sun-goddess, Ama-terasu. Therefore, all are considered to be "God incarnate." *(Nihongi, 2: 198, 210)* This is not a generally accepted doctrine now.

Sikhism—Guru Nanak preached passionately against worshipping any human being as God. He implored, "Why worship any one who is born and dieth? Remember the one God, who pervadeth sea and land."[15] Because of this, many Sikhs reject the concept of Avatars. They feel God does not take birth. One writer qualifies that interpretation explaining that some souls "do not need to take birth anymore. They have been liberated in some prior lifetime. They take birth only for our sake. When a person comes with the spiritual force accumulated through restraint in many such lifetimes, we say it is God manifest in a human body."[16] However, this is not the same as the Hindu idea of a god assuming human form.

There are several passages in the Sikh's holy book that declare Guru Nanak and the other gurus that led Sikhism (ten total) were manifestations of God. For instance, one verse explains, "To save the world the Lord incarnated himself." *(Adi Granth 1409:8)* Verse 12 of the same passage asserts, "There is no difference between God and Guru; Guru Arjun [the fifth guru] is the Personification of the Lord Himself." However, the tenth guru, Guru Gobind Singh, insisted that no one should worship him as God, or for that matter, any of the nine gurus before him. He even stated that those who called him God would have to endure hellfire. *(See Bachitra Natak 218–247.)* Many interpret statements such as this to be sufficient evidence that the Avatar concept should be rejected.

There is some disagreement among Sikhs as to how all of this information should be processed. Many would reduce the explanation to mean that the Spirit of God was powerfully and perfectly expressed through Guru Nanak (and the other gurus) but not one of them was literally God in a body. They were all manifestations of God, but not God born in human form (though some might disagree). Sikhs believe and teach that Guru Nanak and the other nine guru-leaders of their religion lived sinless lives. So, they were certainly not considered ordinary human beings, but expressions of divine perfection. Sikhs definitely do not believe in the doctrine of Avatars exactly as it is found in Hinduism.

Taoism—teaches the existence of Avatars, advanced "beings who choose to mingle among humanity and take on the appearance of mortals to inspire, instruct, and advise...Immortal Lu Tung-pin is such a teacher."[17]

Theosophy—Helena Blavatsky taught that the present world population is the third physical "rootrace" to inhabit this planet. Within each "rootrace" are seven subraces. At the beginning of each subrace, the incarnation of the Supreme World Teacher takes place. Supposedly, at the onset of the fifth subrace, Jesus became the human vessel for the Christ to manifest through. Prior to Jesus being used in this way, there were four other incarnations of the Supreme World Teacher (Buddha in India, Hermes in Egypt, Zoroaster in Persia, and Orpheus in Greece). The world now awaits the sixth manifestation of the Christ as we pass into the next subrace. Annie Besant, president of the Theosophical Society from 1907 until 1933, promoted a Hindu named Jiddu Krishnamurti as this new Messiah. He later refuted this claim and refused the title.

Zoroastrianism—In certain sacred texts, Zoroaster, the founder of this religion, is described as a preexistent, heavenly being who incarnated a unique way. The celestial material that would become his body descended with the rain and was absorbed by his virgin mother as she drank the milk of cows.

MODERN GURUS AND TEACHERS

In the past century, a number of gurus, swamis and religious leaders have claimed 'Avatarship' (or they have been exalted to that position by their followers). Consider the following few examples:

Meher Baba (1894-1969) voiced the unequivocal declaration, "I am God personified."[18] He claimed to be the Avatar of this age, the incarnation of God revealed at the close of this cycle. He insisted that he was the Highest of the High, far above all the sadhus, mahatmas, saints and yogis that can be found in this world. He also explained that he had incarnated as an Avatar "innumerable times...in the last cycle, 5,329 times" (evidently, a reference to the extremely lengthy Cycle-of-cycles) and that he would come back "once more after 450 years."[19] In another reference, his final declaration, he promised to return in 700 years.[20] (Note: followers of Meher Baba point out he taught both Minor and Major Incarnations of the Avatar. For instance, Jesus was a Major Incarnation; Shankara, a noted Hindu philosopher, was a Minor Incarnation. This would seem to justify what seems to be a contradiction. The incarnation after 450 years could be a minor one, while the incarnation after 700 years could be major.)

He maintained silence for nearly forty-four years, communicating only with an alphabet board and hand gestures. He foretold that he would finally break silence and when he did, the entire world would feel the impact of his love, effecting "a worldwide transformation of consciousness."[21] He also asserted, " The whole world will know and recognize me as Jesus returned once I speak."[22] "The breaking of my Silence will reveal to man the universal Oneness of God, which will bring about the universal brotherhood of man."[23] Though conflicting opinions exist, some of his followers claim he did speak just prior to his death. However, they explain that the resulting 'world impact' has been, and will yet be, a gradual process. (In one book, *"Meher Baba, The Awakener,"* it states that he did *not* break his silence.)[24]

Meher Baba also taught that in each cycle of time (which ranges from 700 to 1400 years) there are eleven ages of 65 to 125 years each. From the beginning to the end of each cycle, there are altogether 55 Perfect Masters. That means each age has only five Perfect Masters. In the last, the eleventh age of each cycle, the Avatar *(Saheb-e-Zaman)* is also present. Evidently, this means that every 700 to 1,400 years a new Avatar, or bodily manifestation of God, should make an appearance in this world. Of course, if Meher Baba was the rightful, sole 'heir' of this honorific title, all other claims to Avatarship during his lifespan were perpetrated (according to Meher Baba's own words) by imposters, hypocrites, or persons suffering from spiritual delusion.

Paul Twitchell (1922–1971) who founded ECKANKAR, claimed to be 971st ECK master, a "Mahanta," a living incarnation of God. He taught that "Mahantas" are above the laws of man. They are omnipotent and omniscient. He relegated Jesus to a much lower position, identifying him as "a son of Kal." The name Kal is an ECK word for the devil, King of the lower worlds. Kal is also explained to be the originator of the Christian faith. The present "Mahanta" and leader of ECKANKAR is Harold Klemp.

Guru Maharaj Ji (born in 1957) of Divine Light Mission was esteemed by his followers (quite numerous in the 1970s) to be *the* Perfect Master, *the* Divine Incarnation for this age. He taught against seeking a relationship with God, because doing so suggests that deity is separate from humanity, a departure from the monistic view of oneness that is foundational in Hinduism.

Sai Baba (born in 1926), whose name means *divine mother/father,* was a popular guru with a large following in India. He claimed to be an Avatar for this age. He has been quoted making declarations such as the following: "I am the Self *(Atma)* seated in the hearts of all creatures. I am the beginning, the middle and the end of all beings"…"I am everything, everywhere, omniscient, omnipotent and omnipresent. My power is immeasurable. Tune into it." One of his disciples explains, "The only difference between Sai Baba and ourselves is that he knows his Divine Reality while we have forgotten the fact."[25]

And the list goes on and on and on...

FINAL OBSERVATIONS

While one branch of Hinduism denies the concept of Avatars, classical Hinduism teaches that there can only be one in the world at any given time. Yet Guru Dev, Paul Twitchell, Meher Baba, Guru Maharaj Ji, Sai Baba and others have had overlapping life spans. Some have even claimed exclusive rights to this divine status in their particular era. Who is right? Then again, the question must be asked—How can there presently be any aspirants or contenders for this position since Hindu theology predicts the next Avatar will not arrive for about 425,000 years?

Some of those claiming to be the Avatar for this age, as Meher Baba, have also claimed to be the reincarnation of Jesus Christ. Paul Twitchell, on the other extreme, relegated Jesus to the position of being a son of the devil while identifying himself as God in the flesh.

An evident 'crack in the dike' that quickly erodes the believability of this doctrine is the disagreement among 'Avatars' concerning basic, important issues (like those covered in this book: *the nature of God, the nature of man, the nature of salvation*, etc.). If those persons acknowledged as being Avatars were truly 'inspired,' they should all be in perfect agreement concerning their 'revelations.' But such is certainly not the case.

True biblical teaching confers divinity on only one individual, the Lord Jesus Christ. There is no historical proof that the Avatars of Hinduism, except for Buddha, ever had an actual existence. On the contrary, there is an abundance of historical proof concerning Jesus: what he taught and what he did. Not only did his followers describe him as "God...manifest in the flesh" and the "image of the invisible God." *(1 Timothy 3:16, Colossians 1:15)* Jesus revealed concerning himself, "He who has seen me has seen the Father." *(John 14:9)*

One of Jesus' strongest warnings is found in John 10:8–9: "All who came before me are thieves and robbers...I am the door. If anyone enters by me, he will be saved." In other words, Jesus was explaining that all who have ever claimed to be manifestations of God in this world have 'stolen' from him a position only he has the right to fill. This does not mean that all those heralded as Avatars have been insincere or purposefully deceptive. Admittedly, some have been egoistic frauds with openly sensual, self-serving lifestyles, but others appear to be self-sacrificing persons who generally believed they achieved God-consciousness. However, to put it bluntly, they are victims of spiritual delusion who "grow worse and worse, deceiving and being deceived." *(2 Timothy 3:13)* Also, some of those assigned to this role by their followers never professed it themselves and would be appalled that it happened.

Isaiah, the prophet, described the spiritual condition of all human beings (including those claiming to be Avatars) with the statement, "All we like sheep have gone astray." The end of this verse foretells of the Messiah that "the Lord has laid on Him the iniquity of us all." *(Isaiah 53:6)* Jesus is the good Shepherd, the only One who completely and sacrificially laid his life down for the sheep. Only Jesus, the Son of God, entered this world by a supernatural conception and virgin birth. Only Jesus lived a sinless life. Only Jesus could claim being the Word made flesh: the sum total of all the words that God has ever spoken or will ever speak. *(John1:1-3, 14)* Only Jesus died for the sins of humanity. Only Jesus rose from the dead. Recently, Pope John Paul II released the unequivocal statement (and I agree wholeheartedly), "Christ is absolutely original and absolutely unique. If he were only a wise man like Socrates, if he were a prophet like Mohammed, if he were enlightened like the Buddha, without doubt he would not be what he is."[26]

Finally, if Jesus Christ was an Avatar (within the framework of the generally accepted interpretation of this concept) he would have rejoiced to awaken a similar divine potential in his chief followers. He would have 'passed the torch,' encouraging them to receive worshipful recognition from their own disciples, just as he had received from them. Of course, this was not the case at all.

When Paul, the apostle, prayed for a crippled man in Lystra and he was healed, the people impetuously proclaimed, "The gods are come down to us in the likeness of men." The local populace attempted to worship these followers of Christ, calling Paul, Mercury, and Barnabas, Jupiter. The apostles, if they had been trained in the Far Eastern worldview, would have gladly and serenely allowed this to proceed. They may have denied being incarnations of Roman gods, but they would unashamedly accepted the adoration of the people, affirming their own divinity. Instead, Paul cried aloud, "Why are you doing these things? We also are men with the same nature as you, and preach to you that you should turn from these useless things to the living God, who made the heaven, the earth, the sea, and all things." *(Acts 14:11, 15)*

Having viewed this evidence, we should all come to a firm conclusion. The existence of multiple Avatars is a belief that should be discarded. There has only been one incarnation of God into this world. As many wise observers have concluded—"Religion is man's effort to reach God, but Jesus is God's effort to reach man." Only Jesus can rightfully occupy the role of being God incarnate in this world. In humility, we must submit to heaven's method of reaching earth, if we are to experience earth's only means of reaching heaven.[27] (IMPORTANT NOTE)

10 — What is the true meaning of this celebrated title: "the Christ"?

Many Far Eastern and New Age groups differentiate between the man, Jesus, and "the Christ." Dr. Ernest Holmes, founder of the United Church of Religious Science, stressed:

> *"Christ is the reality of every man, his true inner self."*[28] *"Christ is Universal Idea ...the Higher Self."*[29] *"Christ is the embodiment of divine Sonship which has come, with varying degrees of power, to all people...Christ is a Universal Presence...There is no one particular man predestined to become the Christ. We must understand that Christ is not a person, but a Principle...As the human gives way to the Divine, in all people, they become the Christ."*[30]

George Trevelyan explained the related idea that, "Esoteric Christianity sees Jesus as the human vehicle for the Cosmic Being of the Christ."[31] If this notion is correct, Jesus is demoted to the position of a mere Way-Shower, a Revealer of Mysteries, a Divine Prototype. He is no more than a fellow human being who gave us an excellent example to emulate, that we too might walk in our own 'Christhood.' Believers of this view insist that the 'Christ nature' can be accessed even by those who do not accept Jesus as Lord of their lives. This theory is based on three main assumptions.

(1) **The first assumption is that all human beings have a divine essence.** The Bible does not teach that all men are expressions of God, possessing an inward 'spark of divinity.' It rather explains that men, though made in the image of God, are presently separated from God because of his transcendence and our inherited 'fallen state.' Isaiah 59:2 also warns, "your iniquities have *separated* you from your God." During the experience of salvation, sins are washed away. Christians are then placed in a mystical union with Christ. The Spirit of Christ dwells within them. There is never a point, though, where they actually become God or become Christ, anymore than the tea becomes the cream when the two are mixed together.

(2) The second assumption is that all human beings are, fully and spiritually, children of God. A more thorough examination of this point is found in a later section. In one sense, all human beings are children of God after the creation. Jesus often indiscriminately addressed large crowds of people with general statements such as, "Your Father knows the things you have need of before you ask him." *(Matthew 6:8)* In a spiritual sense, however, only those who receive Jesus into their hearts literally, supernaturally become the "children of God"— through the experience of being "born again." *(See John 1:12–13.)* This experience alone grants full access into the divine family.

Those who have not yet partaken of this experience may be passionate lovers of God and sincere seekers of truth (and I have certainly met many beautiful non-Christians who fit this description). Unfortunately, though, they do not yet possess the indwelling of the true Spirit of God. In attempting to access the 'Christ nature,' at best, they succeed in responding to their conscience (that inward sense of what is morally right or wrong) or tapping into the latent power of the fallen human soul (which, of itself, can result in positive character development in a person's life). At worst, they often inadvertently come under the influence of deceptive, demonic entities who provide counterfeit spiritual experiences in order to mislead those who are spiritually gullible. (Please read the Part 4 article titled, *What really is the "kundalini"?*) This does not negate the sincerity of individual seekers toward God, nor their importance and value in his sight. God intensely loves all who inhabit this world and his deepest desire is to bring them all into a vital and real relationship with himself.

(3) The third assumption is that there is a distinct difference between Jesus and "the Christ." Advocates of this viewpoint believe there was a certain point where Jesus, the human, received an awakening of the Christ nature. However, the angel announced the birth of Jesus to the shepherds saying, "There is born to you this day in the city of David a Savior, who *is* Christ the Lord." *(Luke 2:11*, emphasis by author) Notice the angel did not say he would become the Christ or that he was one of many Christs.

When the anointing of the Holy Spirit descended on him at his water baptism, Jesus did not 'become' the Christ. He was merely empowered to function 'as' the Christ. Even at his birth he was titled this way. Later when Jesus asked his disciples to identify who he was, Peter responded, "You are *the* Christ, the Son of the living God." Jesus did not correct Peter for identifying him as the singular and only Christ. Quite the contrary, he informed this soon-to-be apostle that he was a blessed individual, because this revelation had come to him from the Father. *(See Matthew 16:16–18.)*

The word "Christ" *(Christos)* is the Greek equivalent of the Hebrew "Messiah" *(Mashiyach)* both of which mean "the Anointed One." All true Christians receive an anointing from God, which is a specific application of the Holy Spirit to their lives in order to perform a certain God-ordained task. Thus, they become 'the anointed of the Lord' (Heb. *mashiyach,* Gr. *christianos*) but only in a subordinate sense. *(See 2 Corinthians 1:21, 1 John 2:27.)*

Believers represent the Christ, they take on the nature of Christ, they become part of the body of Christ, but they never replace the Christ (Jesus) in his supreme position or match him in greatness. He is the "Anointed One" over a family of "anointed ones" who represent him in this world. If we yield our lives to Jesus' Lordship we may receive of the "anointing" (the power of the Holy Spirit to accomplish God's purposes), but it all flows from Jesus to his followers. This gift is not available to seekers any other way. Neither is it a latent potential that can be awakened in anyone and everyone, regardless of whether or not there is a discipleship commitment to Jesus.

As writer, Kenneth L. Woodward, pointed out in a Newsweek article, this is an "unbridgeable difference" between the Buddhist and Christian worldview:

> *"A Christian can never become Christ, while the aim of every serious Buddhist is to achieve Buddhahood himself."*[32]

Jesus, the Christ, is the One who always has been and always will be— the eternal Word, the Son of the Living God, inseparably and infinitely a member of the Triune Godhead (a position no other human being could ever claim). The personality of Jesus and the personality of the Christ were not two different things. They are one and the same. We must be careful to identify him correctly. One writer warns, "Faith in a counterfeit Christ will yield a counterfeit salvation."[33]

11 Was the cross merely an example of "at-one-ment," or did it provide "atonement" for the sins of mankind?

As a yoga student, I was taught that Jesus' death on the cross was merely an example of obedience, an inspiring demonstration of the *"at-one-ment"* Jesus possessed with the Oversoul. It graphically showed how far we should all be willing to go in order to fulfill the perfect will of the Absolute. Powerfully portraying death to self, it revealed how we, too, can attain *"at-one-ment"* (oneness with the 'higher Self'). However, the cross did not provide *atonement* (a price paid to remove sin).

This view sounded reasonable and appealing to me at the time, but it didn't match Jesus' own assessment of the purpose of his death and its ultimate effect. Revealing a totally different stance, at the Last Supper Jesus predicted that his blood would be shed, not merely as an example of obedience, but "for the remission of sins." *(Matthew 26:28)* This word "remission" means the act of releasing, pardoning or setting free from sin.

If Jesus was an Avatar and could only speak the truth (as my former gurus and teachers claimed) how could he make such an outlandish claim unless it was true? If this was an accurate appraisal of Jesus' purpose (and I now contend that it is) then the message of the cross should be lifted high over the entire human race (for the sake of mankind's deliverance, not just to enlarge the ranks of a religion).

I am now convinced that Jesus was much more than just another Avatar. He was the only incarnation of God in this world and his death is the only true and complete source of cleansing for the souls of men. Nothing else will remove the stain of sin but the precious blood of Jesus—not lacerating one's own body in self-mortification, or bathing in the River Ganges, or burning holy candles, or turning prayer wheels, or chanting mysterious mantras, or any other sacred rite offered in any religion in this world.

Death is the curse that follows sin. It was pronounced first on Adam. It still hovers over every person who commits sin in this world (which is, unfortunately, an inevitable part of being human). *(See Genesis 2:17, Romans 5:17.)* Thankfully, the Scripture announces that Jesus, by the grace of God, "tasted death for every man." *(Hebrews 2:9)* He became "a curse for us," suffering the consequences of sin in our place, so that we could go free. *(Galatians 3:13)* An occurrence of this spiritual magnitude has never happened before or since. No pivotal religious event can even compare to its importance—not the flight of Mohammed to Medina, nor the supposed enlightenment of Buddha under the Bodhi tree, or even the awesome privilege given to Moses of receiving the Law on Mount Sinai.

Jesus stands unique in executing a substitutionary death in the behalf of a fallen human race. Furthermore, it is totally improbable that his disciples misunderstood the purpose of his death and misrepresented this revelation in their writings, as some have conjectured. The Son of God spent several years carefully instructing his chief followers so they could correctly and effectively perpetuate his message and ministry. Even after his death and resurrection, he instructed them for another forty days before ascending into heaven. *(See Galatians 3:13–14, 1 John 2:1–2, Acts 1:1–3.)*

At the start of Jesus' ministry, John, the Baptist, his forerunner, clearly identified this incomparable purpose for the Christ. As Jesus passed by, John cried aloud to an audience of eager truth-seekers, "Behold, the Lamb of God who takes away the sin of the world." *(John 1:29)* Years later, all the apostles emphasized this substitutionary sacrifice in their preaching. Peter revealed that Jesus was delivered up to die "by the determined purpose and foreknowledge of God." *(Acts 2:23)* Paul even resolved not to dwell on any subject except "Jesus Christ and him crucified." *(1 Corinthians 2:2)*

Comprehending the mystery of Jesus' death is paramount in understanding the purpose of his coming. It is the focal point of Christianity and the hope of every man and woman born into this world. Yes, I concede, it did powerfully portray Jesus' *"at-one-ment"* with the Father (something we should all imitate), but more than that, it also provided *"atonement"* (something we must all appropriate). In almost all other religions, the main emphasis is man sacrificing in order to reach God; in Christianity, the main emphasis is God sacrificing in order to reach man.

12   Are human beings divine in essence, destined to eventually become God?

Involvement in Far Eastern or New Age religions is ordinarily connected to the belief that man is divine. In fact, this is the message conveyed by the traditional Hindu greeting *Namaste*. This Sanskrit word means, "I bow to the Divine in you." The hands, placed palm-to-palm in an upward, prayerful pose, and the polite bow are intended to be a daily reminder, an often-recurring recognition of the 'Universal Self' within all men. The premise is that we are all potential Christs. We are all potential Buddhas. We are all evolving into ultimate, absolute oneness with the Godhead. We all contain this 'seed' of the Divine. Realizing this 'higher Self' is promoted as the key to bliss and enlightenment. Yogi Bhajan propagated this view. He taught, "It is true that between man and God there is no difference. The difference is in the realization. Man has never realized that he is God, man has always realized that he is man."[34]

Many other voices from the East echo this sentiment. Baba Muktananda, swami of Siddha Yoga, urged his adherents, "Kneel to your own self. Honor and worship your own being. Meditate on your own self. God dwells with you *as you*."[35] Sai Baba, a popular, modern guru in India, informed his followers that the person who realizes the *atma*-principle becomes God himself. Maharishi Mahesh Yogi unflinchingly instructed, "Each individual in his true nature is the impersonal God."[36]

Bible doctrine runs contrary to this view. The psalmist David, speaking to the Creator, said, "What is man that you take thought of him, and the son of man that you care for him? Yet you have made him *a little lower than God*, and you crown him with glory and majesty!" *(Psalms 8:4–5 NAU)* Notice, it does not say that man is a manifestation of God or even equal to God, but "*a little lower than God*." We need to remember that it was a desire to be "like God" that brought about the fall of Adam and Eve. *(Genesis 3:5)*

Jesus revealed the correct view of man's state when he explained, "If a man loves Me, he will keep My word, and My Father will love him, and We will come to him and make Our home with him." *(John 14:23 RSV)* Jesus never said that his disciples would become God. He simply pledged that God would make them his abode, his home. He promised that in a personal way, he would indwell their hearts. Jesus also explained to his followers:

> "*I am the vine, you are the branches…without Me you can do nothing. If anyone does not abide in Me, he is cast out as a branch and is withered.*"
> *(John 15:5–6)*

Four things need to be said about this vitally important passage:

(1) There is no permanent, eternal life apart from the vine (Jesus). Those who are not joined to him "wither" spiritually, separated from the Source of life.

(2) Once believers are joined to Jesus, the life-sap of the Spirit of Christ (the Holy Spirit) flows through them, producing the fruit of the divine nature.

(3) Though divine life resides in born-again believers, they never become God—individual branches never actually become the vine as a whole. Branches are dependent on the vine for existence. So we are dependent upon Jesus as our life-source.

(4) If the traditional Eastern view is right, Jesus would have never made this statement. For no one could ever be 'disconnected' from the vine. Even the most evil would still possess a higher Self, identifiable as God.

A yoga devotee is promised 'enlightenment' if he escapes the confines of the senses and achieves what has been termed "I AM Consciousness." This is supposedly an awakening of the understanding that we all, as emanations of the Divine, have an infinite existence—with no beginning and no end. Atman (the soul) and Brahman (the Oversoul) blend together with no lines of distinction. So any person has a right to say, "I AM THAT I AM" or "I AM GOD."

The Christian, biblical position is antithetical. Only God, the omniscient, omnipotent, omnipresent One, has the right to say, "I AM THAT I AM." *(Exodus 3:14–15 KJV)* For any human being to make such a claim is not only wrong; it is blasphemous. The Jews of Jesus' day well understood this and tragically, a number of them—not recognizing Jesus' Messiahship—labeled him a heretic and blasphemer for having said, "Before Abraham was, I AM." *(John 8:58)*

Notice Jesus described Abraham as a created being with a beginning point, yet he described himself as being eternally self-existent with no beginning. If Jesus espoused the idea that all men are divine, he would probably have said something like, "Abraham had an I AM nature, I have an I AM nature and all of you have the I AM nature." Instead, he reserved this status and this declaration to himself, to the consternation of the Israelite leaders. Little did they know that he was the same One who spoke out of the burning bush to Moses, saying, "I AM THAT I AM." *(Exodus 3:14 KJV)* Because Jesus had a preincarnate existence as the eternal image of the invisible God, in his human state, he still had the right to declare his eternal divinity. No other human being could ever make such a bold claim and be correct.

To attribute divinity to all men necessarily involves attributing sinfulness to God. If we are all emanations of the Divine then not only the positive, but the negative, not only the good, but the evil in every human being is an expression of God's very own being. Is it really logical to say, "We are all God!"—when the pronoun "we" includes not only good people, but rapists, murderers, thieves, liars, blasphemous persons and the like? This is once again inconsistent with the revelation that "God is light and in him is no darkness at all." *(1 John 1:5)*

Finally, the belief that we are all God is usually married to a pantheistic view of the universe. God is no more than a cosmic current permeating all things, an impersonal energy force that human beings can manipulate or control. When these viewpoints are married they actually relegate God to a position subservient to man. Yogi Bhajan even offered the analogy, "Man can make God change; God cannot make man change. This is a cosmic law. The key can open the lock; the lock cannot open the key."[37] He also declared, "The Almighty God is very weak before the man of God."[38] The truth is altogether opposite—finite man is very weak before the Infinite God, ethically and morally accountable to him and subject to his laws.

This topic has never been addressed with any better logic than that found in the next two quotes:

↳· *"God cannot bud. He cannot blossom. God has always been in full bloom. That is, God is and always has been God."*[39]

↳· *"The fact that a man 'comes to realize' he is God proves that he is not God. If he were God he would never have to pass from a state of unenlightenment to a state of enlightenment as to who he is."*[40]

An expert on world religions, Dean Halverson also noted, "according to the Upanishads, the goal of enlightenment is for the individual self to lose its separate identity in the universal Self. The end result of biblical salvation, on the other hand, is to have everlasting relationship with God. Eternal life means to be in relational communion with a personal God, not in an undifferentiated union with an impersonal oneness."[41]

---

13   Prior to salvation, is the Creator internal or external?

As a yoga instructor I taught my students that God resides within every human being, that all people possess an inward 'spark of divine nature.' This is basically the stance taken in Far Eastern and New Age religious groups, that the Creator is internal. In order to find him, devotees are instructed to look within. Meher Baba instructed his disciples, "Do not search for God outside of you. God can only be found within you, for his only abode is the heart."[42] Usually, this belief grows out of pantheism: the proposition that creation, with its substance, forces and laws, is an emanation of God. If Deity indwells everything in Nature, it is only logical to believe he already indwells all of us.[43]

In direct contrast, the Bible teaches that men and women are born into this world separated from God. Helen Schucman, author of *A Course in Miracles*, counters the biblical view insisting, "*A sense of separation from God is the only lack you really need correct. This sense of separation* never would have arisen if you had not distorted your perception of truth, and had thus perceived yourself as lacking."[44] However, the Bible does not teach a '*sense of separation*,' but rather, a '*state of separation*.' (Isaiah 59:2 warns that, "your iniquities have *separated* you from your God.") This '*separating*' influence is not only our individual iniquities, but the sin status we have all inherited from Adam. The good news is: the Bible also teaches that we can be reunited with God. This happens when Jesus Christ comes to dwell in our hearts by faith. *(See Romans 8:9–11, Ephesians 3:17–19.)*

An important biblical happening supports this view of man's status with God. Right before Jesus ascended into heaven, he encouraged his disciples to wait in the upper room until the promise of the Holy Spirit came. The Bible explains that on the Day of Pentecost (a Jewish feast day), "there came a sound from heaven, as of a rushing mighty wind." This supernatural 'wind' filled the entire house where the disciples were sitting. *(See Acts 2:1–21.)* Tongues of fire appeared over their heads and they were all *filled* with the Holy Spirit. Notice the Bible says they were *filled*. The Spirit of God came *into* them from *outside* of them. The Holy Spirit was not awakened from *within* their inner being. Seeing this automatically answers the question posed at the beginning of this section.

Yes, without a doubt, God is external prior to a person's experience of salvation. This1 separation between God and man is the chief reason for the emotional and mental misery that racks the human race. No wonder Jesus is entitled the Prince of peace, for "peace with God" and "the peace of God" are gifts he deposits in every heart he reconciles to the Father. *(Philippians 4:7, Romans 5:1)* This really is the cure for our dilemma.

14 What does it mean to be "one with God"?

This concept of being "one with God" can be interpreted two main ways: (1) Undifferentiated oneness and sameness, (2) Differentiated oneness: union with uniqueness, marriage by merging, blending but not the banishing of individuality. In this view, oneness does not mean sameness.

The traditional metaphor used in Hinduism and New Age veins of thought is the drop of water being immersed in the ocean. The droplet of water is *atman* (the soul); the ocean is *Brahman* (the impersonal Oversoul). At the moment of complete absorption into God the 'droplet of water' cannot be differentiated from the 'ocean' into which it is immersed. This symbol fits in with the idea that man in his present ignorance is in the process of realizing that he is God, on a journey that ends in actually 'becoming' God.

After the cycle of reincarnation is finally over, the soul completely loses its connection with 'self-consciousness,' dropping all human personalities in which it was encased through the cycle of rebirths. Unrestrained, the latent divinity in man becomes fully expressed. To the philosophical Hindu, and to most yogis and swamis, this is the ultimate meaning of being "one with God." Progress in life depends on realizing this oneness now and living in the higher consciousness and divine direction provided by the 'higher Self' (which is identical with Brahman).

This view in Indian philosophy is referred to as *Advaita-Vedanta*. (The word *advaita* means "non-dualism.") Its main proponent was Sankara (c.700-750). He taught that man and God are one and the same. We only perceive separate selves and existences because of *maya* (illusion). Actually, the world and everything in it is a manifestation of Brahman and will ultimately return to its original state. This interpretation is based on a monistic and pantheistic view of the universe and its Maker.

An opposing view within the boundaries of Hinduism is called *Dvaita-Vedanta*. (The word *dvaita* means "dualism.") One of its main promoters, Madhva (13th century), taught that Vishnu is the supreme god, and that an evolved soul's ultimate destiny is relational: the final realization of an unhindered, unrestricted relationship or union with a personal God. According to this view, the world is real, not an illusion; and souls, though dependent upon God, are distinct and separate from him. It is interesting to note that Madhva's followers considered him an incarnation of the wind god Vayu, sent by Vishnu to bring deliverance to those who are good, while they described Sankara (who promoted *Advaita-Vedanta*) as being sent by the powers of evil.

Madhva's view is structured somewhat similar to Christian doctrine. However, while proposing man's destiny of relational 'oneness with God,' it fails to supply the correct means of making this happen or the correct revelation of the "One" with whom union is sought. Jesus definitely promised present and ultimate oneness with God for those who follow his teachings. However, the means of accessing this oneness is much different than the methods offered by Far Eastern religions. In his great intercessory prayer for the church *(John 17)*, Jesus revealed how this oneness can be received (not achieved):

> *"Father...I have given to them the words which*
> *You have given Me...that they all may be one, as*
> *You, Father, are in Me, and I in You; that they also*
> *may be one in Us...and the glory which You have*
> *given me I have given them, that they may be one*
> *just as We are one." (John 17:1, 8, 21–22)*

So through the impartation of the words Jesus spoke (the Word of God) and the glory that rested upon him (the Holy Spirit) believers can experience this gift of oneness with the Father. Such a state of being can be actualized during this life, then finalized and perfected at the loss of this mortal body. So what's the difference?

Far Eastern religions teach that this state of being comes through the removal of ignorance and the attaining of higher states of consciousness through various means (meditation, chanting, pilgrimages, devotion, etc). It is considered an inward potential that all human beings possess. It must only be awakened. Christianity, on the other hand, teaches that oneness with God is not an internal possession, latent within all men. It is the product of an external influence, an impartation from God. As a promised gift of God, it is granted only to those who seek it according to his directions.

In Christianity, God is a transcendent God. Mankind is separated from God by sin. It is impossible, therefore, for unredeemed men to be one with the very God from whom they have been separated. This sorrowful condition of soul is wonderfully rectified by the spiritual rebirth Jesus promised. This happens when the Spirit of God enters a person's heart once it is cleansed from sin by the blood of Jesus. This is the only means by which human beings can be reconciled to a right relationship with God.

Prior to this experience any claim to 'oneness with God' may be philosophically correct (as a gift that seekers can acquire), but not experientially correct (as an experience that seekers possess). When I was a teacher of yoga, I sincerely believed that I had oneness with God, but I never actually possessed that oneness. I never truly experienced union with the Divine until I approached God according to the words of Jesus and until I received his Spirit (his glory) into my heart.

This difference becomes most evident when the comparison is between Christianity and the monistic, pantheistic view of philosophical Hinduism. This vein of thought in Hinduism deifies all men. All are manifestations of God. The biblical view, though, is that man is not God and will never be God. Oneness does not mean sameness. Adam and Eve became one in marriage in the beginning, but Eve did not become Adam. Later on, Paul used this marriage analogy explaining, "For this cause shall a man leave his father and mother, and shall be joined unto his wife, and they two shall be one flesh. This is a great mystery: but I speak concerning Christ and the church." *(Ephesians 5:31–32 KJV)*

Some of the Far Eastern viewpoints on this issue are like a house that's been framed up, but not boxed in and furnished. The framework of truth is there (God desires us to experience oneness with him), but the actual means of experiencing that oneness is absent. Of course, I often meet deeply sincere students of yoga and Far Eastern religions who are very godly and loving persons. In living ethical, honorable and self-denying lives, I admit, they have come into harmony with the divine will to a great degree.

Usually their daily goal is to live according to the intuitive promptings of what many of them would term their 'higher Self.''

I believe this inner influence is simply the conscience, that sub-liminal sense of what is morally right and morally wrong. The conscience is a gift *from God*, but it is not evidence of the actual presence *of God* within the heart. Those who yield to this inner influence do achieve oneness with God in a limited sense, by becoming one with his moral demands. But there is a huge difference between keeping God's rules and being filled with his personal presence. I deeply admire people of various religions who live such devoted lives. My heart hurts deeply for them—for I see such consecration, such realness, such thirst for God evidenced in their lives. O, that they could take the next step and discover the Fountainhead of all the joy, peace, and fulfillment they seek: the Lord Jesus Christ.

Finally, it should be mentioned that the Bible forecasts a time when the sons and daughters of God will shine brilliantly in the Kingdom of God. They will reflect the image of God in absolute perfection. These redeemed individuals will experience union with God to a superlative, perfected degree. However, those who inherit eternal life will never become formless, omnipresent spirits filling the universe, nor will they merge into undifferentiated oneness with the Oversoul. The heirs of everlasting life will always have a distinct form (an eternal glorified body) and they will always exist as individual, independent personalities. They will be distinct from God, yet enjoy everlasting, blissful oneness in their relationship with him. Yes, I agree with the apostle Paul—this is a great mystery!

15   What really is "the kundalini"?

Echoing the sentiments of my teachers, as a yoga teacher, I often referred to an inward 'spark of divine nature' that all human beings possess. Yogi Bhajan called this inner divine essence "the kundalini," explaining it to be "the dormant power of infinity," a coiled energy at the base of the spine that must be aroused.[45]

Many swamis, yogis and gurus strangely refer to this dormant energy as the 'serpent power.' They also claim this coiled energy is a manifestation of the goddess Sakti (also spelled Shakti). Theoretically, when this 'awakening' of the kundalini takes place, it travels up the spinal column through five chakras (spiritual energy centers), then through the sixth chakra (the third eye), finally reaching the seventh chakra at the top of the head (called the crown chakra). At that point, within a person's inner being, the goddess Sakti comes into union with the god Shiva. This experience is supposed to bring enlightenment or God-consciousness. It is "the dissolution *(laya)* of the ordinary self into its eternal essence... This experience is also understood as the primordial union of the male and female cosmic principles...It is thus simultaneously a microcosmic, bodily occurrence and a universal one."[46]

Rabi Maharaj recalls from his past experience as a guru, "When aroused without proper control, it [the kundalini] rages like a vicious serpent inside a person with a force that is impossible to resist. It is said that without proper control, the kundalini will produce supernatural psychic powers having their source in demonic beings and will lead ultimately to moral, spiritual, and physical destruction. Nevertheless it is this kundalini power that meditation and yoga are designed to arouse."[47]

The world renowned Swami Muktananda recounted his experience with the 'awakening of the kundalini.' He encountered a naked ascetic blissfully meditating on top of a pile of human excreta. This Hindu 'holy man' invited him to come sit on his lap and lick his head. The ascetic then proceeded to initiate Muktananda into Kundalini Yoga. Later that day he explained, "My mind seemed deluded...I felt I would soon become insane...My entire body started aching and ...the tongue began to move down the throat, and all attempts to pull it out failed...My fear grew...I felt severe pain in the knot *(manipur chakra)* below the navel. I tried to shout but could not even articulate...Next I saw ugly and dreadful demon-like figures. I thought them to be evil spirits...Suddenly I saw a large ball of light approaching me from the front...It merged into my head...I was terrified by that powerfully dazzling light."[48]

Though not all stories dealing with the 'awakening of the kundalini' match the bizarre aspects of this account, still, my concerns are very grave when it comes to this subject. I spent many hours in meditation seeking to 'arouse' the kundalini—and I succeeded, when I was finally lifted out of my body into the experience of 'white light.' However, after becoming a Christian I had a very profound, spiritual encounter that proved to me the dark, negative source of this power. The following points need to be emphasized concerning "the kundalini":

⌣· **Serpent symbol**—Though many New Age groups relate to the serpent as a symbol of esoteric wisdom, biblically, it primarily represents that which is satanic and blatantly evil. A venomous serpent is an agent of death. How could this creature be symbolic of that which leads to goodness, life and the experience of God? *(See Genesis 3:1–15, Revelation 12:9.)*

‿˙ **Sexual overtones**—The experience of 'enlightenment' is compared to a supernatural 'union' between a god and goddess, so there are sexual overtones. Possibly because of this, some fringe sects, especially those involved in what has been termed the 'left-handed' form of Tantric Yoga, have made ritual sex (especially with socially forbidden partners) an aid to developing higher consciousness. Some gurus even include the handling of the genitals in the so-called 'awakening' process. Rajneesh even encouraged nudity and sex orgies among his followers to aid their spiritual 'awakening.' Yet the Bible clearly commands that we abstain from sexual immorality. Regardless of how it is wrapped spiritually, any doctrinal package containing this suggested approach is of darkness and deception. Of course, there are many Hindu ascetics, Buddhist monks and other Far Eastern mystics who seek to live pure lives. They would be appalled at the thought of these immoral practices going on in the name of achieving enlightenment.

‿˙ **Dangerous side effects**—The majority of those who believe in the 'kundalini power' do not pursue its 'awakening' by indulging in illicit or occult sexual practices. Most are sincerely seeking an experience of Ultimate Reality. However, most do agree in the danger of its "unguided" or "premature arousal." I was even cautioned as a yoga student to be extremely careful, because there were instances of some seekers becoming 'locked' in a catatonic-like, meditative state, even for years. In contrast, there is absolutely no account in the Bible of the Spirit of God moving on a person to their detriment. No prophet ever had an encounter with the Most High that caused him to be demonized, or to feel nearly insane (as Swami Muktananda admitted). Only good, healthy, enriching things result from contacting the real Creator. There is no lurking danger present when communing with the Lord of glory. No person filled with the Holy Spirit in the Bible lamented the experience because it resulted in a manifestation of evil, psychic powers.

The true power of God saves, heals, delivers—but never destroys (mentally, emotionally, physically or in any way). Therefore, the source of this 'serpent power' could not be God. It must be the Prince of darkness and his subordinate demons. Those who yield to this dark influence are often granted false supernatural encounters that seem beautiful, enlightening and ecstatic in order to successfully woo them away from the true Source of eternal life. I am well aware of this type of religious deception, having experienced it myself. Remember, Jesus warned that

Satan comes to "steal, and to kill, and to destroy" but he promised "I am come that they may have life." *(John 10:10)* Also, the Bible cautions that Satan often masquerades as "an angel of light." *(2 Corinthians 11:14)*

᠆ᐧ **Chakras**—The whole idea of the "kundalini" is interwoven with a belief in chakras. These are believed to be "energy centers in the body"—"focal points where psychic forces and bodily functions merge and interact with each other." Each chakra is "associated with a specific color, shape, sense organ, natural element, deity and mantra."[49] Though advocating this concept as being true, strangely, Yogi Bhajan insisted chakras are "imaginary and nothing else."[50] There are at least six reasons why I no longer espouse the existence of these psychic centers:

(1) Many teachers who believe in chakras cannot agree on the correct number. Some yogic models include seven, eight, nine and twelve chakras. In Buddhism there are four chakras; in Tibetan Buddhism (Vajrayana) there are five. If there really are rotating, internal energy centers in man, those who 'discover' them should agree on how many actually exist.

(2) Each chakra (in Hinduism) is identified with a different Hindu god. I firmly believe these gods are nothing more than fantasies: mere man-made myths. So, meditating on the chakras only enables a person to engage in false spiritual experiences, based on imaginary deities, which are impersonated by evil spirits committed to the deception and destruction of those who host their indwelling.

(3) The concept of chakras is inextricably connected to the concept of the kundalini (the serpent power) rising up through these 'energy centers' to bring a seeker to new levels of consciousness. Because the kundalini power is not the true power of God, but a demonic counterfeit, then the whole idea of chakras is absolutely unnecessary. The experience of God-consciousness (conscious awareness of the reality of God) comes through the entrance of Jesus Christ into the heart of a person. It has nothing to do with the supposed 'opening up' of internal energy centers.

(4) The concept of chakras is based on the idea that God is an internal, impersonal, energy force that can be controlled by the right incantation, mantra, or ritualistic practice. Yet God *communes* with His people; he is not *controlled* by them. He

is a personal God and he responds to prayer offered to him in a heartfelt, personal way. He is not impressed or motivated by repetitious utterances or magical rites.

(5) Certain gurus have made sweeping claims about the power of meditating on certain chakras. For instance, Sivananda taught that meditating on the first chakra causes all sins to be wiped away; meditating on the second chakra frees a person from desire, wrath, greed and deception; and meditating on the sixth chakra (the third eye) wipes out all karma from previous lives. If these things are true then we do not need the crucifixion of Jesus for the forgiveness of sins, nor the Holy Spirit entering and regenerating our hearts for a character change (which are both absolute necessities). Furthermore, the consequences of our past sins are taken out of God's hands and placed in ours.

(6) The concept of chakras cannot be found in the Bible or the teachings of Jesus.

16 Which view is right: reincarnation or resurrection?

Most Far Eastern religionists cling to the concept of reincarnation (though even in India, this doctrine has been strongly disputed). Basically it involves the theory that the soul-life of every human being 'evolves' from an inanimate state to plant life, then to animal life, then to numerous human forms on its journey toward perfection, ultimate enlightenment and godhood. Many philosophies, religions and modern New Age groups have held up this banner. Even Plato, the Greek philosopher, believed, "The soul is immortal, and is clothed successively in many bodies."[51] Some reincarnationists teach that during transmigration, the 'soul-life' can shuttle back and forth between a human, animal and some teach, even a mineral state. Others believe in only a progressive evolution of the soul. Disagreements do exist concerning the details of this doctrine among those who adhere to it.

I realize that sensitive people behold the anguish of a suffering human race: the heartbreaking disparity between the rich and poor, the healthy and sick, the intelligent and mentally handicapped members of the human family. Often, in their quest for a meaningful answer, reincarnation seems to be the only fair and plausible way of giving all people an equal chance at a fulfilling existence. If individuals are born crippled, demented or surrounded with abject poverty, it explains why (they are suffering for sins committed in a previous existence) and it offers hope (having paid off their karmic debt, they can then be born into a future life offering better conditions and opportunities).

So under the banner of reincarnation, the blatant inequities that abound in this world appear to fall into a sensible order. Instead of negative things happening by random chance, the theory of reincarnation offers a worldview that seems to 'fit the pieces together,' penetrating the chaotic and unpredictable with a multi-faceted system of causes and effects.

For these reasons, I wholeheartedly embraced the idea of reincarnation simultaneous with my involvement in yoga. However, after becoming a Christian I became convinced otherwise. After a thorough search of the teachings of Jesus, I discovered he definitely taught only one incarnation of the soul, one life in this world. He also predicted that at the conclusion of this era, there would be a literal resurrection of the righteous, then later on, of the unrighteous. *(John 5:23–29, Revelation 20)* Furthermore, he validated this teaching by arising victorious over death himself.

In comparison, Mohammed suffered an untimely death (some say he was poisoned), Mahavira, the founder of Jainism, died of starvation, and Buddha apparently died of food poisoning, yet none of them rose again physically. According to legend, Krishna expired of an arrow piercing his foot, but devotees believe his body was all spirit *(sat-cit-ananda)* so he never really died physically anyway. It was just the 'appearance' of a death (some call it *'lila'*—a kind of divine game).

On the contrary, Jesus' resurrection was literal and powerful. Furthermore, the Bible states Christians have been "begotten…again to a living hope by the resurrection of Jesus Christ from the dead." *(1 Peter 1:3)* Jesus is titled "the firstborn from the dead." *(Colossians 1:18)* In other words, he became a living witness of what will happen to all those who place their hope in him. At the end of this age, when Jesus returns, those who have trusted in him as their Savior will either be resurrected or translated, if they are alive when this event takes place.

How will this happen? Concerning the dead, God will use whatever substance remains of their previously inhabited, mortal bodies to create glorious, immortal forms (even if all that remains is infinitesimally small in size). Concerning the living, God will change their flesh, bone, and blood bodies into glorious, radiant, infinite forms in one divine moment.

Someone might ask, "Why is this necessary?" Certainly God could do it another way, but he doesn't choose to. He could have made Adam in the beginning without using a handful of dust. Effortlessly, God could have used the spoken word to produce the first human being, just as he had created the heavens and the earth, but again, God chose to do otherwise. Sometimes God's purposes may not seem logical to us, but who can question God's methods? Thomas à Kempis insisted:

> *"Were the works of God readily understandable*
> *by human reason, they would be neither wonderful*
> *nor unspeakable."*[52]

Probably for this reason Paul used the word "mystery" when describing the resurrection. Speaking to Christian believers he wrote, "Behold, I show you a *mystery*. We shall not all sleep, but we shall all be changed, in a moment, in the twinkling of an eye, at the last trump: for the trumpet shall sound, and the dead shall be raised incorruptible, and we shall be changed." *(1 Corinthians 15:51–52)*

Many Far Eastern and New Age groups teach that the ultimate end of an advanced soul is a merging with the Oversoul, becoming a formless part of the Godhead, an infinite existence beyond all distinction and thought. This final state is termed *Samadhi*: final, absolute bliss. Buddhism interprets this ultimate state somewhat differently calling it *Nirvana*—a word meaning "a blowing out" as in the blowing out of a candle. This metaphor implies the annihilation of desire and suffering at the 'blowing out' or cessation of personal existence. This state could also be described as 'de-personalization,' because it involves final absorption into the impersonal, formless, being-less state of what Buddhists view as final oneness with Ultimate Reality.

Contrary to the assertions of some, Jesus never taught this concept, nor did the early church. John, the apostle, revealed the following concerning the Second Coming of Jesus: "When he is revealed, we shall be like him, for we shall see him as he is." *(1 John 3:2)* Paul, the apostle, taught that we "eagerly wait for the Savior, the Lord Jesus Christ, who will transform our lowly body that it may be conformed to his glorious body, according to the working by which he is able even to subdue all things to himself." *(Philippians 3:20–21)* Our ultimate end, therefore, will not be formlessness, but the obtaining of a glorified and immortal form eternally. Jesus promised a final metamorphosis: that the "righteous will shine forth like the sun in the kingdom of their Father." *(Matthew 13:43)*

Like other yoga teachers I often tried to lend support to the doctrine of reincarnation by using biblical references. We claimed that Jesus taught John, the Baptist, was the reincarnation of Elijah. However, when all the scriptures relating to this particular subject are blended, it becomes clear that the Bible communicates something quite different. The message conveyed is that John the Baptist bore the same anointing of the Holy Spirit that Elijah bore. Though he possessed a similar calling, he was not another incarnation of this great Old Testament prophet. Besides, the Old Testament records the prophet Elijah being bodily translated to heaven. Because He never lost his original body, he certainly could not be incarnated again into a second body. Moreover, when Elijah appeared on the Mount of Transfiguration with Moses and Jesus, had he recently incarnated as John the Baptist, the disciples would have been confused as to the actual identity of the radiant person standing before them. *(See Matthew 11:13–14; 17:3–13.)* Instead of identifying him as Elijah, they would have most likely identified him as John.

In Luke 1:17 the angel Gabriel foretold that John the Baptist would come in the "spirit and power of Elijah." Some non-Christians who read this passage might interpret it as an announcement of Elijah's reincarnation. Yet when we go back and closely inspect traditional biblical language, we find Elisha (the prophet directly after Elijah) asking for, and receiving, a double-portion of the "spirit" that was upon Elijah. *(2 Kings 2:9)* Did that mean that Elijah was reincarnated as Elisha? No, of course not! They lived at the same time. It simply meant that the manifestation of God's Spirit, which rested upon Elijah, was increased in Elisha's life. Did the same anointing of the Holy Spirit that rested upon Elijah and Elisha rest also upon John, the Baptist? Yes it did, in order to accomplish a similar ministry—turning the hearts of the people back to true worship. When Jesus said of John, the Baptist, "He is Elijah which is to come," he meant it, not literally, but figuratively. *(Matthew 11:14)* In Hebrew culture, in the religious vernacular of that day, this was the understood meaning of this mysterious correlation.

One of the strongest and plainest Bible statements concerning this issue is Hebrews 9:27—"It is appointed for men to die once." If we only die once, then it goes without saying: we only live once in a mortal form in this world. I still struggle with the inequities that abound in this world, and I must admit, life does not always appear fair. But I have learned to trust in the wisdom of a loving heavenly Father, the One who is fair and who does understand all things.

Once eternity dawns, surely our questions will be sufficiently answered concerning the pain that racks the inhabitants of this planet. Until then, we are all called to "walk by faith" in the revelation that "God is love" and that the "sufferings of this present time are not worthy to be compared with the glory which shall be revealed in us." *(1 John 4:16, Romans 8:18) In the next section, I will explore in detail thirteen main reasons why I no longer accept the related doctrines of reincarnation and karma.*

---

17   Is our future really determined by past "karma"?

Teachers of Far Eastern religions maintain that the process of reincarnation is necessary for the 'reaping' of what some call 'the karmic debt.' This process supposedly determines the ongoing evolution of the soul. Every action produces either good or bad karma. Ordinarily, good karma cannot cancel bad karma (though some teach it can). Each cause must have its own effect. In his book, *The Teachings of Yogi Bhajan*, my former guru explained, "There are no accidents. Anything that comes to you, you have put out beams for it."[53] According to this theory, if we have an accident or any kind of negative experience, we have drawn it into our lives by some former negative behavior, probably in a previous existence. However, Yogi Bhajan even went as far as saying that, "Every word uttered by you must come back to you within twelve years and it must grip you within the scale of seven years. This is a law of nature."[54]

If Yogi Bhajan's theory is correct (and if I am interpreting his words correctly) karma would usually have to have its effect within the same earthly life span, especially since our words are inseparably tied to our actions. The main 'overflow' of karma that a person would carry into the next life would primarily be the result of the last seven to twelve years of his or her life.

Whether or not this was Yogi Bhajan's intended meaning, most teachers of the doctrine of karma agree that any negative or positive thing we do in life produces either bad or good karma that will inevitably be reaped, either in the same life or a future life. The object of the soul's sojourn in this world is to walk in such righteousness, love and devotion to right religious principles that only good karma is sown. When this happens, when we become so perfected that we have no more negative karma, we attain *moksha* (release from *samsara*, the cycle of rebirths). Supposedly, this process can be quite lengthy. Some adherents of this doctrine feel it can involve hundreds, thousands, even millions of separate existences.

THIRTEEN REASONS
WHY I NO LONGER EMBRACE THE RELATED
DOCTRINES OF REINCARNATION AND KARMA

(1) **If suffering, evil, and imperfection in any individual are a result of negative karma reaped from a former life, then how do suffering, evil, and imperfection make their appearance in a soul's first 'incarnation'?** Since every human being goes through suffering in this world, and every person is subject to evil, and imperfection, there is no person free from this evidence of previous guiltiness. Therefore, there is absolutely no proof that anyone has been born for the first time with a 'clean slate.'

(2) **It is taught that the justice of God demands the concept of reincarnation.** For instance, if a child is born physically debilitated or in abject poverty, there is no other explanation for such a condition than the presupposition that this is repayment for evil behavior in a former life. Otherwise, allowing such a circumstance would be sufficient evidence to indict the Almighty God with the crime of injustice. A loving Creator could never allow such a terrible plight to come upon an innocent child. So negative circumstances can only be the result of karmic indebtedness.

Believing this line of logic supposedly preserves the integrity and justness of God and places the blame on man for his own predicament. But does this really answer the questions we all ask concerning human suffering? Does it not instead catapult the human race into an even greater abyss of despair?

If this scenario is true, then the innocent child is no longer innocent and good people who suffer are no longer good. Instead, they are all guilty parties who should unresistingly submit to the 'punishment' they deserve. How could this possibly be fair and just treatment especially since those who suffer have no recollection of the ill deeds for which they are being 'punished'? Furthermore, because there is no remembrance of the causal action, unfortunate recipients of such 'karmic curses' cannot assess their wrong behavior patterns in order to make necessary adjustments in their character.

The unfairness of this doctrine is magnified even more if the Buddhist doctrine of no-self *(anatta)* is correct. According to this view, there is no enduring self or soul that exists from one incarnation to the next. Instead, five 'aggregates' are disassembled at death and a new person is assembled from five new aggregates in the next incarnation. The only thing transferred from one manifestation to the next is the "unconscious disposition" with its attachment of karma accumulated from previous lives. In this scenario, a person does not suffer for his own evil deeds, but for those performed by altogether different individuals. In the *Garland Sutra (10)* this is verified—"According to what deeds are done, do their resulting consequences come to be; *yet the doer has no existence*: this is the Buddha's teaching." One person being subjected to suffering because of another person's errors is not justice; it is injustice—of cosmic proportions.

(3) **If negative karma must be paid off, then any person used to execute such 'divine justice' unwittingly throws himself into the same vicious cycle.** For instance, if someone lived his life as a compulsive thief, it would be necessary for that same person, in a future life, to be subjected to numerous robberies. But the thieves fated to participate in this 'karmic payoff' would be sowing negative karma that they, too, must reap in future lives, making it necessary for a third generation of robbers to emerge. Further down the karmic road, those fated to fill the role of the fourth generation 'robbers of the robbers of the robbers of the robber' would also incur a load of karmic debt that must be paid off. This would necessitate many more thieves to be born in order for 'robbers of the robbers of the robbers of the robbers of the robber' to make their appearance on the stage of life. So, the process would multiply itself exponentially into an inescapable, never-ending, infinitely-enlarging, impossible-to-solve scenario. Besides, are these thieves making the choice, out of their own free will, to rob others or did fate destine them to be thieves? If the latter is true, a vicious form of injustice reigns over the future of the human race, because people are forced to do wicked things for which they are then punished because of karma. Like swimmers who get caught in an undertow, drown, and are swept out to sea, those 'engulfed' by this law are helpless participants in its execution. They are ignorant and unwilling victims of an irresistible process.

(4) **Belief in the law of karma can result in indifference toward, and even inhumane treatment of, those who are suffering.** Logic would dictate that people in misery are just paying off their karma. So why interfere? In fact, if someone does interfere with the karmic process through an act of charity, it could serve to prolong a person's suffering (even lifetimes) because the repayment of the karmic debt is postponed. So theoretically, the only safe reaction to society's woes would be passive non-involvement, detachment, withdrawal from a pained world. Actually, this paralyzing mindset often dominates societies where this doctrine is embraced.

Taken to an obviously, rarely-embraced extreme, if the doctrine of karma is right, helping others could actually be doing them a disservice. Doctors should not help the sickly; counselors should not help the mentally impaired; benevolent persons should not give alms to the underprivileged. Because in doing these things, those compassionate persons are resisting what fate has dictated for the hurting. If this is the case, is it not even possible that the benevolent person could be earning negative karma himself? By assisting the helpless and the hopeless, he could actually, in some situations, be hurting them and hurting himself. So, the answer would be, not alleviating the misery of others, but escaping into an inner world by striving to attain some 'higher Self.'

Of course, it must be said that many who believe in karma and reincarnation are very compassionate persons who actually make great efforts to reach out to those who are needy. This is commendable, and I am certainly not suggesting that they should do otherwise. But when this doctrine is closely inspected, these facets of interpretation must be seriously considered.

(5) **Certain predictions of karmic retribution in ancient Hindu sacred texts appear much too severe and obviously unjust.** The Puranas are considered sacred and inspired writings by Hindus. The following passage from this portion of Hindu Scripture communicates a detailed warning concerning the severity of the karmic retribution resulting from specific sinful acts:

> *"The murderer of a Brahmin becomes consumptive, the killer of a cow becomes humpbacked and imbecile, the murderer of a virgin becomes leprous—all three born as outcastes. The slayer of a woman and the destroyer of embryos becomes a savage full of diseases; who commits illicit intercourse, a eunuch; who goes with his teacher's wife, disease-skinned. The eater of flesh becomes very red; the drinker of intoxicants, one with discolored teeth... Who steals food becomes a rat; who steals grain becomes a locust...honey, a gadfly; flesh, a vulture; and salt, an ant...Who commits unnatural vice becomes a village pig; who consorts with a Sudra woman becomes a bull; who is passionate becomes a lustful horse...These and other signs and births are seen to be the karma of the embodied, made by themselves in this world. Thus the makers of bad karma, having experienced the tortures of hell, are reborn with the residues of their sins, in these stated forms." (Garuda Purana 5)*

Doesn't it seem unreasonable that these terrible curses are the inevitable plight of those who transgress in these ways? Though some are extremely grave sins, such as murder and adultery, others are quite minor. Just imagine—if all those who worked in slaughterhouses are destined to become humpbacked imbeciles, the world should be full of such persons. Or what if there was a benevolent man who helped thousands, who gave to the poor, who lived and promoted truth his entire life, yet he unfortunately stole some salt when he was a boy? According to this passage, his change of heart and his righteous acts would be of no avail. Because of one ill deed in his youth, this man would be confined to the horrid destiny of becoming an ant until his karmic debt was sufficiently paid off (because good karma normally cannot cancel out bad karma). Such severe treatment could only be labeled unfair and unjust. It isolates individual errors instead of determining a person's destiny by the total contribution of his or her life.

Of course, it must be stated that not all proponents of the doctrine of reincarnation believe in the Puranas or accept the idea of the regression of the soul from human to animal form. For instance, Theosophist Irving Cooper commented, "Progress is forwards, not backwards, so as we advance we always come back in human bodies, each one a little better than the previous one. Sometimes, it is true, for some grievous fault, we may during one incarnation retrace our steps to a slight extent and take birth in a less advanced type of body and under less favorable conditions. But this retrograde movement is apparent and not real, even as the backward movement of an eddy in the flowing water of a river does not change the forward course of the stream."[55] So there is great disagreement even among reincarnationists concerning the correct interpretation of this process.

(6) **The doctrines of karma and reincarnation leave no room for forgiveness coming from God, as promised in the Bible.** In Mark 1:15, Jesus exhorted his listeners to "repent and believe in the Gospel." (The word *gospel* means "good news"—the 'good news' of the message that Jesus preached.) This passage reveals the two necessary prerequisites for those desiring salvation and forgiveness for sins. The first is repentance (which is genuine sorrow for sin resulting in a change of mind). The second is faith toward God (confidence and trust that he will fulfill his promises). Those who fulfill these criteria place themselves in a receptive position to receive that divine forgiveness that wipes sin out of existence; 1 John 1:9 says, "If we confess our sins, He is faithful and just to forgive us our sins, and to cleanse us from all unrighteousness." *(See Matthew 9:13, Romans 6:23, John 3:14–16; 5:24; 10:28, Acts 5:31, Hebrews 6:1.)*

There is no biblical passage that even remotely implies the progressive evolution of the soul by means of self-achieved works of righteousness over a period of multiple lives. Quite the contrary, Titus 3:5 states, "Not by works of righteousness which we have done, but according to His mercy He saved us, through the washing of regeneration and renewing of the Holy Spirit." This "washing" and "renewing" of the soul is a reference to the spiritual rebirth that takes place when the Spirit of Christ indwells any person yielding to his influence. Of course, only a personal and transcendent God can make the decision to forgive and indwell the heart of a remorseful, receptive and believing person. An impersonal, pantheistic, cosmic force could never willfully respond to carry out such a compassionate act of divine intervention.

(7) **There are some means offered through Hinduism and other related religions that enable adherents to escape the accumulated effects of negative karma.** For instance, it is generally accepted that if Hindus die in the city of Varanasi, especially if they have washed away their sins in the nearby River Ganges, such privileged ones will go straight to Shiva, returning immediately upon death to oneness with the Godhead. All negative karma that should forestall such an event is instead bypassed. Another escape from karma is promised in the *Ramayana*, an epic considered sacred and inspired. This portion of Hindu Scripture ends with a pledge that those who "read it" or "hear it read" will have all their sins washed away.

Some propose that meditating on the third eye can destroy karma from previous lives. Yogi Bhajan of Kundalini Yoga explained the value of chanting mantras, "Who is powerful? God or you? When you do the *japa*, chanting repetitiously, then the result is *tapa*, the heat that burns the karma."[56]

Some gurus and swamis claim to be able to dissolve negative karma in the lives of their disciples just by personal contact. Similar to this, Sikhs are encouraged in their holy book: "Whoever meditates on Guru Arjun [the fifth Guru in Sikhism] shall not have to pass through the painful womb of reincarnation ever again." *(Adi Granth 1409:6)*

Animal sacrifices have also been prescribed in Hinduism. In the Brahmanas, the ancient horse sacrifice (which began with the slaughter of 609 animals) was said to be especially efficacious. Though it took a year to finish, it was spoken of as "atonement for everything, the remedy for everything" redeeming all sin.[57]

If Jesus was an Avatar, as some claim, he would have known these means of escaping karmic indebtedness were viable options. Surely, he would have concluded that dying on the cross was unnecessary. Instead, he would have emphasized pilgrimages to the city of Varanasi for the sick and ailing, the reading of the Ramayana, concentration on the third eye, the chanting of mantras or simple interaction with his disciples, karmically rewarding their devotion to him. If Jesus really did study under enlightened masters in India during his hidden years, as some assert, he certainly would have had this information as part of his spiritual portfolio. Yet he never taught or even implied these things. How could someone 'enlightened' withhold such valuable information if it was really true? And above all, why sacrifice yourself when the sacrifice of horses would prove sufficient?

(8) The doctrine of karma and the Hindu belief in cycles of creation seem to be in direct conflict with each other. (See "Hinduism" under *Cycles, Ages, and the Ultimate State of the Universe.*) How could a perfect age (the *Krita Yuga*) in which *dharma* (the moral order) is completely manifested in the human race, ever degenerate into anything less? There would only be positive karma being sown. Likewise, how could this present corrupt age, the *Kali Yuga*, with its overload of negative karma, ever hope to be reborn into another *Krita Yuga*, a golden era of utter perfection? What happens to the huge amount of accumulated negative karma? Furthermore, if the world in its present stage is 'digressing' into the ever-increasing, miry depths of the *Kali Yuga*, how can souls caught in this evil age ever hope to be found 'progressing' toward perfection and godhood? The current of fate's influence is carrying us down, not up. Yet this is the cyclical pattern that is promoted in traditional Hinduism as the true developmental, evolutionary process of this world.

(9) If reincarnation is true, then fatalism is true. The hypothesis is this—"at the moment of reincarnation, the soul (called the subtle body), after making the appropriate karmic calculations, attaches itself to a developing embryo."[58] This would make it necessary for the future of that embryo to be absolutely predetermined, even in minor details. Otherwise the calculations could not be dependable. This leaves very little, if any room for freedom of choice or divine intervention. Men and women are no more than puppets on karmic strings, controlled by an inexorable and inescapable law. While appearing to be masters of their own future, according to this standard, men and women are really prisoners of their own past.

(10) If it is necessary for human beings to work out their 'karmic debt' through many incarnations, Jesus' death was in vain and the

crucifixion was not the pivotal, planetary event that Christianity claims. If Jesus were 'enlightened' to the doctrine of karma, as some insist, he would have known that people's problems may take numerous incarnations to resolve. An attempt to intervene for man on such a grand scale would have been a gross disregard for the karmic process. By his own admission, no man took Jesus' life from him. He gave it up willingly, knowing the infinite value of what he would accomplish. *(See John 10:18.)* The very fact that he did this, expecting it to bring salvation to the world, shows that the related doctrines of reincarnation and karma were not part of his belief system. Therefore, these doctrines should not be a part of our belief system either.

(11) **If it is necessary for human beings to evolve to perfection through numerous incarnations, then both the resurrection of Jesus and the promised future resurrection of all believers, are stripped of validity, value and purpose.** Jesus' physical body went through an agonizing death on the cross. The same body was resurrected three days later. This literal conquering of mortality is something no other religious leader ever accomplished (though Sikhs claim something similar for their founder, Guru Nanak). After Jesus ascended into heaven, he was glorified, receiving a "glorious body," a celestial form that shines like the sun in the kingdom of God. *(Philippians 3:21)* When the biblical patriarch Job faced imminent death, he confessed to God, "All the days of my appointed time will I wait till my change come." *(Job 14:14 KJV)* The Psalmist David also foretold, "I shall be satisfied when I awake in your likeness." *(Psalms 17:15)* In other words, the ultimate hope for God's people is a final, physical change into the likeness of the Lord himself.

While on earth, Jesus promised, "This is the will of him who sent me, that everyone who sees the Son and believes in him may have everlasting life; and I will raise him up at the last day." *(John 6:40)* The Scripture also promises that he is able to "transform our lowly body that it may be conformed to his glorious body." *(Philippians 3:21)* This will happen at the Second Coming of Christ, when the resurrection of the dead takes place.

Jesus explained that after that great event, in the future "kingdom of heaven," God's people will sit down and commune with Abraham, Isaac, and Jacob (the patriarchs of Judaism). *(See Matthew 8:11, Luke 13:28.)* If these men are identifiable eternally as these singular, previous personalities, then what happened to their multiple personalities up to that point? Or what happened to any subsequent personalities they bore later on? No, the implication is clear—they only lived one life!

If reincarnation is true, then the doctrine of the resurrection becomes totally confused. If we wear a number of physical bodies during numerous earthly sojourns, which one is resurrected? Furthermore, if the soul ultimately evolves, through the reincarnation process, into formless union with Brahman, then resurrection is unnecessary. Yet resurrection was the pattern set forth in the prototype of all sons of God. If Jesus, the firstborn Son of God, was literally resurrected from the dead, he went through this experience to set a precedent and to give his followers hope—hope that we, too, will eventually be resurrected from the dead, in a literal sense.

If Jesus was really an Avatar, and if he really studied under Far Eastern masters, why did he teach such a doctrine that is so contradictory to what they would profess. Considering these things, it must be concluded that these two doctrines—reincarnation and resurrection—are completely incompatible. Therefore, only one belief can be retained, at the expense of the other being discarded. (For more information on this particular aspect, see the section directly preceding this section, titled, *"Which is right: reincarnation or resurrection?"*)

(12) Some worldviews teach man's ultimate destiny is to be liberated from 'personhood' in order to achieve an undifferentiated union with an 'impersonal' Cosmic Force. For instance, in philosophic Hinduism the implication is made that passing from a state of being a 'personal entity' to the state of being one with an 'impersonal essence' is actually 'progress.' However, if viewed logically, the loss of personality would have to be gross spiritual digression, not progression. Generally speaking, Buddhism forecasts an even more tragic, spiritual reversal (though a Buddhist would counter that such a view is not pessimistic, but realistic). In this worldview, an individual is finally divested of all the trappings of 'personhood' when he or she enters *paranirvana* (final extinction of personal existence). Embracing such a concept would make some difficult or negative 'personalities' on the evolutionary journey superfluous, expendable and, in a sense, even discardable—reducing the value of the individual. Christianity, on the other hand, grants each person infinite value and promises the perfecting of the individual personality in a final glorified state, as well as an unending love-relationship with a personal and eternal God. It must be said that such a scenario alone constitutes true spiritual progress.

(13) Finally, true salvation is based, not on man's effort to reach perfection, but rather, on God's effort to reach man. The biblical worldview depicts man, caught in a sinful state, seeking God and trusting the Creator to condescend to his level. In response to man's humility and repentance, God grants forgiveness, mercy, restoration, an imparted status of righteousness and the gift of eternal life. The Far Eastern worldview depicts man being awakened out of a state of ignorance, striving to ascend to a place of perfection through human effort. Though striving to live a perfect life is certainly commendable, it is not possible. No human being can be entirely free of imperfections. The Bible does encourage believers to be perfect even as the heavenly Father is perfect, but it does not hinge salvation on the actual attaining of this goal. *(See Matthew 5:48.)* A more thorough explanation of this final argument immediately follows, under the heading, *"Does salvation come by human effort or by the grace of God?"*

18 — Does salvation come by human effort or by the grace of God?

According to the dual doctrines of karma and reincarnation, salvation comes by human effort. Karma Yoga focuses on ridding oneself from all negative karma by achieving perfection in thoughts, words and deeds. When the seeker for 'liberation' attains this goal (through ascetic practices, good deeds, righteous actions, ceremonies, sacrifices, pilgrimages and contemplation), he then begins to sow only positive karma into his future. Once such a character cleansing is consistent, uninterrupted by error, release from the cycle of rebirths is inevitable.

This foundational concept is common to Hinduism, Buddhism, Jainism, and sometimes in Sikhism (though in this religion there is a strong teaching against asceticism and a strong belief in the grace of God). Other esoteric sects and New Age groups embrace reincarnation as the true journey of the soul, such as ECKANKAR, Kabbalism and Theosophy, as well as numerous swamis, gurus, and mystics. These, and almost all other religious expressions in this world—including the Mideastern religions that teach just one earthly existence—place the burden of attaining 'salvation' upon the weary shoulders of human beings.

There is no greater example of this 'salvation by works' perspective than the foundational doctrines of Buddhism. When Buddha was 'enlightened' under the Bodhi tree, he claimed to receive the following insights that became the main foundation stones of his worldview:

"THE FOUR NOBLE TRUTHS"

(1) Life is filled with suffering and pain (*dukkha*, also said to mean "imperfection, emptiness and impermanence").

(2) The cause of suffering is desire (*tanha*, craving, thirst) for things such as existence, prosperity, achievement, and pleasure.

(3) The only way to overcome suffering (*nirodha*) is to overcome desire.

(4) This is accomplished by following the Eightfold Path (*magga*), enumerated below:

"THE EIGHTFOLD PATH"

(1) Right Knowledge (2) Right Thought (3) Right Speech
(4) Right Conduct (5) Right Livelihood (6) Right Effort
(7) Right Mindfulness and (8) Right Meditation.

By doing everything 'right' the sojourner through time can finally experience release from *maya* (the delusion of this realm), from *karma* (in Buddhism *kamma*—the law of cause and effect), and from *samsara* (the cycle of rebirths). Followers of this path are striving to overcome "the four basic evils—sensuality, the desire to perpetuate one's own existence, wrong belief and ignorance." The disciple who so perfects his character, lifestyle and mindset is a candidate for Nirvana (cessation of desire and release from self). For most Buddhists, Nirvana is not interpreted as annihilation, for Buddhists do not believe there is a personal self to annihilate. It is instead, the end of individuality and separateness. One writer explains, "Denial of identity does not imply denial of continuity."[59]

This sought-after peak on the mountain of spirituality is similar in some respects to what other religious groups have called Samadhi, Christ Consciousness, or Ultimate Bliss. However, it is slightly different. Most Hindus believe the self will ultimately be absorbed into Brahman, like a drop of water falling into the ocean. The traditional Buddhist believes that there is no enduring 'self, 'so the end result would be more like that same drop of water evaporating infinitely. Pursuing the "Eightfold Path" and doing everything right is certainly a commendable goal in life (and I respect Buddhists for their passionate pursuit of this objective). However, these categories mean something much different in a Christian context. Furthermore, this whole process is simply "salvation by works."

One writer explains, "Man's position, according to Buddhism, is supreme. Man is his own master, and there is no higher being or power that sits in judgment over his destiny."[60] In contrast, the Bible teaches that we are to trust God for our salvation: "The salvation of the righteous is of the Lord: he is their strength in the time of trouble. And the Lord shall help them, and deliver them...and save them, because they *trust* in him." *(Psalms 37:39–40 KJV)* We are required to come to him with contrition (godly sorrow): "The Lord is near to those who have a broken heart, and saves such as have a *contrite* spirit." *(Psalms 34:18)* Finally, we are expected to exercise simple faith in his promises: "For God so loved the world that he gave his only begotten Son, that whoever *believes* in him should not perish but have eternal life." *(John 3:16)*

Once repentant persons receive Jesus into their hearts, their sins are forgiven, and they have the promise of immediate access into heaven at the moment of death. One scripture says to be "absent from the body" is to be "present with the Lord." *(2 Corinthians 5:8)* No wonder Paul concluded: "And you he made alive, who were dead in trespasses and sins...For by grace you have been saved through faith, and that not of yourselves; it is the gift of God, not of works, lest anyone should boast." *(Ephesians 2:1, 8, 9)*

Not only did Paul believe in salvation by grace (unmerited favor from God), he had a personal experience of the power of this promise. Prior to his conversion experience, he was a persecutor of Christians and even caused the deaths of some believers. According to the doctrine of karma, Paul should have suffered severe retribution for his violent acts. According to his own testimony, he instead obtained mercy. *(See 1 Timothy 1:13–14.)* He was forgiven of God. Immediate upon salvation, he became an heir to eternal life, and later on, one of the greatest apostles to bear the message of the Gospel. What a radical proof of the power of the cross—especially to those who feel lost in a maze of their own failures!

Of course, salvation is not an absolute cure-all for all of life's woes. Those who are saved may still suffer. They may still go through painful situations, some of them quite extreme. Failures may come, sometimes followed by grievous consequences. There is no guarantee of anything different as long as we are in this world. Even though Jesus, the Son of God, walked in perfect oneness with the Father, he still suffered because of the temptations he faced *(Hebrews 2:18)* and the persecution he endured *(1 Peter 1:11)*. He also warned his disciples, "In the world you will have tribulation," but he followed that admonition with the command, "Be of good cheer!" *(John 16:33)*

One of the most glorious Bible promises foretells that "the sufferings of this present time are not worthy to be compared with the glory which shall be revealed in us." *(Romans 8:18, See 2 Corinthians 4:17.)* Suffering will finally cease for the children of God. Once eternity dawns for us, our inheritance of ultimate peace and joy will be "to the praise of the glory of

His grace" by which God has brought us into a relationship with himself. *(Ephesians 1:6)* Yes, in the end, it will rebound to God's credit, not ours.

---

19   What is the correct view of "desire" and "suffering"?

As just reviewed in the previous section, the main objective of Buddha's teaching was escape from suffering. "The Four Noble Truths" succinctly state that life is inevitably going to include suffering, the origin of suffering is ignorance, and the cause of suffering is desire. Cessation of desire ends suffering and that happens through implementation of the "Eightfold Path." Is this true? Is this a correct appraisal of the solution to man's dilemma? The fact of human suffering is not an issue, but the origin, cause, and solution of human suffering are issues that demand our attention.

Suffering is not always caused by desire. What about victims of disease, crime, natural disasters, betrayal, abuse, religious persecution, accidents, or demonic influence? Of course, those who embrace the Buddhist point of view might submit that the suffering resulting from such situations proceeds from the 'desire' to have a life free from complications, problems, disasters, and rejection from others. Those who unfortunately face such situations should react with passive detachment, thus rising above the suffering.

There is a certain element of truth in this portion of Buddhist doctrine, because far too often, those caught in negative circumstances allow themselves to feel overwhelmed. Far too often, they are crushed and even paralyzed emotionally by their sorrow. Sometimes, non-attachment does allow a person to objectively and calmly view his or her situation, so that a rational answer can be reached. However, non-attachment can also produce non-involvement in situations that plead for action. So, achieving a place of non-suffering may not necessarily be the complete answer. A concise, biblical response to these two issues is as follows:

The correct view of "desire"—First, let it be said that legitimate desires are not wrong and should not be purged from our thinking. There is a difference between selfish desire, which ends in death, and godly desire, which ends in life. *(See James 1:13–15.)* The Bible states that God *'desires'* his people to show mercy. During a time of intercession, the Lord Jesus prayed over his people saying, "Father, I *desire* that they also whom you have given me be with me where I am." If it is not wrong for the Lord himself to have righteous desires, it is certainly not wrong for us to have righteous desires. The Scripture does reveal that God "casts away the *desire* of the wicked," but it promises "the *desire* of the righteous will be granted." *(Proverbs 10:3, 24)* The Most High even assures his covenant people, "Delight yourself also in the Lord, and he shall give you the *desires* of your heart." *(Psalms 37:4)* Such righteous desires would logically include the meeting of natural and material needs as well as spiritual. However, if and when these things do not happen the way we *desire*, the Scripture cautions us "to be content." *(Philippians 4:11)* Our highest desire is God himself and when other desires are not realized, we maintain rest in our relationship with him. Inordinate desire is synonymous with lust, a very destructive agent in the human makeup. But holy desire is a motivation that we all definitely need.

The correct view of "suffering"—The goal for a Christian is not to fully escape all suffering, just certain kinds. There are numerous categories of suffering that we are encouraged to avoid, conquer, or rise above. These types of suffering are primarily the result of internal causes. These usually involve wrong thinking patterns that produce wrong behavior—sensuality, sinful cravings, negative emotions, inward temptations, guilt, resisting God's will, and a number of other negatives. We avoid, conquer, or rise above these sources of suffering two ways. First, we maintain a commitment to do all things right. (Actually, Buddha's Eightfold Path itemizes each area we need to deal with quite well—though the interpretation of most of the "right" things would be quite different within a biblical worldview.) Second and most importantly, we draw from the grace, mercy, forgiveness, and strength promised by the personal and loving God we serve (something Buddha did not teach). Our God cleanses us. He forgives us. He empowers us. He fills us with his presence and goodness. As David said, our "help comes from the Lord who made heaven and earth." *(Psalms 121:2)* This divine aid insures our winning all the more.

There are some causes of suffering that are primarily external and inevitably to be faced in life. These include trials, tribulations, outward sources of temptation, demonic influences and mistreatment by others. Even Jesus, the perfect Son of God, "suffered being tempted." *(Hebrews 2:18)* So, if we also "suffer being tempted," it is certainly not a sign of spiritual immaturity. However, in all these situations we are encouraged to react with positive attitudes like: a willingness to endure, a heart that rejoices, and a spirit of trust in God. We overcome the negative with the positive. At times, the negative may still be there, but we rise above it.

Finally, there is a category of suffering that God actually urges his people to embrace. Jesus declared that a true disciple must take up his cross daily and follow him. A cross is a complete death to self for the sake of helping others. This involves, not passive detachment from a hurting world, but active involvement in sharing its burden and meeting its needs. Such sacrificial service is certainly not an easy road to travel. Sometimes, compassion's grip can be quite painful, but it is necessary. Paul zealously laid hold to this challenge, explaining that one of his deepest desires was to know Christ "in the fellowship of his sufferings." *(Philippians 3:10)* He also kindly forewarned true disciples that it is given to us "in the behalf of Christ, not only to believe in him, but also to suffer for his sake." *(Philippians 1:29)* We can be certain, though, that release from all suffering will take place as soon as we are set free from these physical bodies. We will then consciously experience "unspeakable joy" in heavenly places. "Weeping may endure for a night, but joy comes in the morning." *(Psalms 30:5)* Yes, this will be especially true when our souls are finally released into the eternal state.

The sufferings of Jesus—Some claim it is spiritually erroneous to emphasize this aspect of the existence of Jesus. Was it really necessary for Jesus to suffer? Was it really the core purpose of the incarnation of the Son of God? Maharishi Mahesh Yogi commented, "It's a pity that Christ is talked of in terms of suffering...those who count upon the suffering, it is a wrong interpretation of the life of Christ and the message of Christ...How could suffering be associated with the One who has been all joy, all bliss, who claims all that? It's only the misunderstanding of the life of Christ."[61]

In a similar vein of thought, Buddhist teacher Thich Nhat Hanh respectfully offers, "The figure of the crucified Christ is a very painful image to me. It does not contain joy or peace, and this does not do justice to Jesus."[62] Yet the apostle Peter explained, "Those things which God foretold by the mouth of all His prophets, that the Christ would *suffer*, He has thus fulfilled. Repent therefore and be converted, that your sins may be blotted out, so that times of refreshing may come from the presence of the Lord." *(Acts 3:18–19)*

I believe that both Maharishi Mahesh Yogi and Thich Nhat Hanh were probably sincere in their assessment of the nature of Jesus' death. I believe their words were probably motivated by sensitivity to the pain of another. However, my response is this: that the final focus of a Christian's heart is not on the cross, but on the empty tomb. If it were not for the great victory of the latter, the great misery of the former would agreeably be too "painful" to gaze upon. Nevertheless, Jesus "endured the cross," "for the joy that was set before him." *(Hebrews 12:2)* Thankfully, his followers are blessed to also share in this joy even during this earthly sojourn.

Some interpret the sufferings of Jesus to be the result of unwise behavior on his part. Marcus Borg, editor of the book, *"Jesus and Buddha, The Parallel Sayings,"* suggests: "Jesus' activity as a social prophet—as a voice of religious social protest—is the most likely reason that his public activity was so brief compared to the Buddha's." (Jesus' public ministry probably lasted about three years, while Buddha's lasted fifty years.) Borg continues, "Jesus' early death was probably because of his social-political passion; if he had been simply a wisdom teacher and healer, I doubt that he would have been executed."[63]

Jesus' own testimony counters this argument. The Son of God often prophesied the certainty of, and reason for, his soon-to-come death on a cross. He assured, "The Son of man *must* suffer many things, and be rejected of the elders and chief priests and scribes, and be slain, and be raised the third day." Notice the word *must*. This was an unavoidable event. It had to happen. Jesus continued exhorting his disciples, "If any man will come after me, let him deny himself, and take up his cross daily, and follow me." *(Luke 9:22–23)* So, Jesus knew in advance exactly what kind of death he would die. His early demise was not a terrible mistake or backlash from an unwise method of presenting his message. It was simply his destiny, the cup the Father gave him to drink. *(See Matthew 26:39.)* Jesus even claimed that no man took his life from him; he gave it up willingly. *(See John 10:18.)* Irrefutably, it was according to "the definite plan and foreknowledge of God"—the plan for man's redemption. *(Acts 2:23, See Luke 24:13–32.)* No wonder the Bible refers to Jesus, as the "Lamb slain from the foundation of the world." *(Revelation 13:8)*

20   Do we have a "sin-problem" or an "ignorance-problem"?

Most yoga devotees and New Age or Far Eastern advocates declare loudly that man's problem is not sin, but ignorance. However, the subjects of "sin" and the "lower nature" are often addressed in the Scripture base of Hinduism, Buddhism, Jainism and Sikhism, and sometimes with strong language. For instance, the Bhagavad-Gita warns against the "triple gate of hell": lust, anger and greed. *(See Bhagavad-Gita 16:21–22.)*

If ignorance is the source of man's dilemma, the logical deduction is that salvation comes through knowledge. Yogi Bhajan posed the question, "Who is the savior? It is your own higher consciousness which can save you from your own lower consciousness."[64] The premise behind this statement is that human beings are asleep to the fact that they are truly divine. They need to be enlightened, awakened to this realization of their 'higher Self.' They certainly do not need to view themselves as sinners. During the first World Parliament of Religions in Chicago (1983) Swami Vivekananda, founder of the Vedanta Societies, offered the curious comment, "It's a sin to call a man a sinner." Of course, this obvious play on words contradicts itself, because to sin makes one a sinner.

Many of my peers in the study of yoga felt the use of this term was negative, even repulsive—and I must admit that I did too. Yet this word is inseparably integrated into the teachings of Jesus and the purpose for which he came. The angel that foretold Jesus' birth instructed Joseph, "You shall call his name Jesus, for He will save His people from their *sins*." (*Matthew 1:21*, emphasis by author) According to this heaven-sent herald, providing salvation from "*sin*" was the primary reason for the Lord's entrance into this world.

During his earthly ministry Jesus often used this word and dealt with the concept behind it. Once he even protested, "Whoever commits *sin* is a slave of *sin*." (*John 8:34*, emphasis by author) And there is no more powerful statement than Jesus' forceful declaration to those who rejected his claim to Messiahship, "If you do not believe that I am He, you will die in your *sins*." (*John 8:24*, emphasis by author) Such phrases would be inconsistent with a real 'Avatar'—(for those who believe that to be his shared identity)—if the dilemma of the human race is just an 'ignorance problem'.

The teachings of Gnosticism often challenged the early church and its doctrine. The Gnostics proposed that 'salvation' is achieved through knowledge (*gnosis*). Once seekers are awakened to the 'knowledge' of their divinity, they are lifted above the confines of sense-consciousness. When this happens, they conquer negativity in their lives and begin to live on a higher plane of saintliness. So revelation knowledge, not repenting of sin, emerges as the answer. Most likely, in response to the Gnostics of his day, the apostle John wrote, "If we say that we have no *sin*, we deceive ourselves, and the truth is not in us." (*1 John 1:8*, emphasis by author) Erasing the concept of sin enables men to set their own standards, instead of aligning with God's. This can even make aberrant behavior allowable.

The main issue at stake is not the rightness or wrongness of the idea of 'sin,' but rather, the interpretation of the nature of the Godhead. If God is just an impersonal energy force, human beings are not morally accountable to him. Hindu Scripture gives many guidelines concerning a person's moral and ethical behavior. Yet in the story of his conversion to Christianity, former guru, Rabi Maharaj, pointed out, "Hinduism teaches that each man's *dharma*, or rule of conduct, differs and must be discovered individually; there is no moral code binding upon all."[65] This runs parallel to the concept of relativism, the idea that behavioral choices should not be governed by predetermined rules and regulations, but by the sensation of the moment.

If God is a personal Creator, there are definite, moral absolutes to which all human beings must conform. Because God authors these laws, failure to observe them is considered a transgression or a 'sin' against him. A personal God, in great love and fatherly concern, watches over the thoughts, attitudes, and actions of human beings to see if they are in conformity with his will. Those who come to God, acknowledging his standard of proper behavior, are privileged to receive pardon and cleansing upon repentance over wrong choices. The next step is for them to lovingly, worshipfully submit to God's rules and oversight. This should be done in the realization that God's purpose in giving guidelines is not to dominate, but to liberate. He knows what kind of behavior has a destructive, binding, and blinding effect on us and what ushers us into a place of freedom, bounty, illumination, and blessing. His boundaries really are for our protection and comfort.

The Scripture warns that when lust (selfish desire) has "conceived, it gives birth to sin; and sin, when it is full-grown, brings forth death" (emotional death, mental death, spiritual death, physical death and ultimately, eternal death). *(James 1:15)* But Jesus came to give "life... and that more abundantly." *(John 10:10)* Teaching on the concept of sin fills the Bible, as does the cure for this great dilemma of the human race.

This chapter's conclusions does not negate the fact that 'knowledge' is essentially important. The Scripture announces that "the Lord is a God of knowledge" and "through knowledge the righteous will be delivered." *(1 Samuel 2:3, Proverbs 11:9)* It also instructs that those who are bound to their lusts are living in "ignorance." *(1 Peter 1:14)* So being 'awakened' out of 'ignorance' by the influence of the Spirit of God is, and will always be, a primary concern. However, understanding that we have a 'sin-problem' is inextricably a part of this 'knowledge-awakening.'

21 — Maya or deception: which influence is clouding the minds of men?

Some branches of Hinduism teach that *avidya*, or ignorance, hinders the individual self from discerning the non-dual universal nature of pure being *(Brahman)*. Because of the subliminal, all-pervasive influence of *maya* (illusion), human beings tend to perceive only separate selves and things (all that combines to make up this temporal, materialistic world). This view insists that most people fail to perceive that all separate existences are essentially unreal. This false perception results from *maya*, the power of illusion mysteriously inherent in and projected from Brahman.

Theoretically, when the veil of *maya* is lifted, the 'enlightened' person realizes that all things are of one essential substance (the doctrine of monism). The falsehood of dualities then becomes apparent, such as the illusory distinction between *atman* (the human soul) and *Brahman* (the Oversoul), and the doctrinal barriers that exist between various religious expressions. Those who buy into this interpretation of the creation usually conclude, as the Roman Emperor and Stoic Philosopher, Marcus Aurelius, "The universe is a single life comprising one substance and one soul."[66]

Maya is supposedly the result of *lila*, a cosmic game, a kind of divine 'trick' played on the human race. As long as the individual self remains locked in a carnal state, as long as it is devoid of spiritual insight, it will futilely look for fulfillment in the material world with its activities. This spiritual ignorance causes the souls of men to stay trapped within *samsara*, the continuing cycle of birth, death and rebirth.

Christianity *does* agree with the futility of living for things in this world. In the Old Testament, Solomon lamented, "Vanity of vanities, all is vanity." *(Ecclesiastes 1:2)* Vanity is uselessness, senselessness, and emptiness—the dark cloak that covers all the activities of this realm that are not a part of enduring truth. Insightful persons are quick to acknowledge that all these things will eventually bow to the ravages of time. In the New Testament, John, the apostle, explained, "all that is in the world—the lust of the flesh, the lust of the eyes, and the pride of life—is not of the Father but is of the world. And the world is passing away, and the lust of it; but he who does the will of God abides forever." *(1 John 2:16–17)*

Buddhism teaches the related doctrines of "Emptiness" and "Impermanence." Admittedly, all inanimate things and many animate things are "empty" of an enduring essence; and they are "impermanent" (such as rocks and plants). The world as it is now is only temporary. However, Christianity teaches an ultimate "New Earth" that will be permanent and those who know the Lord will permanently be a part of it. Buddhism on the other hand teaches that nothing is permanent, not even personal existence.

Christian doctrine does not support the idea of *maya*: the global grip of illusion supposedly perpetrated by the absolute (Brahman). In Christianity the world is real; it is a substantive and significant expression of the divine plan, to be enjoyed as part of the human experience of life. Moreover, the lessons learned here are relevant and valuable. However, men misuse the world and abuse themselves and each other because of deception.

God does not author this deception. Rather, three main influences have warped the conduct of the human race since the fall of man: (1) The devil (along with his associate demon spirits); (2) The sin that is so rampant here, and; (3) The fallen nature of our own flesh (which actually makes human beings all the more susceptible to the first two sources of deception mentioned). The Scripture indicts these three as being the real perpetrators of deception, explaining that Satan "deceives the whole world," that human beings are "hardened through the deceitfulness of sin" and that the unregenerated human heart is "deceitful above all things, and desperately wicked." *(Revelation 12:9, Hebrews 3:13, Jeremiah 17:9)*

God removed the human race from conscious fellowship with his divine presence because of the entrance of sin in the beginning. However, God does not purposefully delude men or distort the truth. Because of their separation from him and the fallen state of their flesh, human beings are vulnerable to this darkened state of mind. However, God's Spirit is titled the "Spirit of truth," sent forth into this world to guide men into "all truth." *(John 16:13)*

According to the biblical worldview, there will always be a certain measure of what some would term 'duality.' God's people will never actually become God. We will always exist as separate entities, separate and distinct from each other and separate from the Almighty. Once we are given glorified bodies, believers will enjoy a beautiful, eternal oneness with each other and with God, but not to the degree of losing our individual existence. This oneness with God is symbolized in Paul's writings by the oneness of a husband and wife in marriage. *(See Ephesians 5:23–33.)* The mystery is that two persons become one. In the process, however, they never lose their individual identities, though undeniably, there is a uniting of their bodies and a blending of their souls. So it is with the Lord Jesus Christ and his people.

Many 'dualities' will cease with the entrance of what Christian theology terms the "New Creation" (like the opposites of life and death, light and darkness, future and past, etc.). Only life, light and eternity will remain. However, one distinction will continue forever (the Bridegroom, the Lord Jesus—separate and distinct from his eternal bride—though enjoying an indescribably deep and holy union with them forever.)

Meher Baba, who claimed to be *the* Avatar for this age, described creation as a "foolish act" and a "mighty joke."[67] This is much different than the Creator's assessment of the matter, as recorded in the Bible.

After viewing all that he had made in six divine days of creation, God concluded, "Behold, it was very good." *(Genesis 1:31)* Of course, Meher Baba's perspective runs parallel to the Hindu concept of *lila*—explaining all of this to be some kind of divine game. There is possibly no better response to this than Annie Dillard's in *Pilgrim at Tinker Creek*— "Divinity is not playful. The universe was not made in jest, but in solemn incomprehensible earnest by a power that is unfathomably secret and holy and fleet. There is nothing to be done about it but ignore it or see."[68]

22 What is the origin of evil?

According to the Bible, evil streams from four main sources: (1) **The 'Original Sin'** passed down from Adam to all his offspring, which results in a sin nature resident in our human flesh *(Psalms 51:5, Romans 5:12, Ephesians 2:3)*; (2) **Sinful choices** that we, as human beings, make *(John 5:14, James 1:13–14)*; (3) **The world system;** the societies and cultures, created by fallen human beings, that become strongholds of evil *(1 John 2:15-17)*; (4) **Demonic powers** that are constantly tempting the inhabitants of this planet, seducing them to commit evil. Most biblical theologians believe evil spirits were originally righteous angels until they joined Satan in his rebellion against God in the beginning. *(See Isaiah 14:12–19, Ezekiel 28:12–19, 1 Thessalonians 3:5, Revelation 12:1–9.)* Events that result from their influence cannot be attributed to God, since they do not work in submission to his will. The Bible clearly states that God is so holy that he "cannot be tempted by evil nor does he Himself tempt anyone." *(James 1:13)* Logic dictates that if God does not "tempt" human beings, he did not "tempt" the angels to turn against him in the beginning. Neither did God purposefully create demons with an evil nature. The true Creator would never influence demonic beings to do evil. Instead, their evil nature is a result of their original free-will choice to oppose the Creator and his laws.

In Eastern religions, evil is primarily the product of illusion or *maya*. It is considered essentially unreal. (See Question #21.) Liberation consists, not so much in conquering evil, as it does in conquering ignorance. Experiencing Ultimate Reality enables one to be free from the domination of that which is unreal, including the evil that abounds in this world.

Buddhism especially emphasizes that to experience Nirvana, a person must ignore evil and suffering, because these things are alien to the consciousness of true existence. Years ago I met Satguru Sivaya

Subramuniyaswami, a well-known leader in Hinduism. He explained the Eastern View, "There is no intrinsic evil. All is good. All is God. No force in the world or in man opposes God, though the veiling instinctive-intellectual mind keeps us from knowledge of Him."[69] The New Age Movement has inherited this mindset from Hinduism, its spiritual parent. An avid New Ager, Shirley MacLaine, quotes her spirit guide as instructing, "Until mankind realizes that there is, in truth, no good and there is, in truth, no evil, there will be no peace."[70]

Strangely (yet logically, if the related concepts of monism and pantheism are upheld), Brahma, the Creator god in Hinduism, is identified as the Source of both good and evil:

> *"Formerly, all creatures were virtuous, and by themselves they obtained divinity. Therefore the gods became worried, so Brahma created women in order to delude men. Then women, who had been virtuous, became wicked witches, and Brahma filled them with wanton desires, which they in turn inspired in men. He created anger, and henceforth all creatures were born in the power of desire and anger."* (Mahabharata 13.40.5–12)

The perspective of Taoism, with its *yin-yang* theory, also maintains that evil is a manifestation of the Tao (the Universal Force). Both evil and good stream from the same Source, the primal Cause of all causes. Evil flows from the *yin* aspect (the negative principle) of the Absolute, while good flows from the *yang* (the positive principle). Because the Tao is eternal and ultimate, the harmonizing aspects of *yin* and *yang* are eternal and ultimate as well, necessary for spiritual equilibrium in the universe.

Though accepting the story of the fall of Adam and Eve, neither Islam nor Judaism promote the concept of the "Original Sin" being passed on to the offspring of these parents of the human race. In these two religions, man is intrinsically good, and able to live a righteous life if he so chooses. Only Christianity reveals this inherited spiritual dilemma facing the inhabitants of this planet. One scripture warns, "through one man [Adam] sin entered the world, and death through sin." *(Romans 5:12)*[71]

Kabbala, the esoteric offshoot of Judaism, proposes something altogether different. In the Zohar (the "Book of Splendor"—one of the two main sources of Kabbalistic doctrine), it is "implied that the evil in the universe originated from the leftovers of worlds that were destroyed."[72] In Scientology, evil originates in the 'reactive mind.'

With regard to demonic spirits, most religions admit their existence, but they differ greatly concerning the origin of these dark entities. According to the United Church of Religious Science (Ernest Holmes), the "devil" is not an actual entity; "the only devil we shall ever know will be that which appears as the result of our negative thinking."[73] It is "anything which denies the unity of good, the allness of Truth, or our oneness with Spirit."[74] In Ernest Holmes' belief system, evil spirits are reduced to "discordant and chaotic thought patterns consciously retained which tend to influence the conscious faculties negatively."[75] In a similar way, the Bahá'í faith dismisses the idea of Satan and evil spirits, dubbing those concepts as mere superstition. Any reference to something being 'satanic' is metaphorical, not literal.

According to Hinduism, evil spirits came forth from Brahma's side, created with an evil nature, or they could be human beings who lived evil lives or failed to follow their dharma. According to Zoroastrianism, their existence is traceable to Ahriman, the god of evil, who possesses the power to create. Taoism teaches that evil spirits *(kuei)* may actually be disembodied human spirits: those who suffered violent deaths, or those who were buried without the necessary, prescribed rituals. The Qur'an of Islam teaches that these corrupt beings were created out of fire. Only the Bible relates the origin and nature of evil spirits correctly. Much of the ministry of Jesus involved casting out evil spirits and delivering people from their diabolical influence. So it should be still in the ministry of a true man or woman of God. Thankfully, it is also foretold in Scripture that Satan and his subordinate devils will ultimately be exiled from the presence of God forever, confined to the lake of fire. *(See Matthew 8:28–29; 25:41, 2 Peter 2:4, Jude 6, Revelation 12:7-9; 20:1-3, 10, 14.)*

---

23   Mantras: are these repetitious phrases a valid tool in reaching God?

In the Kundalini Yoga classes I attended, I was taught that chanting mantras would aid in penetrating the supernatural and achieving oneness with God. Yogi Bhajan compared God to a great computer into which we could insert these 'mystical formulas' to obtain the desired results. Our primary goal was enlightenment. The mantra we chanted most often was *"Ek Ong Kar, Sat Nam, Siri Wah Guru."* In essence the meaning is, "There is one God, Truth is his name and the Great Spirit is our teacher." Those statements are actually true within the Christian worldview, but the interpreted meaning is much different than what is promoted in yogic teaching. If based on biblical doctrine these three phrases would mean:

Ek Ong Kar—yes, there is "only one God," but there is "only one God" to the exclusion of all others, not the all-inclusive oversoul found in Far Eastern religions. (See Question #1, page 179.)

Sat Nam—yes, "truth" is one of the names or titles of the Lord, for Jesus claimed, "I am the way, the *truth* and the life," but it is not his primary, personal name. *(John 14:6,* emphasis by author) Furthermore, the 'truth' proposed in Far Eastern religions is much different than the actual truth revealed in Christianity.

Siri Wah Guru—yes, the Holy Spirit is sent into our lives to "teach" us all things. *(John 14:26)* However, according to biblical doctrine, we do not truly experience the ongoing leadership and instruction of the Holy Spirit until we become "sons of God" through the born again experience. *(John 1:12)* Also, the Holy Spirit is the personal presence of God, not a mere impersonal, cosmic force.

Supposedly, by repetitiously chanting these words, meditators can be supernaturally drawn into the reality of what the words represent. Yogi Bhajan even claimed that repeating this particular mantra creates "a special heat in which all the karmas get burned." Those participating in this process "become neutralized."[76] So the highest purpose behind this practice is facilitating an earlier release from the cycle of rebirths.

A mantra usually relates to a certain deity or embodies a certain spiritual concept. Devotees of Mantra Yoga believe that if a mantra centers on the name of a deity, chanting that mantra draws the spirit of the meditator into intimate contact with that deity. Chanting a mantra that speaks of a spiritual concept causes the 'represented idea' to pass from the 'conceptual' into the 'actual' for the one meditating. Swami Prabhupada of ISKCON (Krishna Consciousness) warns that unless a seeker is "initiated by a bona fide spiritual master in the disciplic succession, the mantra... received is without any effect."[77] This is a common belief among various swamis, gurus and Far Eastern religious belief systems. There is little agreement, though, concerning which gurus are actually 'qualified' to impart this knowledge.

Most advocates of this methodology believe the primal sound-vibration uttered by the Infinite Oversoul was 'OM,' that this sacred word accompanied the manifestation of the universe, and it continues to resound throughout the entire cosmos. By echoing this subliminal vibration, meditators can 'tune in' to the origin of all things. An ancient Hindu text declares, "When a Yogin is absorbed in the syllable OM, he becomes eternal....He becomes one with Brahman....He wins absorption in Brahman, in the supreme ultimate Self." *(Markandeya Purana 39.6.16)*

One source deepens the explanation, "OM is composed of the three sounds A-U-M... which represent several important triads: the three worlds of earth, atmosphere, and heaven; the three major Hindu gods, Brahma, Vishnu and Shiva; and the three sacred Vedic Scriptures, Rg, Yajus, and Sama."[78]

In opposition to the theory that OM was the original syllable spawning the universe, the Bible teaches this happened because of a number of easily understood commands given by God (See Genesis 1:1–26: "Let there be light," "Let the dry land appear," "Let the earth bring forth," etc.). The Bible never suggests that we should repetitiously chant those commands in order to achieve union with God. **Actually Jesus taught the opposite: that we should never use such "vain repetitions" in prayer. *(Matthew 6:7)***

Every yoga teacher with whom I was associated insisted Jesus studied under Indian gurus during his hidden years in order to discover proper methods to awaken the Christ nature. If this were the case, why did he return from the Far East only to warn others that such methods were futile and should be rejected? Though he gave what has been called "The Lord's Prayer" as a basic outline of effective prayer, he never instructed those who subscribe to its use to sit for hours, repeating these words over and over in a monotone voice. He never trained his disciples in this kind of spiritual exercise, and they never passed it on to future generations of the church. If it were so important, certainly the opposite would be the case.

Why are mantras an incorrect method of prayer? Primarily, because God is not a mere energy force, to be manipulated or controlled in a mechanical way by repeated word-formulas or incantations. We would never expect to make a request of a fellow human being using such a technique. To do so would be considered absurd. After monotonously repeating a request about a hundred times, we would certainly be asked to remove ourselves from the premises. Why should we think that God is responsive to such methodology? He is a personal God to be approached from the heart in a personal way.

The Most High gives the invitation, "Call to Me, and I will answer you, and show you great and mighty things, which you do not know." *(Jeremiah 33:3)* In calling upon the Creator, it is not only important to use right methods, but to use the correct name. Quite often, mantras use names of gods who are not actual, existing entities, but the product of human imagination. This automatically nullifies the effectiveness of the practice and, worse than that, it opens the door to deeper, spiritual deception.

In closing, I must admit that I do respect and appreciate the Far Eastern perception of the power of words. Biblically, this is an emphasis too. All human beings are urged to "confess" with their lips and "believe" in their hearts that God raised Christ from the dead in order to experience true salvation. From that point forward, believers are cautioned to hold the profession of their faith "without wavering." For "death and life are in the power of the tongue and those who love it will eat its fruit." *(Romans 10:8–10, Hebrews 10:23, Proverbs 18:21)*

Quoting the Word of God was the way Jesus defeated Satan during his wilderness temptation. Confessing the promises of God is a practice that believers are encouraged to prayerfully implement—and sometimes confessing promises can become somewhat repetitive. However, these practices are not the same as the Mantra Yoga method focused on reaching enlightenment. Quoting and confessing God's Word (after the initial experience of salvation) is not a methodology aimed at becoming one with God. Rather, it is the rightful exercise of a believer's authority resulting from that oneness with God he or she has already obtained as a gift.

The Bible promises that God will 'inhabit the praise of His people.' *(See Psalms 22:3.)* I admit that sometimes praise can be repetitive, with certain statements being uttered often (e.g., "I love you Lord," "I praise Your name," "I worship You, Father," etc.). Once again, though, these are not mechanically repeated formulas designed to bring a person into a state of enlightenment. These are the celebration of a relationship already established. Even Mahatma Ghandi, that revered leader among Hindus, advised:

> *"Prayer...is a longing of the soul. It is a daily admission of one's weakness...**It is better in prayer to have a heart without words than words without a heart.**"*[79]

Most anyone would agree that repetitive, monotone mantras are always "words without a heart."

---

24   Was Jesus "*a*" Door or "*the*" Door to eternal life?

The general consensus in New Age sects and Far Eastern religious groups is that there are many doors to an ultimate state of being or oneness with the Creator. However, Jesus did not claim, "I am one of the doors to the sheepfold." Promoting an exclusive approach, he asserted, "I am *the* door of the sheep." *(See John 10:1–7, emphasis by author.)*

He did not say, "I am one of many ways." Unashamedly he insisted, "I am *the* way." *(John 14:6,* emphasis by author)

Of course, as a yoga teacher I professed to know what Jesus really meant by these statements—that achieving his "I AM" consciousness, his totally enlightened state, is the 'door' for all humanity and the 'way' to enlightenment. Yet if this was what Jesus meant, he would have plainly said so. He would have used easily understood words like; "You must walk through the door of your own Christ Consciousness, of an awakened 'higher Self,' in order to live in the realm where I abide." Instead, in simple language, he informed, "I am the door" and "I am the way...No one comes to the Father except through Me." *(John 10:9;14:6)*

Without controversy, Jesus was affirming that all must go through him personally to obtain an experience of salvation, to receive the gift of eternal life. This is simple, straightforward language that can only be interpreted in a simple, straightforward way. There are many profound reasons why Jesus could make such an astonishing claim (his deity, his virgin birth, his sinless life, his crucifixion, his resurrection, and his promised return). The following unique insight enhances this concept:

THREE HEAVENS: ONLY ONE DOOR

The Bible speaks of three heavens, probably divided up as follows:

- ⌣' The first heaven is earth's atmosphere and the universe beyond.
- ⌣' The second heaven is an intermediate, spiritual sphere.
- ⌣' The third heaven is the highest realm, the abode of the manifest presence of God, also referred to in the Bible as paradise. *(See 2 Corinthians 12:2–4.)*

These three heavens are concentric, blending together and sharing a common center. The second heaven is apparently an intermediate sphere, bridging the gap between the terrestrial abode of man and the celestial abode of God. Quite possibly, this realm could be similar to what Eastern mystics or New Age thinkers refer to as the "Astral Plane."

Consider this comparison. The soul and the spirit of a human being, though spiritual and invisible, occupy somewhat the same space as the associated physical body. So also, the invisible planes of existence (the second and third heavens), occupy somewhat the same area as the first heaven and yet are spiritual in essence. Though unseen to man, the second heaven is full of angelic and demonic activity that constantly overflows into this natural world affecting us all. Understanding the true nature of these realms pulls back the veil on two highly profound mysteries: (1) Why many religions misinterpret and depersonalize God's nature; (2) Why Jesus could make the astonishing claims showcased at the start of this answer to Question# 24.

The life "of" God or life "from" God—Many who subscribe to a Far Eastern/New Age worldview claim that the 'life-essence' underlying all living things, in both the physical plane and the first two heavens, actually is God—an all-pervasive, impersonal, cosmic life-force. Hindus and yoga advocates call this force *prana*; Taoists call it *chi*—and most advocates of these mindsets would readily suggest these terms are synonymous with what Christians call the Holy Spirit. Yet this cannot be the case. *Prana* or *chi* is described as an *impersonal* force, while the Holy Spirit is the *personal* presence of God. There is a vast and irreconcilable difference between the two concepts.

Why is this important? Because correct revelation presents God as a personal and transcendent Being, existing apart from the physical creation. He dwells in the third heaven (the "high and holy place"—*Isaiah 57:15*). However, he has also filled the physical plane and the first two heavens with a 'life-force' that exists apart from him. This is not the life *of* God; rather, it is a life that comes *from* God. It enables plants, animals and human beings to 'live' in the natural plane; it enables angels, demons and other supernatural entities to exist in higher planes. As already pointed out in Question #3, in the New Testament, there are two main Greek words translated "life." Generally speaking, natural or physical life (life *from* God) is *psuche* (pronounced psoo-khay'); divine life (the life *of* God) is *zoe* (pronounced zo-ay').

When religious seekers in this world (Buddhist, Hindu, Jainist, New Age, etc) open themselves up to a higher spiritual realm through various techniques (like meditating on chakras, chanting mantras or visualizing yantras), they may actually experience the next level above us, but they are unable to proceed into the third heaven. Experiencing this highest realm of the personal presence of God is impossible unless seekers approach God through the 'door' of his Son. Jesus is spoken of as the eternal "image of the invisible God" and the only "mediator between God and men." (*Colossians 1:15, 1 Timothy 2:5*) Those who do not acknowledge this God-appointed 'door' become 'locked' inside a lower spiritual realm—filled with an impersonal life—which they mistakenly label "Ultimate Reality," for that is all they have ever known.

Entities inhabiting the second heaven—It is also important to understand that when Adam and Eve fell, Satan became the ruling force in this world. As "the prince of the power of the air," along with his demonic underlings, he succeeded in surrounding the globe with a suffocating layer of impenetrable spiritual darkness. *(Ephesians 2:2)* No one is exempt from facing such negative influence. According to Revelation 12:9, Satan has succeeded in deceiving "the whole world." Though this "prince of darkness" and his subordinate demons cannot be observed literally moving through the physical atmosphere (the first heaven), they constantly travel through the second heaven, its spiritual counterpart. In this dimension of existence, angelic forces from God oppose satanic activity and work to establish God's purposes in the lives of those who are surrendered to the truth. *(See Hebrews 1:13–14.)* Various orders of angels populate the third heaven, while demons are apparently restrained from entering this celestial sphere (though it is apparent that Satan, in the past, has come into God's presence in the third heaven in an accusatory role—*Job 1:6-12*).

The satanic strategy—The Bible teaches that Satan can appear as an "angel of light." *(2 Corinthians 11:14)* In other words, he and his associate spirits are very adept at granting false supernatural experiences that appear to be of the "True Light." In the beginning, part of his rebellion against God included an attempt to be "like the Most High." *(Isaiah 14:14)* Undoubtedly, he is still endeavoring to accomplish this goal—providing a counterfeit experience of the Divine. Those who open their hearts to the realm of the supernatural, but do not use a proper approach to God (like calling on the name of Jesus and claiming the cleansing effects of his blood) invariably come under this deceptive influence. (I personally experienced visions and out-of-body sensations during meditation that I now know were a product of this negative influence.)

Yes, this is the dilemma! Even those who passionately love God and are sincerely searching for understanding are subject to this predicament. This is exactly why God outlawed various occult practices in the Old Testament such as: necromancy (contacting the dead), astrology, fortune telling, sorcery, channeling, divination and the like. *(See Deuteronomy 18:10–13.)* He was not denying the children of Israel valid experiences in the supernatural realm; he was trying to guard them from demonic deception. He knew such spiritual subterfuge would draw them into false doctrine, and eventually rob them of spiritual reality and the power of truth.

**The following diagram illustrates what happens when
seekers from various religions attempt to reach God,
using non-biblical methods, and why biblical
methods alone are successful.**

THE AWESOME POWER OF SPIRITUAL REBIRTH

As the illustration indicates, the experience of being born again
originates from the third heaven. Jesus said, "Do not marvel that I said
to you, 'You must be born again.' *(John 3:7)* The Greek word translated
"again" is *anothen* (pronounced an´-o-then), which means "from above."
When seekers call on the name of Jesus and ask the Spirit of Christ (the
Holy Spirit) to come into their hearts, he does so, simultaneously creating
a "new spirit" within them. For this reason any 'saved' person is biblically
referred to as a "new creation" *(2 Corinthians 5:17)*. When this inner
transformation takes place, newborn believers are delivered from "the
power of darkness" and translated into "the kingdom of God's dear Son."
(Colossians 1:13) From that moment onward, sons and daughters of God
are 'connected' with the third heaven and can live in an atmosphere of
the presence of God.

Ephesians 2:6 explains how Christian believers "sit together in heavenly places." In other words, though still existing in a natural plane, those who are saved can maintain a daily, supernatural awareness—a blessed sensitivity to the overflow of the kingdom of heaven in their lives. They are filled with divine life *(zoe)* and because of this, able to experience communion with God constantly.

Unfortunately, men's religious bridges always stop short of this goal. Construction always ceases once the builders penetrate the next realm above us. Satanic powers will allow them to progress no further. This is why truth-seekers of good intention and great spiritual fervor can purport to have life-changing supernatural revelations and visionary insights— and yet be wrong. Only God's bridge completely spans the gap between eternity and time. No wonder the axiom is so popular that "religion is man's effort to reach God, but Jesus Christ is God's effort to reach man." And no wonder the Scripture reveals: "He who has the Son has LIFE *(zoe)*; he who does not have the Son of God does not have LIFE *(zoe)*...This is the true God, and eternal LIFE *(zoe)*." *(1 John 5:12, 20, emphasis by author)*

25   Are all human beings "children of God," or is this status only given to those who fulfill certain requirements?

Ordinary human beings, who are focused on earthly and temporal things, are called the "children of this world" in Jesus' teaching. *(Luke 16:8, 20:34 KJV)* They are the offspring of natural parents, born after the natural process of human reproduction, and living within the confines of mere sense-consciousness. Because we all share this common beginning point, we are all part of the same human family. In that sense, we are all brothers and sisters, regardless of race, color, culture, or even creed. The Bible tears down separating walls with the declaration that God "has made from one blood every nation." *(Acts 17:26)*

How wonderfully Jesus expressed God's fatherly care for all people! Those who listened to his public messages had not yet experienced "regeneration," an experience that would only be available only after His resurrection and ascension *(Titus 3:5)*. They were just simple people concerned about life's necessities, yet the great Teacher calmed their hearts by assuring them:

> *"Your heavenly Father knows that you need all these things." (Matthew 6:32)*

If Jesus referred to God as their "Father," it is logical to assume that they were considered "his children." Therefore, we can conclude, on a foundational level, that all human beings are "children of God after the creation" (the earthly, Adamic family). As Paul explained to the Greeks, we are all "His offspring" *(Acts 17:28)*. The Creator loves all people so deeply that He "gave His only begotten Son" to purchase their salvation *(John 3:16)*. He did this in order to lift those who respond to a higher, eternal level of sonship available only through spiritual rebirth.

Unveiling this mystery to Nicodemus, Jesus insisted, "Unless one is born again he cannot see the kingdom of God" (to "see" means to comprehend). Clearly, Jesus was not talking about reincarnation (recurring natural births), but rather a supernatural rebirth. He continued, "Unless one is born of water and of the Spirit, he cannot enter the kingdom of God...Do not marvel that I said to you, 'You must be born again!'" *(John 3:3,5,7)* Being "born of the water" is a reference to what is presently called the 'breaking of the water' during the natural birth process. The amniotic sac tears open and the amniotic fluid spills out as the child exits the womb. This is, of course, our first birth, which is a necessary step in our spiritual evolution.

The Messiah revealed that a second birth must follow if we are to become true heirs of eternal life. This "born-again" experience is totally different than anything provided through the Far Eastern approach. It is not another name for the experience of Nirvana, Samadhi, or Shakti-pat (the awakening of the kundalini through a guru). It is totally unique, best described as the indwelling of the Lord Jesus Christ in a heart sincerely yielded to him. As shared in the last article, the word translated "again" is the Greek word *anothen* that is also translated "from above"—so the English translation could easily be, "You must be born from above." In the Old Testament, God spoke through the prophet Ezekiel of a future time when this experience would be given and what exactly would happen:

> *"I will give you a new heart and put a new spirit*
> *within you; I will take the heart of stone out of your*
> *flesh and give you a heart of flesh.*
> *I will put My Spirit within you and cause you to*
> *walk in My statutes, and you will keep My judgments*
> *and do them." (Ezekiel 36:26-27)*

The Scripture makes it clear that this could not happen until after Jesus ascended into heaven. During a great festival in Jerusalem, the Son of God announced:

"If anyone thirsts, let him come to Me and drink.

He who believes in Me, as the Scripture has said,
out of his heart will flow rivers of living water."

Then the writer of that Gospel explained:

But this He spoke concerning the Spirit, whom
*those believing in Him would receive; **for the Holy***
Spirit was not yet given, because Jesus was
***not yet glorified.** (John 7:37-39)*

Before he went to the cross, the Messiah prayed that this experience would come to those the Father had given him out of the world. *(See John 17:9.)* Notice he did not intercede for every human being, but only his true followers, saying:

"O righteous Father! The world has not known
You, but I have known You; and these have known
that You sent Me. And I have declared to them Your
*name, and will declare it, **that the love with***
which You loved Me may be in them, and I
***in them."** (John 17:25-26)*

This prayer was answered ten days after Jesus ascended into heaven. The disciples were gathered in the upper room when "suddenly there came a sound from heaven, as of a rushing mighty wind, and it filled the whole house where they were sitting. Then there appeared to them divided tongues, as of fire, and one sat upon each of them. And they were all filled with the Holy Spirit. *(Acts 2:2-4)* What an amazing moment that was! What a pivotal point! What a paradigm shift spiritually! What a powerful experience! Men and women were restored to full sonship, adopted into the divine family.

Now this experience has been available for nearly two millennia, for those who fulfill the required approach:

‿· *First, we are called to repent.* The Most High urges the children of this world, "Come out from among them and be separate, says the Lord. Do not touch what is unclean, and I will receive you. I will be a Father to you, and you shall be My sons and daughters, says the Lord Almighty." *(2 Corinthians 6:17–18)*

‿· *Second, we are called to believe.* The Scripture promises that Jesus Christ will "dwell in your hearts through faith." *(Ephesians 3:17)*

‿ ͑ *Third, we must accept and receive.* John, the apostle,
declared, "As many as received him, to them gave he
power to become the sons of God, even to them that
believe on his name." *(John 1:12 KJV)*

So, we repent, believe, and receive—as simple as that. When
we do our part, God does his. Supernatural regeneration takes place,
restoring a person to a vital and real relationship with the Father. God
sends forth "the Spirit of His Son into your hearts, crying out, 'Abba,
Father!'" *(Galatians 4:6, See verses 4-7)* At that moment, we become
God's offspring in a far more powerful sense and join "the whole family in
heaven and in earth" which is named with the name of Jesus. *(Ephesians
3:14, See Romans 8:15, 23, Galatians 4:5.)*

So, becoming a son or daughter of God is a spiritual event, an
acquired status, an inherited position. It does not happen simultaneous
with entrance into this world, though all men have potential access to
this privilege. Because God exists independent of the physical world,
and because we inherit a status of separation from him at conception, we
come into this world devoid of his presence. But spiritual rebirth cures
this problem. No person should dare overlook such a glorious opportunity.

Yogananda suggested that "man reincarnates on the earth until he
has consciously regained his status as a son of God."[80] He also taught
that the secret to experiencing and developing a relationship with God
is to 'look' upon ourselves as his children. However, true divine sonship
is not something acquired through developing a more proper self-image.
Neither is full spiritual sonship a latent potential that can be awakened
in every individual regardless of his or her religious persuasion. Rather,
it is a gift from God and a supernatural impartation. It is received when
the external, transcendent God enters the heart of a repentant person who
has confessed his faith in Jesus' substitutionary death on the cross. Then,
instead of being just the "children of this world," we become "children
of light" and "children of the resurrection." *(Luke 16:8; 20:36 KJV)*

26 What did Jesus mean when he said, "You are gods"?

Taken out of context, this quote of Jesus seems to deify the whole human
race, conferring a divine nature and destiny upon all. When scrutinized
within the framework of the surrounding text, it communicates something
quite different. Certain Israelite leaders were refusing Jesus' claim of
being "the Son of God." He responded by quoting to them a passage from
the Old Testament:

> *"Is it not written in your law, 'I said, **You are**
> **gods?**'"*
>
> *If He called them gods, to whom the word of
> God came (and the Scripture cannot be broken),*
>
> *Do you say of Him whom the Father sanctified
> and sent into the world, 'You are blaspheming,'
> because I said, 'I am the Son of God'?*
>
> *If I do not do the works of My Father, do not
> believe Me;*
>
> *But if I do, though you do not believe Me, believe
> the works, that you may know and believe that the
> Father is in Me, and I in Him."*   (John 10:34–38)

Who were these individuals Jesus referred to as *"gods?"* Over 2,000 times the Hebrew word *elohim* is translated "God" in the Old Testament; over 200 times it is translated into the plural word "gods" (as in the Psalm 82 quote Jesus referenced above). Four times *elohim* is also rendered "judges" in the King James Version of the Bible. *(Exodus 21:6; 22:8–9)* However, the original Hebrew word literally means "God" or "gods." Presumably, the Most High referred to his representative judges in Israel as *elohim*, because if they did their job correctly, they spoke with divine authority. The "word of God" came to them. The God of Israel inspired their judgments. As mouthpieces of the Almighty, they would make pronouncements that aligned with the Word of God and represented the will of God in any case brought to their attention.

Unfortunately, the judges of Israel eventually became quite corrupt: receiving bribes, making false judgments, and abusing their authority. Because they were out of touch with God, they often misrepresented him. In the passage Jesus referenced *(Psalm 82)*, God protested their behavior:

> *"God stands in the congregation of the mighty;
> He judges among **the gods.** How long will you
> judge unjustly, and show partiality to the wicked?
> Selah. Defend the poor and fatherless; do justice to
> the afflicted and needy." (Psalms 82:1–3)*

God was reminding his judges ("the gods," Heb. *elohim*) that he was in their midst, ready to reveal his judgment concerning the situations in question. But the judges were deaf to his counsel. They had their own agenda. Too often, they were self-centered, manipulative, greedy and spiritually insensitive. So God gave them a stern warning:

> *I said, "**You are gods**...but you shall die*
> *like men."* (*Psalms 82:6–7*)

Clearly, this passage teaches the humanity of the judges of Israel, not their divinity. Its correct interpretation is absolutely the opposite of what some construe it to mean. Unquestionably, it cannot be used as proof that all men are evolving into 'godhood.' The Author of the Bible never intended these passages to be interpreted this way.

---

27 **Are there any other quotes of Jesus that some interpret as being supportive of the New Age or Far Eastern doctrinal stance?**

Two biblical references need to be addressed in response to this question. Both deal with man's true nature.

(1) "**The light of the body is the eye**"—Most yoga practitioners believe in seven energy centers in the body called chakras. The position of the sixth is supposedly in the middle of the forehead. It is often referred to as the "third eye." This chakra is described as being one of the main exits out of the body into the 'astral realm' (a spiritual dimension said to be directly above this natural plane). Some feel that Jesus was referring to this concept when he explained, "The light of the body is the eye: if therefore thine eye be single, thy whole body shall be full of light. But if thine eye be evil, thy whole body shall be full of darkness. If therefore the light that is in thee be darkness, how great is that darkness!" (*Matthew 6:22–23 KJV*)

When subjected to proper methods of interpretation, this one isolated passage is definitely not sufficient evidence that Jesus believed in chakras or specifically, in the third eye. Jesus was rather talking about the way we 'see' or 'perceive' what is important in life, how we set our priorities. These two verses are sandwiched between passages dealing with 'materialism versus spirituality.' Jesus started by saying, "Do not lay up for yourselves treasures on earth" and he concluded by saying, "You cannot serve God and mammon" (material riches). (*Matthew 6:19, 24*) Plainly, Jesus was encouraging his disciples to stay focused on that which is spiritual and eternal, even if they have to function in a secular world. No one can be a slave to material possessions and enjoy the abundant life that the Savior promised.

A popular, modern translation changes the archaic English of the King James Version to say, "If therefore your eye is good, your whole body will be full of light. But if your eye is bad, your whole body will be full of darkness." *(Matthew 6:22–23 NKJV)* Other Bible versions use words like, "sound," "healthy," "clear" or "unclouded" for the word "good." The exact meaning becomes all the more obvious in these newer renditions. Very simply, if you 'look' at life with a good attitude—if your values are sound and healthy, and your perceptions, clear and unclouded—the light of truth radiates in you and through you. If Jesus were actually attempting to enlighten his disciples concerning the existence of internal psychic energy centers, he surely would not have been so vague.

(2) **"The kingdom of God is within you**"—One of the most misunderstood statements of Jesus is recorded in Luke 17:20–21, "Now when He was asked by the Pharisees when the kingdom of God would come, He answered them and said, 'The kingdom of God does not come with observation; nor will they say, 'See here!' or 'See there!' For indeed, *the kingdom of God is within you*" (emphasis by author).

Jesus was answering skeptical Pharisees who were hoping God's dominion on earth would immediately appear. They were expecting Jesus, if he were truly the Messiah, to liberate the Jews from Roman control and restore the Promised Land to Abraham's seed. For their sakes, Jesus explained that the kingdom "does not come with observation." This word "observation" implies viewing something over a protracted period. In other words, he was informing his hearers that they would not see a gradual removal of the Romans from the land of Israel, with the Israelites recapturing one city at a time.

I do not believe that Jesus was indicating his audience actually possessed an inward experience of the kingdom of God. Rather, he was making a hypothetical statement. He was proposing, *"If* you experience the kingdom of God, it will be an inward experience." In a similar sense, Jesus could have exhorted a group of depressed persons saying, "You will not find true joy in external, material things, for behold, true joy is within you." Such a statement would not be an acknowledgment that joy was actually resident within their hearts, but rather, that if they ever found true joy, it would be an internal experience.

When all the New Testament scriptures on this subject are blended together, they clearly reveal that the kingdom did not become an inward, personal experience in the hearts of the disciples until much later, on the day of Pentecost. On that pivotal day, when the Holy Spirit swept into the upper room like a wind, men were 'born of the Spirit' for the first time. It was then that one of Jesus' prophecies came to pass: a prediction that a number of his disciples would not "taste of death" until they saw "the kingdom of God come with power." *(Mark 9:1 KJV)*

In John 3:3–7 Jesus clearly indicated that this "born-again" experience is the main prerequisite for 'seeing' (comprehending) and 'entering' the kingdom of God. So Luke 17:20–21 is not a description of the inward spiritual condition of the whole human race. Instead, it only indicates a potential inheritance that can be realized through the biblical experience of salvation.

28 How will this present age end, and what is the meaning of the "Second Coming of Christ"?

Many religious groups have doctrines forecasting the "Second Coming of Christ" or more correctly, the return of the Messiah (from the Hebrew *Masiyach*, which means the "Anointed One," *Daniel 9:25-26, John 1:41)*. The interpretation of this grand prophetic event is quite varied:

Bahá'ís believe that Bab (founder of Babism and forerunner of the Bahá'í faith) was "the spiritual return of John the Baptist" and Bahá'u'lláh (founder of Bahá'í) was "Christ returned in the glory of the Father."[81]

Helen Schucman, in her book, *A Course in Miracles*, writes, "Christ's Second coming, which is sure as God, is merely the correction of mistakes, and the return of sanity...It is the invitation to God's Word to take illusion's place; the willingness to let forgiveness rest upon all things without exception and without reverse...Forgiveness lights the Second Coming's way, because it shines on everything as one...It needs your eyes and ears and hands and feet. It needs your voice. And most of all it needs your willingness."[82]

Ernest Holmes of the United Church of Religious Science defined the Second Coming of Christ as "the dawning in the individual consciousness of the meaning of the teachings of Jesus."[83]

Yogananda of Self-Realization Fellowship taught that the real explanation of Jesus descending out of the clouds is "metaphysical." On an individual basis, the Second Coming of Christ happens when a person overcomes the darkness of this world by recognizing the "inner light." In a universal sense, "through his oneness with the divine Christ Consciousness [Jesus] is incarnate in all that lives. If you have eyes to behold, you can see him enthroned throughout creation."[84] This constitutes Jesus' 'return.'

David Spangler, a popular New Age writer, also spiritualizes this event. He insists, "The Second Coming of Christ in our age will be fundamentally, most importantly, a mass coming. It will be the manifestation of a consciousness within the multitudes."[85] Of course, this concept is based on the premise that all men have a spark of divine nature, a dormant 'Christ consciousness' that needs to be awakened. This planetary awakening is expected to usher in what has been termed the 'Aquarian Age,' a time of enlightenment and peace on this planet.

Dr. Rudolph Steiner, another New Age voice, echoes a similar opinion. This founder of the German offshoot of Theosophy (The Anthroposophical Society) explained that Christ is now seeking to "mass incarnate." In the 1920's he foretold that the "Christ impulse will penetrate humanity...He belongs to the whole earth and can enter all human souls, regardless of nation and religion."[86] It should be noted, though, that there are major disagreements in the 'New Age' arena concerning the exact nature of this pivotal planetary event.

Benjamin Creme, head of the Tara Center in Los Angeles, claimed divine revelation on a cosmic 'change of plans.' Some twenty years after Steiner's death, Creme supposedly received communications from a higher sphere that the Christ had reversed his previous decision and decided, not to incarnate *en masse* in humanity, but to visit this world in his own "body of manifestation."[87] Creme now insists that the 'Second Coming of Christ' has been realized in an individual known as Maitreya. He contends that Maitreya is the presiding head of the "Planetary Hierarchy"—a group of Ascended Masters who oversee the spiritual progress of the human race.

Supposedly, Maitreya has been secretly living among human beings since 1977 when his consciousness entered a supernaturally materialized human-type body called the "Mayavirupa." He descended from the Himalayas to a major city in India by airplane (Creme believes this fulfilled the prophecy concerning Christ "coming in the clouds"—*Matthew 24:30*). Maitreya then flew to a more modern part of the world. Though Maitreya was predicted to reveal himself to the world telepathically in 1982, via television and radio, it never happened. Human and media apathy were cited as the main hindrance. Creme suggests Maitreya will yet manifest himself and that he will remain in the world for the rest of the Aquarian Age (approximately 2,350 years) to lead mankind.

OTHER RELIGIONS HAVE PREDICTIONS FOR THE FUTURE THAT SEEM SIMILAR—YET THEY CONTAIN DETAILS THAT ARE EVIDENTLY DIFFERENT

Buddhism—Some Buddhists anticipate the arrival of the next Buddha (presently a bodhisattva also named *Maitreya*) who will descend to earth from his present residence in the *Tushita* heaven. This fifth Buddha (some say twenty-fifth) will restore the teachings *(dharma)* of Gautama Buddha and convert this earth into a Buddhist paradise at the climax of this present mappo age (a time of increasing degeneracy). One reference states that Maitreya is slated to make his appearance "4,000 years after the disappearance of Buddha Gautama"[88] (about 1,400 to 1,500 years from now). Other references speak of Maitreya coming 30,000 years in the future. Some believe he will preach for 60,000 years, then enter Nirvana. His spiritual influence will linger on the planet for another 10,000 years.[89]

Not all Buddhists are necessarily awaiting an actual person to fill this role. In *The Heart of the Buddha's Teaching*, Thich Nhat Hanh suggests that "the Buddha of the twenty-first century—Maitreya, the Buddha of Love—may well be a community rather than an individual."[90] The assumed meaning of this statement is that the coming of Maitreya may be a time when such compassion abounds in numerous communities of devoted Buddhist disciples that a supreme place of refuge (a sangha) is provided for all humanity.

Hinduism—Many Hindus believe Kalki (also spelled Kalkin) will be the last Avatar of Vishnu and that he will appear in about 425,000 years. One writer explains, "Kalkin will be born a Brahmin and will glorify Vishnu. Destroying all things, he will bring in a new age. As king of kings he will...restore order and peace to the world. At a great horse-sacrifice he will give away the earth to the Brahmins and retire to the forest...he will also roam the earth and destroy thieves and robbers." Kalki, similar to the apocalyptic presentation of Christ in the book of Revelation, is depicted "riding a white horse and holding a flaming sword."[91]

Islam—Certain Muslim groups believe in the emergence of an enlightened leader called the Imam Mahdi ("the Guided One"), who will usher in a golden era of Muslim expansion that will only last seven to nine years before the end of the world and the final judgment of God. However, they actually believe that the Imam Mahdi will come before the return of Jesus Christ. Some feel the Imam Mahdi has been alive in the world for centuries.

Judaism—Jews are looking for the coming of the Messiah, who will usher in the resurrection and restore supremacy to Israel.

Zoroastrianism—Members of this religion believe that a third and last savior will be born into the world named Saoshyant. He will usher in the final judgment, grant the drink of immortality to men and bring about a New World.

The Kalachakra Tantra, an ancient Tantric text, predicts a time when evil forces will engulf this world. Shambhala, a mythical kingdom in the Himalayan Mountains, will then manifest visibly and its righteous King will go forth with his armies to conquer evil and reestablish the moral order (the *dharma*).

And there are other sects and groups that have global aspirations, ultimately to be realized under an 'inspired leader.' Are all of these just slightly different descriptions of the same event and different names for the same individual? The answer is absolutely and irrefutably, "No," and for the following six reasons:

(1) **The coming of Christ will be a visible, bodily descent from heaven; it will not be an invisible mass incarnation in the whole human race.** As the resurrected Christ ascended into heaven two men in white apparel were standing nearby (probably two angels who assumed human form). These prophesied to the disciples, "This same Jesus, who was taken up into heaven, will so come in like manner as you saw him go into heaven." *(Acts 1:11)* Notice he will return "in like manner." It will not be just a 'Christ principle' surfacing in humanity, but the very person of Jesus in bodily form. He will return in the very same glorious, resurrected body he had when he departed. His descent will once again be supernatural, after the pattern of his ascension. Rolling clouds of the glory of God will accompany him. He will not return in an airplane, as suggested in Benjamin Creme's story concerning Maitreya.

(2) **The coming of Christ will be universally witnessed, but will not be universally received.** The Bible declares that Jesus will gloriously descend from heaven "with his mighty angels, in flaming fire" and that "every eye will see him." *(2 Thessalonians 1:7–8, Revelation 1:7)* However, the whole human race will not undergo some spiritual renewal that lifts everyone into God-consciousness. The positive effects of the coming of Christ are reserved primarily "to those who eagerly wait for him." *(Hebrews 9:28)* The Antichrist will be "destroyed by the brightness of his coming." *(2 Thessalonians 2:8, See Revelation 19:19–21)* Then "the angels will come forth" and "separate the wicked from among the just." *(Matthew 13:49)* Clearly, only those who are saved and born again will receive the full benefits of the Second Coming.

(3) **Jesus foretold that one of the main signs of the "last days" will be the appearance of many false Christs in the world.** If the Second Coming of Christ is, as some propose, an awakening of Christ

Consciousness in the masses, as we near the end of the age, many 'Christs' should emerge in various parts of the world. This is only logical. Individuals walking in Christ Consciousness should be encountered everywhere: a pleasant and wonderful indication of the predicted 'blossoming of planetary awareness.' However, Jesus warned against this scenario in no uncertain terms.

When asked what signs would precede his return, the Savior of the world cautioned, "Take heed that no one deceives you," and also, "If anyone says to you, 'Look, here is the Christ!' or 'There!' do not believe it. For false Christs and false prophets will rise and show great signs and wonders to deceive, if possible, even the elect. See, I have told you beforehand. Therefore if they say to you, 'Look, He is in the desert!' do not go out; or 'Look, He is in the inner rooms!' do not believe it. For as the lightning comes from the east and flashes to the west, so also will the coming of the Son of Man be." *(Matthew 24:4, 23–27)*

(4) Great opposition to the kingdom of God will precede the coming of Christ. Benjamin Creme cited world and media apathy as the main reason that Maitreya (the Christ) did not make his appearance in 1982. Yet the Bible plainly forecasts, not just apathy, but antipathy preceding the coming of Christ. The Antichrist will seize world dominion and attempt to stamp out any evidence of Christian faith in the world (as well as other faiths that do not acknowledge the Antichrist's supremacy and divinity).

The Antichrist will "make war against the saints." *(Revelation 13:7)* He will oppose and exalt himself "above all that is called God or that is worshipped, so that he sits as God in the temple of God, showing himself that he is God." *(2 Thessalonians 2:4)* In a final bid for world sovereignty, he will gather his armies together to the place in Israel known as Armageddon. However, none of this will hinder the coming of the true Christ. Amid circumstances far worse than media apathy, the Lord Jesus will descend with all his holy angels. He will quickly and successfully wrench this world free from the grip of this counterfeit Christ that the Bible dubs "the man of sin" and "the son of perdition." *(2 Thessalonians 2:3)*

(5) The heavenly source, the exact earthly destination of the returning Christ, and the length of the resulting kingdom of God are all important factors. According to the Bible, the Messiah will descend, not from a kingdom in the Himalayan Mountains, but from heaven. He will not be "born a Brahmin" (a Hindu priest). In fact, he will not be born at all, in a physical sense (that already happened). He will manifest himself in spectacular, celestial splendor. His feet will "stand on the Mount of Olives…and the Mount of Olives shall be split in two" as a result of the intensity of his coming. *(Zechariah 14:4)* Jesus will then set up the seat of his kingdom on earth in the holy city, Jerusalem; not in Shambhala, or a forest in India, or any other location.

Some Muslims, who believe in the Imam Mahdi, teach that this messianic leader will usher in a golden era of justice, goodness and true religion in the earth, but it will only last seven to nine years before the end of the world. The Bible, however, teaches that when Jesus returns, this present evil age will come to an end. If the timeline of Revelation 20:1-6 is taken literally, Jesus will then set up the kingdom of God on earth for a thousand years. Immediately after this millennial period of 'heaven on earth,' a fiery universal renovation will bring about a final and climactic New Creation. *(See Revelation 19–20.)* Messianic predictions from many other religions do not include a permanent transformation of the universe, but rather, a temporary age-change in an endless series of spiritual cycles.

(6) **At the end of the age, God's people will experience, not a spiritual awakening, but something far more profound: either resurrection (if they have died) or translation (if they are alive) at the coming of the Lord.** "For the Lord Himself will descend from heaven with a shout, with the voice of an archangel, and with the trumpet of God. And the dead in Christ will rise first. Then we who are alive and remain shall be caught up together with them in the clouds to meet the Lord in the air. And thus we shall always be with the Lord. Therefore comfort one another with these words." *(1 Thessalonians 4:16–18)*

The Scripture also explains concerning true believers, "We shall not all sleep, but we shall all be changed—in a moment, in the twinkling of an eye, at the last trumpet. For the trumpet will sound, and the dead will be raised incorruptible, and we shall be changed…So when this corruptible has put on incorruption, and this mortal has put on immortality, then shall be brought to pass the saying that is written: 'Death is swallowed up in victory.'" *(1 Corinthians 15:51–54)*

Final conclusion—When all of this information is reviewed, it is evident that all of these various predictions from different religious sources cannot coexist harmoniously. There are too many irreconcilable contradictions. The biblical view is not only unique; it is the correct projection of those future events that are soon to unfold. How can a person be assured of this? Once a seeker experiences the reality of Jesus, the dependability and infallibility of his Word become an inner assurance.

---

29   **Which is the correct view of the future: endless cycles of creation and destruction (the view of Hinduism and other Far Eastern worldviews), or one ultimate, universal change (the view of Christianity)?**

As brought out in the second section of this book (under *Cycles, Ages, and the Ultimate State of the Universe*), classical Hinduism maintains that the universe is destined to pass through repetitive cycles of creation and destruction, manifestation and non-manifestation...*ad infinitum. (See Kaushitaki Upanishad 3,3.)* Astrology also teaches a cyclical view of the future, foretelling the unfolding of a number of astrological ages that repeat themselves endlessly. Jainism, Sikhism and other religions of Far Eastern origin also view the future cyclically. In all of these cases, there is no lasting conclusion and no hope for any final, victorious outcome.

Some advocates of this cyclical view contend that once a soul is liberated from *samsara* (the cycle of rebirths), it will never be subjected to this process again. Others maintain that all spiritual entities (including gods) will face the inevitable and be 'pulled under' by this spiritual 'undertow,' again and again, eternally. At the end of each "day of Brahma," when this Creator god causes the creation to pass into an Unmanifest state (after an era of Manifestation lasting 4,320,000,000 years) all beings—even gods and demigods—will also, in a sense, be 'dissolved' into an Unmanifest state. They will then begin *samsara* afresh (the cycle of rebirths) with the beginning of the next period of Manifestation. Again and again, they will be forced to ascend step-by-step up the evolutionary ladder. Whichever view is held, there is still no ultimate state of stability promised for the universe as a whole.

One of the basic doctrines of Buddhism is the impermanence of all things *(anicca)*. Primarily this speaks that nothing has a lasting condition of existence. The universe is in a constant state of flux. The universe will never reach a place of unchanging, unalterable constancy.

Christianity and its root source, Judaism, offer a different view altogether. Both teach a final dissolution of all things that will result in a New Creation, containing a New Heaven and a New Earth. Once God's people are resurrected and glorified, they will reign on the earth as king/priests of God, and live forevermore in absolute perfection. Ultimately, their dwelling place will be New Jerusalem, the permanent capital city of the permanent New Creation. God has promised concerning this eternal state, *"Behold I make all things new." (Revelation 21:4–5)* Of all the opposing religious scenarios for the future mentioned in this book, this is undoubtedly the most glorious.

---

30   **Do doctrinal differences between various sects have any relevance since, according to some belief systems, we are all headed for the same ultimate destiny anyway?**

I believe that the sum of all the information we have covered in this book creates a serious theological hurdle for those who believe all religions are one. At this juncture, most likely, we are in full agreement that only one of the following two conclusions can be embraced:

(1) A person's religious belief system is relatively unimportant (because all the varied doctrines and rituals are just shadowy representations, often misrepresentations, of some Ultimate Reality into which all will eventually be absorbed anyway), or...

(2) A person's religious belief system is of absolute importance (because there is only one correct interpretation of truth, one path that leads from this present existence into that ultimate destiny which is eternal and glorious).

If the former is true, it would be impossible for the adherents of various sects to place their complete trust in any religious book: the Qur'an of Islam, the Bible of Christianity, the Torah of Judaism, the Adi Granth of Sikhism, the Avesta of Zoroastrianism, the Tao Te Ching of Taoism, or the Vedas of Hinduism. None of these 'holy writings' can be taken literally anyway. There is no standard by which to judge the truthfulness of the doctrinal claims of any religious group. Totally contradictory beliefs can all be blended together into one homogeneous whole. Exploring different religious theories may satisfy the intellectual curiosity of the 'seeker for truth,' but no dependable, lasting conclusions can ever be reached.

If the latter is true, it is absolutely essential to discover that unchanging standard of unquestionable truth that grants a successful passage from time into eternity. Yes, the vital essence of life is to identify the "True Light" and walk in its brilliance all the days of our earthly sojourn. The next section in this book will help you do that very thing.

PART 5

IDENTIFYING THE TRUE LIGHT

"From the unreal lead me to the real; from darkness lead me to the light; from death lead me to immortality."

Brihadaranyaka Upanishad 1.3.28

(*See special note: p. 329)

"He who has no vision of eternity has no hold on time."

Thomas Carlyle[1]

"Join thyself to the eternal God, and thou shalt be eternal."

Augustine[2]

Thoreau rightly observed that "the mass of men lead lives of quiet desperation."[3] Some get more desperate than others, though[3]—and they break the silence to cry out for truth. Thankfully, my cry was heard, and precious revelation came to me. Nevertheless, in subjecting my belief system to such critical analysis, deciding what to retain and what to discard was no easy matter.

After experiencing the reality of God, I struggled to get a grip on what doctrines, concepts and spiritual experiences could rightly be labeled "True Light." Then, after much study and a great deal of introspection and prayerful communion with God, the heaven-sent answer apprehended my heart. I concluded that the worldview I held as a yoga teacher and the teachings of the Bible were doctrinally and spiritually incompatible. Having made such a strong statement, I feel I must reinforce two major concessions already made clear in this book:

First, I do not disregard the sincerity, goodness, and spiritual zeal that are often discovered in persons whose beliefs are sometimes non-biblical. Buddha gave up the comforts of a royal lifestyle to pursue a life of self-denial and contemplation. Mahavira, founder of Jainism, subjected himself to such rigid asceticism in his search for answers that he eventually died of starvation. Zoroaster persisted in preaching ten years with only one convert to his credit. Confucius lived a life of such exemplary conduct that when he died, one of his disciples faithfully remained at his grave for six years. The Bab, forerunner of the Baha'i faith, was imprisoned numerous times and finally executed for the revelations he held to be true. For many years, Guru Nanak traveled all over Asia with a Muslim musician doing all he could to unite Hindus and Muslims.

Who can deny that these men—and thousands of other monks, sadhus, ascetics, mystics and religious thinkers—have been passionate about what they believed, and most likely, deeply sincere in pursuing a glimpse of Ultimate Reality? Who can deny that in a bad world they were probably exemplary in their goodness? They all command our attention and even, at times, our respect.

How genuine rings the admission of Paramahansa Yogananda, "Fervently I implored Christ to guide me in divining the true meaning of his words!"[4] I *do not* doubt that Yogananda was deeply sincere in asking for such guidance. I *do* doubt that he actually obtained it. Anyone who reads the prayers of Yogananda will quickly sense that he was probably a true lover of God (just as I was prior to salvation). Unfortunately, though—just as I did, and as many others do—he tried to fit the message and life of Jesus into the framework of a Far Eastern worldview. He tried to assign to Jesus a role similar to a yogi or an eastern mystic. To do so is like attempting to force a square peg into a round hole. Even the Dalai Lama admitted that trying to meld Jesus into a Buddha-like figure "is like putting a yak's head on a sheep's body."[5] It doesn't work. The two are just not compatible. Their messages and methods are oceans apart.

Most likely, Yogananda deeply desired to resolve this issue in his own mind. Nevertheless, his case proves once again that genuineness of intent and fervency of soul are not always sufficient gauges to determine the correctness of opinions regarding the "True Light."

Second, I do not deny that there are common elements in almost all religions that have great worth. In fact, I shudder to think what kind of horrid conditions this world would suffer if there were no positive religious systems in the world defining proper moral behavior and challenges to the 'higher life.' Thank God for the influence of even non-religious, philosophical worldviews that accomplish this goal. Confucianism, for instance, is certainly not mystical and spiritual, but practical and world-affirming. *Li*, the Chinese term for the ideal standard of conduct in Confucianism, encourages goodness, kindness, respect and honesty in human relationships. Such standards are of great value, worthy of implementation in any of our lives. So again, I concede: there are some aspects of truth in many religions that are universally acceptable and universally beneficial. However, the presence of some truth does not authenticate, validate or substantiate an entire belief system. Besides, as Augustine so aptly put it, "All truth is God's truth" wherever you may find it.[6]

Mahatma Ghandi, whose life and character I deeply admire, felt that all "religions are true," yet evidently flawed. Lamenting the situation, he explained they have been "interpreted with poor intellects, sometimes with poor hearts, and more often misinterpreted."[7] Though I cannot agree that all worldviews are basically true, I must admit that they have all been subject to misinterpretation—even Christianity. One has only to look at the history of Christianity over the last two millennia to see the horrendous ways that the loving message of Christ has been twisted, sanctioning such things as forced conversions, the severe treatment of the Jewish people or the harsh and even murderous persecution of one Christian sect by another. I strongly assert that those who committed such atrocities were themselves Christian in name only, not in truth.

There are actually two different types of Christians in this world: professing Christians and possessing Christians. Professing Christians have a historical view of Jesus, what he accomplished and the message he preached, yet they lack a personal relationship with him. Possessing Christians not only know and appreciate the former; they possess the latter. Their 'Christianity' is not based on being christened at birth into some Christian denomination or being born into a predominantly Christian society. It does not hinge on rituals and ceremonies. Rather, it rests on the heart-changing experience of being "born again." While on earth, Jesus revealed to his disciples, "This is eternal life, that they may know You, the only true God, and Jesus Christ whom You have sent." *(John 17:3)* It is not enough to *know about* the Lord Jesus Christ; it is necessary to actually *know* him.

Thankfully, there have been many instances of individuals and organizations correctly representing the Lord Jesus Christ to this world during the past two millennia. It is through them—through the true church of the New Testament—that the correct revelation of God has flowed to quench the spiritual thirst of a parched human race.

Prior to the establishment of Christianity, revealed truth was deposited primarily within one nation (Israel) and its associated worldview (Judaism). Notwithstanding, according to the apostle Paul, God still did not "leave himself without witness" in regions of the world not exposed to the truth through God's chosen nation. *(Acts 14:17)* When read in context, this scripture primarily refers to God *'witnessing'* his reality and care by providing rain, crops and natural provisions that create gladness in the hearts of all men. Another important passage *(Ecclesiastes 3:13 NIV)* unveils that God "has also set eternity in the hearts of men; yet they cannot fathom what God has done from beginning to end." In other words, God has given men an inward sense that there is an eternal reality available, but how to possess it is a mystery they cannot comprehend.

Furthermore, Romans 2:11-16 also indicates that God deals with all men, even those never exposed to his Word, through the vehicle of conscience. Certainly, this worldwide subliminal influence of the Spirit of God—quickening the consciences of all men—has caused basic, correct insights such as the following to rise to surface in various worldviews:

- ⌣· **Buddhism** teaches that misery results from self-centeredness and that to change this condition, we must strive to do all things right. This is true.

- ⌣· **Confucianism** emphasizes the essential goodness of human nature, as a potential implanted by God. This is true.

- ⌣· **Hinduism** teaches that union with the Divine is the goal of existence. This is true.

- ⌣· **Islam** teaches that man's goal should be submission to a sovereign and omnipotent God who administers both judgments and rewards. This is true.

- ⌣· **Jainism** teaches that self-renunciation is essential to salvation. This is true.

- ⌣· **Sikhism** teaches discipleship to the one true God, reverencing and trusting in his name. This is true.

- ⌣· **Shinto** teaches reverence for the beauty of creation and for purity of heart. This is true.

- ⌣· **Taoism** teaches that understanding life involves discerning and comprehending the dualities and opposites that make up this world. This is true.

- ⌣· **Zoroastrianism** teaches active cooperation with a cosmic Power of goodness in a struggle against evil. This is true also.[8]

All of these doctrinal generalizations are basically true (though the words, ideas, and concepts communicated must be placed within the framework of a Christian worldview in order to be interpreted correctly). Still, it is noteworthy that these parallel perceptions, concerning both the human condition and man's connection with the Divine, have been evidenced in many world religions.

As R. Eugene Sterner points out:

> *"The laws of God are written in the tissues of our bodies, in the process of our minds, in the avenues of our souls, and in the fabric of society...They are part of your very nature."*[9]

And as Plato insisted:

> *"The world is God's epistle to mankind—his*
> *thoughts are flashing upon us from every direction."*[10]

Once again, this does not imply that the bulk of doctrinal beliefs in all world religions are accurate and universally acceptable. Though the seed-like concepts listed on the previous page are all found planted in the soil of Christianity, many other beliefs of these various religions would not be found growing in the ground of biblical revelation.

When it comes to the most important points of theology like the exact nature of God, the full plan of salvation, the securing of a right relationship with the Creator and the precise means of inheriting eternal life, Christianity stands alone as a singular beacon of hope to the entire human race.

WHAT IS THE NATURE OF TRUTH?

If we are to find the truth, we must become acquainted with the exact nature of truth. Of all human pursuits, this is the most necessary, fulfilling and rewarding. Ralph Waldo Emerson insisted, "Every violation of truth...is a stab at the health of society."[11] Certainly the opposite is also correct. Discovering and upholding the truth greatly improves the spiritual health, first, of the individual soul, then second, of that person's sphere of social influence.

One of the most important determinations any person will ever make concerns truth being objective or subjective. If truth is objective, it is the same for all people, whether it is consciously affirmed or not. If truth is subjective, every person can 'create' his or her own reality. One person can have his 'truth' and another person can claim another 'truth' and both be right simultaneously. This is the foundation stone of "Pluralism": "the belief that the world is far too complex for any one philosophy to explain everything" and that all religions are equally effective means of achieving the Ultimate State.[12]

The following quote by John Hay Allison exemplifies this viewpoint well:

> *"Truth is the disciple of the ascetic, the quest of*
> *the mystic, the faith of the simple, the ransom of the*
> *weak, the standard of the righteous, the doctrine of*
> *the meek, and the challenge of Nature. Together, all*
> *these constitute the Law of the Universe."*[13]

If truth really is the *"disciple of the ascetic,"* then it can be manipulated or altered by a single person to fit a worldview imagined by him to be genuine. If it is simply the *"faith of the simple,"* then any simple person could have faith in any desirable, spiritual concept and for him it would be correct. If the *"standard of the righteous"* automatically qualifies as truth, then any righteous person could set any moral or religious standard and for him it would be "truth": perfectly just and right.

If this is the criterion for acceptable doctrine, then authority for setting standards rests in the hands of men, not the hands of God. We must make a quality decision concerning this central and crucial issue. Either the "Law of the Universe" is a product of human intellect (to which God himself is subject) or a product of the wisdom of God (to which man must be submitted in order to have a fruitful and meaningful life—both now and forevermore).

The following parable pleads the case of truth being objective:

> A man climbs to the top of the Empire State Building. A number of persons are sitting there who appear knowledgeable. So he poses the question, "What will happen to me if I jump off the edge of this building?" Several responses indicate drastically differing opinions. One person asserts, "You will sprout wings and fly over the Atlantic Ocean." Another informs, "You will free-fall ten stories, then a net will automatically swing out from the building and catch you. You will have a very exhilarating experience." Finally, a third warns in no uncertain terms, "You will fall all the way to the ground and be immediately killed by the impact."

Though this proposed situation is certainly unrealistic, it illustrates an important point. Choosing the correct view is absolutely essential, because the outcome is a matter of life and death. Of course, only one answer is true, that which is objectively correct for all, regardless of personal opinion. So the question we must ask ourselves is this—If someone would show extreme caution over a choice like this (stepping off the edge of the Empire State Building) should we not all show even more care over a far greater transition (stepping from time into eternity)?

Certain natural laws rule the natural realm—like gravity, friction, inertia, magnetic fields, and so on. Whether we acknowledge these laws or not, they are constantly influencing us and will ever remain a permanent fact of our physical existence. In like manner, it makes sense to believe that definite spiritual laws govern the spiritual realm—which remain the same for all human beings and affect us all, whether we acknowledge them or not.

One permanently established divine law is the declaration that reconciliation with God is only available through the cross. The very beams of the cross—being vertical and horizontal—speak of God and man reunited. The cross of Jesus is the connecting point between time and eternity and the main thing that sets the Christian faith apart from all other religions. The apostle Paul declared that "the preaching of the cross" is the "power of God." *(1 Corinthians 1:18)* At the very place where it appeared that God himself became utterly weak, he imparts his awesome power to men—power to overcome sin, power to master the flesh, power to overcome this world. Our appraisal of this truth should be similar to Lyn Landrum's:

> *"That the Potter should die for his clay is a stupendous miracle."*[14]

O, that all men could see the wonder of this mystery!

"God Is One! We Are All One!"

Since my conversion to Christianity in the fall of 1970 I have asked hundreds of advocates of various Far Eastern religions if they have ever considered receiving Jesus into their hearts. Quite often I receive a kindly spoken answer like:

> *"God is one. We all are one. We are all seeking the same God different ways."*

I deeply appreciate the humility, compassion, and consideration for others a response like this indicates. But I must say, humbly, compassionately, and out of deep consideration for others, that I cannot embrace this point of view. I agree wholeheartedly that *God is one*. There definitely is *only one God*. However, through the millennia, many theories have surfaced in this world about the Creator, some of which are right and some of which are wrong.

In a similar, analogous way, the solar system is one—there is only one solar system containing the planet Earth. However, there have been various ideas promoted regarding its nature, some of which have been right and some wrong. For instance, in the second century, an astronomer named Ptolemy promoted the idea that our solar system is earth-centric (earth-centered): that the sun, moon and other planets all revolve around the earth on a backdrop of unmoving stars. Over a thousand years later, the Polish astronomer, Nicolaus Copernicus, offered an opposing view: that the solar system is instead heliocentric (sun-centered), that all the planets, including the earth, revolve around the sun.

Both of these ideas cannot be true simultaneously. If one is right, the other must necessarily be wrong. Of course, modern astronomy has proven Copernicus' viewpoint—though scorned and rejected in his day—to be the correct one. Had Ptolemy and Copernicus lived at the same time, and were it possible for them to dialogue concerning their beliefs, Copernicus would have never suggested to Ptolemy, "*Truth is relative. Truth is subjective. You can have your truth and I can have my truth and we can both be right simultaneously.*" To even consider such a merging of ideas would have been absurd. One viewpoint had to be accepted at the expense of the other being rejected.

Based on similar logic, we can further deduce that God is either internal or external before the experience of salvation. Both concepts cannot be true simultaneously. Ultimate Reality is either an impersonal cosmic energy or a personal God—it cannot be both. The 'self' in man is either identical with God or distinct from God—it cannot be both. True religion is either man-centric, focusing on man's superlative greatness and his ability to tap into and control some mysterious, inner, divine energy, or it is God-centric, focusing on the matchless wonder of the Redeemer God and submitting lovingly and worshipfully to his Word and his will. The human race is either saved by grace or by self-effort. We each have only one life or we have many incarnations. Either Jesus was the only incarnation of God or he was just another Avatar, another prophet, another teacher. In all these areas, only one of the two opposing beliefs can be retained while the other is discarded.

Hindus, Buddhists and Jainists, seem to express a great deal of sympathetic open-mindedness concerning other worldviews. However, when their foundational beliefs are closely inspected, they are found to be very exclusive. Geoffrey Parrinder offers this penetrating observation:

> *"It is sometimes thought that only the Semitic religions believe that they have revelations, which tend towards exclusiveness, and that Hindus accept anything and believe that anybody can be saved by doing, or not doing, what any religion teaches. But Hindus have been as insistent as Christians and Muslims that they have a divine relationship, which is the only way to salvation...Sankara [a teacher of Advaita Vedanta, born 788 A.D.] believed that only the Vedas could give knowledge of Brahman... Buddhists and Jains also claimed to have the final truth; the Jains holding that he alone is righteous who believes the true teaching [of Mahavira], and Buddhists that anything which contradicted the Buddha's teaching could not be true. So modern exponents of Hinduism should make it explicit that such statements as 'All religions are true' are made only on their own authority, and do not represent the orthodox Hindu tradition."[15]*

Rabi Maharaj also explains that "the Vedanta Society, founded by Vivekananda, the successor of Ramakrishna, with centers around the world, professes to teach tolerance for all religions. However, the 'unity of all religions' it espouses is really not liberal or broad-minded, but is based upon this uncompromising monism which says that everything is One."[16] Divided opinions on major issues even exist between many religious groups that trace their roots back to Far Eastern religions. For instance, in defining his "Krishna Consciousness" Movement, Swami Prabhupada unashamedly promotes exclusivity. He quotes Krishna as saying, "Abandon all varieties of religion and just surrender unto Me."[17] Adding to this, he gives his own suggestion, "Give up all other ideas of so-called dharma, or religiosity...Krsna is the authority."[18]

Another popular Eastern leader in the Western world, Maharishi Mahesh Yogi, describes Transcendental Meditation in glowing terms, "If this teaching is followed, effectiveness in life will be achieved. Men will be fulfilled on all levels and the historical need of the age will be fulfilled also."[19] Yet Swami Prabhupada responds to the Transcendental Meditation movement quite negatively, "They do not know what real meditation is. Their meditation is simply a farce."[20] So who is right? Or could it be that neither of them is interpreting truth and reality correctly?

The Dalai Lama, exiled leader of Tibetan Buddhism, admitted the irreconcilable differences between Buddhism and Christianity in a recent interview:

> *"The entire Buddhist worldview is based on a philosophical standpoint in which...all things and events come into being purely as a result of interactions between causes and conditions. Within that philosophical worldview it is almost impossible to have any room for an atemporal, eternal, absolute truth. Nor is it possible to accommodate the concept of a divine Creation.*
>
> *Similarly, for a Christian whose entire metaphysical worldview is based on a belief in the Creation and a divine Creator, the idea that all things and events arise out of mere interaction between causes and conditions has no place within that worldview. So in the realm of metaphysics it becomes problematic at a certain point, and the two traditions must diverge."*[21]

Many years ago I instructed my yoga students that they could find God by looking within and that from within, the divine nature would be awakened. Now, as a follower of Jesus and a minister of the Gospel, I share instructions that are much different: that God is transcendent, separate from human beings, and he must be invited to come and dwell within their hearts. I also teach that this experience can only happen through the name of the Lord Jesus Christ and his redemptive work. As a believer in the Bible, I now fully realize that this revealed path cannot include any other worldview. As the Dalai Lama honestly and correctly disclosed, they *"must diverge."* Jesus himself warned, "Narrow is the gate...which leads to life, and there are few who find it." *(Matthew 7:14)*

Having experienced both the Christian and the Far Eastern mindset, I can speak with absolute certainty on this issue. Jesus' life and teachings are unique and unmatched by any other religious belief system in the world. The New Testament refers to this as "the mystery which has been hidden from ages and generations...Christ in you, the hope of glory." *(Colossians 1:26–27)* Though it was hidden from the human race for millennia, thank God, the mystery has now been revealed! And though many of us have wandered far from God, he still beckons lovingly from above.

According to Jesus' teachings, we are all "lost"—groping through spiritual darkness and grasping for reality—yet to all of us the Good Shepherd extends a gracious invitation:

> *"Behold, I stand at the door and knock. If any-*
> *one hears My voice and opens the door, I will come*
> *in to him and dine with him, and he with Me."*
> *(Revelation 3:20)*

You may have seen the famous painting titled, "The Light of the World," that portrays this promise. Jesus is shown standing at night in a garden, holding a lamp with one hand and knocking on a heavily paneled door with the other.

I was told years ago that when the artist, Holman Hunt, formally unveiled this work of art, a number of art critics were present. One of them noticed what seemed to be an obvious flaw.

He abruptly pointed out, "Mr. Hunt, you haven't finished your work!"

"O yes, it is finished," the artist replied.

"But there is no handle on the door," countered the critic.

With calmness Holman Hunt responded, as if his answer was well rehearsed, "That is the door of the human heart, and it can only be opened from the inside."

I would urge you to hold this statement suspended in the inner chamber of your soul as you finish the remaining pages of this book. Why? Because the kernel of truth it offers needs to be replanted in our thinking again and again....

> *Yes, it is so very true...the human heart can only*
> *be opened from the inside.*

MAN'S NATURE AND BASIC NEED

Why is it is so important that we open our hearts to the entrance of God's Spirit? This question is answered when we discover man's true nature and his basic need. As the illustrations on the following page reveal, man is a triune being (in the image of the Triune God)—comprised of spirit, soul, and body. *(See 1 Thessalonians 5:23, Hebrews 4:12.)*

Prior to the experience of salvation, human beings are "dead in trespasses and sins." *(Ephesians 2:1)* This condition affects our whole being and is first an inherited status. When Adam transgressed God's command in the beginning, he died spiritually and began dying physically. This condition was passed to all of Adam's offspring ("for in Adam all die"). *(1 Corinthians 15:22)* So, we all enter this world spiritually dead. Inevitably, we pass through damaging experiences in life that can further darken the soul with death-dealing attitudes like anger, fear, guilt, depression, lust, selfishness, and so on.

THE TRIUNE NATURE OF MAN: SPIRIT—SOUL—BODY

Most would agree that the spiritual part of man is actually larger than his body. However, in these illustrations, the larger, outer ring represents the body. Why? Because the spirit is the 'centermost' part of man's being, while the flesh is only a temporary 'outer' shell. Remember, the body, being the abode of the senses, makes us 'world-conscious;' the soul, 'self-conscious' and the spirit, 'God-conscious' (consciously aware of the reality and presence of God).

O R I G I N A L   S T A T E

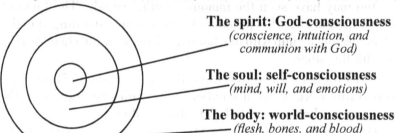

The spirit: God-consciousness
*(conscience, intuition, and
communion with God)*

The soul: self-consciousness
(mind, will, and emotions)

The body: world-consciousness
(flesh, bones, and blood)

Illustration #1—Man is a triune being: body, soul and spirit. Each part is a trinity within itself: (1) **The body**—flesh, bones, and blood; (2) **The soul**—mind, will, and emotions; (3) **The spirit** (in the original and restored states)—conscience, intuition, and communion with God. Intuition includes revelation, inspiration, and creativity. In a perfected state (depicted above), all three parts are filled with the light of God and in harmony with him.

F A L L E N   S T A T E

The spirit
*(conscience and intuition—partially
functional, communion with God—
non-functional)*

The soul
*(the mind and emotions darkened,
the will weakened)*

The body
(controlled by senses and passions)

Illustration #2—In a fallen state (depicted above) human beings are described as being "dead in trespasses and sins," *(Ephesians 2:1)*. Dark, death-dealing influences affect all three parts of man. In the spirit, true **communion** with God is no longer possible (unless initiated by God). **Intuition** may occur, but it is usually intellectual or artistic. Correct revelation is rare until a person is born again. Though its perceptions are imperfect, the **conscience** abides as the primary 'guardian of the soul.'

R E S T O R E D   S T A T E

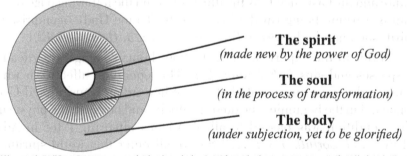

The spirit
(made new by the power of God)

The soul
(in the process of transformation)

The body
(under subjection, yet to be glorified)

Illustration #3—Once restored (depicted above), the whole man comes under divine influence. (1) **The body**—still in a fallen state, must be brought under subjection daily; (2) **The soul**—mind, will, and emotions are progressively transformed into the image of the Lord Jesus by God's Word and Spirit; (3) **The spirit**—once renewed, becomes the abode of a cleansed **conscience**, restored **intuition**, and true **communion** with God.

Many human beings are flesh-ruled, driven by their passions and locked inside of their senses. The soul is the primary functioning part of the invisible nature of persons who are not born again. Because the soul is the abode of the mind, will, and emotions, prior to the experience of God's reality, our problems are often soulish—involving mental and emotional struggles. Furthermore, a weak will often causes us to fall short of the inner dictates of the conscience. This often causes a deadly cycle—more failures, more inner struggles—more inner struggles, more failure. When the soul finally 'overloads,' people are driven to make a choice: either give up on higher ideals and give in to the flesh, succumbing to its deadening influence, or make an attempt to change in a positive way. A great deal of intellectual, emotional and moral reformation can take place without God's intervention simply by self-analysis, self-denial, self-discipline and self-help: psychological, philosophical and religious. However, these means always fall short of the full work that must be done to fill the void in man. 'Soulish problems' in human beings cannot be fixed until their 'spirit problem' is solved.

The human spirit, in the original perfect man, was the fully functional abode of conscience, intuition, and communion with God. Once sin separated man from God, a state of spiritual death set in. Real communion with the Creator ceased and is no longer possible (by man's effort) unless a relationship is initiated by God, and usually, until true salvation takes place. Intuition (which includes revelation, inspiration and creativity) descended primarily into a lesser, non-spiritual expression (intellectual, scientific or artistic). True intuitive knowledge about God became quite limited and rare. Being out of touch with God, men have made many assumptions about the nature of God. Some have been right; many have been erroneous. Only those who received direct revelation about God's character and purposes (like Abraham or Moses) got a firm grip on truth. Other seekers may have received some elementary, intuitive glimpses into the nature of Ultimate Reality, but often these 'insights' became mixed with other false, man-made views. Many religions have developed correct guidelines about moral behavior, yet this has resulted not as much from intuition, as from the influence of the conscience.

This third aspect of the spirit remained most active after the fall, though according to the Bible, it too is darkened, defiled and undependable. The conscience is a gift from God, but it is not the evidence of the presence of God within the heart. The conscience is that inward sense of what is morally right and morally wrong, that carries with it a desire to do what is morally right. However, the conscience is a barely burning ember where there used to be a raging fire of sensitivity to God. When a person becomes born again, the conscience is cleansed "from dead works to serve the living God." *(Hebrews 9:14)*

So when the Bible describes unsaved people as being "dead in trespasses and sins," this does not mean a state of absolute death, or we would not be functioning at all. This is biblical hyperbole—intended exaggeration that shows the seriousness of man's plight. It is not dead in an absolute sense, but a relative sense—(related to what it was originally in a perfected state).

The new birth—When a person is "born again," this curse of death is reversed. Three primary things happen: (1) The blood of Jesus cleanses the inner man from sin; (2) The human spirit is regenerated (made new); (3) The Spirit of God takes up his abode within the spirit. Notice it is the spirit that is initially reborn, not the body or the soul. This is far different than just a moral reformation brought about by a response to conscience. Ezekiel, the prophet, foretold God's promise concerning the spiritual transformation that would be available under the New Covenant, "I will give you a new heart and put a new spirit within you; I will take the heart of stone out of your flesh and give you a heart of flesh." *(Ezekiel 36:26)* Once man's spirit is regenerated, it once again becomes the abode of true communion with God, correct intuition and a revived conscience (all of which manifest according to the level of a person's consecration to God).

From that point forward, the spirit should daily influence the soul toward a strong will, godly emotions and a mind filled with correct interpretations of the truth. The goal of a true Christian is for the spirit to become the dominating influence in his or her life, daily transforming the soul, and bringing the body under subjection—anticipating the final 'rebirth' of the body also, into a glorified state, at the Second Coming of Christ.

IDENTIFYING THE TRUE LIGHT

Recently I happened on a simple, yet striking metaphor, penned by a man named Samuel Rutherford:

> *"If you saw a man shut up in a small room,*
> *idolizing a set of lamps and rejoicing in their light,*
> *and you wanted to make him truly happy, you would*
> *begin by blowing out all his lamps and throwing*
> *open the shutters to let in the light of heaven."*[22]

Though I related to this analogy and sensed its worth, I couldn't help feeling uneasy. The sequence of events just wasn't right. Extinguishing someone's only source of light could easily be misinterpreted. An act that was truly kind and compassionate could be construed to be a belligerent and aggressive one. Besides, if you strip a person of his dependencies before giving him a superior replacement, he will quickly rise to his own defense. Had I composed the allegory, I would have worded it differently:

> *"If you saw a man shut up in a small room, idolizing a set of lamps and rejoicing in their light, and you wanted to make him truly happy, you would begin by throwing open the shutters to let in the light of heaven. Automatically, with exceeding joy, the man would then proceed to extinguish all man-made lights himself, realizing their inferiority."*

One of my chief desires in writing this book is to make others "truly happy." In the preceding pages, therefore, I have attempted to throw open the shutters of truth to let in the "light of heaven," the glorious light of the living God! I pray that I have achieved this goal. If I have, then those who read my words will quickly discern the insufficiency of artificial, man-made 'lights,' extinguish them, leave them behind and turn their faces toward man's true and only Source.

One Old Testament prophet portrayed the coming Savior as "the Sun of righteousness" who would arise with healing in his wings. *(Malachi 4:2)* When Jesus came into the world, how brilliantly he radiated the truth! And when he arose from the dead, what a healing, revitalizing, enlightening effect he shed forth toward all those who would ever come to him in faith! No wonder one of his chief disciples explained:

> *"In Him was life, and the life was the light of men...that was the **True Light** which gives light to every man coming into the world." (John 1:4, 9)*

This passage speaks two very important things:

First, it reveals that Jesus shines his eternal light upon every person born into this world. I believe this is more than just an admonition that the Gospel should be preached to every people-group in the earth. It rather implies that Jesus, as the Light of the world, spiritually influences every individual inhabiting this planet. Sometimes the signs of his influence are quite evident; sometimes they are subtle and barely discernible. Often the results of his influence are not even attributed to him. Instead, other gods or non-biblical teachings may be credited for the changes that take place in people's lives. However, it is the Spirit of the Lord Jesus Christ worldwide that constantly, subliminally convicts the souls of men concerning their sin, stirs their consciences and draws their hearts toward a life of devotion to righteous principles. This could very well explain why there is some evidence of truth in almost all religions. Tragically though, many have not heard the story of Jesus, so they fail to understand how salvation through Jesus can be obtained. *(See John 6:44, Romans 2:1–16.)*

Dealing with this calamity, the Scripture goes on to explain that "the light shines in the darkness and the darkness did not comprehend it." *(John 1:5)* I believe this happens often. After being inwardly influenced by the Spirit of Christ—by the stirring of the conscience—men and women truly repent of their sin and alter their lifestyle. But they fail to *comprehend* the next steps that need to be taken (most often, because of lack of biblical instruction), so they embrace religious ideas more readily accessible to them regionally or more comfortable to them culturally.

I now recognize that years before I became a Christian, God was dealing with me. His Spirit was drawing me, influencing my choices, convicting me of sin and creating in me a deep thirst for spiritual realities. Though I did not recognize it at the time, "the True Light which gives light to every man" was beginning to light up my life. I was only fully 'enlightened' when I acknowledged the Source of the light, when I called on that Name the Bible says is "above every name," accepting Jesus as Lord of my life. *(Philippians 2:9)*

Second, the declaration that Jesus is the "True Light" implies that there is a false light as well. Even though I gleaned some valuable truth from the books I studied and teachings I received as a student of yoga, it is clear to me now that the majority of those teachings were untrue—they were 'false light.' They were spurious attempts to analyze the nature of the Creator and man's relationship with him.

I also realize that the supernatural experiences I received were deceptive. The times my soul exited my body into the astral plane, or into 'white light,' were all counterfeit occurrences, false light. Of course, no one could have convinced me of such a thing at that time. Yet I should have heeded Jesus' warning, "Be careful lest the light in you be darkness." *(Luke 11:35 RSV)* Once I experienced the "True Light" it became very simple for me to identify the false. It will work the same for you. Once he illuminates your heart with his indwelling presence, he will illuminate your mind with the correct interpretation of truth.

Many New Age and Far Eastern teachers emphasize the heart above the mind. For instance, Meher Baba insisted, "All religions are basically dear to me. It is not so much what you believe that counts, but what you are."[23] Though I absolutely agree that character, in one sense, is much more important than creed—I must add that the latter, in many ways, gives birth to the former. What you believe actually determines what you are, so it is of the utmost importance. Even the Bhagavad-Gita states, "Man is made by his belief. As he believes, so he is." *(Bhagavad-Gita 17.3)* And Jesus exhorted that true worshippers must "worship the Father in spirit and in truth"—so character ("spirit") and creed ("truth") are both vitally and equally important. *(John 4:23)*

Of course, you may still have many questions about certain aspects of the teachings of Christianity, but please don't allow these to prevent you from experiencing the reality of Jesus. Only after you come into a personal relationship with this everlasting Messiah will all the answers fall in place. I cannot emphasize this too much. Knowing him is the priority; knowing about him is the result. In his day, Jesus answered some of his critics with the statement:

> *"My teaching is not My own. It comes from Him who sent Me. If anyone chooses to do God's will, he will find out whether My teaching comes from God or whether I speak on My own." (John 7:16–17 NIV)*

Again, this is the key—those who make an effort to approach God according to his will (according to God's revealed plan of salvation) will inevitably experience the reality of Jesus. Once a person experiences that reality, he or she will know the validity of the doctrine Jesus promoted. Do not seek to be convinced of the doctrine first; meet the One who authored it.

Shri Brahmananda Sarasvati suggests, "Your first and foremost duty is to know who you are. Without knowing oneself real life does not begin."[24] I respectfully offer that our first and foremost duty is rather to know the true God—because when we discover him, automatically, we discover ourselves. So let me encourage you with the same words Kent Sullivan spoke to me in the Fall of 1970—*"Just try Jesus!"* Once you experience his reality, everything else will fall into place. So this really is the answer... and once again, I share it in deep, heart-felt compassion:

✧ ✧ ✧ ✧ ✧ ✧ ✧ ✧

Just try Jesus.

✧ ✧ ✧ ✧ ✧ ✧ ✧ ✧

A PRAYER THAT CAN TRANSFORM YOUR LIFE FOREVER!

Allow me to share with you some very important, final instructions. In the previous pages of this book, you have been exposed to the words of Jesus—the One who is also titled the "Word...made flesh." *(John 1:14)* Because his words are the absolute standard of truth, all that is labeled truth must be in absolute agreement with his words. I pray you will make the choice to embrace these 'heaven-sent' insights. But again, it may seem difficult, or nearly impossible, to wholeheartedly accept these concepts, until you have a personal experience with the Author of Truth himself.

Blaise Pascal, defender of the Christian religion, passed to us an observation similar to the following:

> *"In every heart there is a God-shaped vacuum,*
> *and until that vacuum is filled with God, every other*
> *part remains empty."*

This 'emptiness of heart' is every person's basic problem—and it cannot be remedied even by studying every book on religion available in this world (including this one). As William Cowper pointed out:

> *"God never meant that man should scale the*
> *heavens by strides of human wisdom."*
> *(The Task, Bk. III.1.221)*

We need more than what the human intellect can provide, even at its zenith of expression. We need more than just an 'explanation,' no matter how sound or how logical it may be. What we need is an invigorating spiritual experience, a revelation to the heart—something that comes through 'spontaneous openness' to the reality of God.

Yes, I urge you to come to the Lord with this dual attitude; spontaneity and openness—and pray the prayer on the next page with all of your heart, just as it is worded. I also encourage you to be creative, expressing yourself in a very personal way to God. This prayer is not a mantra-like, mechanical formula; it is a suggested approach, an outline of appropriate ways to communicate with the Creator.

The most important thing is to pray from the heart and continue praying until you feel the assurance that God has heard you and responded. You can use these words, or similar statements using your own words, that express the concept of biblical salvation correctly.

The posture of the body is not important. You can be standing, kneeling or prostrate before God. You can be walking briskly or sitting quietly. Your location is not that important either. You can be in a church, in your home, or in a flower garden. What *is* important is that you come to God with sincere love, deep humility, and strong faith—and that you spend quality time seeking God without any distractions.

Sometimes there is a very joyous spiritual sensation that accompanies the experience of salvation. Sometimes there is no actual supernatural 'feeling' associated with the praying of this prayer and submission to Jesus' Lordship. The Bible explains we are saved through faith *(Ephesians 2:8)*; so the significant thing is to believe, whether you feel an inward sensation or not. These divine 'witnesses' to the soul may come later on.

The main issue is that all who approach Jesus for salvation must do so trusting in the promises contained in his Word. One reassuring pledge he gave is this:

> *"Come to me, all you who are weary and burdened,*
> *and I will give you rest." (Matthew 11:28 NIV)*

Notice, Jesus did not say with uncertainty, "I could" or "I might"; he declared emphatically, "I *will* give you rest!" So by faith, come to him now with a request and a confession similar to the following:

> *"Dear Lord Jesus, I ask you to manifest yourself*
> *to me. Please reveal your salvation. I believe you died*
> *on the cross for the sins of the human race and I*
> *believe you arose from the dead. I ask you to come*
> *and live in my heart and wash away all my sin by*
> *the blood that you shed.*
>
> *Thank you for saving my soul and granting me*
> *eternal life. Be Lord of my life and Lord of my future.*
> *I believe with my heart and I confess with my lips*
> *that you are the way to salvation and I accept you*
> *by faith as my source of hope, joy and fulfillment.*
>
> *Fill my heart with your love, your peace and*
> *your truth. Fill me with the gift of the Holy Spirit.*
> *And by the help of your grace, I will serve you the*
> *rest of my days. Amen."*

Now the promise belongs to you that Jesus spoke while he was still on the earth:

> *"I am the Light of the world. He who follows*
> *me shall not walk in darkness, but have the light*
> *of life." (John 8:12)*

Now that you have received him—follow him. If you do, you will never walk in darkness again. You will have the "Light of life."

✤ ✤ ✤ ✤ ✤ ✤ ✤ ✤ ✤ ✤ ✤ ✤ ✤

A FINAL COMMITMENT

Ralph Waldo Emerson once commented:

> *"I hate the giving of the hand unless the whole man accompanies it."*[25]

By reading this book, you have, in essence, reached out to receive my extended hand. Please be assured that *"the whole man accompanies it."* I am committed to help, in any way possible, those who need assistance in their search for "True Light." Please do not hesitate to communicate with me if you need to, and please be sure to visit our website for more stories of personal, spiritual transformation (www.thetruelight.net). Surely it was by God's design that this book came into your hands.

A BASIC HISTORY
OF THE RELIGIOUS
GROUPS INCLUDED IN THIS BOOK

THE ELEVEN MAIN LIVING RELIGIONS

Buddhism—Around 528 B.C., Buddhism was founded by Siddhartha Gautama (later to be known as Buddha). Siddhartha's father, Suddhodana, was an Indian rajah, the head of the Sakya warrior caste. Legend has it that prior to Gautama's birth, his mother, Mahamaya, dreamed a beautiful silver-white elephant with six tusks entered her womb from the side. The Vedic priests interpreted this to mean that she would have a son who would either be a universal monarch or a great Buddha. Therefore, she named him Siddhartha, meaning *one whose aim is accomplished.*

Though his family was elite, wealthy, and influential, Siddhartha found his royal heritage empty and unfulfilling. He left in search of enlightenment, adopting the life of a wandering monk (*sadhu*). Siddhartha rejected traditional Hinduism because he found the Hindu caste system repulsive, extreme Hindu asceticism futile and the sensuality of the Hindu gods unacceptable.

The turning point in his life came while meditating under a fig tree (later to be called the "Bodhi Tree"—the tree of wisdom). Siddhartha claimed to receive the experience of Nirvana (enlightenment). Hence, he was called the "Buddha," the *"enlightened one."* He then began preaching his message of liberation from suffering, an approach he called the "Middle Path." He began with five disciples and taught for about fifty years. He lived to be eighty years old, dying about 480 B.C. There are many sects in Buddhism. Those mentioned in this book include: Theravada, Mahayana, Amidha, Nichiren, Zen and Tibetan Buddhism.

The main sources of Scriptural inspiration for Buddhists are the *Tripitaka* (the Three Baskets). These are three collections of writings: the *Sutra Pitaka* (primarily dialogues between Buddha and other people), *Vinaya Pitaka* (over 225 rules that govern the monastic path), and *Abhidharma Pitaka* (philosophical and doctrinal explanations and categorizations).

Christianity—This is the correct path and true revelation of God to man. It is based on the belief that Jesus Christ, born of the virgin Mary in Bethlehem of Judea approximately 2,000 years ago, was the longed-for Messiah to the Jews, the Son of God, the manifestation of the God of Abraham in a physical body. His death, burial, resurrection, and ascension were all pivotal events in the history and spiritual development of this world. His crucifixion provided forgiveness of sins and restoration to fellowship with God; his resurrection displayed the hope of eternal life for all who believe. Christianity teaches the return of Jesus to this earth, when the kingdom of God will be fully established in this world. The Scripture base of Christianity is the *Bible*, comprised of the Old Testament (adopted from Judaism) and the New Testament.

Confucianism—This worldview originated with the respected Chinese philosopher Confucius (551–479 BC) and was further developed by some of his followers, such as Mencius (372–289 BC) and Zhu Xi (1130–1200 AD). His philosophy dealt more with ethics than religion. Confucius lived in a time when moral standards were lacking. He advocated a return to the ancient Chinese ideal of ethical living. He taught that rulers could be great only if they themselves lead exemplary lives. Effective leaders must be willing to be guided by moral principles. If they do so, their states will inevitably become prosperous and happy.

Confucius put his theories into practice when he became the magistrate of Zhongdu and the minister of crime for the state of Lu. His reforms were very successful, causing the prosperity of Lu to grow and greatly reducing crime. He was dismissed, however, due to the influence of leaders in another Chinese state who felt threatened by the increased prosperity of Lu. Confucius then devoted himself to traveling and teaching. During his last years, he spent most of his time writing commentaries on ancient Chinese literature.

The principles of Confucianism have been preserved in nine ancient Chinese writings, authored by either Confucius or one of his followers: the Five Classics and the Four Books. The Four Books *(Shih Shu)* impart many of the philosophic sayings of Confucianism. They are: *Analects*, *The Great Learning*, *The Doctrine of the Mean*, and *The Book of Mencius* (one of Confucius' most revered followers).

Hinduism—The word "Hindu" stems from the Sanskrit word *sindhu* meaning river (specifically the Indus River that flows through India and Pakistan). Dating historically from 1500 B.C., Hinduism is one of the oldest of the eleven main living religions. It boasts over 700 million adherents. A wide variety of beliefs exist in Hinduism, sometimes complementary and sometimes contradictory. Most likely this syncretism has resulted because of Hinduism's ease in absorbing ideas from other cultures and religions. Millions of gods are revered (the traditional number is 330 million), but the source of all personal deities is the Impersonal Absolute, that Ultimate Reality referred to as Brahman.

No ecclesiastical hierarchy, no specific doctrinal parameters, and no universally defined moral boundaries are promoted in Hinduism. Each man discovers his own dharma, the divine order for his life. Commonly held beliefs include: reincarnation, the divinity of man, and the quest for enlightenment. The highest source of written truth for Hindus is found in the four Vedas (a word meaning "knowledge" or "sacred teaching"). The most ancient is the Rig Veda, probably created between 1,300 and 1,000 B.C.

Hindus differentiate between *shruti*—"hearing" (texts that adherents believe stream from divine revelation and are therefore infallible, absolute truth) and *smriti*—"recollection, tradition" (texts based on traditions that are valid and authoritative only when drawing from *shruti*). *Shruti* includes certain portions of the *Vedas* (the *Samhitas*, *Brahmanas*, *Upanishads*, and certain *Sutras*). *Smriti* includes certain traditional texts (including the *Puranas* and two lengthy Sanskrit epics: the *Mahabharata* and the *Ramayana*). One of the most popular texts is the *Bhagavad-Gita* ("The Song of the Lord"), which is actually part of the *Mahabharata*.

Islam—Mohammed (570–632 AD), the founder of Islam, is considered in this religion to be the last and greatest of all prophets. Born an orphan, he was raised by his uncle and grandfather. Although he was a member of a poor family in Mecca, his family was still well respected. Known for his organizational ability and honesty, he was employed by a wealthy widow who he eventually married. Mohammed periodically went to a cave outside of Mecca for prayer and meditation. According to Muslim tradition, it was there that the archangel Gabriel appeared to Mohammed, declaring him to be a prophet of God.

Mohammed's teaching stressed his belief in only one God, social and economic justice, and the final judgment. His emphasis on social reform

A Basic History of Religious Groups • 303

brought him into conflict with the wealthy merchants of Mecca. In 619 A.D., he was offered a prominent position in arbitrating feuds in the city of Medina. Mohammed accepted the position and encouraged his followers to immigrate there. In Medina, he began to lay the foundation for Islamic practices and continued his efforts toward societal improvement. The city of Mecca finally surrendered to Mohammed in 630 A.D. after warring against Medina for a season. Soon after this, tribes from all over Arabia were converted to Islam. There are presently over 150 Islamic sects in the world.

The *Qur'an* is the main Scripture base for Muslims. Believed to be divinely inspired, the *Qur'an* was allegedly revealed to Mohammed by Gabriel over a period of approximately twenty-two years. The second source is the *Sunna* (the example of the prophet) known through *Hadith* (traditions concerning the sayings or actions of Mohammed as he dealt with various issues). The *Qur'an* is considered infallible; *Hadith* is not.

Jainism—The word "Jain" refers to a follower of the *Jinas* (a word meaning "those who conquer"). Individuals known as *Jinas* were, therefore, "conquerors" of this world and of their own fleshly existence. Twenty-four such persons are revered in Jainism, the last of which was Mahavira, the founder of this religion. These are also known as *Tirthankaras*, word that meaning "Ford-makers" (great teachers who guide others across the "river" of transmigration).

His name was originally Vardhamana Jnatiputra. Born in 599 B.C., he was a contemporary of Buddha. Later on, he was given the name Mahavira (pronounced mah-hah-vee-rah), meaning "great hero," because of his courage and self-control. As the son of a king, Mahavira was raised in royal and opulent surroundings. When both his parents died, Mahavira wanted to renounce the world, but his brother convinced him to stay home for two years. For these two years, he practiced self-discipline and abstaining from luxuries. During the last year of this stage in his life, Mahavira gave charity to beggars every day.

At age thirty, he totally renounced his princely life including his wife, wealth, home, and clothing and for the next twelve years spent his time in silence and deep meditation, fasting often. During this time, Mahavira carefully avoided harming any living thing, including plants. According to Jainist tradition, at the end of this period he achieved *keval-jnana* or "perfect perception, knowledge, and bliss." Mahavira then spent the next thirty years traveling as a barefoot mendicant preaching his message on non-violence and renunciation of the world.

Though it emerged in a predominantly Hindu culture, Jainism rejects the idea that the Vedas are divinely inspired. However, they similarly embrace a belief in reincarnation and the need for enlightenment in order to escape the cycle of rebirths. Jainism, like Buddhism, is basically non-theistic, though the worship of certain saints *(siddhas)* is promoted, and, most importantly, the adoration of the *Tirthankaras (the Jinas)*. Non-violence to any living thing is a dominant doctrine in Jainism.

Judaism—This modern term relates to the religious culture of the Jews, those who are identified historically and presently as the remnant of biblical Israel. Though Jews, as God's chosen people, trace their history back to the first man, Adam, their origin is primarily identified with the visitation Abraham received from God. At that time Abraham's seed were set apart as a special treasure to God. Moses is one of the most revered prophets in this religion. Through him came the revelation and codification of foundational religious laws of Judaism.

Judaism has developed into a religious and cultural system of regulations, traditions, and ceremonies that govern the entire life of a Jew. The goal is the sanctification of all Israelites from the world as a people consecrated to the Most High God. *Halakah* is the "way" to live according to Jewish laws, customs, and rituals. It primarily involves abiding in a covenant relationship with God *(*Heb. *berith)* by observing His commandments *(*Heb. *mitzvoth)*. A right relationship with God is further maintained by repentance for any shortcomings and faith in the God who mercifully forgives and restores the remorseful to a righteous standing.

Rooted deeply in monotheism, Judaism emphasizes the oneness of God. The most revered of all Scripture passages is the *Shema*—"Hear, O Israel: the Lord our God, the Lord is one!" *(Deuteronomy 6:4)* To a Jew, the one and only true God is the God of Abraham, Isaac, and Jacob: transcendent, omnipresent, omnipotent, omniscient, and personal.

Pivotal events in the history of Judaism include: the calling of Abraham (separating him from a polytheistic family and culture), the enslavement of his offspring in Egypt, the supernatural deliverance of the children of Israel from Egypt, the receiving the Law at Mount Sinai, their conquest of the Land of Canaan, their enslavement in Babylon, the subsequent restoration of the Israelite people to their homeland seventy years later, their dispersion *(diaspora)* into all the world after the destruction of Jerusalem in 70 A.D., and their regathering in 1948.

The doctrinal foundation of Judaism is fivefold: (1) The *Torah* (the Pentateuch—the most revered, first five books of the Hebrew Bible); (2) The rest of the *Tenach*, which is divided into three parts: the *Torah*, the *Nebiim* (the prophetic writings) and the *Ketubim* (other writings). (3) The compilation of handed-down oral traditions, which resulted in the *Mishnah* (meaning "that which is learned"). (4) Commentaries on the *Mishnah*, which produced the *Talmud* (meaning "that which is studied"). (5) Other exegetical studies on the Scripture, and works of *Halakhah*, philosophy and thought.

Shinto—This is fundamentally and primarily the religion of the Japanese people. The word "Shinto" means "the way of the gods," a name adopted in the sixth century A.D. to distinguish it from Buddhism and Confucianism. The origin of this religion is prehistoric. In its earliest expression it offered no orthodox sacred writings, no universal standard of moral behavior, and no fixed doctrinal base. It primarily focuses on the worship of a pantheon of deities or spirits *(kami)*. The *kami* range from deities associated with aspects of nature (the sky, the sun, a mountain, etc.) to those that perform specific functions. Examples include: Fudo, who guards against danger or misfortune; Yakushi, who imparts healing for the mind and the body; or Inari, the rice god who brings an abundant harvest.

Two other major facets of Shintoism have been: *Emperor worship*— stemming from a belief that the Mikado (the emperors that ruled Japan) descended from Ama-terasu Omikami, the sun goddess. Defeat during the Second World War produced a great deal of skepticism toward, and rejection of, this doctrine. *Ancestor worship*—stemming from the belief that thirty-three years after death, every Shinto person becomes divine, joining the ranks of the *kami*. For many centuries, Shintoism lost its uniqueness and independent existence, being mixed with its two chief rivals: Buddhism and Confucianism. In the 18th century, however, a nationalistic revival took place under the influence of a number of scholars who sought to rid Japan of foreign influence and reestablish Shinto as the state religion.

The revered texts of this religion are: *Kojiki* (Records of Ancient Matters—712 A.D.) *Nihongi* or *Nihon Shoki* (Chronicles of Japan—720 A.D.) and *Engishiki* or *Yengishiki* (Procedures of the Engi Era—927 A.D.).

Sikhism—Guru Nanak, founder of Sikhism, was born in a Hindu family of merchants (1469–1539 A.D.). From a young age, he rejected many of his family's ways. In his latter twenties, he claimed to experience a divine revelation and calling. This spurred him to make a number of long trips to help spread this viewpoint. One of his primary objectives was to create a completely God-centered, egalitarian society, free of injustice. His life story shows a high level of dedication to his ideals. Along with a Muslim musician, he journeyed all over the Far and Middle East teaching the oneness of God (the concept that Muslims and Hindus, as well as other religions, are all actually worshipping the same God). He also taught that salvation or liberation was easily accessible to all people, not just ascetics (as found in Hinduism). He vigorously promoted the equality of men and women.

Nine gurus succeeded Guru Nanak. The tenth and last guru, Guru Gobind Singh, decreed that at his demise there would no longer be a human guru at the head of the Sikh religion. Rather, their holy book, the *Adi Granth*, would become their "Guru" (their spiritual guide). All initiated Sikhs (the *Guru Panth*) also act as guides to others who are seeking truth. Though they have branched out worldwide, Sikhs are primarily found in the Punjab region of Northern India.

Taoism—Pronounced "Dowism," this Chinese philosophical and religious worldview is believed to have begun around the sixth century B.C. Taoism claims Lao-Tzu as its founder, believed to be a contemporary of Confucius. His name means either "wise old child" or "old master." Certain traditions claim Lao-Tzu was born a white-haired philosopher, after being carried seventy-two years in the womb of his mother. Some Taoist scholars admit he is only a legendary figure. However, according to the *Shih-chi*, he was actually a custodian of the archives in the court of the King of Chou. Disagreeable situations in this royal court motivated Lao-Tzu to resign and travel west.

At the mountain pass of Hsien-ku he was constrained by Yin Hsi, the guardian of that pass, to preserve his views by putting them into writing. The result was the *Tao-te Ching*, a document made up of 5,000 pictograms. It is the main sacred text on which this religion is based. After transferring his beliefs to paper, Lao-Tzu disappears, walking off the pages of history. He was later deified by his followers, some even suggesting that he was a manifestation of the primordial chaos and that he had previously reincarnated numerous times in order to guide the human race with his teaching. Another famous and greatly influential leader in Taoism is Chuang-tzu (369-286 B.C.).

Eva Wong, in *The Shambhala Guide to Taoism*, identifies five different and primary paths within Taoism: Magical Taoism (the Way of Power), Divinational Taoism (the Way of Seeing), Ceremonial Taoism (the Way of Devotion), Internal-Alchemical Taoism (the Way of Transformation), and Action and Karma Taoism (the Way of Right Action).

The *Tao-te Ching* describes the Source of all things as being *Tao* (meaning "the Way"). It is "eternal, nameless." Yet whenever it is manifested, it is given "different names." *(Tao-te Ching 1, 32)* Any name given to a manifestation of Tao is only earthly and temporary—"The name that can be named is not the eternal name." *(Tao-te Ching 1)* On the highest level, Ultimate Reality is an impersonal energy force.

In Taoism, the secret to a successful life is to come into harmony with *Tao*. This harmonious union is called *wu-wei* (quiet non-striving). The superiority of this way of life is compared to water (that appears shapeless and weak) wearing away stone (that appears permanent and strong). The "parent of all teachings" is that "the violent man will come to a violent end." *(Tao-te Ching 42, 78)*

Zoroastrianism—This unique religion stems from ancient Persia and is based on the teachings of Zoroaster (630–550 B.C). Considered a prophet by his followers, he declared Ahura Mazda ("Wise Lord") to be the chief deity and god of light, opposed by Angra Mainyu, the god of darkness. Both gods are self-existent, co-equal and able to create. Darius I, who reigned from 521 to 486 B.C., was probably the first Persian king to embrace Zoroastrianism. It was established as the state religion of Persia centuries later, from 224 to 641 A.D. Persia was eventually conquered by the Arabs and gradually converted to Islam during the seventh century A.D. Zoroastrianism was then suppressed, but still managed to survive. In India, Zoroastrians are called Parsis ("Persians"). Adherents revere fire as a symbol of the divine Presence. Their sacred Scripture is the *Avesta*.

OTHER RELIGIONS, SECTS OR TEACHERS

Astrology—This is the study of how the sun, moon, planets and stars affect events in this world, not only culturally, nationally and globally, but personally and individually as well. The positioning of all astronomical bodies at a person's birth, and throughout his or her life, are said to determine both character and destiny. Astrological charts are called horoscopes. The Chaldeans were practicing astrology in Babylonia as early as 3000 B.C. There is evidence that astrology was being practiced about 1,000 years later in China and by the year 500 B.C. in ancient Greece. There are many schools of thought in astrology giving rise to a wide spectrum of speculations concerning the meaning of planetary and solar positions. It was based originally on a Ptolemaic view of the solar system (the belief that the earth is the center of the solar system and the sun, moon and planets revolve around the earth on a backdrop of unmoving stars).

Bahá'í—This faith grew out of Babism, which itself sprang out of the Shiite branch of the Muslim faith. On May 23, 1844, Sayyid 'Alí Mohammed Shírazí began to proclaim in the land of Persia the fundamentals of his theology. He became known as the Bab (a Persian term meaning "the Gate") because he was revered as a 'gate' of true revelation. He announced that various prophets of the past were divine Manifestations and that he was a Prophet and a Manifestation of God. He claimed greatness equal to Mohammed, yet identified himself only as a forerunner of an even greater Manifestation of God destined to emerge nineteen years later. A strong advocate of monogamy, the Bab preached against the polygamy so prevalent in the society of his day. Though greatly opposed, this sect survived. In 1863, a disciple of the Bab named Mírzá Husayn-'Alí Núrí declared that he was the "Manifestation" foretold by the Bab. He took the name Bahá'u'lláh (which means "the glory of God").

Bahá'ís believe strongly in the oneness of the human race and the establishment of a universal religion for all. It has no official priesthood and no system of sacraments in its belief system. There is no preaching in Bahá'í temples, simply the reciting of scriptures from the sacred texts of all religions. Especially in its beginning years, members of this faith suffered severe persecution.

Benjamin Creme (Share International Foundation)—Benjamin Creme, founder of Share International, was born in Glasgow, Scotland, in 1922. At an early age he was recognized as an accomplished artist (modern style). He also became quite studious in the pursuit of spiritual insights through esoteric philosophy, especially the teachings of Helena Blavatsky (co-founder of the Theosophical Society) and Alice Bailey, who was one of the first writers to popularize the term "New Age." Through their influence, Benjamin Creme came to believe in a hierarchy of Ascended Masters who are the spiritual custodians of this planet. He claims that in 1959 one of these Masters of Wisdom contacted him—revealing that about twenty years later, Maitreya, the long awaited World Teacher for this age, would manifest himself in the earth. Benjamin Creme was also informed that he would be instrumental in this planetary event if he accepted the responsibility.

In 1972 he began preparing for this task, and eventually began lecturing all over the world. His primary message has always been the declaration of the arrival of Maitreya. He insists Maitreya is the fulfillment of the messianic hope found in many religions. According to Benjamin Creme's worldview, Maitreya is the fulfillment of the Christian expectation of the coming of Christ, the Jewish longing for Messiah, the Muslim hope for the Imam Mahdi, the Hindu's longing for the next Avatar named Kalki and the Buddhist anticipation of Maitreya Buddha. All these religious projections for the future, he claims, will be realized in one individual. On his website (www.shareintl.org), Benjamin Creme lists numerous incidents worldwide that he claims were supernatural manifestations of Maitreya, usually to large groups of people. He has written a number of books and pamphlets on this subject.

Brahma Kumaris World Spiritual Organization (Raja Yoga)— In 1876, the founder of this religious group, Lekh Raj, was born in Hyderabad, Sindh (now Pakistan). He was the child of a village headmaster, certainly a humble beginning. Later in life, he became a very successful and wealthy diamond merchant, known for his philanthropic treatment of the poor. Around the age of sixty, "Dada" (as he was affectionately called—meaning "elder brother") felt compelled to spend a great deal of his time in solitude. His focus was the contemplation of the true nature of God and the self.

During meditation he claimed to receive a series of divinely inspired visions. A dominant prophetic theme involved a soon-to-come era of great destruction on the earth—through natural calamities, war, and the use of powerful weapons (his followers believe this was a reference to what would later be known as nuclear arms). Another vision revealed souls descending like tiny stars to the earth. Upon arriving here these souls were transformed into divine beings in a restored world of celestial-like peace, love, harmony, and happiness.

One vision was most pivotal to Lekh Raj's view of his own role. He claimed to see the four-armed god, Vishnu, who said to him, "I am you." It is also taught that around 1937, god Shiva began descending into Lekh Raj's body expressing his wisdom and insights concerning the closing of a dark cyclical era (called "the Iron Age") and the dawning of a new and glorious era (called "the Golden Age"). When Shiva allegedly spoke through one of Lekh Raj's disciples, the name Prajapita Brahma was supernaturally bestowed on him. It was also communicated that he would be Brahma's instrument to awaken the ancient yoga system of India and to establish the new world. He was especially known for preaching the equality of women with men in a society and during an era in which the opposite view was much more dominant and widespread.

This religious group explains that on January 18, 1969, Brahma Baba reached *karmateet*—the stage of being freed from all karmic accounts. It is taught that his soul departed to higher spiritual realms where he continues to work toward this goal of a transition into a golden-aged new world. Those who follow his teachings are known as Brahmins (the "twice-born"). Brahma Kumaris World Spiritual University (or Organization) has many centers all over the world. Their system of meditation and spiritual discipline is referred to as "Raja Yoga." Their views on key doctrinal issues are quite unique as compared to other yoga groups.

ECKANKAR (Paul Twitchell and Sri Harold Klemp)—Heralded by its founder, Paul Twitchell, to be the channel of ancient wisdom revived, this sect made its appearance in 1965. Twitchell also claimed to be the 971st Living ECK Master. He insisted that he received his revelations from two former ECK Masters: Sudar Singh in India and Rebazar Tarzs in the Himalayas, and that the terminology used in this religion came from the Amdo dialect of the Tibetan language.

The present leader, Sri Harold Klemp, became the 973rd ECK Master in 1981. The ECK Master is also called the Mahanta. Whoever fills this role is said to be God in the flesh, omniscient and omnipresent, one who abides in the highest state of God-consciousness. The ECK Master's calling is to lead other souls into the realm of spirit which is called the Kingdom of Heaven. The primary means by which this takes place is the leadership of the Mahanta and an experience called "Soul Travel." Interpretation of dreams is also an important part of one's spiritual development. To its initiates and members, ECKANKAR is taught to be the only true path to God.

The sacred text of this religious group is the *Shariyat-Ki-Sugmad*, said to be twelve volumes long, most of which are viewable only in the spiritual worlds. Paul Twitchell claimed to have transcribed the first two volumes while visiting higher planes.

Gnosticism—A religious movement that emerged strongly in the second and third centuries, Gnosticism presented a strong challenge to orthodox Christianity. Its emphasis was esoteric knowledge *(gnosis)* acquired through various means. Gnostics refuted or altered the meaning of many Christian doctrines. Members of this movement felt they possessed secret insights into the nature of God and of man. Gnosticism taught that matter is essentially evil, the creation of an evil god. Human beings possess a spark of divinity that is unfortunately trapped in matter and in ignorance, and must be liberated. To overcome this condition, some Gnostics embraced asceticism, while others embraced licentiousness, teaching that any indulgence in the flesh did not affect the state of the soul. Man does not need 'salvation from sin,' but an 'awakening out of spiritual ignorance.'

Helen Schucman (*A Course in Miracles*)—This book and the worldview it promotes resulted from a mutual decision between two professors of medical psychology at Columbia University's College of physicians and Surgeons in New York City: Helen Schucman and William Thetford. They were professionals, working together in a highly academic setting, but by their own admission, their relationship was strained, full of anger and marred by aggressiveness. One day, William, the head of the department, announced that there must be a better way. Around June of 1965, they proceeded to seek it out.

Though at one time a professed atheist, Helen began receiving symbolic dreams and perceiving strange images. After several months, she felt compelled to write down her impressions, sensing what she felt was the guidance and inspiration of the Holy Spirit in her task. Over a course of seven years, Helen Schucman dictated to William what she felt the 'Voice' communicated to her. She claimed her source was Jesus Christ (though her teachings are very non-biblical). William typed the course, making it a collaborative effort. The book, *A Course in Miracles*, was published in 1975 by the Foundation for Inner Peace. Helen Schucman died February 9, 1981. William Thetford passed away seven years later, July 4, 1988.

ISKCON (International Society of Krishna Consciousness)—This religious group is a modern continuation of a movement that adherents claim predates Hinduism. The central theme is devotion to Krishna as the highest personality of the Godhead. Devotees state their lineage goes all the way back to Lord Brahma, creator of this particular universe around 105 trillion earth-years ago. One of the most revered proponents of this worldview is Caitanya (1486-1534 A.D.), recognized as an Avatar ("one who descends")—a manifestation of both Krishna, and Radha, his chief consort. Radha is described as a gopi (a shepherdess), who is so overwhelmed with a longing for Krishna that she leaves all other earthly attachments. Thus, she becomes the personification of the ecstatic love existing between God and every devotee. Radha is also worshipped as a goddess herself.

In 1922, a philosophy and economics major at the Scottish Churches College named Abhay Charan De was initiated into this worldview. He was greatly influenced by an Indian Guru and Spiritual Master *(Acharya)*, Srila Bhaktisiddhanta Sarasvati Thakura Goswami Maharaja, who was spearheading a revival of devotion to Krishna in the early 1900s. At the age of 54, Abhay Charan De withdrew from business and family associations, only to assume the *sannyasa* order of life as a renunciate ten years later. At the age of 70, he came to the Western world and founded ISKCON. He then became known as His Divine Grace A. C. Bhaktivedanta Swami Prabhupada. The main source of the religious philosophy of ISKCON is the *Bhagavad-Gita*. Other Vedic sacred books are revered.

Kabbala (Mystical Judaism)—This is the esoteric offshoot of Judaism. One of its main sacred texts is called the *Zohar*. Some propose this book was authored by Rabbi Simeon Ben Yohai in the second century A.D. Others contend it was authored by a group of mystics associated with Moses de Leon, a Jew who lived in Spain in the latter part of the thirteenth century. Kabbalistic doctrine overflows with spiritual symbolism, mathematical and numerological projections, metaphysical insights, and a unique method of interpreting Scripture. Its doctrines, at times, conflict with traditional Judaism. However, Kabbalistic 'revelations' are so interwoven into traditional Jewish thought that often they are indistinguishable one from the other. Most of the quotes in this book are from modern Kabbalistic sources.

Kriya Yoga (Swami Sri Yukteswar and Paramahansa Yogananda)— Paramahansa Yogananda was born January 5, 1893. His parents were Bengalis of the *Kshatriya* caste. He studied Kriya Yoga under Swami Sri Yukteswar who later encouraged him to carry this belief system to the West. (The word *Kriya* means "action" or "to do.") In 1920, he came to the United States, eventually establishing the Church of All Religions and the Self-Realization Fellowship, building a large headquarters and yoga center in 1949 in Los Angeles, California. Since then Self-Realization Fellowship Centers have sprung up all over the world. Yogananda was one of the first Indian gurus to receive widespread recognition in the Western world. One of his most popular and well-known works is the book entitled, *The Autobiography of a Yogi*. He died in 1952.

Kundalini Yoga (Yogi Bhajan)—In 1969, at the age of forty, Yogi Bhajan came to the Western world from India. He formed the 3HO Foundation (Happy, Healthy, Holy Organization) and began spreading the message of achieving a happy, healthy and holy life through the practice of Kundalini Yoga. Some Sikhs acknowledge Yogi Bhajan as the Siri Singh Sahib, the chief religious and administrative authority of Sikh Dharma of the Western Hemisphere. There are other Sikhs who question his right to bear this honorific title. Kundalini Yoga is professed to be a combination of many other types of yoga (hatha yoga, mantra yoga, raja yoga, etc.). It is called the "Yoga of Awareness." Its emphasis is the arousal of the "kundalini" power in order to achieve enlightenment.

Meher Baba—Born February 25, 1894, Meher Baba's name was originally Merwan Sheriar Irani. According to tradition, five Perfect Masters (*Qutub*—a God-conscious individual) influenced him over a period of seven years to achieve the realization that he was the Avatar of this cycle. The first was an elderly woman of the Muslim faith, Hazrat Babajan, who initiated the process when she kissed him on the forehead. The word "Avatar" means an embodiment or manifestation of God on earth. Followers of Meher Baba believe he was the most recent manifestation of God, having previously visited the earth as Zoroaster, Rama, Krishna, Buddha, Jesus, Mohammed, and others. Meher Baba maintained silence for the last forty-three years of his life, communicating primarily with hand gestures and an alphabet board. He never sought to establish a religious sect, but proclaimed the unity of all religions. A large following of disciples, from many different faiths, continues to grow worldwide. Meher Baba established a Universal Spiritual Center in Myrtle Beach, South Carolina. He died January 31, 1969, at Meherazad, India.

Scientology—In 1952, American author, L. Ron Hubbard founded the Scientology religion. The first Church of Scientology was established by several of Mr. Hubbard's students in February of 1954. The main emphasis is on "clearing" a person of "engrams" (negative perceptions in the subconscious mind) by a pastoral counseling process called "Dianetics" (a word meaning "through the soul"). Fundamentally, the goal of Scientology is to empower an individual to experience a greater understanding of life and to improve himself and the world in which he lives. There are many laws, axioms and techniques that the Scientologist applies to his day-to-day living to achieve this goal. Scientologists believe that truth is a subjective experience, a voyage of self-discovery. Scientology claims to draw wisdom from all the great religions of this world, although its closest spiritual 'cousin' is Buddhism.

Sufism (Mystical Islam)—Around the ninth century Sufism began to grow out of the ground of the Muslim faith. The Arabic word *sufi* means "mystic." It stems from *suf*, meaning "wool"—most likely an allusion to the traditional woolen garment that early Muslim ascetics wore. Others contend is comes from the Arabic word *tassawuf* meaning "purification." Though most Muslims teach a transcendent God, beyond personal encounter, the Sufi Muslims believe otherwise. They pursue mystical experiences with Allah through various means, especially a whirling kind of dance designed to project the worshipper into a trance-like state of blissful union with God. Other practices include *fikr* (meditation) and *dhikr* (the remembrance of God by frequent repetition of his names). Being a lover of the Beloved (God) is the emphasis in Sufism.

Sufis have long been noted for their spiritual 'love poetry' concerning this theme. The *Qur'an* is revered, though Sufis add levels of symbolic, inner meanings. Though many ascetics are found among Sufis, still, this religion does not 'demand' an ascetic-like withdrawal from the world. Rather, it emphasizes the goal of seeking God while involved in the world. Sheikh Muzaffer explains, "Keep your hands busy with your duties in this world, and your heart busy with God."[1] There are many different Sufi brotherhoods. Given the emphasis of 'dying to self' in Sufism, some of its adherents claim the best description of this religious group is the enigmatic statement—"The Sufi is the one who is not."[2]

Theosophy (Helena Blavatsky, Henry Steel Olcott and Annie Besant)—The word "Theosophy" comes from two Greek words, *theos* meaning "god," and *sophos* meaning "wise." In essence, it means those who seek the wisdom of God by searching through philosophy or by the pursuit of mystical experiences, or both. Proponents of Theosophical concepts can be found in Hinduism, Taoism, Gnosticism, Neo-Platonism and the like.

In recent years, this term became closely linked with Helena Petrovna Blavatsky who formed the Theosophical Society in New York City in 1875, along with Henry Steel Olcott. Blavatsky claimed to be in touch with spiritually evolved human beings dedicated to the service of the world whose teachings formed the basis of her belief system. She promoted a monistic and pantheistic view of the relationship between God and the universe. She also taught that mankind is evolving through reincarnation toward perfection, and those who are near, or reach such a goal are responsible to guide less evolved souls.

Annie Besant succeeded Blavatsky as the spiritual leader of the society after the latter's death in 1891 and as international president after the death of the president-founder, Henry Steel Olcott, in 1907. She was quite involved, not only as a proponent of Theosophy, but in governmental, educational and social work in the land of India. It was Annie Besant who introduced Jiddu Krishnamurti as the Messiah of this age. He later refuted the claim.

There is no set dogma in the Theosophical Society. However, three foundational beliefs normally embraced are: "(1) the fundamental unity of all existence, so that all pairs of opposites—matter and spirit, the human and the divine, I and thou—are transitory and relative distinctions of an underlying absolute Oneness, (2) the regularity of universal law, cyclically producing universes out of the absolute ground of being, and (3) the progress of consciousness developing through the cycles of life to an ever-increasing realization of Unity."[3]

Transcendental Meditation (Maharishi Mahesh Yogi)—Maharishi Mahesh Yogi was born in India around 1910. After graduating from Allahabad University with a degree in physics, he began pursuing a higher purpose in life, becoming a disciple of Guru Dev for thirteen years. Maharishi first taught TM in India and then, at Guru Dev's urging, he brought this system of thought to the West in 1959. Promoted as the Science of Creative Intelligence, TM offers its practitioners a means of achieving peace, harmony, inner joy, creativity, and enlightenment primarily through meditation and the chanting of various Sanskrit mantras.

Adherents claim these are designed to lift a person to higher levels of consciousness. TM has been one of the more popular movements out of India and has numerous centers around the world.

United Church of Religious Science (Dr. Ernest Holmes)—This religious sect is a part of what has been termed the "New Thought Movement." It is based on a belief that the human mind is an expression of the Universal Mind. The universe is its physical manifestation. Something called "affirmative prayer" is used to bring healing to the mind or the body. Ministers and practitioners give spiritual mind treatments. Dr. Ernest Holmes published his beliefs in the book, *The Science of Mind*, in 1926. The next year he formed the Institute of Religious Science and Philosophy in Los Angeles, California, to disseminate his doctrinal views. In 1949, the United Church of Religious Science was established.

Yoga—The word "yoga" means *yoke*. It implies being yoked or harnessed with God, brought into harmony with the Divine. Yoga is one of the six primary systems of orthodox thought in Indian philosophy. Adherents claim that its practice can, first, free the aspirant from the illusion and ignorance that characterizes this earthly realm, and second, enable the seeker, through various self-disciplines, to achieve oneness with the Divine. There are many types of yoga, such as: Hatha Yoga (the path of physical disciplines), Karma Yoga (the path of selfless action), Bhakti Yoga (the path of devotion to an individual god), Jnana Yoga (the path of transcendental knowledge), Mantra Yoga (the path of chanting mantras to achieve enlightenment) and others. Primary sacred texts are the *Yoga Sutras* written by Patanjali (c. 200 BC). He taught that there are "eight limbs" of yoga: (1) *Yama* (discipline, including avoidance of violence, dishonesty and greed); (2) *Niyama* (restraint, spiritual devotion); (3) *Asana* (physical postures); (4) *Pranayama* (breath control); (5) *Pratyahara* (sense-withdrawal); (6) *Dharana* (concentration); (7) *Dhyana* (meditation); (8) *Samadhi* (ecstasy or enlightenment). Most westerners only associate "yoga" with numbers (3) and (4).

ENDNOTES

PART 1—THE QUEST OF EVERY HEART

[1] Frank S. Mead, *12,000 Religious Quotations* (Grand Rapids, Michigan: Baker Book House, 1989) p. 169.

[2] Ibid., p.123.

[3] *The World's Great Religions* (New York: Time Incorporated, 1957) p. 16.

[4] Frank S. Mead, *12,000 Religious Quotations*, p. 374.

[5] Albert M. Wells Jr., *Inspiring Quotations, Contemporary & Classical* (Nashville, Tennessee: Thomas Nelson Publishers, 1989) p. 169.

[6] Bhau Kalchuri, *Lord Meher*, vol. 12 (Asheville, North Carolina: Manifestation, Inc.) p. 809.

[7] www.katinkahesselink.net/blavatsky/articles/v6/y1884_016.htm (accessed September 20, 2018).

[8] www.brainyquote.com/quotes/edmund_burke_118578 (accessed September 20, 2018).

[9] Kahlil Gibran, *The Prophet* (Ware, Hertfordshire, Great Britain: Wordsworth Editions, Ltd., 1996) p. 48

[10] www.brainyquote.com/quotes/albert_einstein_148864 (accessed September 20, 2018).

[11] https://en.wikiquote.org/wiki/Religiousness (accessed September 20, 2018).

[12] Frank S. Mead, *12,000 Religious Quotations*, p. 372

[13] Maharishi Mahesh Yogi, *Science of Being and Art of Living* (New York: Meridian, an imprint of Dutton Signet, a division of Penguin Books, 1995) p. 253.

[14] https://en.wikipedia.org/wiki/Opium_of_the_people (accessed September 20, 2018).

[15] Citation not available.

[16] Robert E Hume, *The World's Living Religions* (New York: Charles Scribner's Sons, rev. ed., 1936) p. 2.

[17] Peter Smith, "Golden Rule," *A Concise Encyclopedia of the Bahá'í Faith* (Oxford, England: Oneworld Publications, 2000) p. 165.

[18] www.christianquotes.info/images/f-b-meyer-quote-allow-yourself-to-receive-christs-blessings/#axzz5Re3NGdDx (accessed 2/18/2019).

[19] Meher Baba, *Beams for Meher Baba on the Spiritual Panorama*, ed. Ivy Duce (Walnut Creek, California: Sufism Reoriented) n.p.*

[20] Bhagavan Dass, *The Essential Unity of All Religions* (Kila, Montana: Kessinger Publishing Company, rev. ed. 1939) p. 479.

[21] Ernest Holmes, *The Science of Mind* (New York: R.M McBride and Co., 1938, New York: Penguin Putnam, Inc., rev. and enl. ed., 1966) p. 155 (page citation is to reprint edition).

[22] www.brainyquote.com/quotes/socrates_388541 (accessed 2/18/2019).

[23] www.brainyquote.com/quotes/ralph_waldo_emerson_118592 (accessed 2/18/2019).

[24] Ernest Holmes, *The Science of Mind* (New York: R.M McBride and Co., 1938, New York: Penguin Putnam, Inc., rev. and enl. ed., 1966) p. 159 (page citation is to reprint edition).

[25] www.brainyquote.com/quotes/petrarch_211775 (accessed 2/18/2019).

[26] Joel Beversluis, ed., *Sourcebook of the World's Religions* (Novato, California: New World Library, 2000) p. 6.

[27] Benjamin Shield and Richard Carlson, eds., *For the Love of God* (Novato, California: New World Library, 1997) p. 3.

[28] James Fadiman, ed., and Robert Frager, ed., *Essential Sufism* (Edison, New Jersey: Castle Books, 1998) pp. 14, 18.

[29] Quoted by al-Ghazali in Margaret Smith, trans., *Readings from the Mystics of Islam*, p. 35. This is not a quote from the Qur'an, but a so-called *Hadith Qudsi*; quoted in John Alden Williams, ed., *Islam* (New York City, New York: George Braziller, Inc., 1962) p. 146.

[30] Kahlil Gibran, *The Prophet*, p. 6.

[31] David N. Elkins, Ph. D., "Compassion: A Way of Being in the World, An Interview with Sharon Salzberg," *Personal Transformation* (Winter 1999): p. 58 (Sharon Salzberg is actually quoting the German monk and scholar, Nyanaponika Thera).

[32] John Alden Williams, ed., *Islam* (New York City, New York: George Braziller, Inc., 1962) pp. 156, 158, Note: the last four lines are from the very end of the poem.

[33] Huston Smith, "Sufism," *The Illustrated World's Religions: A Guide to our Wisdom Tradition*, Labyrinth Publishing (UK) Ltd., 1994) p. 171.

[34] Annie Besant, *Four Great Religions*, p. 7; quoted in Robert E Hume, *The World's Living Religions* (New York: Charles Scribner's Sons, rev. ed., 1936) p. 10.

[35] www.allaboutreligion.org/religion.htm (accessed 9/20/2018).

[36] Frank S. Mead, *12,000 Religious Quotations* (Grand Rapids, Michigan: Baker Book House, 1989) p. 17. This particular translation is not a strict one. A more precise translation of the same passage is: "Do not go upon what has been acquired by repeated hearing; nor upon tradition; nor upon rumor; nor upon what is in a scripture; nor upon surmise; nor upon an axiom; nor upon specious reasoning; nor upon a bias towards a notion that has been pondered over; nor upon another's seeming ability; nor upon the consideration, 'The monk is our teacher.' Kalamas, when you yourselves know: 'These things are good; these things are not blamable; these things are praised by the wise; undertaken and observed, these things lead to benefit and happiness,' enter on and abide in them." (Translated from the Pali by Soma Thera)

[37] https://simple.wikiquote.org/wiki/Voltaire (accessed 2/18/2019).

PART 2—WORLDVIEWS CONTRASTED

¹ The author is not proposing that the identities of the "Seven Pillars of Wisdom" in this book are identical to the intended meaning of this passage in the Bible. However, he feels that this categorization is an appropriate and effective use of this biblical symbol.

Pillar of Wisdom #1 - The Origin and Nature of the Universe

¹ https://en.wikiquote.org/wiki/Thomas_Browne (accessed 2/18/2019).

² Nyanaponika Thera, "Seeing Things as They Are," *An Introduction to the Buddha and His Teachings,* Samuel Bercholz, ed., and Sherab Chodzin Kohn, ed., (New York: Barnes and Noble Books, Inc., by arrangement with Shambhala Publications, Inc., 1997) p. 85.

³ "Dvaita," *Miriam-Webster's Encyclopedia of World Religions* (Springfield, Massachusetts: Merriam-Webster, Incorporated, 1999) p. 307.

⁴ Bansi Pandit, *The Hindu Mind* (Glen Ellyn, Illinois: B & V Enterprises, Inc., 3rd ed., 1998) p. 32.

⁵ F. Max Muller, ed., *The Sacred Books of the East* (Oxford, 1879-1910) 45: 245 (from Uttaradhyayana Sutra and Sutrakritanga Sutra); quoted in Robert E. Hume, *The World's Living Religions* (New York: Charles Scribner's Sons, rev. ed. 1936) p. 49.

⁶ "Jainism," *Miriam-Webster's Encyclopedia of World Religions* (Springfield, Massachusetts: Merriam-Webster, Incorporated, 1999) p. 551.

⁷ Abraham Cohen, *Everyman's Talmud* (New York: Schocken Books, 1949) p. 32.

⁸ Ibid.

⁹ Preet Mohan S. Ahluwalia, "Sikhism - Guru Nanak's Concept of Nature, Part One," Last modified April 17, 2001. www.sikhnet.com (accessed 4/19/2001).

¹⁰ "Taoism," *Miriam-Webster's Encyclopedia of World Religions,* p. 1066.

¹¹ The information in this paragraph was obtained by personal communication with Livia Kohn, a renowned authority on Taoism.

¹² Livia Kohn, ed., *The Taoist Experience, An Anthology* (Albany, New York: State University of New York Press, 1993) p. 169.

¹³ Peter Smith, "Creation," *A Concise Encyclopedia of the Bahá'í Faith* (Oxford, England: Oneworld Publications, 2000) p. 116.

¹⁴ Ibid., p. 116, See also "Metaphysics," p. 245.

¹⁵ Benjamin Creme, *Maitreya's Mission* (London: Share International Foundation, 1997) p. 353.

¹⁶ "Gnosticism: II Mythology," *Microsoft Encarta Encyclopedia 99.*

¹⁷ "Chaos," *Microsoft Encarta Encyclopedia 99.*

¹⁸ Srimad-Bhagavatam 1:3:28 (Bhaktivedanta Book Trust, n.d.).

¹⁹ A.C. Bhaktivedanta Swami Prabhupada, *The Science of Self Realization* (Los Angeles, California: The Bhaktivedanta Book Trust, 1998) p. 89.

²⁰ Rabbi David A. Cooper, *God is a Verb: Kabbalah and the practice of mystical Judaism* (New York, New York: Riverhead Books, The Berkeley Publishing Group, a division of Penguin Putman, Inc., 1998) p.95.

²¹ Michael Berg, *The Way: Using the Wisdom of Kabbalah for Spiritual Transformation and Fulfillment* (New York: John Wiley & Sons, Inc., 2001) p. 26.

²² Ibid., p. 39, 41.

²³ Paramahansa Yogananda, *Journey to Self-Realization* (Los Angeles, California: Self-Realization Fellowship) p. 241.

²⁴ Bhau Kalchuri, *Lord Meher,* vol. 3 (Asheville, North Carolina: Manifestation, Inc.) p. 855, Meherabad, October 7, 1926.

²⁵ Ibid., pp. 988-989, Meherabad, December, 1927.

²⁶ Meher Baba, *The Everything and the Nothing,* ed. Francis Brabazon (Myrtle Beach, South Carolina: Sheriar Press, Inc., 1995) pp. 95-96.

²⁷ Bhau Kalchuri, *Lord Meher,* vol. 3, p. 1148, Meherabad, March 28, 1929.

²⁸ Meher Baba, *The Path of Love,* ed. Filis Frederick (Myrtle Beach, South Carolina: Sheriar Press, Inc, n.d.) p. 32, also *The Awakener (Magazine)* 10:4, ed. Filis Frederick, p. 1.

²⁹ Meher Baba, *Discourses* (Myrtle Beach, South Carolina: Sheriar Press, Inc., 7th rev. ed.,1987) p. 24.

³⁰ T.K Ramanujam, *Much Love,* (1994) p. 529, Notes dictated by Meher Baba.

³¹ L. Ron Hubbard, *The Factors,* 1954, as re-printed in *What is Scientology?* (Los Angeles, California: Bridge Publications, Inc., 1993, 1998) p. 660.

³² Church of Scientology International, *Scientology Theology & Practice of a Contemporary Religion,* 2000, www.bonafidescientology.org/Append/02/page22.htm, (accessed 10/22/2002). The book on which this website is based was published in 1998.

[33] Inayat Khan, *The Soul, Whence and Whither* (London / The Hague: East-West Publications, 1984) p. 41; quoted in Dr. H. J. Witteveen, *Universal Sufism* (Rockport, Massachusetts: Element, 1997) p. 64.

[34] Helena P. Blavatsky, *The Key to Theosophy* (Pasadena, California: Theosophical University Press, 1995) p. 83-84 (unabridged printing of original 1889 ed., with new index).

[35] Ernest Holmes, *The Science of Mind* (New York: R.M McBride and Co., 1938, New York: Penguin Putnam, Inc., rev. and enl. ed., 1966) p. 582 (page citation is to reprint edition).

[36] Ernest Holmes, *A Dictionary of New Thought Terms* (Marina del Rey, California: DeVorss Publications, 1991) p. 30.

Pillar of Wisdom #2 - The Nature of God

[1] This is the strict interpretation of an 'Impersonal Cosmic Energy Force' as Ultimate Reality. Some seekers who say they believe in an Impersonal God as Ultimate Reality also, at times, grant some personal attributes to what they would term an 'Impersonal God.' Such a practice is not consistent with the terminology being used.

[2] Ernest Valea, "God or the Ultimate Reality, and Creation," *Many Paths to One Goal?* www. comparativereligion.com. (accessed 6/20/2000). On his excellent website, Ernest Valea offers these three categories as the fundamental interpretations of Ultimate Reality in world religions.

[3] J. Isamu Yamamoto, *Buddhism, Taoism & Other Far Eastern Religions* (Grand Rapids, Michigan: Zondervan Publishing House, 1998) p. 61.

[4] Reginald A. Ray, "Religion Without God," *Shambala Sun* (July 2001) p. 26.

[5] Bansi Pandit, *The Hindu Mind* (Glen Ellyn, Illinois: B & V Enterprises, Inc., 3rd ed., 1998) p. 54.

[6] "Concepts of Hinduism," *Eerdman's Handbook to the World's Religions* (Grand Rapids, Michigan: Wm. B. Eerdman's Publishing Company, 1982) p. 185.

[7] Philip Wilkinson, "Jain History and Beliefs," *Illustrated Dictionary of Religions* (New York, New York: DK Publishing, 1999) p. 46.

[8] Stevenson, *Heart of Jainism,* p. 270; quoted in Robert E. Hume, *The World's Living Religions* (New York: Charles Scribner's Sons, rev. ed. 1936) p. 51.

[9] From the Kirtan Sohila, an evening prayer.

[10] "God," *Microsoft Encarta Encyclopedia 99.*

[11] F. Max Muller, ed., *The Sacred Books of the East* (Oxford, 1879-1910) 40:68-69; quoted in Robert E. Hume, *The World's Living Religions* (New York: Charles Scribner's Sons, rev. ed. 1936) p. 141.

[12] Eva Wong, *The Shambhala Guide to Taoism* (Boston: Shambhala Publications, Inc. 1997) p. 160.

[13] See the explanation of the beliefs of Bahá'í under the question in Part 4, "Was Jesus just one of many Avatars or was he the only incarnation of God?"

[14] Peter Smith, "God," *A Concise Encyclopedia of the Bahá'í Faith* (Oxford, England: Oneworld Publications, 2000) pp. 164-165.

[15] Ibid., "Bahá'u'lláh: Theological Status," p. 79.

[16] *New Beginnings* (Pandav Bhawan, Mount Abu, Rajasthan, India: Brahma Kumaris Ishwariya Vishwa Vidyalaya, 1996) p. 45.

[17] Ibid., p. 50.

[18] Ibid., p. 50–51.

[19] Louis Berkhof, *The History of Christian Doctrine* (Grand Rapids: Baker Book House, 1981) p. 47; quoted in Ron Rhodes, *The Counterfeit Christ of the New Age Movement* (Grand Rapids, Michigan: Baker Book House, 1990) p. 17.

[20] A.C. Bhaktivedanta Swami Prabhupada, *Bhagavad-Gita As It Is* (New York: Collier Books, 1972) p.365.

[21] A.C. Bhaktivedanta Swami Prabhupada, *The Science of Self Realization* (Los Angeles, California: The Bhaktivedanta Book Trust, 1998) p. 8.

[22] "Sefirot," *Miriam-Webster's Encyclopedia of World Religions* (Springfield, Massachusetts: Merriam-Webster, Incorporated, 1999) p. 982.

[23] These names and numbering of the *Sefirot* were primarily obtained from the *Encyclopedia Judaica,* in the article titled "Kabbalah," (Jerusalem, Israel: Keter Publishing House, Ltd., 1971) Columns 570-571.

[24] Kenneth Boa, *Cults, World Religions and the Occult* (Wheaton, Illinois: Victor Books, 1990) p. 178.

[25] Paramahansa Yogananda, *How You Can Talk with God* (Los Angeles, California: Self-Realization Fellowship, 1997) p. 14.

[26] Ibid.

[27] Ibid., p. 21.

[28] Ibid., p. 22.

[29] Paramahansa Yogananda, *Journey to Self-Realization* (Los Angeles, California: Self-Realization Fellowship) p. 437, under "Trinity."

[30] Yogi Bhajan (Siri Singh Sahib Bhai Sahib Harbhajan Singh Kalsa Yogiji), *The Teachings of Yogi Bhajan, The Power of the Spoken Word* (Pamona, California: Arcline Publications, 1977) p. 77, #277.

³¹ Meher Baba, *The Everything and the Nothing* (Myrtle Beach, South Carolina: Sheriar Press, Inc., 1995) p. 98.

³² Meher Baba, *God Speaks* (Walnut Creek, California: Sufism Reoriented, 1973) pp. 158-159.

³³ Bhau Kalchuri, *Lord Meher,* vol. 3 (Asheville, North, Carolina: Manifestation, Inc.) pp. 988-989, Meherabad, December 1927.

³⁴ Church of Scientology International, *What is Scientology?* (Los Angeles, California: Bridge Publications, Inc., 1993, 1998) p. 530.

³⁵ Church of Scientology International, *Scientology Theology & Practice of a Contemporary Religion,* 2000, www.bonafidescientology.org/chapter/02/page20.htm (accessed 10/22/2002). The book on which this website is based was published in 1998.

³⁶ Inayat Khan, *The Soul, Whence and Whither* (London / The Hague: East-West Publications, 1984) p. 9;quoted in Dr. H. J. Witteveen, *Universal Sufism* (Rockport, Massachusetts: Element, 1997) p. 65.

³⁷ Annemarie Schimmel, *Mystical Dimensions of Islam* (Chapel Hill, North Carolina: The University of North Carolina Press, 1975) p. 266.

³⁸ Helena P. Blavatsky, *The Key to Theosophy* (Pasadena, California: Theosophical University Press, 1995) p. 61 (unabridged printing of original 1889 ed., with new index).

³⁹ L.W. Rogers, *Elementary Theosophy* (Wheaton, Illinois: The Theosophical Press, 1956) p. 23.

⁴⁰ Maharishi Mahesh Yogi, *Science of Being and Art of Living* (New York: Meridian, an imprint of Dutton Signet, a division of Penguin Books, 1995) p. 268.

⁴¹ Ibid., p. 267.

⁴² Maharishi Mahesh Yogi, *Transcendental Meditation,* p. 266; quoted in Josh McDowell and Don Stewart, *Handbook of Today's Religions* (Nashville, Tennessee: Thomas Nelson Publishers, 1983) p. 83.

⁴³ Ernest Holmes, *What Religious Science Teaches* (Los Angeles: Science of Mind Publications, 1975) p. 61.

⁴⁴ Ibid., p. 64.

⁴⁵ Ibid., p. 65.

⁴⁶ Ernest Holmes, *A Dictionary of New Thought Terms* (Marina del Rey, California: DeVorss Publications, 1991) p. 28.

⁴⁷ Ernest Holmes, *The Science of Mind* (New York: R.M McBride and Co., 1938, New York: Penguin Putnam, Inc., rev. and enl. ed., 1966) p. 362 (page citation is to reprint edition).

Pillar of Wisdom #3 - The Origin and Nature of Man

¹ "Cosmology, www.britannica.com/eb/article?query=buddhism&eu=108290&tocid=68705 (accessed 1/5/2002).

² This reference to 'God-consciousness' does not means, as it is often used, the awakened awareness of a person's higher Self as God. In a Christian, biblical context, it merely means an awakened awareness of the reality of God and the possibility of relationship with him, as opposed to the spiritual dullness of being a 'flesh-ruled' person.

³ James Legge, *Mencius,* 70, 150; quoted in Robert S. Hume, *Treasure-House of the Living Religions* (New York: Charles Scribner's Sons, 1932) p. 78.

⁴ James Legge, *The Chinese Classics with a Translation* 4.2.505 (Oxford University Press, 1871); cf. Sacred Books of the East 3.410-411; quoted in Robert S. Hume, *Treasure-House of the Living Religions* (New York: Charles Scribner's Sons, 1932) p. 78.

⁵ Swami Prabhavananda, *The Spiritual Heritage of India* (Hollywood, California: Vedanta Press, n.d.) p. 140.

⁶ "Sharira," *The Encyclopedia of Eastern Philosophy and Religion* (Boston, Massachusetts: Shambhala Publications, 1994) p. 316.

⁷ Herbert Stroup, *Four Religions of Asia* (New York: Harper and Row, 1968) p. 99; quoted in Josh McDowell and Don Stewart, *Handbook of Today's Religions* (Nashville, Tennessee: Thomas Nelson Publishers, 1983) p. 297.

⁸ "Man, The Nature of" *Encyclopedia Judaica* (Jerusalem, Israel: Keter Publishing House, Ltd., 1971) vol. 11, column 843.

⁹ "Soul," *Encyclopedia Judaica,* vol. 15, column 172.

¹⁰ Ibid.

¹¹ George Robinson, *Essential Judaism, A Complete Guide to the Beliefs, Customs and Rituals* (New York: Pocket Books, 2000) p. 88.

¹² "Man, the Nature of," *Encyclopedia Judaica,* vol. 11, column 847.

¹³ Rag Malar, *Hymns of Guru Nanak:* Macauliffe, *The Sikh Religion: Its Gurus, Sacred Writings, and Authors* 1.374, 375; quoted in Robert S. Hume, *Treasure-House of the Living Religions* (New York: Charles Scribner's Sons, 1932) p. 80.

¹⁴ Eva Wong, *The Shambhala Guide to Taoism* (Boston: Shambhala Publications, Inc. 1997) p. 173.

[15] Ibid.

[16] Livia Kohn, *Living with the Dao: Conceptual Issues in Daoist Practice* (Three Pines Press, downloaded book from www.threepinespress.com, Feb. 2002) p.17, Quoting from the Taoist sacred text *Chu sanshi jiuchong baosheng jing.*

[17] Ibid., p. 17.

[18] Ibid., p. 18.

[19] Ibid., p. 18.

[20] Eva Wong, *The Shambhala Guide to Taoism,* p. 47.

[21] Livia Kohn, *Living with the Dao: Conceptual Issues in Daoist Practice,* p. 72.

[22] Ibid., p. 18.

[23] Ibid., p. 19.

[24] "Gayomart," *Miriam-Webster's Encyclopedia of World Religions* (Springfield, Massachusetts: Merriam-Webster, Incorporated, 1999) p. 367.

[25] Joel Beversluis, ed., *Sourcebook of the World's Religions* (Novato, California: New World Library, 2000) p. 121.

[26] Peter Smith, "Soul," *A Concise Encyclopedia of the Bahá'í Faith* (Oxford, England: Oneworld Publications, 2000) p. 325.

[27] Ibid., "Human Nature," p. 186.

[28] Benjamin Creme, *Maitreya's Mission* (London: Share International Foundation, 1997) pp. 354-355.

[29] *New Beginnings* (Pandav Bhawan, Mount Abu, Rajasthan, India: Brahma Kumaris Ishwariya Vishwa Vidyalaya, 1996) p. 14.

[30] Ibid., p. 16.

[31] Ibid., p. 62.

[32] Ibid., p. 13.

[33] "Quotes," www.eckankar.org, (accessed 9/16/2000).

[34] Paul Twitchell, *The Flute of God* (Minneapolis: ECKANKAR, 1969) p. 7.

[35] Ibid., p. 19.

[36] Ibid., p. 17.

[37] Ibid., p. 20.

[38] A.C. Bhaktivedanta Swami Prabhupada, *The Science of Self Realization* (Los Angeles, California: The Bhaktivedanta Book Trust, 1998) p. 242.

[39] Ibid., p. 243.

[40] "Kabbalah," *Encyclopedia Judaica,* vol. 10, column 611.

[41] David A. Cooper, *God is a Verb, Kabbalah and the practice of mystical Judaism* (New York: Riverhead Books, 1998) pp. 98-99

[42] Kenneth Boa, *Cults, World Religions and the Occult* (Wheaton, Illinois: Victor Books, 1990) p. 179

[43] "Kabbalah," *Encyclopedia Judaica,* vol. 10, column 609.

[44] Ibid., column 610

[45] Ibid., column 611

[46] Ibid., column 607.

[47] Michael Berg, *The Way: Using the Wisdom of Kabbalah for Spiritual Transformation and Fulfillment* (New York: John Wiley & Sons, Inc., 2001) pp. 101-102.

[48] Paramahansa Yogananda, *Man's Eternal Quest* (Los Angeles, California: Self-Realization Fellowship, sec. ed., 1998) pp. 263-264.

[49] Paramahansa Yogananda, *How You Can Talk with God* (Los Angeles, California: Self-Realization Fellowship, 1997) p. 13.

[50] "About Self-Realization Fellowship," www.yogananda-srf.org, (accessed 1/4/2002). A quote found on the opening page.

[51] Shakti Parwha Kaur Khalsa, *Kundalini Yoga, The Flow of Eternal Power* (New York: The Berkley Publishing Group, 1996) pp. 183-186.

[52] Yogi Bhajan, *The Mind, Its Projections and Multiple Facets* (Espanola, New Mexico: Kundalini Research Institute, 1998) p. 135 (diagram), p. 207 (fold-out diagram).

[53] Bhau Kalchuri, *Lord Meher,* vol. 5 (Asheville, North Carolina: Manifestation, Inc.) pp. 1871-1873, Meherabad, May 23, 1934.

[54] Church of Scientology International, *What is Scientology?* (Los Angeles, California: Bridge Publications, Inc., 1993, 1998) p.70.

[55] Ibid., p. 546.

[56] Ibid., p. 64.

[57] Kabir Helminski, *The Knowing Heart: A Sufi Path of Transformation* (Boston, Massachusetts: Shambhala Publications, 1999) p. 262.

⁵⁸ Carl W. Ernst, Ph. D., *The Shambhala Guide to Sufism* (Boston, Massachusetts: Shambhala Publications,1997) p. 107.

⁵⁹ http://naqshbandi.org/teachings/suhbat-association/sohbats-of-mawlana-shaykh-hisham-kabbani/the-heart-of-the-believer-is-the-house-of-god/ (accessed 9/20/2018).

⁶⁰ https://en.wikipedia.org/wiki/Shath (accessed 2/18/2019).

⁶¹ Carl W. Ernst, Ph. D., *The Shambhala Guide to Sufism*, p. 117.

⁶² Dr. H. J. Witteveen, *Universal Sufism* (Rockport, Massachusetts: Element, 1997) p. 73.

⁶³ Helena P. Blavatsky, *The Key to Theosophy* (Pasadena, California: Theosophical University Press, 1995) pp. 91-92 (unabridged printing of original 1889 ed., with new index).

⁶⁴ Ibid., pp. 91-92,175-176.

⁶⁵ Helena P.Blavatsky, *Studies in Occultism* (Theosophical University Press, n.d.) p. 134; quoted in Josh McDowell and Don Stewart, *Handbook of Today's Religions* (Nashville, Tennessee: Thomas Nelson Publishers, 1983) p. 87.

⁶⁶ L.W. Rogers, *Elementary Theosophy* (Wheaton, Illinois: The Theosophical Press, 1956) p. 22-25

⁶⁷ Maharishi Mahesh Yogi, *Science of Being and Art of Living* (New York: Meridian, an imprint of Dutton Signet, a division of Penguin Books, 1995) p. 271.

⁶⁸ Ernest Holmes, *The Science of Mind* (New York: R.M McBride and Co., 1938, New York: Penguin Putnam, Inc., rev. and enl. ed., 1966) p. 388 (page citation is to reprint edition).

⁶⁹ Ernest Holmes, *A Dictionary of New Thought Terms* (Marina del Rey, California: DeVorss Publications, 1991) p. 86.

Pillar of Wisdom #4 - The Nature of Salvation, Liberation, or Enlightenment

¹ Kenneth Boa, *Cults, World Religions and the Occult* (Wheaton, Illinois: Victor Books, 1990) p. 33.

² J. Isamu Yamamoto, *Buddhism, Taoism & Other Far Eastern Religions* (Grand Rapids, Michigan: Zondervan Publishing House, 1998) p. 50.

³ Thich Nhat Hanh, *Living Buddha, Living Christ* (New York, New York: Riverhead Books, 1995) p. 204.

⁴ Samuel Bercholz and Sherab Chodzin Kohn, eds., *An Introduction to the Buddha and His Teachings* (New York: Barnes and Noble Books, Inc., by arrangement with Shambhala Publications, Inc., 1997) p. 320.

⁵ Thich Nhat Hanh, *Living Buddha, Living Christ*, pp. 187, 202.

⁶ Chogyam Trungpa, "The Bodhisattva Path," *An Introduction to the Buddha and His Teachings*, Samuel Bercholz and Sherab Chodzin Kohn, eds., p. 169.

⁷ Philip Wilkinson, "Jain History and Beliefs," *Illustrated Dictionary of Religions* (New York, New York: DK Publishing, 1999) p. 46.

⁸ Abraham Ezra Millgram, ed., *Great Jewish Ideas* (Clinton, Massachusetts: Colonial Press, Inc., B'nai B'rith Department of Adult Jewish Education 1964) p. 179.

⁹ Moses Luzatto, *Mesillat Yesharim*, chapter 5.

¹⁰ "Olam Ha-Ba," *Encyclopedia Judaica* (Jerusalem, Israel: Keter Publishing House, Ltd., 1971) vol. 12, column 1357.

¹¹ Andrew Wilson, ed., *World Scripture, A Comparative Anthology of Sacred Texts* (St. Paul, Minnesota: Paragon House, 1995) p. 37.

¹² "Noachide Laws," *Encyclopedia Judaica*, vol. 2, column 1189.

¹³ Eva Wong, *The Shambhala Guide to Taoism* (Boston: Shambhala Publications, Inc. 1997) p. 49.

¹⁴ Livia Kohn, *Living with the Dao: Conceptual Issues in Daoist Practice* (Three Pines Press, downloaded book from www.threepinespress.com, accessed Feb. 2002) p.19.

¹⁵ Ibid.

¹⁶ Eva Wong, *The Shambhala Guide to Taoism*, p. 186.

¹⁷ Peter Smith, "Salvation," *A Concise Encyclopedia of the Bahá'í Faith* (Oxford, England: Oneworld Publications, 2000) p. 303.

¹⁸ "Bahá'í Faith," *Miriam-Webster's Encyclopedia of World Religions* (Springfield, Massachusetts: Merriam-Webster, Incorporated, 1999) p. 107.

¹⁹ *New Beginnings* (Pandav Bhawan, Mount Abu, Rajasthan, India: Brahma Kumaris Ishwariya Vishwa Vidyalaya, 1996) p. 25.

²⁰ Ibid., p. 12.

²¹ Ibid., p. 63.

²² Ibid.

²³ Ibid., p. 64.

²⁴ Stephen A. Hoeller, *Gnosticism: New Light on the Ancient Tradition of Inner Knowing* (Wheaten, Illinois: Quest Books, Theosophical Publishing House, 2002) p. 122.

²⁵ Helen Schucman and William Thetford, *A Course in Miracles* (Tiburon, California: Foundation for Inner Peace, 1976) "Text," p. 53.

[26] Ibid., "Text," p. 186.

[27] Ibid., "Workbook for Students," p. 118.

[28] Ibid., "Workbook for Students," p. 119.

[29] Ibid., "Text," p. 264.

[30] Ibid., "Manual For Teachers," p. 79.

[31] A.C. Bhaktivedanta Swami Prabhupada, *The Journey of Self-Discovery* (Botany, Australia: The Bhaktivedanta Book Trust, 1997) pp. 105-106.

[32] A.C. Bhaktivedanta Swasmi Prabhupada, *The Science of Self Realization* (Los Angeles, California: The Bhaktivedanta Book Trust, 1998) p. 7.

[33] Ibid., p. 313.

[34] Paramahansa Yogananda, *God Talks with Arjuna, The Bhagavad Gita* (Los Angeles, California: Self-Realization Fellowship, sec. ed., 1999) pp. 213-214.

[35] Yogi Bhajan (Siri Singh Sahib Bhai Sahib Harbhajan Singh Kalsa Yogiji), *The Teaching of Yogi Bhajan, The Power of the Spoken Word* (Pamona, California: Arcline Publications, 1977) p.177 #709.

[36] Ibid., p.129 #510.

[37] Information brochure from Meher Spiritual Center, Myrtle Beach, South Carolina, *A Place of Pilgrimage For All Time*, p. 5.

[38] C. D. Deshmukh, *Sparks of the Truth: From Dissertations of Meher Baba* (Myrtle Beach, South Carolina: Sheriar Press, Inc., 1971, Reprinted from "The Awakener" Magazine) p. 91.

[39] Church of Scientology International, *What is Scientology?* (Los Angeles, California: Bridge Publications, Inc., 1993, 1998) p. 66.

[40] According to Kabir Helminski's teaching, three levels of understanding effect this process: realizing that there are no actions but God's actions, no qualities but God's qualities, and no existence but God's existence.

[41] Kabir Helminski, *The Knowing Heart: A Sufi Path of Transformation* (Boston, Massachusetts:Shambhala Publications, 1999) p. 49.

[42] Barrie and Jenkins, *The Sufi Message of Inayat Khan*, vol. XI (London: Servire Publishers, Katwijk,Holland, 1960-1982) p. 163; quoted in Dr. H. J. Witteveen, *Universal Sufism*, p. 101.

[43] James Fadiman and Robert Frager, eds., *Essential Sufism* (Edison, New Jersey: Castle Books, 1998) p. 15.

[44] Ibid., p. 12.

[45] Ibid., pp. 9-10.

[46] Helena P. Blavatsky, *The Key to Theosophy,* (Pasadena, California: Theosophical University Press, 1995) p. 152 (unabridged printing of original 1889 ed., with new index).

[47] Annie Besant, *Karma* (London: Theosophical Publishing Society, 1904) p.23; quoted in Ron Rhodes, *New Age Movement* (Grand Rapids, Michigan: Zondervan Publishing House, 1995) p. 65.

[48] Helena P. Blavatsky, *The Key to Theosophy,* p. 223.

[49] Ibid., p. 155.

[50] Ibid., p. 223.

[51] Ibid., p. 237.

[52] Maharishi Mahesh Yogi, *Science of Being and Art of Living* (New York: Meridian, an imprint of Dutton Signet, a division of Penguin Books, 1995) p. 322.

[53] Maharishi Mahesh Yogi, *Maharishi Mahesh Yogi on the Bhagavad-Gita,* New York, New York: ARKANA: Penguin Putnam, Inc., 1990) p 15.

[54] Ibid.

[55] Ernest Holmes, *The Science of Mind* (New York: R.M McBride and Co., 1938, New York: Penguin Putnam, Inc., rev. and enl. ed., 1966) p. 633 (page citation is to reprint edition).

[56] Ernest Holmes, *What Religious Science Teaches* (Los Angeles, California: Science of Mind Publications, 1975) p. 25.

[57] Ibid., p. 65.

Pillar of Wisdom #5 - Dimensions or Planes of Existence

[1] John Bowker, "Buddhism," *World Religions* (New York, New York: DK Publishing, Inc., 1997) p. 64, under "Cosmology."

[2] Vasudha Narayanan, "Hinduism," *The Illustrated Guide to World Religions*, Michael D. Coogan, gen. ed. (New York: Oxford University Press, 1998) p. 157, under "Hindu Heavens and Hells."

[3] Most of the names for these various realms were obtained from the lexicon offered on www. himalayanacademy.com though the information is not rendered verbatim. The exact address for the lexicon is www.himalayanacademy.com/books/dws/lexicon/t.html. The names for these various realms are found under "Three Worlds" (accessed 5/12/2001).

[4] "Hell," *Miriam-Webster's Encyclopedia of World Religions* (Springfield, Massachusetts: Merriam-Webster, Incorporated, 1999) p. 421.

⁵ Abraham Cohen, *Everyman's Talmud* (New York: Schocken Books, 1949) p. 30.

⁶ George Foot Moore, *Judaism in the First Centuries of the Christian Era, The Age of Tannaim,* vol 1 (Cambridge: Harvard University Press, 1962) p. 368.

⁷ Abraham Cohen, *Everyman's Talmud,* p. 31.

⁸ The Greek equivalent is *Hades:* a word translated "hell" and "grave" in the New Testament (Christianity).

⁹ "Netherworld," *Encyclopedia Judaica* (Jerusalem, Israel: Keter Publishing House, Ltd., 1971) vol. 12, column 996.

¹⁰ "Netherworld," *Encyclopedia Judaica,* vol. 12, column 997.

¹¹ "Eschatology: Gehennna," *The Jewish Encyclopedia* (New York: KATV Publishing House, Inc., n.d.) vol. 5, p. 217.

¹² "Eschatology," *Encyclopedia Judaica,* vol. 6, column 876.

¹³ Peter Smith, "Metaphysics: God and the World," *A Concise Encyclopedia of the Bahá'í Faith* (Oxford, England: Oneworld Publications, 2000) pp. 245-246.

¹⁴ Ibid., "Heaven and Hell," p. 180.

¹⁵ *New Beginnings* (Pandav Bhawan, Mount Abu, Rajasthan, India: Brahma Kumaris Ishwariya Vishwa Vidyalaya, 1996) p. 34.

¹⁶ A.C. Bhaktivedanta Swami Prabhupada, *The Journey of Self-Discovery* (Botany, Australia: The Bhaktivedanta Book Trust, 1997) p. 6.

¹⁷ Rabbi David A. Cooper, *God is a Verb: Kabbalah and the practice of mystical Judaism* (New York, New York: Riverhead Books, The Berkeley Publishing Group, a division of Penguin Putman, Inc., 1998) pp. 95-99.

¹⁸ Swami Sri Yukteswar, "Sutra 13," *The Holy Science* (Los Angeles, California: Self-Realization Fellowship, 8ᵗʰ ed., 1990) pp. 33-34.

¹⁹ Bhau Kalchuri, *Lord Meher,* vol. 4, (Asheville, North, Carolina: Manifestation, Inc.) p. 1264, Nasik, January 12, 1930.

²⁰ Meher Baba, *Discourses* (Myrtle Beach, South Carolina: Sheriar Press, Inc., 7ᵗʰ rev. ed., 1987) p. 307.

²¹ Annemarie Schimmel, *Mystical Dimensions of Islam* (Chapel Hill, North Carolina: The University of North Carolina Press, 1975) p. 270.

²² Helena P. Blavatsky, *The Key to Theosophy* (Pasadena, California: Theosophical University Press, 1995) p. 138 (unabridged printing of original 1889 ed., with new index).

²³ Ernest Holmes, "Heaven," *A Dictionary of New Thought Terms* (Marina del Rey, California: DeVorss Publications, 1991) p. 58.

²⁴ Ibid., "Hell," p. 58.

²⁵ Ibid., "Hades," p. 56.

Pillar of Wisdom #6 - The Spiritual Journey and Ultimate Destiny of Man

¹ John Bowker, "Buddhism," *World Religions* (New York, New York: DK Publishing, Inc., 1997) p. 64, under "Cosmology."

² Special Collections Department, University of Virginia, "Transitions to the Other World," *The Tibetan Book of the Dead,* March 14, 1998, www.lib.virginia.edu/exhibits/dead/index.html (accessed 10/31/2000). Most of the information on the Tibetan Book of the Dead was obtained from this source.

³ David G. Bradley, *A Guide to the World's Religions* (Englewood Cliffs, New Jersey: Prentice-Hall, Inc., 1963) p. 147.

⁴ Bansi Pandit, *The Hindu Mind* (Glen Ellyn, Illinois: B & V Enterprises, Inc., 3rd ed., 1998) p. 30.

⁵ Ibid., p. 119.

⁶ "Islam," *Miriam-Webster's Encyclopedia of World Religions* (Springfield, Massachusetts: Merriam-Webster, Incorporated, 1999) p. 519.

⁷ Robert E Hume, *The World's Living Religions* (New York: Charles Scribner's Sons, rev. ed., 1936) p. 55.

⁸ "Jainism Simplified," *Gati,* www.umich.edu/~umjains (accessed 10/21/2000).

⁹ "Man, The Nature of," *Encyclopedia Judaica* (Jerusalem, Israel: Keter Publishing House, Ltd., 1971) vol. 11, column 845.

¹⁰ "Heaven," *Miriam-Webster's Encyclopedia of World Religions,* p. 418.

¹¹ "Soul, Immortality of," *Encyclopedia Judaica,* vol. 15, column 175.

¹² "Netherworld," *Encyclopedia Judaica,* vol. 12, column 998, italic emphasis by author.

¹³ Ibid.

¹⁴ "Paradise," *Encyclopedia Judaica,* vol. 13, column 83.

¹⁵ "Soul, Immortality of," *Encyclopedia Judaica,* vol. 15, column 175.

¹⁶ "Afterlife," *Encyclopedia Judaica,* vol. 2, column 338.

¹⁷ "Olam Ha-ba," *Encyclopedia Judaica,* vol. 12, column 1356.

[18] Michael D. Coogan, gen. ed., *The Illustrated Guide to World Religions, Japanese Traditions*, by C. Scott Littleton (New York: Oxford University Press, 1998) p. 267.

[19] Livia Kohn, *Daoism and Chinese Culture* (Cambridge, Massachusetts: Three Pines Press, 2001) p. 184.

[20] Eva Wong, *The Shambhala Guide to Taoism* (Boston: Shambhala Publications, Inc. 1997) p. 182.

[21] Ibid., p. 183.

[22] Ibid., p. 59.

[23] John Bowker, "Zoroastrianism," *World Religions*, p. 13.

[24] Peter Smith, "Death and the Afterlife," *A Concise Encyclopedia of the Bahá'í Faith* (Oxford, England: Oneworld Publications, 2000) p. 326.

[25] Ibid., "Soul: the Afterlife," p. 119.

[26] Ibid., "Angels," pp. 38-39.

[27] *New Beginnings* (Pandav Bhawan, Mount Abu, Rajasthan, India: Brahma Kumaris Ishwariya Vishwa Vidyalaya, 1996) p. 33.

[28] Ibid., p. 71.

[29] A.C. Bhaktivedanta Swami Prabhupada, *Coming Back: the Science of Reincarnation* (Los Angeles, California: The Bhaktivedanta Book Trust, 1982) pp. 122-123; quoted in Norman L. Geisler & J. Yutaka Amano, *The Reincarnation Sensation* (Wheaton, Illinois: Tyndale House Publishers, Inc., 1986) p. 35.

[30] Ibid., pp. 16, 33; quoted in Norman L. Geisler & J. Yutaka Amano, *The Reincarnation Sensation*, p. 34.

[31] Ibid., pp.122-123; quoted in Norman L. Geisler & J. Yutaka Amano, *The Reincarnation Sensation*, p. 35.

[32] "Kabbalah," *Encyclopedia Judaica*, vol. 10, column 613.

[33] "Afterlife," *Encyclopedia Judaica*, vol. 2, column 339.

[34] "Eschatology," *Encyclopedia Judaica*, vol. 6, column 882.

[35] "Kabbalah," *Encyclopedia Judaica*, vol. 10, column 610.

[36] David A. Cooper, *God is a Verb, Kabbalah and the practice of mystical Judaism* (New York: Riverhead Books, 1998) p. 107.

[37] "Kabbalah," *Encyclopedia Judaica*, vol. 10, column 610.

[38] Ibid., vol. 10, column 613.

[39] Ibid., vol.10, column 612.

[40] David A. Cooper, *God is a Verb, Kabbalah and the practice of mystical Judaism*, p. 96.

[41] Ibid., p. 262, In pages 263-264 of *God is a Verb*, the author outlines the ways that a *nefesh* can be redeemed: (1) By serving *Tzaddikim* (saints) in reclaiming the world for righteousness, invisible, yet active in this world in ways similar to angels; (2) By the intercessory prayers of loved ones; (3) By the merits of ancestors; (4) By the compassion of God. Inc., 2001) p. 142

[42] Perle Epstein, *Kabbalah, The Way of the Jewish Mystic* (Boston, Masschusetts: Shambhala Publications, Inc., 2001) p. 142.

[43] "Eschatology," *Jewish Encyclopedia* (New York: KATV Publishing House, Inc., n.d.) vol. 6, p. 881.

[44] Shakti Parwha Kaur Khalsa, *Kundalini Yoga, The Flow of Eternal Power* (New York: The Berkley Publishing Group, 1996) p. 55.

[45] "Meher Baba," *Miriam-Webster's Encyclopedia of World Religions*, p. 706.

[46] Meher Baba, *Discourses* (Myrtle Beach, South Carolina1: Sheriar Press, Inc., 7ᵗʰ rev. ed., 1987) p. 320.

[47] Bhau Kalchuri, *The Nothing and the Everything*, p. 291-292, From dictated notes, Meherabad, 1968.

[48] Meher Baba, *Discourses* (Myrtle Beach, South Carolina: Sheriar Press, Inc., 7ᵗʰ rev. ed., 1987) p. 63.

[49] James Fadiman and Robert Frager, eds., *Essential Sufism* (Edison, New Jersey: Castle Books, 1998) pp. 20-23.

[50] Ibid., p. 17.

[51] Carl W. Ernst, Ph. D., *The Shambhala Guide to Sufism* (Boston, Massachusetts: Shambhala Publications,1997) pp. 43-44.

[52] Ibid., p. 43.

[53] Irving S. Cooper, *Reincarnation: A Hope of the World* (Wheaton, Illinois: Theosophical Publishing House, 1979) p. 25; quoted in Norman L. Geisler & J. Yutaka Amano, *The Reincarnation Sensation*. p. 40.

[54] Irving S. Cooper, *Theosophy Simplified*, Wheaton, Illinois: The Theosophical Publishing House, sec. Quest ed., pp. 70-71.

[55] Helena P. Blavatsky, *The Key to Theosophy* (Pasadena, California: Theosophical University Press, 1995) pp. 91-92 (unabridged printing of original 1889 ed., with new index).

[56] Ibid., p. 143.

[57] Ibid., p. 148.

[58] Ibid.

⁵⁹ Ernest Holmes, *The Science of Mind* (New York: R.M McBride and Co., 1938, New York: Penguin Putnam, Inc., rev. and enl. ed., 1966) p. 384 (page citation is to reprint edition).

⁶⁰ Ibid., p. 383.

⁶¹ Ibid.

⁶² Ibid., pp. 386-387.

⁶³ Ibid., p. 387.

⁶⁴ Ibid., pp. 374-375.

Pillar of Wisdom #7 - Cycles, Ages, and the Ultimate State of the Universe

¹ J. Isamu Yamamoto, *Buddhism, Taoism & Other Far Eastern Religions* (Grand Rapids, Michigan: Zondervan Publishing House, 1998) p. 43.

² Explanation supplied by Reverend Himaka of the Enmanji Buddhist Temple in Sebastopol, CA.

³ "Kalpa," *The Encyclopedia of Eastern Philosophy and Religion* (Boston, Massachusetts: Shambhala Publications, 1994) p. 171.

⁴ Ibid.

⁵ Satguru Sivaya Subramuniyaswami, a leading voice in Hinduism, offers a slightly different interpretation and timing for these cosmic cycles. To see his view, go to www.himalayanacademy.com and go to the Online Lexicon. Look up the key words: *cosmic cycles, yuga* and *kalpa*.

⁶ Heinrich Zimmer (Edited by Joseph Campbell) *Myths and Symbols in Indian Art and Civilization* (Princeton, New Jersey: Princeton University Press, 1946) p. 15.

⁷ "Yuga," *Miriam-Webster's Encyclopedia of World Religions* (Springfield, Massachusetts: Merriam-Webster, Incorporated, 1999) p. 1159.

⁸ "Eschatology: The Days of the Messiah," *The Jewish Encyclopedia* (New York: KATV Publishing House, Inc., n.d.) vol. 5, p. 209.

⁹ "Eschatology," *Encyclopedia Judaica* (Jerusalem, Israel: Keter Publishing House, Ltd., 1971) vol. 6, columns 879-880.

¹⁰ "Eschatology: The Days of the Messiah," *The Jewish Encyclopedia*, vol. 5, p. 213.

¹¹ "Eschatology," *Encyclopedia Judaica*, vol. 6, column 882.

¹² Ibid., vol. 6, column 880.

¹³ George Robinson, *Essential Judaism, A Complete Guide to the Beliefs, Customs and Rituals* (New York: Pocket Books, 2000) p. 88.

¹⁴ "Beatitude," *Encyclopedia Judaica* (Jerusalem, Israel: Keter Publishing House, Ltd., 1971) vol. 4, column 359.

¹⁵ Peter Smith, "Manifestations of God," *A Concise Encyclopedia of the Bahá'í Faith* (Oxford, England: Oneworld Publications, 2000) p. 231. Though a full list of "Manifestations of God" is not available, the fourteen persons accepted by Bahá'ís are listed in Part 4 of this book under the heading, "*Was Jesus just one of many Avatars or was he the only incarnation of God?*"

¹⁶ Ibid., p. 338.

¹⁷ "Unity and Peace: The Bahái Faith," *Eerdman's Handbook to the World's Religions* (Grand Rapids, Michigan: Wm. B. Eerdman's Publishing Company, 1982) p. 270.

¹⁸ Benjamin Creme, *Maitreya's Mission* (London: Share International Foundation, 1997) p. 356.

¹⁹ Ibid., p. 357.

²⁰ *New Beginnings* (Pandav Bhawan, Mount Abu, Rajasthan, India: Brahma Kumaris Ishwariya Vishwa Vidyalaya, 1996) p. 118.

²¹ A.C. Bhaktivedanta Swami Prabhupada, *The Journey of Self-Discovery* (Botany, Australia: The Bhaktivedanta Book Trust, 1997) pp. 186-187.

²² "Kabbalah," *Encyclopedia Judaica*, vol. 10, column 582. Bracketed words inserted by author.

²³ Ibid.

²⁴ Gershom Scholem, *Origins of the Kabbalah* (Princeton, New Jersey: Princeton University Press, in association with the Jewish Publication Society, first paperback printing, 1990) p. 467.

²⁵ Paramahansa Yogananda, *Autobiography of a Yogi* (Los Angeles, California: Self-Realization Fellowship, 13th ed., 1998) pp. 193-194.

²⁶ Swami Sri Yukteswar, *The Holy Science* (Los Angeles, California: Self-Realization Fellowship, 8th ed., 1990) p. 7-15, 19-20.

²⁷ Paramahansa Yogananda, *Journey to Self-Realization* (Los Angeles, California: Self-Realization Fellowship) p. 438, under "Yuga."

²⁸ Meher Baba, *God Speaks* (Walnut Creek, California: Sufism Reoriented, 1973) p. 254.

²⁹ Bhau Kalchuri, *Lord Meher*, vol. 4 (Asheville, North Carolina: Manifestation, Inc.) p. 1264, Nasik, January 12, 1930; *Lord Meher*, vol. 5, p. 1871-1873, Meherabad, May 23, 1934.

³⁰ Carl W. Ernst, Ph. D., *The Shambhala Guide to Sufism* (Boston, Massachusetts: Shambhala

Publications,1997) p. 44.

[31] Ernest Holmes, *The Science of Mind* (New York: R.M McBride and Co., 1938, New York: Jeremy P. Tarcher/Putman, a member of Penguin Putnam, Inc., rev. and enl. ed., 1966) pp. 492-493 (page citation is to reprint edition).

Acknowledging the Contradictions

[1] S. Radhakrishnan, *East and West, The End of Their Separation* (New York: Alen & Uniwin, Humanities Press, 1954) p. 164.

[2] https://www.brainyquote.com/quotes/nicolaus_copernicus_127510 (accessed 9/20/2018).

[3] https://en.wikiquote.org/wiki/Ren%C3%A9_Descartes (accessed 2/18/2019).

[4] Shuxian, Liu, *Understanding Confucian Philosophy* (Greenwood Press, 1998) p. 58.

PART 3—MY SPIRITUAL JOURNEY

[1] https://en.wikipedia.org/wiki/The_unexamined_life_is_not_worth_living (accessed 9/20/2018).

[2] *The Illustrated World's Religions*, Huston Smith

[3] www.goodreads.com/quotes/38640-earth-s-crammed-with-heaven-and-every-common-bush-afire-with (accessed 9/20/2018).

[4] Citation not available.

[5] *The World's Great Religions* (New York: Time Incorporated, 1957) p. 38.

[6] Thich Nhat Hanh, *Living Buddha, Living Christ* (New York, New York: Riverhead Books, 1995) p. xvi.

[7] https://www.azquotes.com/quote/672969 (accessed 9/20/2018).

PART 4—STRIKING THE TOUCHSTONE

[1] Frank S. Mead, *12,000 Religious Quotations* (Grand Rapids, Michigan: Baker Book House, 1989) p. 116.

[2] Ibid., p. 131.

30 Relevant Questions and Answers

[1] Admittedly, there are some unique cultural groups in which a belief exists in a personal, perfect, omnipresent Supreme Deity who transcends the physical creation. When this Supreme Being (Lord of heaven) is not represented by false idols or images and when his character is not marred by false doctrine, fabricated legends, or wrongly applied personality traits, there are rare situations in which the names applied to him *may* be regarded as legitimate. Sometimes, these names are not only suitable ways of describing the Creator. They are even adaptable in explaining the full revelation of God to those particular people groups. However, such names are not sufficient to bring the users into real salvation experience and/or personal fellowship with God. (See *Eternity in their Hearts* by Don Richardson.)

[2] The word *Tao* means "the Way." Actually, this is a correct title of the true God, who in his incarnate state declared, "I am THE WAY, the truth and the life." *(John 14:6)* However, "the Way" in Taoism differs significantly from "the Way" as outlined in Christianity.

[3] Kenneth L. Woodard, "The Other Jesus," *Newsweek Magazine* (March 27, 2000) p. 56, Excerpt from *The Good Heart* by the Dalai Lama.

[4] Dr. H. J. Witteveen, *Universal Sufism* (Rockport, Massachusetts: Element, 1997) p. 95.

[5] Yogi Bhajan (Siri Singh Sahib Bhai Sahib Harbhajan Singh Kalsa Yogiji), *The Teachings of Yogi Bhajan, The Power of the Spoken Word* (Pamona, California: Arcline Publications, 1977) p. 71, #250 (bracketed statement by author).

[6] Ibid., p. 129, #508.

[7] Ibid., p 180, #724.

[8] A.C. Bhaktivedanta Swami Prabhupada, *The Science of Self Realization* (Los Angeles, California: The Bhaktivedanta Book Trust, 1998) p. 20.

[9] *The World's Great Religions* (New York: Time Incorporated, 1957) p. 16.

[10] Dr. Anis A. Shorrosh, *Islam Revealed* (Nashville, Tennessee: Thomas Nelson Publishers, 1988) p. 101.

[11] Ron Rhodes, *The Counterfeit Christ of the New Age Movement* (Grand Rapids, Michigan: Baker Book House, 1990) p. 52.

[12] Peter Smith, "Manifestations of God," *A Concise Encyclopedia of the Bahá'í Faith* (Oxford, England: Oneworld Publications, 2000) p. 231.

[13] Ernest Valea, "The Divine Incarnation in Hinduism and Christianity," *Many Paths to One Goal?* www.comparativereligion.com (accessed 6/2000). Those examining this concept of Avatars should definitely read this informative article on this excellent website. Ernest Valea explores this subject much more extensively.

[14] Rabi R. Maharaj, *The Death of a Guru* (Eugene, Oregon: Harvest House Publishers, 1977) pp. 199-200.

[15] Macauliffe, M. A., "Life of Guru Nanak," *The Sikh Religion: Its Gurus, Sacred Writings, and Authors* (Oxford, 1909) p. 280; quoted in Robert E Hume, *The World's Living Religions* (New York: Charles Scribner's Sons, rev. ed., 1936) p. 95.

[16] An explanation offered by Yuktanand Singh, a contributing writer on www.sikhnet.com and other websites.

[17] Eva Wong, *The Shambhala Guide to Taoism* (Boston: Shambhala Publications, Inc. 1997) p. 162.

[18] Meher Baba, *The Everything and the Nothing*, ed. Francis Brabazon (Myrtle Beach, South Carolina : Sheriar Press, Inc., 1995) p. 4.

[19] Ivy Duce, *How a Master Works*, Kahmir, April 20, 1933 (Walnut Creek, California: Sufism Reoriented) p. 451-454.

[20] Avatar Meher Baba's Final Declaration, Clarification, etc. (booklet) p. 3-6, September 30, 1954, Meherabad; Kitty Davy, *Love Alone Prevails* (Myrtle Beach, South Carolina: Sheriar Press, Inc., 1981) p. 700-701; Bal Natu, *Glimpses of the God-Man Meher Baba*, vol. 6 (Myrtle Beach, South Carolina: Sheriar Press, Inc., 1994) p. 166-169.

[21] Adi K. Irani, ed., *Messages of Meher Baba, East and West* (India: Meher Baba Trust) p. 95, May 31, 1932, Hollywood, part of a message read out at a reception at the Knickerbocker Hotel.

[22] Bhau Kalchuri, *Lord Meher*, vol. 5 (Asheville, North Carolina: Manifestation, Inc.) p. 1670, A message to his followers in 1932.

[23] Meher Baba, *The Everything and the Nothing*, ed. Francis Brabazon, p. 75.

[24] Charles Haynes, *Meher Baba, The Awakener* (N. Myrtle Beach, South Carolina: The Avatar Foundation, Inc., 1993) p. 67.

[25] Mohan Prasad, "Bhagavan Shri Sathya Sai Baba," www.geocities.com/Athens/Forum/5464 (accessed 5/2/2001).

[26] Kenneth L. Woodard, "The Other Jesus," *Newsweek Magazine* (March 27, 2000) p. 51.

[27] It should be mentioned that in philosophical Hinduism, it is contradictory to the nature of truth to seek a relationship with God, or to worship God, because WE ARE GOD! If enlightened wisdom would lead us not to worship a Divine 'Life Force' that is invisible, why should devotees offer worship to supposed Avatars (or incarnations of God) who are visible?

[28] Ernest Holmes, *What Religious Science Teaches* (Los Angeles, California: Science of Mind Publications, 1975) p. 12.

[29] Ibid., p. 55.

[30] Ernest Holmes, *The Science of Mind* (New York: *Mind* (New York: R.M McBride and Co., 1938, New York: Jeremy P. Tarcher/Putman, a member of Penguin Putnam Penguin Putnam, Inc., rev. and enl. ed., 1966) p. 359 (page citation is to reprint edition).

[31] George Trevelyan, *Operation Redemption: A Vision of Hope in an Age of Turmoil* (Walpole, New Hampshire: Stillpoint, 1985) p. 37.

[32] Kenneth L. Woodard, "The Other Jesus," *Newsweek Magazine* (March 27, 2000) p. 60.

[33] Ron Rhodes, *The Counterfeit Christ of the New Age Movement*, p. 168.

[34] Yogi Bhajan, *The Teachings of Yogi Bhajan, The Power of the Spoken Word*, p. 76, #274.

[35] Jack and Betty Cheetham, *An Age of Meditation* (Plainfield, New Jersey: Logos International, 1976) p.15.

[36] Maharishi Mahesh Yogi, *Science of Being and Art of Living* (New York: Meridian, an imprint of Dutton Signet, a division of Penguin Books, 1995) p. 271.

[37] Yogi Bhajan, *The Teachings of Yogi Bhajan, The Power of the Spoken Word*, p. 79, #288.

[38] Ibid., p. 131, #522.

[39] Norman L. Geisler and Ronald M. Brooks, *Christianity Under Attack* (Dallas: Quest Publications, 1985) p. 18; quoted in Ron Rhodes, *New Age Movement* (Grand Rapids, Michigan: Zondervan Publishing House, 1995) p. 60.

[40] Ibid., p. 43; quoted in Ron Rhodes, *New Age Movement*, p. 60.

[41] Dean C. Halverson, ed., *The Compact Guide to World Religions* (Minneapolis: Bethany House, 1996) p. 91; quoted in J. Isamu Yamamoto, *Hinduism, TM & Hare Krishna* (Grand Rapids, Michigan: Zondervan, 1998) p. 45.

[42] Information brochure from Meher Spiritual Center, Myrtle Beach, South Carolina, *A Place of Pilgrimage For All Time*, p. 5.

[43] Actually, this argument would be offered by both pantheists and panentheists.

[44] Helen Schucman and William Thetford, *A Course in Miracles* (Tiburon, California: Foundation for Inner Peace, 1976) "Text," p. 11.

[45] Yogi Bhajan, *The Teachings of Yogi Bhajan, The Power of the Spoken Word*, p. 182, #733.

[46] "Kundalini," *Miriam-Webster's Encyclopedia of World Religions* (Springfield, Massachusetts: Merriam-Webster, Incorporated, 1999) p. 651.

[47] Rabi R. Maharaj, *The Death of a Guru*, p. 203.

[48] Amma, *Swami Muktananda Paramhamsa*, (Ganeshpuri, 1971) p. 32ff.; quoted in Vishal Mangalwadi, *Yoga: Five Ways of Salvation in Hinduism* (unpublished manuscript, 2001) pp. 11-12.

[49] "Chakra," *Miriam-Webster's Encyclopedia of World Religions*, p. 193.

[50] Shakti Parwha Kaur Khalsa, *Kundalini Yoga, The Flow of Eternal Power* (New York: The Berkley Publishing Group, 1996) p. 61.

[51] https://books.google.com/books?id=sunzBz04mJkC&pg=PA516&lpg=PA516#v=onepage&q&f=false (Under the article titled, "The last word on Reconditioned souls," accessed 9/20/2018).

[52] Frank S. Mead, *12,000 Religious Quotations* (Grand Rapids, Michigan: Baker Book House, 1989) p. 459

[53] Yogi Bhajan, *The Teachings of Yogi Bhajan, The Power of the Spoken Word*, p. 171, #673

[54] Ibid., p. 177, #710.

[55] Irving S. Cooper, *Theosophy Simplified* (Wheaton, Illinois: The Theosophical Publishing House, sec. Quest ed., 1989) p. 57.

[56] Yogi Bhajan, *The Teachings of Yogi Bhajan, The Power of the Spoken Word*, p. 173, #684.

[57] F. Max Muller, *Sacred Books of the East* (Oxford 1879-1910) Brahmana translation: 44:328; quoted in Robert E Hume, *The World's Living Religions* (New York: Charles Scribner's Sons, rev. ed.,1936 p. 23.

[58] John H. Hick, "Reincarnation," *The Westminster Dictionary of Christian Theology* (Philadelphia, Pennsylvania: Westminster Press, 1983) p. 491; quoted in Norman L. Geisler & J. Yutaka Amano, *The Reincarnation Sensation* (Wheaton, Illinois: Tyndale House Publishers, Inc., 1986) p. 29.

[59] David J. Kaluapahana, *Buddhist Philosophy: A Historical Analysis* (Honolulu: University Press of Hawaii, 1976); quoted in Norman L. Geisler & J. Yutaka Amano, *The Reincarnation Sensation* (Wheaton, Illinois: Tyndale House Publishers, Inc., 1986) p. 174, footnote #13.

[60] Walpola Rahula, *What the Buddha Taught* (New York: Grove Press, 1974) p. 1; quoted in J. Isamu Yamamoto, *Buddhism, Taoism & Other Far Eastern Religions* (Grand Rapids, Michigan: Zondervan Publishing House, 1998) p. 45.

[61] Maharishi Mahesh Yogi, *Meditations of Maharishi Mahesh Yogi*, pp. 123-124; quoted in Josh McDowell and Don Stewart, *Handbook of Today's Religions* (Nashville, Tennessee: Thomas Nelson Publishers, 1983) p. 84.

[62] Kenneth L. Woodard, "The Other Jesus," *Newsweek Magazine* (March 27, 2000) p. 60.

[63] Marcus Borg, ed., *Jesus and Buddha, The Parallel Sayings* (Berkeley, California: Seastone, 1997) Editor's Preface, pp. xi-xii.

[64] Yogi Bhajan, *The Teachings of Yogi Bhajan, The Power of the Spoken Word*, p. 129, #510.

[65] Rabi R. Maharaj, *The Death of a Guru*, p. 159.

[66] https://www.azquotes.com/quote/1225942 (accessed 9/20/2018).

[67] Meher Baba, *The Everything and the Nothing*, ed. Francis Brabazon, p. 22.

[68] Annie Dillard, *Pilgrim at Tinker Creek* (New York: Harper's Magazine Press, 1974) p. 270.

[69] Satguru Sivaya Subramuniyaswami, *How to Become a Hindu* (Himalayan Academy, sec. ed., 2000) p. 243.

[70] Martin Gardner, "Issues is Her Business," *New York Review*, 1987; quoted in Kenneth Boa, *Cults, World Religions and the Occult*, Wheaton, Illinois: Victor Books, 1990, from Shirley MacLaine, *Dancing in the Light*.

[71] See "Christianity" under *The Origin and Nature of Man*, pp. 68-69.

[72] "Kabbalah," *Encyclopedia Judaica* (Jerusalem, Israel: Keter Publishing House, Ltd., 1971) vol. 10, column 583.

[73] Ernest Holmes, *The Science of Mind*, p. 584 (page citation is to reprint edition).

[74] Ernest Holmes, *A Dictionary of New Thought Terms* (Marina del Rey, California: DeVorss Publications, 1991) p. 34.

[75] Ibid., p. 41.

[76] Yogi Bhajan, *The Teachings of Yogi Bhajan, The Power of the Spoken Word*, p. 173, #682.

[77] A.C. Bhaktivedanta Swami Prabhupada, *The Science of Self Realization*, p. 81.

[78] "OM," *Miriam-Webster's Encyclopedia of World Religions*, p. 826.

[79] *The World's Great Religions*, p. 16, similar to a quote by John Bunyan.

[80] Paramahansa Yogananda, *Autobiography of a Yogi* (Los Angeles, California: Self-Realization Fellowship, 1998) p. 199.

[81] Peter Smith, "Christianity," *A Concise Encyclopedia of the Bahá'í Faith*, p. 105.

[82] Helen Schucman and William Thetford, *A Course in Miracles*, "Workbook for Students," p. 439.

[83] Ernest Holmes, *A Dictionary of New Thought Terms*, p. 22.

[84] Paramahansa Yogananda, *Man's Eternal Quest* (Los Angeles, California: Self-Realization Fellowship, sec. ed., 1998) p. 232, see pp. 229-236.

[85] David Spangler, *Towards a Planetary Vision* (Forres, Scotland: Findhorn, 1977) p. 108; quoted in Ron Rhodes, *New Age Movement* (Grand Rapids, Michigan: Zondervan Publishing House, 1995) p. 72.

[86] Rudolph Steiner, *The Four Sacrifices of Christ* (Spring Valley, New York: Anthroposophic Press, 1944) pp. 19-20; quoted in Ron Rhodes, *The Counterfeit Christ of the New Age Movement* (Grand Rapids, Michigan: Baker Book House, 1990) p. 124.

[87] Benjamin Creme, *The Reappearance of Christ and the Masters of Wisdom* (Los Angeles, California: The Tara Center, 1980) pp. 54-55.

[88] Richard Gard, *Great Religions of Modern Man: Buddhism* (New York: George Braziller, 1962) p. 93.

[89] "Maitreya," *The Encyclopedia of Eastern Philosophy and Religion* (Boston, Massachusetts: Shambhala Publications, 1994) p. 217. See also "Maitreya," *Microsoft Encarta Encyclopedia 99*.

[90] Thich Nhat Hanh, *The Heart of the Buddha's Teaching* (New York: Broadway Books, 1998) p. 167.

[91] Geoffrey Parrinder, *Avatar and Incarnation, The Divine in Human Form in the World's Religions* (Oxford, England: Oneworld Publications, 1970) p. 26.

PART 5—IDENTIFYING THE TRUE LIGHT

[1] Frank S. Mead, *12,000 Religious Quotations* (Grand Rapids, Michigan: Baker Book House, 1989) p. 123.

[2] Though commonly assigned to Augustine, this quote has been attributed to several other sources as well.

[3] https://en.wikiquote.org/wiki/Henry_David_Thoreau (accessed 9/20/2018).

[4] Paramahansa Yogananda, *Autobiography of a Yogi* (Los Angeles, California: Self-Realization Fellowship, 1998) p. 558.

[5] Kenneth L. Woodard, "The Other Jesus*," Newsweek Magazine* (March 27, 2000) p. 60.

[6] www.nae.net/the-truth-competition (accessed 9/20/2018).

[7] "Ghandi, Mohandas Karamchand," *Miriam Webster's Encyclopedia of World Religions* (Springfield, Massachusetts: Merriam-Webster, Incorporated, 1999) p. 366.

[8] Robert E Hume, *The World's Living Religions* (New York: Charles Scribner's Sons, rev. ed., 1959) pp. 273-274, The basic information for this list of statements was drawn from this source, though transferred in slightly different wording.

[9] Citation not available.

[10] Frank S. Mead, *12,000 Religious Quotations* (Grand Rapids, Michigan: Baker Book House, 1989) p. 476.

[11] Ralph Waldo Emerson, *Essays: "Prudence"* (First Series, 1841).

[12] "Pragmatism: III History," *Microsoft Encarta Encyclopedia 99.*

[13] http://greatthoughtstreasury.com/author/john-hay-allison (accessed 9/20/2018).

[14] http://theranch.org/2009/01/18/lynn-landrum-that-the-potter-should-die (accessed 9/20/2018).

[15] Geoffrey Parrinder, *Avatar and Incarnation, The Divine in Human Form in the World's Religions* (Oxford, England: Oneworld Publications, 1970) pp. 124-125 (Also refer to K.S. Jurty, *Revelation and Reason in Advaita Vedanta*, p. 219, 2 Gita 10, 13-14.) Bracketed words by author.

[16] Rabi R. Maharaj, *The Death of a Guru* (Eugene, Oregon: Harvest House Publishers, 1977) p. 207, in the Glossary under "Vedanta."

[17] A.C. Bhaktivedanta Swami Prabhupada, *The Journey of Self-Discovery* (Botany, Australia: The Bhaktivedanta Book Trust, 1997) p. 49.

[18] Ibid., Note: "Krsna" is Swami Prabhupada's preferred spelling of "Krishna."

[19] Yogi, Maharishi Mahesh. *Maharishi Mahesh Yogi on the Bhagavad-Gita, A New Translation and Commentary Chapters 1-6* (London: Arkana, Penguin Books, 1990) back cover.

[20] A.C. Bhaktivedanta Swami Prabhupada, *The Science of Self Realization* (Los Angeles, California: The Bhaktivedanta Book Trust, 1998) p. 181.

[21] His Holiness, the Dalai Lama, *The Good Heart: A Buddhist Perspective on the Teachings of Jesus* (Boston: Wisdom, 1996) pp. 81-82.

[22] https://en.wikiquote.org/wiki/Samuel_Rutherford (accessed 9/20/2018).

[23] Bob Larson, Larson's Book of World Religions and Alternative Spirituality (Wheaton, Illinois Copyright 1982, 1989, 2004) p. 64.

[24] Citation not available. See www.anandaashramyoga.org.

[25] www.brainyquote.com/quotes/ralph_waldo_emerson_118170 (accessed 9/20/2018).

BASIC HISTORY

[1] James Fadiman and Robert Grager, *Essential Sufism* (Edison, New Jersey: Castle Books, 1998) p. 35.

[2] Abu al-Hasan Kharaqani, in Jami, *Nafahat*, p. 298; quoted in Carl W. Ernst, Ph. D., *The Shambhala Guide to Sufism* (Boston, Massachusetts: Shambhala Publications, 1997) p. 228.

[3] FAQ, "What does this Wisdom Tradition Teach?," www.theosophical.org (accessed September 30, 2001).

SPECIAL NOTE (from pages 33, 163 & 279)

* Whenever passages from the sacred books of other religions are quoted, or authors whose worldviews are not Christianity, this is NOT an endorsement on my part of these books being a source of truth for those who are seeking. Only the Bible fills this role. I am merely quoting a single passage or line that supports the point I am making and is my way of acknowledging commonalities that are universally acceptable.

SELECTED BIBLIOGRAPHY

Books Cited

Amma. *Swami Muktananda Paramhamsa*. Ganeshpuri, 1971, p. 32ff. Quoted in Vishal Mangalwadi, *Yoga: Five Ways of Salvation in Hinduism*, 11-12, unpublished manuscript, 2001.

Baba, Meher. *God Speaks*, sec. ed., rev. and enl., Walnut Creek, California: Sufism Reoriented, 1973.

_____, *Beams for Meher Baba on the Spiritual Panorama*. Edited by Ivy Duce, Walnut Creek, California: Sufism Reoriented.*

_____, *Discourses*, 7ᵗʰ rev. ed., Myrtle Beach, South Carolina: Sheriar Press, Inc., 1987.

_____, *The Everything and the Nothing.* edited by Francis Brabazon, Myrtle Beach, South Carolina: Sheriar Press, Inc., 1995.

_____, *The Path of Love.* edited by Filis Frederick, Myrtle Beach, South Carolina: Sheriar Press, Inc., n.d.*

Barrie and Jenkins. *The Sufi Message of Inayat Khan*, vol. XI. London: Servire Publishers, Katwijk, Holland, 1960-1982, 163. Quoted in Dr. H. J. Witteveen. *Universal Sufism*, 101, Rockport, Massachusetts: Element, 1997.

Bercholz, Samuel, ed., and Sherab Chodzin Kohn, ed. *An Introduction to the Buddha and His Teachings.* New York: Barnes and Noble Books, Inc., by arrangement with Shambhala Publications, Inc., 1997.

Berg, Michael. *The Way: Using the Wisdom of Kabbalah for Spiritual Transformation and Fulfillment.* New York: John Wiley & Sons, Inc, 2001.

Berkhof, Louis. *The History of Christian Doctrine.* Grand Rapids: Baker Book House, 1981, 47. Quoted in Ron Rhodes. *The Counterfeit Christ of the New Age Movement,* 17, Grand Rapids, Michigan: Baker Book House, 1990.

Besant, Annie. *Four Great Religions,* 7. Quoted in Robert E Hume, *The World's Living Religions,* rev. ed., 10, New York: Charles Scribner's Sons, 1936.

_____, *Karma.* London: Theosophical Publishing Society, 1904, 23. Quoted in Ron Rhodes, *The New Age Movement,* 65, Grand Rapids, Michigan: Zondervan Publishing House, 1995.

Beversluis, Joel, ed. *Sourcebook of the World's Religions.* Novato, CA: New World Library, 2000.

Bhajan, Yogi (Siri Singh Sahib Bhai Sahib Harbhajan Singh Kalsa Yogiji). *The Teachings of Yogi Bhajan, The Power of the Spoken Word.* Pamona, California: Arcline Publications, 1977.

_____, *The Mind, Its Projections and Multiple Facets.* Espanola, New Mexico: Kundalini Research Institute, 1998.

Blavatsky, Helena P. *The Key to Theosophy.* Pasadena, California: Theosophical University Press, 1995 (unabridged printing of original 1889 ed., with new index).

_____, *The Secret Doctrine.* Pasadena, California: Theosophical University Press, 1999.

_____, *Studies in Occultism.* Theosophical University Press, n.d., 134. Quoted in Josh McDowell and Don Stewart, *Handbook of Today's Religions,* 87, Nashville, Tennessee: Thomas Nelson Publishers, 1983.

Boa, Kenneth. *Cults, World Religions and the Occult.* Wheaton, Illinois: Victor Books, 1990.

Borg, Marcus, ed. *Jesus and Buddha, The Parallel Sayings.* Berkeley, California: Seastone, 1997.

Bowker, John. *World Religions.* New York, New York: DK Publishing, Inc., 1997.

Bradley, David G. *A Guide to the World's Religions.* Englewood Cliffs, New Jersey: Prentice-Hall, Inc., 1963.

Campbell, Joseph, ed. *Myths and Symbols in Indian Art and Civilization.* Princeton, New Jersey: Princeton University Press, 1946.

Cheetham, Jack and Betty. *An Age of Meditation.* Plainfield, New Jersey: Logos International, 1976.

Clymer, R. Swinburne. *The Secret Schools.* Oceanside, California: Philos Publishing, 19. Quoted in Josh McDowell and Don Stewart. Handbook of Today's Religions, 223, Nashville, Tennessee: Thomas Nelson Publishers, 1983.

Cohen, Abraham. *Everyman's Talmud.* New York: Schocken Books, 1949.

Coogan, Michael D., Gen. ed. *The Illustrated Guide to World Religions.* New York: Oxford University Press, 1998.

Cooper, Irving S. *Reincarnation: A Hope of the World.* Wheaton, Illinois: Theosophical Publishing House, 1979, 25. Quoted in Norman L. Geisler & J. Yutaka Amano, *The Reincarnation Sensation,* 40, Wheaton, Illinois: Tyndale House Publishers, Inc., 1986.

_____, *Theosophy Simplified,* sec. Quest ed. Wheaton, Illinois: The Theosophical Publishing House, 1989.

Cooper, Rabbi David A. *God is a Verb, Kabbalah and the practice of mystical Judaism.* New York, New York: Riverhead Books, The Berkeley Publishing Group, a division of Penguin Putman, Inc., 1998.

Creme, Benjamin. *Maitreya's Mission.* London: Share International Foundation, 1997.

_____, *The Reappearance of Christ and the Masters of Wisdom.* Los Angeles, California: The Tara Center, 1980.

Davy, Kitty. *Love Alone Prevails.* Myrtle Beach, South Carolina: Sheriar Press, Inc., 1981.*

Dass, Bhagavan. *The Essential Unity of All Religions,* rev. ed., Kila, Montana: Kessinger Publishing Company, 1939.

Deshmukh, C. D. *Sparks of the Truth: From Dissertations of Meher Baba* (Reprinted from "The Awakener" Magazine) Myrtle Beach, South Carolina: Sheriar Press, Inc., 1971.

Dillard, Annie. *Pilgrim at Tinker Creek.* New York: Harper's Magazine Press, 1974.

Duce, Ivy. *How a Master Works.* Walnut Creek, California: Sufism Reoriented.*

Eerdman's Handbook to the World's Religions. Grand Rapids, Michigan: Wm. B. Eerdman's Publishing Company, 1982.

Encyclopedia of Eastern Philosophy and Religion, The. Boston, Massachusetts: Shambhala Publications, 1994.

Encyclopedia Judaica, 16 vol., Jerusalem, Israel: Keter Publishing House, Ltd., 1971.

Epstein, Perle. *Kabbalah, The Way of the Jewish Mystic.* Boston, Massachusetts: Shambhala Publications, Inc., 2001.

Ernst, Carl W., Ph. D. *The Shambhala Guide to Sufism.* Boston, Massachusetts: Shambhala Publications, 1997.

Fadiman, James, and Robert Frager, eds. *Essential Sufism.* Edison, New Jersey: Castle Books, 1998.

Gard, Richard, ed. *Great Religions of Modern Man: Buddhism.* New York: George Braziller, 1962.

Geisler, Norman L., and J. Yutaka Amano. *The Reincarnation Sensation.* Wheaton, Illinois: Tyndale House Publishers, Inc., 1986.

Geisler, Norman L. and Ronald M. Brooks. *Christianity Under Attack.* Dallas: Quest Publications, 1985.

Gibran, Kahlil. *The Prophet.* Hertfordshire: Wordsworth Editions Ltd., 1996.

Halverson, Dean C., ed. *The Compact Guide to World Religions.* Minneapolis: Bethany House, 1996, 91. Quoted in J. Isamu Yamamoto. *Hinduism, TM & Hare Krishna,* 45, Grand Rapids, Michigan: Zondervan, 1998.

Hanh, Thich Nhat. *Living Buddha, Living Christ.* New York, New York: Riverhead Books, 1995.

_____, *The Heart of the Buddha's Teaching.* New York: Broadway Books, 1998.

Haynes, Charles. *Meher Baba, The Awakener.* N. Myrtle Beach, South Carolina: The Avatar Foundation, Inc., 1993.

Helminski, Kabir. *The Knowing Heart: A Sufi Path of Transformation.* Boston, Massachusetts: Shambhala Publications, 1999.

Hick, John H. *The Westminster Dictionary of Christian Theology,* "Reincarnation," Philadelphia, Pennsylvania: Westminster Press, 1983, 491. Quoted in Geisler, Norman L., and J. Yutaka Amano. *The Reincarnation Sensation,* 29, Wheaton, Illinois: Tyndale House Publishers, Inc.,1986.

Hoeller, Stephan A. *Gnosticism: New light on the Ancient Tradition of Inner Knowing.* Wheaten, Illinois: Quest Books, Theosophical Publishing House, 2002.

Holmes, Ernest. *A Dictionary of New Thought Terms.* Marina del Rey, California: DeVorss Publications, 1991.

_____, *The Science of Mind.* New York: R.M McBride and Co., 1938, New York: Penguin Putnam, Inc., rev. and enl. ed., 1966.

_____, *What Religious Science Teaches.* Los Angeles: Science of Mind Publications, 1975.

Hubbard, L. Ron. *What is Scientology?* (A compilation and explanation of Hubbard's works produced by the Church of Scientology staff) Los Angeles, California: Bridge Publications, Inc., 1993.

Hume, Robert E. *The World's Living Religions,* rev. ed., New York: Charles Scribner's Sons, 1936.

_____, *Treasure-House of the Living Religions, Selections from Their Sacred Scriptures,* rev. ed., New York: Charles Scribner's Sons, 1932.

Irani, Adi K., ed., *Messages of Meher Baba, East and West,* India: Meher Baba Trust.*

Khan, Inayat. *The Soul, Whence and Whither.* London / The Hague: East-West Publications, 1984, 9 & 41. Quoted in Dr. H. J. Witteveen, *Universal Sufism,* 64-65, Rockport, Massachusetts: Element, 1997.

Jewish Encyclopedia, The, 12 vols. New York: KATV Publishing House, Inc., n.d.

Kalchuri, Bhau. *Lord Meher,* 12 vol. Asheville, North Carolina: Manifestation, Inc.*

_____, *The Nothing and the Everything.* Asheville, North Carolina: Manifestation, Inc.*

Kaluapahana, David J. *Buddhist Philosophy: A Historical Analysis.* Honolulu: University Press of Hawaii, 1976. Quoted in Norman L. Geisler & J. Yutaka Amano, *The Reincarnation Sensation,* 174, chapter 2, footnote #13, Wheaton, Illinois: Tyndale House Publishers, Inc., 1986.

Khalsa, Shakti Parwha Kaur. *Kundalini Yoga, The Flow of Eternal Power.* New York: The Berkley Publishing Group, 1996.

Kohn, Livia, *Daoism and Chinese Culture.* Cambridge, Massachusettes: Three Pines Press, 2001.

_____, *Living with the Dao: Conceptual Issues in Daoist Practice.* Three Pines Press, downloaded book from www.threepinespress.com, Feb. 2002.

_____, *The Taoist Experience, An Anthology.* Albany, New York: State University of New York Press, 1993.

Lama, His Holiness the Dalai. *The Good Heart: A Buddhist Perspective on the Teachings of Jesus.* Boston: Wisdom, 1996.

Legge, James. *The Chinese Classics with a Translation.* Oxford University Press, 1871, 4.2.505; cf. *Sacred Books of the East* 3.410-411. Quoted in Robert S. Hume, *Treasure-House of the Living Religions,* 78, New York: Charles Scribner's Sons, 1932.

_____, *Mencius* 70, 130. Quoted in Robert S. Hume, *Treasure-House of the Living Religions,* 78, New York: Charles Scribner's Sons, 1932.

LIFE, *The World's Great Religions.* New York: Time Incorporated, 1957.

Lockyer, Herbert, edited by Herbert Lockyer, Jr. *All the Angels of the Bible.* Peabody Massachusetts: Hendrickson Publishers, 1997.

Macauliffe, M. A. *The Sikh Religion: Its Gurus, Sacred Writings, and Authors.* Oxford, 1909, 280, "Life of Guru Nanak." Quoted in Robert E Hume, *The World's Living Religions,* rev. ed., 95, New York: Charles Scribner's Sons, 1936.

_____, Hymns of Guru Nanak, 1, 365-365, quoted in Robert S. Hume, *Treasure-House of the Living Religions.* New York: Charles Scribner's Sons, 1932, 80.

Maharaj, Rabi R. *The Death of a Guru.* Eugene, Oregon: Harvest House Publishers, 1977.

McDowell, Josh and Don Stewart, *Handbook of Today's Religions.* Nashville, Tennessee: Thomas Nelson Publishers, 1983.

Mead, Frank S. *12,000 Religious Quotations.* Grand Rapids, Michigan: Baker Book House, 1989.

Millgram, Abraham Ezra, ed. *Great Jewish Ideas.* Clinton, Massachusetts: Colonial Press, Inc., B'nai B'rith Department of Adult Jewish Education, 1964.

Miriam-Webster's Encyclopedia of World Religions. Springfield, Massachusetts: Merriam-Webster, Inc., 1999.

Moore, George Foot. *Judaism in the First Centuries of the Christian Era, The Age of the Tannaim,* vol. 1. Cambridge: Harvard University Press, 1962.

Muller, F. Max, ed. *The Sacred Books of the East* (Oxford, 1879-1910) 40:68-69, 45: 245. Quoted in Robert E. Hume, *The World's Living Religions,* rev. ed., 49, 141, New York: Charles Scribner's Sons, 1936.

Natu, Bal. *Glimpses of the God-Man Meher Baba,* vol. 6, Myrtle Beach, South Carolina: Sheriar Press, Inc., 1994.*

Pandit, Bansi. *The Hindu Mind.* Glen Ellyn, IL: B & V Enterprises, Inc., 1998.

Parrinder, Geoffrey. *Avatar and Incarnation, The Divine in Human Form in the World's Religions.* Oxford, England: Oneworld Publications, 1970.

Place of Pilgrimage For All Time, A. Information brochure from Meher Spiritual Center, Myrtle Beach, South Carolina.

Prabhavananda, Swami. *The Spiritual Heritage of India.* Hollywood, California: Vedanta Press, n.d. (copyright date 1963, 1979).

Prabhupada, A.C. Bhaktivedanta Swami. *Bhagavad-Gita As It Is.* New York: Collier Books, 1972.

_____, *Coming Back: the Science of Reincarnation.* Los Angeles, California: The Bhaktivedanta Book Trust, 1982, 16, 33, 122-123. Quoted in Norman L. Geisler & J. Yutaka Amano. *The Reincarnation Sensation,* 34-35, Wheaton, Illinois: Tyndale House Publishers, Inc., 1986.

_____, *The Journey of Self-Discovery.* Botany, Australia: The Bhaktivedanta Book Trust, 1997.

_____, *The Science of Self Realization.* Los Angeles, California: The Bhaktivedanta Book Trust, 1998.

Radhakrishnan, S. *East and West, The End of Their Separation.* New York: Allen & Unwin, Humanities Press, 1954.

Rahula, Walpola. *What the Buddha Taught.* New York: Grove Press, 1974, 1. Quoted in J. Isamu Yamamoto. *Buddhism, Taoism & Other Far Eastern Religions,* 45, Grand Rapids, Michigan: Zondervan Publishing House, 1998.

Ramanujam, T.K. *Much Love.* India: Meher Baba Trust,1994.*

Rhodes, Ron. *The Counterfeit Christ of the New Age Movement.* Grand Rapids, Michigan: Baker Book House, 1990.

_____, *New Age Movement.* Grand Rapids, Michigan: Zondervan Publishing House, 1995.

Robinson, George. *Essential Judaism, A Complete Guide to the Beliefs, Customs and Rituals.* New York: Pocket Books, 2000.

Rogers, L.W. *Elementary Theosophy.* Wheaton, Illinois: The Theosophical Press, 1956.

Schucman, Helen and William Thetford. *A Course in Miracles* (The Paperback Version containing three sections that were originally three separate books: the "Text," "Workbook for Students," and "Manual for Teachers"). Tiburon, California: Foundation for Inner Peace, 1976.

Shield, Benjamin, ed. and Richard Carlson, ed. *For the Love of God.* Novato, California: New World Library, 1997.

Schimmel, Annemarie. *Mystical Dimensions of Islam.* Chapel Hill, North Carolina: The University of North Carolina Press, 1975.

Scholem, Gershom. *Origins of the Kabbalah.* Princeton, New Jersey: Princeton University Press, in association with the Jewish Publication Society, first paperback printing, 1990.

Shorrosh, Dr. Anis A. *Islam Revealed.* Nashville: Thomas Nelson Publishers, 1988.

Smith, Huston. *The Illustrated World's Religions: A Guide to our Wisdom Traditions.* Labyrinth Publishing (UK) Ltd., 1994.

Smith, Peter. *A Concise Encyclopedia of the Bahá'í Faith.* Oxford, England: Oneworld Publications, 2000.

Spangler, David. *Towards a Planetary Vision.* Forres, Scotland: Findhorn, 1977, 108. Quoted in Ron Rhodes, *New Age Movement,* 72, Grand Rapids, Michigan: Zondervan Publishing House, 1995.

Srimad-Bhagavatam 1:3:28. Bhaktivedanta Book Trust, n.d.

Steiner, Rudolph, *The Four Sacrifices of Christ*. Spring Valley, New York: Anthroposophic Press, 1944, 19-20. Quoted in Ron Rhodes, *The Counterfeit Christ of the New Age Movement*, 124, Grand Rapids, Michigan: Baker Book House, 1990.

Stern, David H. *Complete Jewish Bible*. Clarksville, Maryland: Jewish New Testament Publications, Inc., 1998.

Stevenson, *Heart of Jainism*, 270. Quoted in Robert E. Hume, *The World's Living Religions*, rev. ed., 141, New York: Charles Scribner's Sons, 1936.

Stroup, Herbert. *Four Religions of Asia*. New York: Harper and Row, 1968, 99. Quoted in Josh McDowell and Don Stewart, *Handbook of Today's Religions*, 297, Nashville, Tennessee: Thomas Nelson Publishers, 1983.

Subramuniyaswami, Satguru Sivaya. *How to Become a Hindu*, sec. ed., Himalayan Academy, 2000.

Trevelyan, George. *Operation Redemption: A Vision of Hope in an Age of Turmoil*. Walpole, New Hampshire: Stillpoint, 1985.

Trumpp, Ernst. *The Adi Granth, or Holy Scriptures of the Sikhs*. Trubner, 1877, 174-179. Quoted in Robert E. Hume, *The World's Living Religions*, rev. ed., 88, New York: Charles Scribner's Sons, 1936.

Twitchell, Paul. *The Flute of God*. Minneapolis: ECKANKAR, 1969.

Wells Jr., Albert M. *Inspiring Quotations, Contemporary & Classical*. Nashville: Thomas Nelson Publishers,1979.

Wilkinson, Philip. *Illustrated Dictionary of Religions*. New York, New York: DK Publishing, 1999.

Williams, John Alden, ed. *Islam*. New York City, New York: George Braziller, Inc., 1962.

Wilson, Andrew, ed., *World Scripture, A Comparative Anthology of Sacred Texts*. St. Paul, Minnesota: Paragon House Publishers, 1995.

Witteveen, Dr. H. J. *Universal Sufism*. Rockport, Massachusetts: Element, 1997.

Wong, Eva. *The Shambhala Guide to Taoism*. Boston: Shambhala Publications, Inc., 1997.

Yamamoto, J. Isamu. *Buddhism, Taoism & Other Far Eastern Religions*. Grand Rapids, Michigan: Zondervan Publishing House, 1998.

_____, *Hinduism, TM & Hare Krishna*. Grand Rapids, Michigan: Zondervan Publishing House, 1998.

Yogananda, Paramahansa. *Autobiography of a Yogi*, 13ᵗʰ ed., Los Angeles, California: Self-Realization Fellowship, 1998.

_____, *How You Can Talk With God*. Los Angeles, California: Self-Realization Fellowship, 1997.

_____, *Journey to Self-Realization*. Los Angeles, California: Self-Realization Fellowship, 1997.

_____, *Man's Eternal Quest*. sec. ed., Los Angeles, California: Self-Realization Fellowship, 1998.

Yogi, Maharishi Mahesh. *Maharishi Mahesh Yogi on the Bhagavad-Gita, A New Translation and Commentary Chapters 1-6*. London: Penguin Books, 1990.

_____, *Meditations of Maharishi Mahesh Yogi*, 123-124; Quoted in Josh McDowell and Don Stewart, *Handbook of Today's Religions*, 84, Nashville, Tennessee: Thomas Nelson Publishers, 1983.

_____, *Science of Being and Art of Living*. New York: Meridian, an imprint of Dutton Signet, a division of Penguin Books, 1995.

_____, *Transcendental Meditation*, 266. Quoted in Josh McDowell and Don Stewart, *Handbook of Today's Religions*, 83, Nashville, Tennessee: Thomas Nelson Publishers, 1983.

Yukteswar, Swami Sri. *The Holy Science*, 8ᵗʰ ed., Los Angeles, California: Self-Realization Fellowship, 1990.

Zimmer, Heinrich. *Myths and Symbols in Indian Art and Civilization*, edited by Joseph Campbell. Princeton, New Jersey: Princeton University Press, 1972.

*A single asterisk in the bibliography indicates those quotes drawn from that book were actually obtained one of two ways: either in conversations with Mar   kar, a devotee of Meher Baba or from postings on his website which no longer exists: www.members.aol.com/markar1.

Magazine Articles Cited

Elkins, David N., Ph. D. "Compassion: A Way of Being in the World, An Interview with Sharon Salzberg." *Personal Transformation*, Winter 1999.

Gardner, Martin, "Issues is Her Business." *New York Review*, 1987. Quoted in Boa, Kenneth. *Cults, World Religions and the Occult*. Wheaton, Illinois: Victor Books, 1990.

Reginald A. Ray, "Religion Without God." *Shambala Sun*, July 2001.

Woodard, Kenneth L. "The Other Jesus." *Newsweek Magazine*, March 27, 2000.

Computer CD Programs Cited

Microsoft® Encarta®® Encyclopedia 99, © 1993-1998, Microsoft Corporation, All rights reserved.

Websites Cited

www.brittanica.com - an excellent website for in-depth research, based on the entire Encyclopedia Brittanica.

www.comparativereligion.com - an excellent site produced by Ernest Valea, primarily focusing on the beliefs of Far Eastern religions, as compared to the Christian belief system.

www.eckankar.org - an official website for the ECKANKAR religious group, founded by Paul Twitchell. The current leader is Sri Harold Klemp.

www.geocities.com/Athens/Forum/5464 - a site by Mohan Prasad, dedicated to the teachings and person of Sathya Sai Baba, professed to be an Avatar for this age.

www.himalayanacademy.com - a site containing a great deal of information on Hinduism. It is also the web location for the "Hinduism Today" magazine. Though no quotes were taken verbatim from this site, the author decided to mention it as a rich resource for research on Hinduism.

www.lib.virginia.edu/exhibits/dead/index.html - Most of the information on "The Tibetan Book of the Dead" was obtained from this source.

www.members.aol.com/markar1 - dedicated to the teachings of Meher Baba.

www.bonafidescientology.org - a site created by The Church of Scientology International that presents a reference work titled, *Theology & Practice of a Contemporary Religion.*

www.shareintl.org - the website explaining the beliefs of Benjamin Creme, especially with respect to Maitreya, who he believes is the promised World Teacher, presently manifesting himself in this world.

www.sikhnet.com - a Sikh website. Two contributing writers, Preet Mohan and Yuktanand Singh, were especially helpful, directing me to needed information.

www.srigurugranthsahib.org - a Sikh website especially dedicated to the teachings of Baba Nand Singh Ji Maharaj.

www.theosophical.org - the official site of the Theosophical Society in America.

www.umich.edu/~umjains - a website offering information on Jainism.

www.unification.net/ws/ - This is a site that lists and categorizes similar quotes from the scripture base of various world religions.

www.yogananda-srf.org - the official site of the Self-Realization Fellowship founded by Paramahansa Yogananda.

Bible Versions Cited

Unless otherwise noted, all scriptures are from the NEW KING JAMES VERSION®. Copyright© 1982 by Thomas Nelson, Inc. Used by permission. All rights reserved.

Scripture references marked (KJV) are from the KING JAMES VERSION of the Bible. Public domain.

Scripture quotations marked (NIV) are taken from THE HOLY BIBLE, NEW INTERNATIONAL VERSION®. Copyright© 1973, 1978, 1984, 2011 by Biblica, Inc.™. Used by permission of Zondervan.

Scripture quotations marked (RSV) are taken from the REVISED STANDARD VERSION, Grand Rapids: Zondervan, 1971. Used by permission. All rights reserved.

Image Credit

Crucifixion picture, p. 283, Quickverse 4.0 New Bible Reference Collection for CD-Rom (Parson's Technology, Hiawatha, IA: 1997 Edition) Findex bitmap image LP201, Used by permission.

THE TRUE LIGHT PROJECT—Various outreaches have been included in our ongoing effort to share truth with those who embrace a far eastern and/or new age belief system. The primary hub of this project is our associated website. On it, we feature the personal stories of many sincere seekers who passed through yoga, meditation, the new age, or various non-Christian religions on their way to an encounter with the Lord Jesus Christ. We also post informative articles, interviews, TV shows, and podcast teachings that will help you discover and fully explore the truth. A mini-book of Mike Shreve story titled *The Highest Adventure: Encountering God* is offered as a free download. You are welcome to email us your questions and comments: www.thetruelight.net

THE CATHOLIC PROJECT—Mike Shreve also has an outreach geared toward those who embrace Catholicism. He was raised Catholic, served as an altar boy, and at one point, was on his way to the monastery when a close encounter with death caused him to reevaluate his direction in life. His book, *The Beliefs of the Catholic Church*, examines the differences between Catholicism and authentic New Testament, Bible-based Christianity in twenty-five essential areas of doctrine, practices, and traditions. Visit the website: www.toCatholicswithlove.org

DEEPER REVELATION BOOKS
Revealing "the deep things of God" (1 Corinthians 2:10)

We are a co-publishing company: a bridge between self-publishing and traditional publishing. We come alongside authors who embrace an authentic, Christian worldview and assist them in producing their books. www.deeperrevelationbooks.org / 423-478-2843 / Our four divisions:

Non-fiction Division

Children's Division

Fiction Division

Success Division

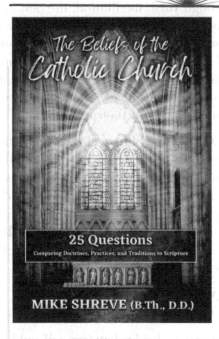